Taking SIDES

Clashing Views on Controversial Issues in Gender Studies

Edited, Selected, and with Introductions by

Alison D. Spalding

State University of New York, College at Brockport

Dushkin/McGraw-Hill
A Division of The McGraw-Hill Companies

For B. Spalding,
A Being like no other.

And for Mom,
With very special thanks.

Cover Art Acknowledgment

Charles Vitelli

Library of Congress Cataloging-in-Publication Data

Main entry under title:
    Taking sides: clashing views on controversial issues in gender studies/edited, selected, and with introductions by Alison D. Spalding.—1st ed.
    Includes bibliographical references and index.
    1. Sex role—United States. I. Spalding, Alison D., *comp.*

                                  301.41
0-697-38550-7   ISSN: 1094-7574

 Printed on Recycled Paper

PREFACE

Many of the selections contained in this book represent extreme positions and views of gender studies. *Extremism* may be defined as "outermost or farthest," "most remote in any direction," or "representing the extreme edge of the field." In addition, some of the viewpoints expressed may be perceived as dogmatic, overly positive, or even arrogant, given the fact that many of the writers' assertions are based on unproved or unprovable principles. In studying controversial issues, it is crucial to hear from a wide range of women and men across many disciplines. Thus, this book centers on works from many fields, including sociology, psychology, political science, women's studies, men's studies, gay and lesbian studies, medicine, and ethnic studies. The continuing work by people in these fields has provided an exciting and rich base of new information that continues to grow. This book includes essays, research, and autobiographical material from this base.

This book contains 38 selections presented in a pro-con format. A total of 19 controversial gender studies issues are debated. Although only two positions are presented for any one issue, it is recommended that the reader consider the likely perspective of the group or groups that are not included in each discussion. It is also important to analyze each position, highlight the critical concepts and constructs, and carefully follow the writer's line of logic. Key arguments from each issue selection should be compared with those from its opposing selection. It is hoped that readers will learn to support their own positions, critique their own positions, and note areas that the writers of the selections may have failed to cover.

Presumably, readers of this book will start out with their own perspectives, which will invariably be colored by their own gender, class, race, age, values, and personal life experiences. Readers are challenged to listen in an open way to the viewpoints of others and to openly debate these issues with their peers. Considering alternative viewpoints will teach readers how to deal with objections to their own viewpoints. In criticizing the arguments of others, readers will learn to anticipate criticisms of their own views, to formulate responses to those arguments, and to make a more convincing case for their own viewpoints in the future. The issues addressed in this book are of tremendous import to our continuing social development, and major world changes have already been made in response to political and social activism in these areas. Readers are encouraged to become—and to remain —socially and politically active, to express viewpoints persuasively, and to seek positive social change.

Organization of the book   Each issue begins with an *issue introduction*, which sets the stage for the debate as it is argued in the YES and NO selections.

Each issue concludes with a *postscript* that makes some final observations and points the way to other questions related to the issue. In reading the issues and forming your own opinions, you should not feel confined to adopt one or the other of the positions presented. There are positions in between those of the selections provided as well as alternatives outside of the viewpoints presented. The *suggestions for further reading* that appear in each postscript should assist you in finding resources for continued study. At the end of the book you will find a *list of contributors* to this volume, which will give you information on the various writers whose views are debated here. Also, each part opener contains a list of Internet sites to assist students in further exploring topics of interest.

A word to the instructor   An *Instructor's Manual With Test Questions* (multiple-choice and essay) is available through the publisher for the instructor using *Taking Sides* in the classroom. A general guidebook, *Using Taking Sides in the Classroom*, which discusses methods and techniques for integrating the pro-con approach into any classroom setting, is also available. An online version of *Using Taking Sides in the Classroom* and a correspondence service for Taking Sides adopters can be found at www.dushkin.com/usingtakingsides/. For students, we offer a field guide to analyzing argumentative essays, *Analyzing Controversy: An Introductory Guide,* with exercises and techniques to help them to decipher genuine controversies.

Taking Sides: Clashing Views on Controversial Issues in Gender Studies is only one title in the Taking Sides series. If you are interested in seeing the table of contents for any of the other titles, please visit the Taking Sides Web site at http://www.dushkin.com/takingsides/.

Acknowledgments   I would like to thank my colleagues, friends, and family for their encouragement and support during the time that it took to prepare this book. I would especially like to thank my faculty mentor, Eileen Daniel, for her advice and assistance; Kathleen Hunter for her contribution of materials and support; and my critical reader, who prefers to remain anonymous. I would also like to thank Olie and Edith Spalding for the use of their computer equipment and supplies, and David Dean, list manager for the Taking Sides program, and David Brackley, developmental editor, for their helpful assistance in organizing materials, preparing the manuscript, making suggestions, and corresponding with contributors. Finally I would like to thank the faculty of the SUNY Brockport Women's Studies Program, headed by Jenny Lloyd, for their recommendations and guidance.

Alison D. Spalding
State University of New York, College at Brockport

CONTENTS IN BRIEF

CONTENTS

Sociology professor Steven Goldberg asserts that male dominance is rooted in the physiological differences between men and women. Attorney Deborah L. Rhode argues that it is not nature but rather how we interpret it that accounts for gender inequalities in society today.

Author Elayne A. Saltzberg and associate professor of psychology Joan C. Chrisler suggest that the value of beauty for women is not worth the high price paid by many in terms of emotional changes and physical side effects. Elizabeth Fox-Genovese, a professor of humanities, asserts that femininity empowers women and gives them a source of connection with other women.

Edward Gilbreath, associate editor of *New Man* magazine, says that Promise Keepers (PK) is a socially positive organization. John Swomley, a professor of theology, contends that Promise Keepers serves as a cover for a takeover by the fundamentalist religious right.

Political science professor Sheila Jeffreys maintains that male ownership of female bodies via the sex industry provides an arena for male supremacy and oppression. Professor of humanities Camille Paglia argues that prostitutes and women in pornography are powerful, autonomous, and in control.

Robert L. Allen, senior editor of the *Black Scholar*, argues that prevention through community education should be utilized to reduce sexual harassment. Author Jonathan Rauch asserts that the hostile environment rule is now the most virulent threat to free speech in the United States.

Michele Commeyras and Donna Alvermann, both associates at the University of Georgia, assert that history textbooks contain serious omissions, misrepresentations, and insensitivity in gender positioning. Historians Robert Lerner, Althea Nagai, and Stanley Rothman maintain that federal regulations calling for systematic recasting of American history are unnecessary.

Assistant business professors Amy Oakes Wren, Roland E. Kidwell, Jr., and Linda Achey Kidwell argue that workplace discrimination against pregnant women continues to be rampant in spite of pregnancy discrimination laws. The late cultural critic William A. Henry III states that women are disproportionately grouped on lower rungs of the economic ladder because they are less committed to their careers.

Author Rene Denfeld asserts that women's presence in all areas of the military is supported by most Americans. Writer Stephanie Gutmann maintains that the integration of women into the military compromises the integrity of the American national security system.

M. T. Stepaniants, a professor of philosophy, maintains that patriarchal religious denominations overtly discriminate against women. Writer Kenneth L. Woodward asserts that sociological aspects of American religious life privilege the feminine over the masculine.

David Gelernter, a professor of computer science, argues that the "motherhood revolution," which was grounded on the assumption that paid employment would make women happier, has failed. Sociologist Sharon Hays contends that "intensive mothering" is neither natural nor desirable.

John J. DiIulio, Jr., a professor of politics, asserts that the institution of marriage is cheapened and detraditionalized by divorce. John Taylor, senior writer for *Esquire*, contends that divorce may be the necessary choice in some instances. He feels that it may serve to lift an intellectual and emotional fog and may lead to increased energy and reduced self-doubt.

Attorney Debra Dickerson maintains that African American women would like to marry but that the dearth of marriageable African American males is a crisis. Linda Blum, an associate professor of sociology, and Theresa Deussen, a doctoral candidate in sociology, assert that African American women seek to carve out alternative relationships based on nonmarital relationships with male partners.

Attorney Jeffrey M. Leving and professor of psychology Kenneth A. Dachman argue that mothers are disproportionately more likely to benefit from judiciary protections in family courts than are fathers. Editor and author Phyllis Chesler asserts that most women do not win custody unfairly.

Writer Joan Nestle maintains that the butch-femme experience is a natural way of life for a majority of lesbian couples. Psychotherapist Beverly Burch argues that typical lesbian relationships are not likely to function within the context of a butch-femme dichotomy.

Health writer Gayle Feldman contends that almost every disease outside of the female reproductive system has been studied almost exclusively in men. Physician Andrew G. Kadar maintains that American health care delivery and research efforts actually benefit women at the expense of men.

Psychiatrist Sally K. Severino and physician Margaret L. Moline argue that premenstrual syndrome (PMS) is a legitimate illness. Psychology professor

Maria Gurevich suggests that PMS is a complex, culturally constructed category that imposes a label that is socially damaging to women.

Freelance reporter Celeste McGovern states that induced abortion is often psychologically harmful. Technical writer Joyce Arthur asserts that most women who elect to have an abortion experience little or no psychological harm.

Lynette J. Dumble, a research fellow in the Department of Surgery at the University of Melbourne, asserts that silicone breast implants have caused recipients to become ill. Author Michael Fumento states that solid research has proven that silicone breast implants are not dangerous.

Efua Dorkenoo, a World Health Organization (WHO) consultant on women's health, argues for worldwide regulation of ritual female genital surgery (RFGS) based on human rights standards. Scholar Eric Winkel suggests that Islamic legal discourse be utilized as a forum for resolving issues associated with RFGS.

INTRODUCTION

Perceptions and Processes in Gender Studies

Alison D. Spalding

WHAT IS GENDER?

The *PDR Medical Dictionary* (1995) defines *gender* as "a category to which an individual is assigned by self or others, on the basis of sex." The *New Websters Dictionary and Thesaurus of the English Language* (1993) defines *gender* as "the classification of words, or the class to which a word belongs by virtue of such classification, according to the sex of the referent (natural gender) or according to arbitrary distinctions of form and syntax (grammatical gender)." *Longman's Dictionary of Psychology and Psychiatry* (1984) defines *gender role* as "the pattern of masculine or feminine behavior that characterizes an individual, defining masculine and feminine in terms accepted by the particular culture. The gender role is largely determined by one's rearing and may or may not conform to the individual's biologically determined sexual identity." Immediately it becomes clear that controversy over gender-related topics begins with something as simple as a definition.

The division of the human race by gender has introduced controversy beyond that which has emanated from other social human divisions. Across cultures, the male-female distinction has been assigned meanings and importance that have implications for virtually all aspects of society. Yet controversy exists over how various meanings and significance should be assigned to gender. Have assigned meanings been accurately based on human nature and intrinsic biological and physiological inevitabilities? Are they the result of socialization processes? Or are they based on some combination of the two? This question lies at the heart of many of the controversial issues addressed in this book.

Issues of gender can generate many questions when it comes to definitions of femininity and masculinity. Are such definitions shaped and limited by cultural perceptions of femininity and masculinity? Are female and male human behaviors traceable to such social factors as stereotyping, self-fulfilling prophecy, conformity to social pressure, or expectancy effects? Or, alternatively, do cultural definitions of femininity and masculinity simply reflect reality or the natural order of existence? Does behavior typically exhibited by men and women reflect the evolutionary concept of natural selection? Examination of the issues presented in this volume will provide a sampling of the many ways in which the topic of gender is addressed.

THE NATURE OF WOMEN'S STUDIES AND
GENDER STUDIES PROGRAMS

Women's studies programs, which predate gender studies programs, began by embodying a feminist critical approach to knowledge. Feminism is an ideology that, in its most basic form, directly opposes sexism by supporting gender equality and by portraying females as essentially equal to males. Feminism has been a modern force in shaping the American women's movement and in shaping women's studies programs. These programs started with the assumption that men and women live within historical contexts that had been previously ignored or hidden.

Women's studies courses traditionally encourage students to develop an awareness of context by learning about the ways in which their personal gender identities, and those of their friends and loved ones, have been shaped by sociological, psychological, and biological contexts and forces. In other words, these classrooms provide an environment in which students can interpret their own social contexts from the perspective of their personal experiences. The process is designed to assist students in developing critical awareness, which lends itself to discussion of gender-related variables and factors that may be transformed, reinforced, changed, or strengthened as deemed appropriate. Student-teacher relationships are also used to highlight awareness of gender via in-class dialogue and negotiation. The classroom has provided a model for learning about the process of gender interaction and has promoted different contexts through which to view gender.

WOMEN'S MOVEMENTS AND MEN'S MOVEMENTS
IN THE UNITED STATES

On July 14, 1848, four women drafted an announcement for a meeting to be held in Seneca Falls, New York, for the purpose of discussing the social, civil, and religious conditions and rights of women. The group was interested in elementary rights for women, including the right to divorce without losing property and children, the right to be educated, the right to vote, and the right to legal equality. As a result of the Seneca Falls Convention, the first women's movement began in the mid-nineteenth century and was articulated most famously by Susan B. Anthony and Elizabeth Cady Stanton.

By the end of the nineteenth century women's appeals for change had been challenged, and the first wave of the women's movement seemed to have stalled. Many gains had been reversed. The term *feminism* entered the popular vocabulary in the early 1910s, and women launched a nationwide political campaign in the struggle for suffrage. In 1916 the National Women's Party was organized, a campaign for an Equal Rights Amendment was launched, and working women formed their own trade unions, demanding decent pay and better working conditions. But, again, postfeminist sentiment surfaced in the press, just after women had won the right to vote. In the 1920s the women's movement stalled again. Some saw this decline in the women's movement as a sign of completion rather than as a sign of failure.

The women's movement finally resurfaced in the 1970s when concerned parties forged historic and record numbers of antidiscrimination and equal employment policies and helped to legalize abortion. But although support for the women's movement and the Equal Rights Amendment reached a peak in 1981, the amendment was defeated the following year. By the mid-1980s postfeminism had returned, and resistance to the women's movement and especially to feminism in its original form had acquired mass social and political support once again.

Also in the 1970s and 1980s the first men's movements were introduced. Warren Farrell, author of *The Liberated Man* (Random House, 1974), organized hundreds of men's groups, which were intended to be counterparts to women's consciousness-raising groups. Within these sessions men were encouraged to listen to women rather than dominate them, to explore the political underpinnings of their marriages and relationships, and to explore the link between machismo and violence. Farrell also founded 60 "men's liberation" chapters in the National Organization for Women in the 1970s. He was hailed in the *Chicago Tribune* as the "Gloria Steinem of men's liberation."

The newest of the men's movements, Promise Keepers, is an all-male social movement that was founded in 1990 by Bill McCartney, a former football coach at the University of Colorado. Promise Keepers was ostensibly organized in response to men's failures to fulfill their roles as husbands, fathers, and moral leaders, a failure that leaders say led to a breakdown of family values and of society. The movement has grown from a local fellowship of 72 men joining for prayer to a multidenominational national phenomenon.

GENDER AND SOCIETY

All societies create and define gender roles and reinforce behaviors that are consistent with their prescriptions. Whether or not these prescriptions should be challenged and possibly altered continues to be a matter of debate. Important though it may be to reach a consensus with respect to societal values and gender, no such consensus exists. Indeed, issues concerning gender—in interaction with other variables such as race, class, and age—present many questions and challenges for social and political leaders and advocacy groups.

Are sex differences in behavior, perceptions, temperament, and the like the inevitable outcome of the anatomical and physiological differences between the sexes? Are gender roles socially constructed, or are they biologically inevitable? These questions lie at the heart of the first issue in this volume, which raises questions about patriarchy and male dominance in American society. Feminists assume that current inequalities are a direct result of socialization and are thus malleable. Other writers argue that feminists falsely reconstruct gender realities to deny the fact that biological differences contribute significantly to gender inequalities.

The second controversy involves the "beauty industry." Many service providers and consumers see appearance-related services as self-image enhancers for women, offering strategies for expanding women's opportunities. Engaging in beauty rituals, practices, and procedures is seen as taking control of one's own appearance. Opponents of the beauty industry, however, argue that the multiple costs of pursuing beauty, including physical danger and emotional, financial, and temporal costs, far exceed any potential enhancements that could be made.

Issue 3 involves a debate over the social benefit of the recent large-scale mobilization of male Promise Keepers. This all-male social movement of Christian fundamentalist religious origins has mushroomed into a national phenomenon and is at the core of a major social controversy. While conservative politicians and fundamentalist Christian religious groups see this movement as a panacea and a positive challenge for men, critics fear that Promise Keepers is one of the most dangerous political organizations active in the United States today.

The changing political and social climate of the past three decades has led to a variety of views on the effects of the sex industry for women, the focus of Issue 4. Early research on the effects of explicit erotic stimuli on behavior was limited. In 1970 the President's Commission on Obscenity and Pornography concluded that there was no evidence that exposure to sexually explicit materials is harmful in any significant way. The growth of the women's movement led to renewed attention to the role of the sex industry as it affected women. Since the early 1970s a steady stream of researchers have investigated a possible connection between pornography and sexual aggression. Although the 1986 *Final Report of the Attorney General's Commission on Pornography* stated that there was evidence of a causal link between pornography and both aggressive behavior and the degradation of women, there remains widespread disagreement on this topic among behavioral scientists.

GENDER, WORK, AND SCHOOL

Contemporary feminism has altered the structure of American society by promoting changes in traditional gender role expectations for men and women in education and employment. In the interest of advancing the causes of women, feminism has supported an expanded women's presence in a wide variety of work and school settings. While these changes are seen by many as healthy and positive, others have concerns about the impact of the changes on society and about the new problems that are brought about when work settings integrate males and females. Still others remain unsatisfied with the changes and believe that more progress needs to be made for women.

The gap between men's perceptions and women's experiences when it comes to the issue of workplace harassment (Issue 5), according to some writers, reflects a substantial level of denial in the American population. Other Americans believe that sexual harassment is highly exaggerated and argue that women tend to invite or condone the behaviors they later report as harassment. People object to sexual harassment rulings in the workplace mainly because they are unwilling to allow intrusive governmental regulations due to the free speech implications of monitoring offensive expression. Others believe that sexual harassment laws play an important role in underscoring the power differential between men and women in society.

Issue 6 involves the appropriate role of women in history courses and textbooks. From 1980 to the present, the field of women's history has grown spectacularly both in institutional and intellectual terms. For the past 15 years, students of women's history have challenged conceptual frameworks and methods of history documentation with new categories and with interdisciplinary work. Some write in favor of the expanded importance of women in history, indicating that this process should continue, while others argue that history textbooks have already included women more extensively and in more biased ways than is appropriate.

The next topic of debate is that of workplace discrimination. Some commentators argue that women want certain privileges such as shorter work hours and more flexible scheduling because of their "unique inclinations" to nurture young, elderly, and ill family members. However, they also maintain that women cannot have "special" treatment in the workplace and still expect to receive equal opportunity for advancement. Such theorists believe that workplace discrimination does not exist *per se* but that women make their own decisions because of their different priorities. On the other side are writers who maintain that women should not be the focus of discrimination simply because they want to have children or because they are pregnant.

Another workplace controversy involving gender surrounds the role of women in the military. Society's perception of appropriate roles for men and women together with concerns about national security have provided the rationale for restricting female involvement in the U.S. armed forces. Although the 1970s brought some changes for women in this regard, positions for women in active duty have remained limited, especially combat positions. Many Americans remain unprepared to acknowledge females as fighters who are capable of killing. Alternatively, some theorists maintain that technology neutralizes any reasonable concern over the military effectiveness of women.

Issue 9 concerns the role of women in the religious hierarchy. This debate became sharply defined in 1989, when a group of women launched a challenge against fundamentalism in religion. Feminist thinkers have long asserted that the Catholic Church, along with most other religious dominations, invariably sanctifies the unequal status of women in society. Opposing groups suggest that women have already gained so much ground that they have essentially taken over some religious denominations completely.

The final issue in Part 2 (Issue 10) involves the question of whether or not mothers of young children should work outside the home. The popular view that mothers should stay home was reinforced by early research in the 1940s and 1950s that pointed to adverse effects resulting from repeated separation of infants and mothers. In the 1970s the numbers of working mothers increased, which sparked new research and different findings. There is tremendous controversy over how much parenting children need and over what constitutes "appropriate" parenting.

GENDER AND RELATIONSHIPS

A variety of themes runs through gender controversies with regard to the appropriate construction of social relationships at interpersonal levels. Some groups believe that a traditional family structure and traditional parenting behaviors are in the best interests of society, while other groups believe that these traditional arrangements are inappropriate in today's progressive, modern world. To complicate matters further, certain governmental policies may reinforce or alter existing structures, and debates often occur over what constitutes appropriate governmental intervention.

The first issue in Part 3 (Issue 11) addresses the risks and benefits of divorce for men and for women in terms of physical and mental health. Most scholars acknowledge that health may be affected by a combination of economic, social, and behavioral factors, and a variety of works have emphasized the effects of family relations on physical well-being. In some studies, married individuals have been found to enjoy greater health and well-being than nonmarrieds. Disagreement remains, however, as to why married people tend to be in better health. Critics point to alternative variables, such as the social acceptability of the role of marriage, or the possibility that healthier individuals may be more likely to get (and stay) married in the first place. They also point to literature showing that marriage may be damaging to those whose relationships are largely characterized by negative interactions.

While the risks and benefits of marriage itself are a source of controversy, the subject of marriage among African American individuals contains yet additional areas of disagreement (Issue 12). Currently, in the United States about 43 percent of African American homes are headed by women, while numbers of African American males who are available for marriage to black women continues to decline. Some writers report that the shortage of marriageable black males is disturbing and frustrating for black women. Others define the role of the African American woman in a unique context that diminishes the importance of marriage.

Another controversial issue that remains prevalent in the United States is that of child custody following divorce. The current "best interest of the children" standards are not strictly adhered to, some critics of family courts say, and they maintain that male discrimination in child custody hearings is rampant. Others maintain that most fathers do not want custody anyway and that, of those who do, at least half will be awarded custody of their children. Whether or not women are consistently and unfairly awarded custody is at the heart of this debate.

Issue 14 concerns the presence (or lack) of gender roles in lesbian couples. In the 1950s and 1960s, some say, lesbians were also more inclined to enact gender roles within their relationships than they are today. The enactment of such gender roles became a focus of criticism by lesbian-feminists in the 1970s, who saw the portrayal of gender roles as an imitation of a heterosexual norm. Currently there is controversy in this area: some writers support gender roles as entirely normal, natural, and prevalent, completely distinct from heterosexual gender roles. Others continue to support the focus on gender role neutrality that was put forth in the 1970s.

GENDER AND HEALTH

Men and women in the United States continue to face a variety of severe health problems. With traditional gender roles and values continually changing, some health issues have become gender issues. Competing groups debate the importance of health research and health care allocations for one sex versus the other, and political controversy surrounds a variety of issues that may disproportionately affect one gender over the other.

A current controversy in the field of medicine involves the question of whether or not males receive more than their fair share of medical resources with regard to research, medical care, surgical procedures, and money. Some writers have highlighted details suggesting that men have been the primary beneficiaries of these resources. Others maintain that greater expenditures of all types of resources have been devoted to medical needs that are exclusive to women.

Another debate in the area of health and gender involves the construct of premenstrual syndrome (PMS). The health care system has been accused of medicalizing women's lives to the point where normal female life events such as menstruation, pregnancy, childbirth, and menopause are considered diseases. PMS is often cited as a prime example of this phenomenon. PMS has been described from a medical perspective, and various treatment options have been proposed. However, opponents have voiced a number of concerns about PMS, ranging from reservations about research methodology and treatment to questions about the very existence of the syndrome.

Issue 17 focuses on whether or not women experience negative aftereffects following elective abortion. This is one of the more highly charged controversial issues of these times. Some research studies prior to the legalization of abortion in 1973 suggested that women who had abortions suffered serious emotional trauma after the fact. However, later findings (subsequent to the legalization of abortion) indicated that there are no psychological aftereffects associated with abortion or that any such effects were negligible. Nevertheless, there is concern that to minimize the negative aftereffects of abortion is to overlook the needs of women who do have such problems.

Another current issue associated with health and gender addresses the alleged medical danger of silicone breast implants. Critics of the 1992 moratorium placed on manufacturers and distributors of silicone breast implants believe that credible evidence linking implants to disease has not been presented and that settlements given to women simply reflect the inappropriate power of the U.S. Food and Drug Administration and the breakdown of the tort system. In contrast, groups that are concerned about the possible effects of silicone implants on the human body see implant availability as evidence of a lingering medical negligence toward women. The central locus of the debate presented herein is about the appropriateness of, motive for, and ramifications of removing silicone breast implants from the market.

Finally, one of today's most controversial issues regarding gender and health is the cultural practice of ritual female genital surgery (RFGS), also known as female genital mutilation (FGM). RFGS, a widespread practice in Africa and the Middle East, entails the removal of part of or all of the external female genitalia and/or injury to the female genital organs for cultural or other nonmedical reasons. Those who object to the procedure are fighting to have it banned in all areas of the world in the name of human rights. On the other hand, many of the representatives from the cultures that practice RGFS are offended by the regulatory attempts of countries like the United States. They claim that it is inappropriate for one nation to interfere with the decision-making autonomy of another.

CONCLUSION

Whether or not any of the debates presented in this book can ever be conclusively resolved depends on a number of considerations. For example, how much of what the writers present is based on empirical evidence? Do writers on each side of the issues offer a fair representation of the research, or do they select research that supports their personal points of view while omitting findings that may cast doubt on their claims? Do the writers present research findings within their proper context? Empirical research, which may be defined as research that tests theories against observable facts, serves as an excellent tool for either unmasking and discrediting or promoting and reinforcing assumptions about sex and gender. However, many of the topics that do lend themselves to empirical examination have yet to be resolved in any consistent way. Some claim that in the controversial area of gender studies it is not possible for the research process itself to remain unbiased because opinions are formed and knowledge is gathered within a social context.

One of the underlying assumptions of this book is that the study of gender, as it applies to these issues, requires continuous dialogue. Differences of opinion and dissent will inevitably occur. The two selections presented for each issue do not always represent the definitive position on either side. The format is provided to give students a chance to draw their own conclusions as they observe the prejudices of the speakers and the strengths and limitations of the research and the arguments.

On the Internet . . .

http://www.dushkin.com

Feminism and Women's Resources
This listing of feminism and women's resources includes information on and links to women's organizations, women's studies resources, and other organizations and links of interest. *http://zeno.ibd.nrc.ca/~mansfield/feminism*

The Men's Issues Page
This site on men's issues includes news and a "hierarchical topic index." The alphabetical subject index contains links to topics such as battered men, false rape/abuse/molestation reporting, men's physical and mental health, men's organizations, and periodicals of men's movements. *http://www.vix.com/men/index.html*

The Well
This site is a forum for Feminists for Free Expression (FFE). It provides information on FFE as well as links to bibliographies of books, books by FFE members, and the FFE's Free Speech Pamphlet Series. FFE serves as a leading voice opposing state and national legislation that threatens free speech. It supports the rights of artists who have had their work suppressed or censored, provides expert speakers to universities, and defends the right to free expression in court cases.
http://www.well.com/user/freedom/

WomensNet
WomensNet supports women's organizations worldwide by providing and adapting telecommunications technology to enhance their work. The information on women's issues at this site is organized into an action alerts archive; a headlines archive; current highlights, headlines, and features; and an issue index.
http://www.igc.org/igc/womensnet

PART 1

Gender and Society

However important it may be to reach a consensus with respect to societal values and gender, no such consensus exists. Indeed, issues concerning gender in interaction with other variables, such as race, class, and age, present many questions and challenges for social and political leaders and advocacy groups. All societies create and define gender roles and reinforce behaviors that are consistent with their prescriptions. Whether or not these prescriptions should be challenged or even altered in our society continues to be a matter of debate. Issues that highlight the extent of controversy in the area of gender and society include male dominance, the beauty industry, men's movements, and the sex industry. Analysis of these issues involves strongly held and often opposing values and beliefs.

■ Is Male Dominance Rooted in Biology?

■ Is the Quest for Beauty Necessarily Damaging to Women?

■ Is the Men's Movement "Promise Keepers" Socially Positive?

■ Is the Sex Industry Harmful to Women?

ISSUE 1

Is Male Dominance Rooted in Biology?

YES: Steven Goldberg, from "Is Patriarchy Inevitable?" *National Review* (November 11, 1996)

NO: Deborah L. Rhode, from *Speaking of Sex: The Denial of Gender Inequality* (Harvard University Press, 1997)

ISSUE SUMMARY

YES: Sociology professor Steven Goldberg asserts that the social environment is a dependent variable that is limited by the constraints of our physiological construction. He claims that male dominance is rooted in these physiological differences.

NO: Attorney Deborah L. Rhode argues that it is not nature but rather how we interpret it that accounts for gender inequalities in society today.

America is considered a patriarchal society. More than 95 percent of corporate executives and 85 percent of elected officials are male. Meanwhile, more than two-thirds of poor adults are female. White males account for about 40 percent of the population but compose about 95 percent of senior managers, 90 percent of newspaper editors, 80 percent of congressional legislators, and 80 percent of *Forbes* magazine's list of the richest Americans. Women continue to perform the vast majority of work in the home, which serves to limit their representation as leaders in the outside world. Recent research indicates that when children are ill, mothers stay home about 70 percent of the time. In many of the remaining circumstances, women make alternative arrangements that will not disrupt their husbands' schedules. American workplaces are gender segregated and gender stratified, with female minorities at the bottom of the occupational hierarchy. Full-time female employees earn less than 75 cents for every dollar earned by men.

The nature-nurture controversy lies at the heart of the debate over whether or not males are innately destined to assume the majority of leadership positions outside of (and possibly within) the home. "Nature" suggests that men's leadership roles are related to biological differences between men and women, while "nurture" suggests that men lead and women follow only because they have been socialized to do so. The nature argument proposes that male dominance derives from aggressive tendencies of the male, which are grounded in their physiological composition. One of the most salient behavioral differences discussed by gender researchers from the nature perspective is the assertion that most men are more aggressive than most women and are more inclined to take risks. Theorists argue that men's innate attraction to thrills propels them toward social status and dominance, often expressed as the urge to assume a leadership position or challenge for supremacy. Whether or not this innate inclination to take charge is solely the result of male hormones, men are born to lead, say proponents of patriarchy.

The nurture argument provides an alternative explanation for the human history of patriarchy. Scholars on this side of the debate believe that there is an array of processes through which women are socialized, indoctrinated, and "coerced" into cooperation with patriarchal systems. For example, women have been (and often still are, according to some views) prevented from fully participating in such empowering activities as education (including learning women's history), politics, and the use of economic resources. This may have led to women's internalizing the idea of their own inferiority. Living under male domain throughout history, often exclusively as wives and daughters, women may have exchanged submission for protection and unpaid labor for economic maintenance.

The core issue is whether this tendency toward patriarchy is the result of purely historical and social forces or whether there is some natural human tendency toward male dominance. Supporters of the former argument agree that Western society has been dominated by men, but they dispute the idea that the dominance has resulted from inherent biological traits. Biology, they argue, does not necessarily dictate the forms that gender differences will assume. Roles and characteristics associated with gender differ considerably across time and culture. Gender disparities, they believe, reflect inequality and injustice as social problems.

In the following selections, Steven Goldberg views the social environment as a *dependent* variable whose limits are set by the physiological construction of humans (i.e., the *independent* variable). He argues that human anatomy and physiology ensure that patriarchy is inevitable. Deborah L. Rhode argues that it is not nature but rather how we interpret its endowments that accounts for gender inequalities in society today. She debates the universality of the sex-linked traits often presented as proof that the male is superior, suggesting instead that recent anthropological evidence casts doubt on such theories.

3

YES
Steven Goldberg

IS PATRIARCHY INEVITABLE?

In five hundred years the world, in all likelihood, will have become homogenized. The thousands of varied societies and their dramatically differing methods of socialization, cohesion, family, religion, economy, and politics will have given way to a universal culture. Fortunately, cultural anthropologists have preserved much of our present diversity, which may keep our descendants from too hastily allowing their natural human ego- and ethnocentricity to conclude that theirs is the only way to manage a society.

However, the anthropological sword is two-edged. While diversity is certainly apparent from anthropological investigations, it is also clear that there are realities which manifest themselves no matter what the varied forms of the aforementioned institutions. Because these universal realities cut across cultural lines, they are crucial to our understanding of what society *by its nature* is and, perhaps, of what human beings are. It is important, then, that we ask why, when societies differ as much as do those of the Ituri Pygmy, the Jivaro, the American, the Japanese, and a thousand others, some institutions are universal.

It is always the case that the universal institution serves some need rooted in the deepest nature of human beings. In some cases the explanation of universality is obvious (e.g., why every society has methods of food gathering). But there are other universalities which are apparent, though without any obvious explanation. Of the thousands of societies on which we have any evidence stronger than myth (a form of evidence that would have us believe in cyclops), there is no evidence that there has ever been a society failing to exhibit three institutions:

1. *Primary hierarchies always filled primarily by men.* A Queen Victoria or a Golda Meir is always an exception and is always surrounded by a government of men. Indeed, the constraints of royal lineage may produce more female societal leaders than does democracy—there were more female heads of state in the first two-thirds of the sixteenth century than there were in the first two-thirds of the twentieth.

2. *The highest status roles are male.* There are societies in which the women do most of the important economic work and rear the children, while the men

seem mostly to hang loose. But, in such societies, hanging loose is given higher status than any non-maternal role primarily served by women. No doubt this is partly due to the fact that the males hold the positions of power. However, it is also likely that high-status roles are male not primarily because they are male (ditch-digging is male and low status), but because they are high status. The high status roles are male because they possess—for whatever socially determined reason in whichever specific society—high status. This high status exerts a more powerful influence on males than it does on females. As a result, males are more willing to sacrifice life's other rewards for status dominance than are females.

In their *Not in Our Genes*, Richard Lewontin, Leon Kamin, and Stephen Rose—who, along with Stephen Jay Gould are the best-known defenders of the view that emphasizes the role of environment and de-emphasizes that of heredity—attempt to find fault with my work by pointing out that most family doctors in the Soviet Union are women. However, they acknowledge that in the Soviet Union "family doctoring [had] lower status than in the United States."

Which is precisely the point. No one doubts that women can be doctors. The question is why doctors (or weavers, or load bearers, etc.) are primarily women only when being a doctor is given lower status than are certain roles played mostly by men—and furthermore, why, even when this is the case (as in Russia) the upper hierarchical positions relevant to that specific area are held by men.

3. *Dominance in male–female relationships is always associated with males.* "Male dominance" refers to the feeling, of both men and women, that the male is dominant and that the woman must "get around" the male to attain power. Social attitudes may be concordant or discordant with the reality of male dominance. In our own society there was a time when the man's "taking the lead" was positively valued by most women (as 30s' movies attest); today such a view is purportedly detested by many. But attitudes toward male-dominance behavior are causally unimportant to the reality they judge—and are not much more likely to eliminate the reality than would a social dislike of men's being taller be able to eliminate men's being taller.

*   *   *

Over the past twenty years, I have consulted every original ethnographic work invoked to demonstrate an exception to these societal universalities. Twenty years ago many textbooks spoke cavalierly of "matriarchies" and "Amazons" and pretended that Margaret Mead had claimed to find a society in which sex roles were reversed. Today no serious anthropologist is willing to claim that any specific society has ever been an exception.

It is often claimed that "modern technology renders the physiological differentiation irrelevant." However, there is not a scintilla of evidence that modernization alters the basic "motivational" factors sufficiently to cast doubt on the continued existence of the universals I discuss. The economic needs of modern society probably do set a lower limit on the status of women; no modern society could give women the low status they receive in some non-modern societies. But modernization probably also sets an upper limit; no modern society is likely to give women the status given to the maternal roles in some other matrilineal societies.

Scandinavian nations, which have long had government agencies devoted to equalizing women's position, are often cited by social scientists as demonstrating modernization's ability to override patriarchy. In fact, however, Norway has 454 municipal councils; 443 are chaired by men. On the Supreme Court, city courts, appellate courts, and in Parliament, there are between five and nine times as many men as there are women. In Sweden, according to government documents, men dominate "senior positions in employer and employee organizations as well as in political and other associations" and only 5 of 82 directors of government agencies, 9 of 83 chairpersons of agency boards, and 9 per cent of judges are women.

One may, of course, hope that all this changes, but one cannot invoke any evidence implying that it will.

Of course, there are those who simply try to assert away the evidence. Lewontin *et al.* write, "Cross cultural universals appear to lie more in the eye of the beholder than in the social reality that is being observed." In fact, with reference to the universalities mentioned above, they do not. If these universals were merely "in the eye of the beholder," the authors would merely have to specify a society in which there was a hierarchy in which males did not predominate and the case would be closed.

The answer to the question of why an institution is universal clearly must be parsimonious. It will not do to ascribe causation of a universal institution to capitalism or Christianity or modernization, because many hundreds of societies lacked these, but not the universal institutions. If the causal explanation is to be at all persuasive, it must in-voke some factor present in every society from the most primitive to the most modern. (Invoking the male's physical strength advantage does meet the requirement of parsimony, but does not counter the evidence of the central importance of neuro-endocrinological psycho-physiological factors.)

When sociologists are forced to acknowledge the universals, they nearly always invoke "socialization" as explanation. But this explanation faces two serious problems. First, it does not explain anything, but merely forces us to ask another question: *Why* does socialization of men and women always work in the same direction? Second, the explanation implicitly assumes that the social environment of expectations and norms acts as an *independent* variable capable of acting as counterpoise to the physiological constituents that make us male and female.

In individual cases, of course, anything can happen. Even when a causation is nearly entirely hereditary, there are many exceptions (as tall women demonstrate). Priests choose to be celibate, but this does not cast doubt on the physiological basis of the "sex drive." To be sure, there is also feedback from the environmental to the physiological, so that association of physical strength with males results in more males lifting weights. However, in principle, a society could find itself with women who were physically stronger than men if women lifted weights throughout their lives and men remained sedentary.

But, in real life, this can't happen because the social environment is a *dependent* variable whose limits are set by our physiological construction. In real life we all observe a male's dominance tendency that is rooted in physiological differences between males and females and, because values and attitudes are not of primary causal importance here, we develop expectations concordant with the male–female behavioral differences.

Most of the discussion of sex differences has emphasized the neuro-endocrinological differentiation of males and females and the cognitive and behavioral differentiation this engenders. This is because there is an enormous amount of evidence demonstrating the role of hormones in fetally differentiating the male and female central nervous systems, CNS response to the potentiating properties of certain hormones, and the thoughts and actions of males and females.

There is not room here for detailed discussion of the neuro-endocrinological mechanism underlying dominance behavior. But a useful analogy is iron and magnet. Iron does not have a "drive" or a "need" to find a magnet, but when there is a magnet in the area, iron, as a result of the very way it is built, tends to react in a certain way. Likewise, the physiological natures of males and females predispose them to have different hierarchies of response to various environmental cues. There is no response that only one sex has; the difference between men and women is the relative strengths of different responses. Males react more readily to hierarchical competitiveness than do females; females react more readily to the needs of an infant-in-distress. Norms and socialization do not cause this difference, but reflect it and make concrete a specific society's specific methods for manifesting the response. (Cleaning a rifle and preparing Spaghetti-Os are not instinctive abilities).

The iron–magnet analogy makes clear the role of social environment. Were there to be a society without hierarchy, status, values, or interdependence of the sexes, there would be no environmental cue to elicit the differentiated, physiologically rooted responses we discuss. But it is difficult to imagine such a society and, indeed, there has never been such a society.

Even if we had no neuro-endocrinological evidence at all, the anthropological evidence alone would be sufficient to force us to posit a mechanism of sexual psycho-physiological differentiation and to predict its discovery. We do, however, possess the neuro-endocrinological evidence and the anthropological evidence permits us to specify the institutional effects—the limits of societal variation that the neuro-endocrinological engenders.

For thousands of years, everyone, save perhaps some social scientists and others ideologically opposed to the idea, have known perfectly well that men and women differ in the physiological factors that underlie masculine and feminine thought and behavior. They may not have known the words to describe the linkage of physiology with thought and behavior, but they knew the linkage was there. (I recently read a comment of a woman in Pennsylvania: "They keep telling us that men and women are the way they are because of what they've been taught, but you can go a hundred miles in any direction and not find a single person who really believes that.") And even the most feminist parent, once she has children, can't help but notice that it is nearly impossible to get small boys to play with dolls not named "Killer Joe, the Marauding Exterminator," or at least with trucks—*big* trucks.

* * *

None of this is to deny tremendous variation on the level of roles. Even in our own society, in just a century the role of secretary changed from virtually solely male to virtually solely female. With the exception of roles associated with child nurturance, political leadership, warfare, security, and crime, virtually every specific role is male in some societies and female in others. No one doubts that the women who exhibit the dominance behavior usually exhibited by men encounter discrimination. But the question remains: why is dominance behavior usually exhibited by *men?*

The implication of all this depends on context. Clearly the correctness or incorrectness of the theory I present is important to an understanding of human behavior and society. But to the individual man or woman, on the other hand, the universals are largely irrelevant. The woman who wishes to become President has a sufficient number of real-life equivalents to know that there is not a constraint rendering impossible a female head of state. But there is no more reason for such a woman to deny that the motivation to rule is more often associated with male physiology than there is for the six-foot woman to pretend that women are as tall as men.

NO

Deborah L. Rhode

THE IDEOLOGY AND BIOLOGY OF GENDER DIFFERENCE

"Is it a boy or a girl?" This is usually the first question we ask at the birth of a child. And the answer remains of crucial importance throughout the child's life. In every known society, gender differences structure human identity and social relationships. Yet biology by no means dictates the form that those differences assume. The roles and characteristics that we associate with males and females vary considerably across time and culture. Still, one similarity remains striking. As anthropologist Margaret Mead once noted, there are cultures in which men weave and women fish, and ones in which women weave and men fish. But in either case, the work that women perform is valued less.

What accounts for both the variations and the uiversalities in sex-linked differences? This is one of the central paradoxes of gender. If biology does not explain the inequalities in men's and women's social positions, why are those inequalities so pervasive and persistent? Alternatively, if biology is the central force in determining male and female identity, why do societies differ so widely in the tasks and traits that are associated with each sex?

Over the past several decades, both the similarities and variations in gender roles have become increasingly apparent. In the West, women's opportunities and employment patterns have changed considerably, but traditional gender stereotypes remain much the same. Despite some variation across class, race, ethnicity, and sexual orientation, the characteristics that American and European societies associate with men and women have changed little from the ones Aristotle described more than two thousand years ago. Masculine traits still include strength, courage, independence, competitiveness, ambition, and aggression. Feminine qualities still include emotional sensitivity, patience, caution, nurturance, passivity, and dependence. Men are taught to place higher value on power, and women to place higher value on interpersonal relationships.

Challenging these gender stereotypes and expanding opportunities for both sexes has been a primary objective of the women's movement. But this objective points to another central paradox. In an important sense, feminism rests on the very differences that it challenges. Those concerned with gender equality seek to prevent traditional gender roles from limiting individuals' aspirations and achievements. Yet by definition, the women's movement also requires some sense of group identity and interests. In effect, feminism assumes the very shared experience that it seeks in part to eliminate.

This tension has pushed the campaign for sexual equality in multiple directions. The American women's movement has long struggled both to challenge and to celebrate gender difference. For many contemporary feminists, the dilemma is how to affirm the value of women's traditional role without perpetuating its constraints. A related concern is how to build on "women's experience" without losing sight of its diversity across time, culture, class, race, ethnicity, and sexual orientation. Progress on both fronts requires rethinking conventional views about the "inherent" nature of women's nature.

THE BIOLOGY OF DIFFERENCE

The biological basis of sex-linked differences is complicated, contested, and confused. It is also increasingly irrelevant. Even those who believe that masculine and feminine traits have a physiological basis acknowledge that society can prevent these differences from translating into social disadvantages or from unnecessarily limiting individual opportunities.

However, assumptions about biology still affect assumptions about fairness —about the appropriateness of current gender roles and the possibilities for change. Popular accounts, such as Robert Wright's "Feminists Meet Mr. Darwin" and Ann Moir and David Jessel's best-selling book *Brain Sex* warn us that "there are some biological facts of life that, with the best and most sexually liberated will in the world, we just cannot buck." Many Americans agree. In one representative poll, 40 percent believed that biology was as important as or more important than culture in creating masculine and feminine attributes. Such perceptions account for many individuals' failure to perceive gender inequality as a significant problem. In their view, as a 1995 ABC-TV documentary suggested, "perhaps instead of suing about difference we should honor it."

Given these assumptions, most debates about sexual equality sooner or later bump up against beliefs about sexual physiology. So it makes sense to start out where we almost always seem to end up: What do we know and what do we only think we know about sex-based difference?

Even to speak of "knowledge" on this subject requires considerable poetic license. "Scientific" wisdom concerning gender traditionally has rested more on ideology than on biology. Until quite recently, the prevailing assumption was that women's nature was to nurture, and that the sexes' distinctive social roles reflected physiological imperatives. Innumerable theories of female incapacity emerged. Leading medical authorities identified a deadly brain-womb conflict. Women had limited "vital forces," and those who concentrated on intellectual rather than reproductive pursuits risked chronic disabilities and permanent sterility.

Many contemporary assertions about sex-based differences bear an equally dubious relationship to the evidence. The differences that figure most prominently in explanations for sex-based inequality deserve particularly close attention. They include reproductive capacity, brain structure, hormonal drives, and physical size and strength.

... [T]he traditional "scientific" explanation for sex-based inequality has rested on sex-based differences in reproductive physiology. Sociobiologists offer the most elaborate rationale. In essence, their theories assume that male dominance and female nurturance are universal traits in humans and in most biologically similar animals. From this vantage, the pervasiveness of these sex-linked traits demonstrates their "adaptiveness" and their genetic basis. Individuals who exhibit adaptive traits leave behind more offspring, and over long cycles of evolution only their genes survive.

Under leading sociobiological accounts, the genetic grounding for sexual differences lies in the structure of sex cells. The female's egg is relatively large because it contains the yolk that nourishes the embryo during early development. By contrast, the male's sperm is small, mobile, and easily replicated. Men can make millions of sperm and therefore have the capacity to spread their genes through promiscuous sex. Women perpetuate their genes by prolonged nurturance of each embryo. In the view of prominent sociobiologists such as Edward Wilson and Richard Dawkins, "female exploitation begins here." Under the primitive subsistence conditions that prevailed throughout most human evolution, women depended on men during periods of pregnancy and breast feeding. Males supposedly were the hunters, while females were the gatherers and nurturers, and each sex developed traits adaptive to those roles. Natural selection thus favored characteristics that encouraged sexual hierarchy: physical strength, aggression, and promiscuity in men; caretaking and fidelity among women.

According to sociobiologists, discriminatory patterns like the double standard of sexual morality rest on this biological foundation. Before the arrival of reliable contraceptives, men best ensured survival of their genes by sleeping around, but not settling down with a woman who did the same. Although recent birth control developments may have "short circuited this [evolutionary] logic, we're still stuck with the minds the logic created."

Popular accounts of sexual difference often reach similar conclusions through simpler routes. To many individuals, it seems obvious that women's capacity for childbirth and breast feeding has encouraged nurturing instincts and priorities that account for contemporary gender roles. As one recent survey participant put it, "Just like in the animal kingdom, the mother takes care of the kids—it's instinctive." Fathers can learn to do certain tasks, "but a man cannot be a mother."

Moreover, according to many commentators, the rigid gender linkages that the women's movement deplores are a result not only of biological differences but also of women's responses to those differences. Sociobiologists often argue that male drives for power and control of resources are partly the result of female preferences for successful, ambitious mates. These preferences, operating repeatedly over thousands of generations, are to blame for traits that now perpetuate gender inequality. This leads to the somewhat "startling" conclusion that women are in important respects responsible for their own subordination, as well as for male casualties in the competitive struggle; shorter life spans and higher homicide rates are just "the tip of the iceberg of the cost of competition to men."

From this perspective, because the root of gender roles is biological, society's attempts at interference are costly and futile. If the sexes have not come out equal in the process, no one is to blame. The problem, as sociobiologists see it, is simply that "Mother Nature is a sexist." Women are both products and prisoners of their reproductive history.

Yet a careful review of the evidence suggests that the problem lies elsewhere, as does the sexism. It is not nature but what we make of her endowments that accounts for gender inequalities. Recent anthropological evidence casts doubt both on the universality of sex-linked traits and on our inheritance of rigid gender role divisions from early hunter-gatherer societies. Contrary to many sociobiologists' assertions, it does not appear that men in these societies were the only major providers while women were constantly preoccupied with childrearing. Rather, birthrates were relatively low and the sexes shared breadwinning responsibilities.

Sociobiologists' frequent reliance on other primates for evidence of universal male and female traits is equally suspect. Popular articles like "Sexual Harassment: Why Even Bees Do It" provide an amusing read but an inadequate foundation for sweeping generalizations. The animal kingdom is large enough to provide both examples and counterexamples of most gendered behaviors, and of environmental influences on prevailing patterns. Instances of female dominance and male nurturance are readily available. For example, among ruffled lemurs and South American night monkeys, males tend infants while females forage.

Variations are also apparent among human patterns of male aggression and female nurturing. Mothers have not always assumed primary childcare responsibilities. Upper-class European women once relied heavily on wetnurses, governesses, tutors, and male boarding school teachers. Men in some nonindustrial cultures also have shared power and parenting tasks. So too, in contemporary American society, fathers who become primary caretakers (even involuntarily because of a wife's death) do not display any less nurturing capacity than mothers. Nor is there an adequate biological explanation for why other men, when they take on childrearing tasks, generally end up with the most enjoyable ones—playing with infants, not changing their diapers.

Yet rather than addressing these counterarguments, many sociobiologists simply ignore or categorically dismiss their critics. In a telling passage, exceptional only in its candor, Robert Wright announces that "there is not a single well-known feminist who has learned enough about modern Darwinism to pass judgment on it." Yet... there may not be a single prominent sociobiologist who has learned enough about modern feminist critiques to pass judgment on *them*. Those critiques rest on a vast array of scientific research that casts doubt on physiological explanations for gender hierarchies. Summarizing this evidence, Harvard biologist Ruth Hubbard reminds us that stereotypical patterns of male dominance and female nurturance "do not characterize all human societies and there is no reason to believe that our biology determines the ways we construct them."

Related assumptions about women's intellectual incapacities reflect similar problems and a similarly troubled history. Nineteenth-century experts (mis)-measured women's brains and declared them smaller, lighter, and therefore inferior. It later turned out that women did not have smaller brains relative to their body size. Nor did the size of the brain determine intellectual capacity, as should have been apparent from even casual comparisons of intelligence among certain large and small animals. But no matter. When scientists did not find the anatomical difference they were seeking, they often simply shifted the location of their search and their methods for measurement. For example, experts originally considered the left hemisphere of the brain to be the source of intellect and reason and the right to be the site of passion and irrationality. Not coincidentally, these scientists also believed that men had greater brain capacity on the left, and that women had greater capacity on the right. In the 1960s and 1970s, when experts began to suspect that the right hemisphere was the source of genius and creative inspiration, male superiority in brain function promptly migrated. So, too, in the 1920s, after women scored higher on the first IQ tests, authors changed the questions.

Despite this undistinguished legacy, the search for sex differences in the brain doggedly continues....

Yet the point on which there is great scholarly consensus is that experts have reached no consensus on these issues. Researchers have not produced consistent findings on sex-based differences in brain structure. Nor is there agreement on the way that this structure affects cognitive functions and interacts with environmental influences. Moreover, the inequalities that supposedly result from brain structure are extremely small and unstable, a fact that the popular media usually obscure. Gender accounts for a very small part of the reported variations among individuals in math, verbal, and visual/spatial skills, usually between 1 and 5 percent. Such small disparities scarcely support sociobiologists' sweeping assertions about natural differences in the sexes' occupations, interests, and capacities....

Although there is much we still do not know about sex-based differences in math capabilities, there is much we do know about differences in math education.... [U]ntil we address biases in our instructional approaches, we cannot begin to disentangle genetic and cultural influences.

The same is true for theories about hormonal influences....

Treating women as "naturally abnormal" in response to hormonal levels can mask the importance of other explanations. Much of the depression or irritability that Americans often attribute to women's "time of life" or "time of the month" may have much more to do with stressful external conditions than with internal hormonal changes. Stereotyping women as imbalanced may simply add to the stress. Such stereotyping seems especially dubious in light of recent research suggesting that men also experience hormone-related fluctuations in mood and behavior.

Assumptions about a hormonal basis for male dominance and aggression require similar qualification. Sociobiological and popular discussion often assumes that male aggression is a "fact of life" (although not beyond modest "cultural improvement") and that woman's less assertive nature has "sealed her fate for millions of years." Such discussion frequently lumps together widely disparate behaviors—everything from rape to reckless driving, rough-and-tumble play, and political ambition. Yet it does not seem likely that the same hormonal drives explain all of these behaviors, particularly since they vary so widely across cultures. In some societies rape is almost unknown; in others, such as ours, it is all too common.

Moreover, in most cultures, certain forms of female aggression are unexceptional. American women generally have been no less supportive than men of wartime efforts and no less effective in military, police, and prison security work. Nor is the relationship of hormones to aggression well established. Many studies find no correlation between levels of testosterone and violence, hostility, or aggression.

This is not to discount the significance of sex-based differences in many aggressive behaviors or to suggest that biology plays no part in explaining them.... [T]here are ways in which "boys will be boys" despite their parents' best efforts. It may also be significant that girls with sex-related abnormalities, such as high exposure to testosterone during prenatal development, reportedly display increased aggression and preferences for "male" toys.

Yet it by no means follows that the extent of current gender differences in aggression is physiologically determined or that we can separate biological from cultural influences. Recent research finds that gender accounts for only about 5 percent of the variation among individuals in aggressive behavior, and that both parents and peers are more tolerant of such behavior in males than in females. Even the best human behavior studies cannot view nature in the raw. The adults who reported masculine tendencies in girls with abnormal hormonal exposure knew of those abnormalities. Parents' and teachers' expectations about the effects of testosterone may have influenced

how they interpreted and reacted to the girls' behaviors.

Like other cultures, America encourages and values aggression more in males than in females. What often looks appropriately assertive in men appears abrasive in women. Games, sports, media images, parental attitudes, and peer pressures all amplify gender differences.... [V]iolence is, in large measure, learned behavior. Whatever their biological predispositions, males acquire models for aggression from family and societal settings. As social critic Barbara Ehrenreich notes, "However science eventually defines it, 'la différence' can be amplified or minimized by human cultural arrangements. The choice is up to us, and not to our genes."

A final cluster of "real differences" between the sexes involves size and strength. For centuries, men's physical advantages have served to enforce and justify their cultural dominance. These advantages in certain military, athletic, and employment contexts help rationalize other inequalities. The use or threat of physical coercion also discourages women's resistance. Of course, in any advanced industrial nation, technology has dramatically reduced the importance of gender differences in size and strength....

[S]ex-based disparities in height and weight, like other ostensibly innate differences, vary considerably in response to cultural influences. In societies where neither men nor women perform much physical labor, the gender gap in body sizes is considerably smaller. And in America, sex-based differences in speed and strength have narrowed as opportunities for women have broadened. Increased support for female athletes has enabled them to improve their performance in many sports at rates much greater than those of men. Given current patterns, sex disparities in some events may disappear altogether in the next half-century....

Although there is much about [sex-based] differences that we have yet to understand, one general point seems clear. Mind, body, and culture interact in ways that scientific research cannot wholly disentangle. And while we cannot definitively resolve the nature/nurture debate, we can look more critically beneath and beyond it. John Dewey once noted that progress often occurs not when we solve questions but when "we get over them." If equality between the sexes is our ultimate goal, we need to care less about the biological origins of difference and more about its social consequences.

THE CULTURE OF DIFFERENCE

To challenge the biological foundations of gender differences is not to discount the importance of those differences in shaping individual identity.... [G]ender matters in profound ways. Men and women differ in virtually every aspect of their life experience, including power, physical security, work, reproduction, sexuality, and family roles. The problem is not that we exaggerate the importance of gender. It is rather that we do so selectively and simplistically in ways that disadvantage women.

For those writing about gender-related issues, " 'difference' is where the action is," notes columnist Katha Pollitt. For those concerned with gender inequality, this focus is a mixed blessing. Emphasizing women's distinctive contributions can serve as a useful counterweight to traditional biases. But the cost is to overstate

the difference in sex-linked traits, and to overlook the disadvantages that follow from it.

The strengths and limitations of difference-oriented frameworks are apparent in an increasing body of gender-related analysis. One cluster of work is largely descriptive. For example, some feminist and pop-psychological accounts of conversational patterns aim to increase understanding without passing judgment on males' and females' distinctive styles. Other works are explicitly evaluative. From their perspective, women are not just different but, in important respects, better: more caring, compassionate, and cooperative. On this view, the greater involvement of women may help transform our professional and political life.

Unlike sociobiological accounts, these analyses generally do not assume that gender differences are biologically rooted. Nor do adherents agree about the causes of such differences. Some feminists believe that women's experience of mothering, or of being expected to perform nurturing roles, accounts for a wide range of sex-specific traits and values. Other theorists emphasize more general processes of socialization and subordination. Their frameworks stress the cultural pressures on women to gain status and approval by conforming to traditional feminine standards.

What unites these diverse analyses is their tendency to make broad generalizations about sex-linked characteristics. Theorists such as Deborah Tannen chart the differences in male and female conversation. In their view, men are more likely to use language to maintain status, establish control, attract attention, solve problems, and exhibit knowledge. Women are more likely to use language to establish connection, give support, and reach consensus. Philosophers and psychologists like Carol Gilligan argue that women tend to reason in a "different voice." According to these theorists, men attach greater priority to abstract analysis, formal rights, and competitive structures; women give greater value to social context, caring relationships, and cooperative interaction. . . .

A quarter-century ago, in *Man's World, Woman's Place,* Elizabeth Janeway referred to stereotypes about male achievers and female nurturers as an idea whose time won't go. Our renewed fixation on difference confirms her point. We have not yet found ways to acknowledge sex-linked qualities without perpetuating their constraints. When the subject is gender, we may never entirely escape this dilemma of difference. But we can at least refocus our inquiry. Our universe of pinks and blues could acquire a more complicated color scheme. We should focus less on the quest for inherent differences and more on the inequality they create.

We also need a clearer understanding of the limits of gender in structuring our analysis. To divide the world solely by sex is to ignore the ways in which biological status is experienced differently by different groups in different contexts. There is no "generic woman," and more attention must center on variations in culture, class, race, ethnicity, age, and sexual orientation. We must become equally sensitive to the contextual forces that lead the same women to vary in the feminine characteristics that they express in different social circumstances.

This focus on context offers a way around the dilemmas of difference that have long plagued the women's movement. Such a framework can acknowledge the qualities traditionally associated with women without exaggerating their extent or assuming that they are biologically determined. As an increasing body of research makes clear, changes in social expectations and in the gender composition of a particular setting significantly affect women's willingness to express gender-related traits.

Our daily experiences bear this out. I have noticed the shift in my own willingness to raise "women's issues" in workplace settings now that I have ten female colleagues rather than one. Women's "different voice" speaks in more than one register; and the same is true for men. Boys may be boys, but they express that identity differently in fraternity parties than in job interviews with a female manager.

The advantage of focusing on context is that we can acknowledge gender differences but resist dichotomies. We can avoid sweeping assertions about women's and men's essential natures while noting the importance of sex-linked experiences. Whatever our biological predispositions, we shape gender differences through a complex set of forces. Much depends on childhood socialization and structural constraints such as status, wealth, and power. A better understanding of all our differences also permits a better understanding of our similarities—of women's and men's common needs, aspirations, and capacities for change.

POSTSCRIPT

Is Male Dominance Rooted in Biology?

While Goldberg argues that men have been the leaders in every culture throughout time, there are many theorists and anthropologists who would disagree. For example, Peggy Reeves Sanday, in *Female Power and Male Dominance: On the Origins of Sexual Inequality* (Cambridge University Press, 1981), models three different types of societies: equal, unequal, and mythical male dominant. An example of the latter would be peasant societies where a mix of formal male authority and informal female power is found. In these societies, women give public deference to men who monopolize public positions, but neither the males nor the females believe that men are really dominant.

Anne Campbell, in *Men, Women and Aggression* (Basic Books, 1993), puts aggression in perspective by noting that people who believe that aggression is a loss of control will express anger in a different manner than those who believe that it is a way of exerting control. There is no shortage of plausible explanations for men's heightened aggression, according to Campbell. Biologists argue that testosterone, the male androgen, is the key. Some psychologists attribute it to the different, gender-specific ways in which parents teach their children about the acceptability and utility of aggression. Other theorists pinpoint adult roles that males and females are expected to assume.

Michael Segell, in "The Second Coming of the Alpha Male," *Esquire* (October 1996), states that there is a subgroup of males who are the true aggressors. About 15 percent of men, he says, are simply fearless. Segall believes that physiology is only part of the story. He maintains that presumed common male traits such as insensitivity and the ability to suppress human emotion have adaptive usefulness. In the boardroom and other competitive arenas, betraying emotions can be interpreted as a weakness. Segell defines characteristics of success to include willingness to take risks, aggressiveness, and passion for success. He claims that women's aversion to risk and to the single-minded pursuit of status "stifles their rise to the top in the Darwinian business world."

Rene Denfeld, in *Kill The Body, The Head Will Fall* (Warner Books, 1997), contends that women are just as aggressive as men, and she cites a plethora of examples to make her case. She notes that aggression is held to be a defining aspect of masculinity but asserts that this perception itself is frequently inaccurate. Denfeld believes that a great deal of social confusion results from ignoring women's aggressiveness. Like men, women can be ruthlessly aggressive and competitive at work, unable to control their tempers, and dangerously violent, but when women display these behaviors, their actions are overlooked or reinterpreted.

ISSUE 2

Is the Quest for Beauty Necessarily Damaging to Women?

YES: Elayne A. Saltzberg and Joan C. Chrisler, from "Beauty Is the Beast: Psychological Effects of the Pursuit of the Perfect Female Body," in Jo Freeman, ed., *Women: A Feminist Perspective,* 5th ed. (Mayfield, 1995)

NO: Elizabeth Fox-Genovese, from *Feminism Is Not the Story of My Life: How Today's Feminist Elite Has Lost Touch With the Real Concerns of Women* (Doubleday, 1996)

ISSUE SUMMARY

YES: Author Elayne A. Saltzberg and associate professor of psychology Joan C. Chrisler suggest that the value of beauty for women is not worth the high price paid by many in terms of emotional changes, physical side effects, time, money, and even, in some instances, death.

NO: Elizabeth Fox-Genovese, a professor of humanities, asserts that femininity does not prevent women from pursuing power and independence but rather provides ways for them to create their own images, empowering them and giving them a source of connection with other women.

According to surveys by the Kinsey Institute, American women have more negative feelings about their bodies than women in any other culture studied. In the late 1800s the Victorian beauty press warned women that their move toward employment and higher education was "spoiling complexions" and causing a "general lapse in attractiveness." It was then, too, that a "wasting away" look led, in part, to the nation's first dieting mania and the emergence of eating disorders in young women. The media campaign to promote a preferred standard of beauty has not diminished over time.

Campaigns against aging have been effective with women of the baby boom generation. By 1985 a cosmetics trade association of skin care professionals found that 97 percent had noticed that their clients were markedly more concerned about the threat of aging than just a few years earlier. By 1986 annual skin cream sales had escalated to $1.9 billion, double what they had been five years earlier. In 1997 advertising tended to focus on how beauty products can produce effects similar to those brought about by surgeons or dermatologists.

The rise of the women's movement in the 1970s brought with it a decade of flat or declining sales in beauty products. In 1981 the cosmetic company

Revlon's earnings began to fall for the first time in over a decade, and by 1982 the company's profits had declined by 40 percent. But starting in 1983 the American Society of Plastic and Reconstructive Surgeons began to bill "body sculpting" as safe, effective, affordable, and even essential for women's mental health. By 1988 the cosmetic surgeons' caseload had more than doubled to 750,000 annually, and more than 100,000 women had undergone liposuction surgery priced at $4,000 and up. A 1987 survey by a plastic surgery association found that about half of their patients made less than $25,000 a year, with some taking out loans and mortgaging their homes to pay surgery bills.

Beauty became medical in the 1980s and many women who followed the directions of "beauty doctors" became physically ill as a result. They endured acid face peels, which burned their skin; antiwrinkle treatment, which exposed them to carcinogens; silicone injections, which left deformities; and cosmetic liposuction, which caused infections, complications, and even death. During the Reagan era, the U.S. Food and Drug Administration (FDA) issued cease and desist warnings to companies claiming that their products provided "age reversal," "DNA repair," or "cell renewal."

With regard to plastic surgery, a 1988 congressional investigation turned up widespread fraud, major injuries, ill-equipped facilities, and even death from botched operations. Studies found that at least 15 percent of cosmetic surgery caused facial nerve damage, bad scars, hemorrhages, or complications from anesthesia. A reference manual of over 1,000 pages offered follow-up procedural options for plastic surgeons who were devoting as much as one-quarter of their practices to correcting the errors of their colleagues.

In support of the beauty industry, however, many providers and consumers see various services as self-image enhancers for women and as strategies for expanding women's opportunities. The Center for Aesthetic and Reconstructive Surgery, for example, points to women's ability to "exercise a choice" and claims that cosmetic surgery has been associated with improved career performance and enhanced self-confidence. Engaging in beauty rituals, practices, and procedures is often seen as "taking control" of one's own appearance. *Ms.* magazine deemed plastic surgery a way for women to "reinvent" themselves. Individuals who support this position maintain that women do not change their appearance only to comply with male wishes or to please a potential mate; rather, this behavior reflects their power to do what pleases them personally. Furthermore, some ideologies promote a fun, playful perspective on beauty, which reinforces the importance of narcissistic and erotic pleasure created and maintained within beauty rituals.

In the following selections, Elayne A. Saltzberg and Joan C. Chrisler argue that the costs of pursuing beauty exceed the benefits; physical danger and emotional, financial, and temporal costs far exceed any potential enhancements that could be made. Elizabeth Fox-Genovese, on the other hand, promotes the acceptance of "traditional femininity," suggesting that the image women want to present embodies personal choice and women's ability to take charge of their own appearance.

YES

Elayne A. Saltzberg and
Joan C. Chrisler

BEAUTY IS THE BEAST

Ambrose Bierce (1958) once wrote, "To men a man is but a mind. Who cares what face he carries or what he wears? But woman's body is the woman." Despite the societal changes achieved since Bierce's time, his statement remains true. Since the height of the feminist movement in the early 1970s, women have spent more money than ever before on products and treatments designed to make them beautiful. Cosmetic sales have increased annually to reach $18 billion in 1987 ("Ignoring the economy . . . ," 1989), sales of women's clothing averaged $103 billion per month in 1990 (personal communication, U.S. Bureau of Economic Analysis, 1992), dieting has become a $30-billion-per-year industry (Stoffel, 1989), and women spent $1.2 billion on cosmetic surgery in 1990 (personal communication, American Society of Plastic and Reconstructive Surgeons, 1992). The importance of beauty has apparently increased even as women are reaching for personal freedoms and economic rights undreamed of by our grandmothers. The emphasis on beauty may be a way to hold onto a feminine image while shedding feminine roles.

Attractiveness is prerequisite for femininity but not for masculinity (Freedman, 1986). The word *beauty* always refers to the female body. Attractive male bodies are described as "handsome," a word derived from "hand" that refers as much to action as appearance (Freedom, 1986). Qualities of achievement and strength accompany the term *handsome;* such attributes are rarely employed in the description of attractive women and certainly do not accompany the term *beauty,* which refers only to a decorative quality. Men are instrumental; women are ornamental.

Beauty is a most elusive commodity. Ideas of what is beautiful vary across cultures and change over time (Fallon, 1990). Beauty cannot be quantified or objectively measured; it is the result of the judgments of others. The concept is difficult to define, as it is equated with different, sometimes contradictory, ideas. When people are asked to define beauty, they tend to mention abstract, personal qualities rather than external, quantifiable ones (Freedman, 1986; Hatfield & Sprecher, 1986). The beholder's perceptions and cognitions influence the degree of attractiveness at least as much as do the qualities of the beheld.

Because beauty is an ideal, an absolute, such as truth and goodness, the pursuit of it does not require justification (Herman & Polivy, 1983). An ideal, by definition, can be met by only a minority of those who strive for it. If too many women are able to meet the beauty standards of a particular time and place, then those standards must change in order to maintain their extraordinary nature. The value of beauty standards depends on their being special and unusual and is one of the reasons why the ideal changes over time. When images of beauty change, female bodies are expected to change, too. Different aspects of the female body and varying images of each body part are modified to meet the constantly fluctuating ideal (Freedman, 1986). The ideal is always that which is most difficult to achieve and most unnatural in a given time period. Because these ideals are nearly impossible to achieve, failure and disappointment are inevitable (Freedman, 1988).

Although people have been decorating their bodies since prehistoric times, the Chinese may have been the first to develop the concept that the female body can and should be altered from its natural state. The practice of foot binding clearly illustrates the objectification of parts of the female body as well as the demands placed on women to conform to beauty ideals. The custom called for the binding of the feet of five-year-old girls so that as they grew, their toes became permanently twisted under their arches and would actually shrink in size. The big toe remained untouched. The more tightly bound the feet, the more petite they became and the more attractive they were considered to be (Freedman, 1986; Hatfield & Sprecher, 1986; Lakoff & Scherr, 1984). The painful custom of foot binding finally ended in the twentieth century after women had endured over one thousand years of torture for beauty's sake (Brain, 1979).

In the sixteenth century, European women bound themselves into corsets of whalebone and hardened canvas. A piece of metal or wood ran down the front to flatten the breasts and abdomen. This garment made it impossible to bend at the waist and difficult to breathe. A farthingale, which was typically worn over the corset, held women's skirts out from their bodies. It consisted of bent wood held together with tapes and made such simple activities as sitting nearly impossible. Queen Catherine of France introduced waist binding with a tortuous invention consisting of iron bands that minimized the size of the waist to the ideal measurement of thirteen inches (Baker, 1984). In the seventeenth century, the waist was still laced, but breasts were once again stylish, and fashions were designed to enhance them. Ample breasts, hips, and buttocks became the beauty ideal, perhaps paralleling a generally warmer attitude toward family life (Rosenblatt & Stencel, 1982). A white pallor was also popular at that time, probably as an indication that the woman was so affluent that she did not need to work outdoors, where the sun might darken her skin. Ceruse, a white lead-based paint now known to be toxic, was used to accentuate the pallor.

Tight corsets came back into vogue in Europe and North America in the mid-nineteenth century, and many women were willing to run the risk of developing serious health problems in order to wear them. The tight lacing often led to pulmonary disease and internal organ damage. American women disregarded the advice of their physicians, who spoke against the use of corsets because of their potential to displace internal organs. Fainting, or "the vapors," was the result of wearing such tightly laced clothing that normal breathing became impossible. Even the clergy sermonized against corsets; miscarriages were known to result in pregnant women who insisted on lacing themselves up too tightly. In the late nineteenth century, the beauty ideal required a tiny waist and full hips and bustline. Paradoxically, women would go on diets to gain weight while, at the same time, trying to achieve a smaller waistline. Some women were reported to have had their lower ribs removed so that their waists could be more tightly laced (Brain, 1979).

In the twentieth century, the ideal female body has changed several times, and American women have struggled to change along with it. In the 1920s, the ideal had slender legs and hips, small breasts, and bobbed hair and was physically and socially active. Women removed the stuffing from their bodices and bound their breasts to appear young and boyish. In the 1940s and 1950s, the ideal returned to the hourglass shape. Marilyn Monroe was considered the epitome of the voluptuous and fleshy yet naive and childlike ideal. In the 1960s, the ideal had a youthful, thin, lean body and long, straight hair. American women dieted relentlessly in an attempt to emulate the tall, thin, teenage model Twiggy, who personified the 1960s' beauty ideal. Even pregnant women were on diets in response to their doctors' orders not to gain more than twenty pounds, advice physicians later rejected as unsafe (Fallon, 1990). Menopausal women begged their physicians to prescribe hormone replacement therapy, which was rumored to prevent wrinkles and keep the body

youthful, and were willing to run any health risk to preserve their appearance (Chrisler, Torrey, & Matthes, 1989). In the 1970s, a thin, tan, sensuous look was "in." The 1980s' beauty ideal remained slim but required a more muscular, toned, and physically fit body. In recent decades the beauty ideal has combined such opposite traits as erotic sophistication with naive innocence, delicate grace with muscular athleticism (Freedom, 1988), and thin bodies with large breasts. The pressure to cope with such conflicting demands and to keep up with the continual changes in the ideal female body is highly stressful (Freedman, 1988) and has resulted in a large majority of American women with negative body images (Dworkin & Kerr, 1987; Rosen, Saltzberg, & Srebnik, 1989). Women's insecurity about their looks has made it easy to convince them that small breasts are a "disease" that require surgical intervention. The sophisticated woman of the 1990s who is willing to accept the significant health risks of breast implants in order to mold her body to fit the beauty ideal has not progressed far beyond her sisters who bound their feet and waists.

The value of beauty depends in part on the high costs of achieving it. Such costs may be physical, temporal, economic, or psychological. Physical costs include the pain of ancient beauty rituals such as foot binding, tattooing, and nose and ear piercing as well as more modern rituals such as wearing pointy-toed, high-heeled shoes, tight jeans, and sleeping with one's hair in curlers. Side effects of beauty rituals have often been disastrous for women's health. Tattooing and ear piercing with unsanitary instruments have lead to serious, sometimes fatal, infections. Many women have been poisoned by toxic chemicals in cosmetics (e.g., ceruse, arsenic, benzene, and petroleum) and have died from the use of unsafe diet products such as rainbow pills and liquid protein (Schwartz, 1986). The beauty-related disorders anorexia nervosa and bulimia have multiple negative health effects, and side effects of plastic surgery include hemorrhages, scars, and nerve damage. Silicone implants have resulted in breast cancer, autoimmune disease, and the formation of thick scar tissue.

Physical costs of dieting include a constant feeling of hunger that leads to emotional changes, such as irritability; in cases of very low caloric intake, dieters can experience difficulty concentrating, confusion, and even reduced cognitive capacity. The only growing group of smokers in the United States are young women, many of whom report that they smoke to curb their appetites (Sorensen & Pechacek, 1987). High heels cause lower back pain and lead to a variety of podiatric disorders. Furthermore, fashion trends have increased women's vulnerability in a variety of ways; long hair and dangling earrings have gotten caught in machinery and entangled in clothing and led to injury. High heels and tight skirts prevent women from running from danger. The *New York Times* fashion reporter Bernardine Morris was alarmed to see in Pierre Cardin's 1988 summer fashion show tight wraps that prevented the models from moving their arms (Morris, 1988).

Attaining the beauty ideal requires a lot of money. Expensive cosmetics (e.g., makeup, moisturizers, and hair dyes and straighteners) are among the most popular and are thought to be the most effective, even though their ingredients cost the same (and sometimes are the same) as those in less expensive products (Lakoff & Scherr, 1984). Health spas have become

fashionable again as vacation spots for the rich and famous, and everyone wants to wear expensive clothing with designer labels. Plastic surgery has become so accepted and so common that, although it's quite expensive, surgeons advertise their services on television. Surgery is currently performed that can reduce the size of lips, ear lobes, noses, buttocks, thighs, abdomens, and breasts; rebuild a face; remove wrinkles; and add "padding" to almost any body part. Not surprisingly, most plastic surgery patients are women (Hamburger, 1988).

Beauty rituals are time-consuming activities. Jokes about how long women take to get ready for a date are based on the additional tasks women do when getting dressed. It takes time to pluck eyebrows, shave legs, manicure nails, apply makeup, and arrange hair. Women's clothing is more complicated than men's, and many more accessories are used. Although all women know that the "transformation from female to feminine is artificial" (Chapkis, 1986, p. 5), we conspire to hide the amount of time and effort it takes, perhaps out of fear that other women don't need as much time as we do to appear beautiful. A lot of work goes into looking like a "natural" beauty, but that work is not acknowledged by popular culture, and the tools of the trade are kept out of view. Men's grooming rituals are fewer, take less time, and need not be hidden away. Scenes of men shaving have often been seen on television and in movies and have even been painted by Norman Rockwell. Wendy Chapkis (1986) challenges her readers to "imagine a similar cultural celebration of a woman plucking her eyebrows, shaving her armpits, or waxing her upper lip" (p. 6). Such a scene would be shocking and would remove the aura of mystery that surrounds beautiful women.

Psychological effects of the pursuit of the perfect female body include unhappiness, confusion, misery, and insecurity. Women often believe that if only they had perfect looks, their lives would be perfectly happy; they blame their unhappiness on their bodies. American women have the most negative body image of any culture studied by the Kinsey Institute (Faludi, 1991). Dissatisfaction with their bodies is very common among adolescent girls (Adams & Crossman, 1978; Clifford, 1971; Freedman, 1984), and older women believe that the only way to remain attractive is to prevent the development of any signs of aging. Obsessive concern about body shape and weight have become so common among American women of all ages that they now constitute the norm (Rodin, Silberstein, & Striegel-Moore, 1985). The majority of women in the United States are dieting at any given time. For them, being female means feeling fat and inadequate and living with chronic low self-esteem (Rodin, et al., 1985). Ask any woman what she would like to change about her body and she'll answer immediately. Ask her what she likes about her body and she'll have difficulty responding.

Those women who do succeed in matching the ideal thinness expected by modern beauty standards usually do so by exercising frenetically and compulsively, implementing severely restrictive and nutritionally deficient diets, developing bizarre eating habits, and using continuous self-degradation and self-denial. Dieting has become a "cultural requirement" for women (Herman & Polivy, 1983) because the ideal female body has become progressively thinner at the same time that the average female body has be-

come progressively heavier. This cultural requirement remains in place despite the fact that physiology works against weight loss to such an extent that 98 percent of diets fail (Chrisler, 1989; Fitzgerald, 1981). In fact, it is more likely for someone to fully recover from cancer than for an obese person to lose a significant amount of weight and maintain that loss for five years (Brownell, 1982). Yet a recent study (Davies & Furnham, 1986) found that young women rate borderline anorexic bodies as very attractive. Thus, even the thinnest women find it nearly impossible to meet and maintain the beauty ideal.

The social pressure for thinness can be directly linked to the increasing incidence of anorexia nervosa and bulimia among women (Brumberg, 1988; Caskey, 1986). There are presently at least one million Americans with anorexia nervosa, and 95 percent of them are women. Between sixty thousand and 150,000 of them will die as a result of their obsession (Schwartz, 1986). Although cases of anorexia nervosa have been reported in the medical literature for hundreds of years (Bell, 1985), it was considered to be a rare disorder until the 1970s. Today's anorexics are also thinner than they were in the past (Brumberg, 1988). It is estimated that at least seven million American women will experience symptoms of bulimia at some point in their lives (Hatfield & Sprecher, 1986). A recent study (Hall & Cohn, 1988) found that 25 to 33 percent of female first-year college students were using vomiting after meals as a method of weight control. An accurate estimate of the number of women who are caught in the binge-purge cycle is difficult because women with bulimia are generally secretive about their behavior and the physical signs of bulimia are not nearly are obvious as those of anorexia nervosa.

Exercise has become for many women another manifestation of their body dissatisfaction. Studies have found that most men who exercise regularly do so to build body mass and to increase cardiovascular fitness; most women who exercise do so to lose weight and to change the shape of their bodies in order to increase their attractiveness (Garner, Rockert, Olmstead, Johnson, & Coscina, 1985; Saltzberg, 1990). Exercise has lost its status as a pleasurable activity and become yet another way for women to manipulate their bodies, another vehicle for narcissistic self-torture. Reports of the number of women exercising compulsively are increasing and may become as widespread as compulsive calorie counting and the compulsive eating habits of anorexics and bulimics.

Beauty ideals are created and maintained by society's elite. Racism, class prejudice, and rejection of the disabled are clearly reflected (Chapkis, 1986) in current American beauty standards. For example, women from lower socioeconomic groups typically weigh more than women in higher socioeconomic groups (Moore, Stunkard, & Srole, 1962); they are thus excluded by popular agreement from being considered beautiful. The high costs of chic clothing, cosmetics, tanning salons, skin and hair treatments, weight loss programs, and plastic surgery prevent most American women from access to the tools necessary to approach the ideal. Furthermore, the beauty standard idealizes Caucasian features and devalues those of other races (Lewis, 1977; Miller, 1969). In recent years, Asian American and African-American women have sought facial surgery in order to come closer to the beauty ideal (Faludi,

1991), and psychotherapists have noted increased reports from their black women clients of guilt, shame, anger, and resentment about skin color, hair texture, facial features, and body size and shape (Greene, 1992; Neal & Wilson, 1989; Okazawa-Rey, Robinson, & Ward, 1987). Obviously, women with visible disabilities will never be judged to have achieved "perfection." Whoopi Goldberg's routine about the black teenager who wrapped a towel around her head to pretend it was long, blonde hair and Alice Walker's (1990) essay about her psychological adjustment after the eye injury that resulted in the development of "hideous" scar tissue provide poignant examples of the pain women experience when they cannot meet beauty standards.

The inordinate emphasis on women's external selves makes it difficult for us to appreciate our own internal selves (Kano, 1985). The constant struggle to meet the beauty ideal leads to high stress and chronic anxiety. Failure to meet the beauty ideal leads to feelings of frustration, low self-worth, and inadequacy in women whose sense of self is based on their physical appearance. The intensity of the drive to increase attractiveness may also contribute to the high rate of depression among women.

Insecurity is common even among beautiful women, and studies show that they are as likely as their plain sisters to be unhappy about their looks (Freedman, 1988). Beautiful women are all too aware of the fleeting nature of their beauty; the effects of aging must be constantly monitored, and these women worry that the beauty ideal they've tried so hard to match may change without warning. When such women lose their beauty due to illness or accidents, they often become depressed and are likely to have difficulty functioning in society and to believe that their entire identity has been threatened.

Given the high costs of striving to be beautiful, why do women attempt it? Attractiveness greatly affects first impressions and later interpersonal relationships. In a classic study titled "What Is Beautiful Is Good," psychologists Kenneth Dion, Ellen Berscheid, and Elaine Walster Hatfield (1972) asked college students to rate photographs of strangers on a variety of personal characteristics. Those who were judged to be attractive were also more likely to be rated intelligent, kind, happy, flexible, interesting, confident, sexy, assertive, strong, outgoing, friendly, poised, modest, candid, and successful than those judged unattractive. Teachers rate attractive children more highly on a variety of positive characteristics including IQ and sociability, and attractive babies are cuddled and kissed more often than unattractive babies (Berscheid & Walster, 1974). Attractive people receive more lenient punishment for social transgressions (Dion, 1972; Landy & Aronson, 1969), and attractive women are more often sought out in social situations (Walster, Aronson, Abrahams, & Rottman, 1966; Reis, Nezlek, & Wheeler, 1980).

Furthermore, because unattractive people are more harshly punished for social transgressions and are less often sought after social partners, failure to work toward the beauty ideal can result in real consequences. Television newswoman Christine Craft made the news herself when she was fired for being too old and too unattractive. Street harassers put women "in their place" by commenting loudly on their beauty or lack of it. Beauty norms limit the opportunities of women who can't or won't meet them. Obese women, for example, have experienced discrimination in a number of instances including hiring and promotion (Larkin & Pines, 1979; Rothblum, Miller, & Gorbutt, 1988) and college admissions (Canning & Mayer, 1966). Obese people even have a harder time finding a place to live; Lambros Karris (1977) found that landlords are less likely to rent to obese people. Even physicians view their obese patients negatively (Maddox & Liederman, 1969).

There is considerable evidence that women's attractiveness is judged more harshly than men's. Christine Craft was fired, yet David Brinkley and Willard Scott continue to work on major television news shows; their abilities are not thought to be affected by age or attractiveness. Several studies (Adams & Huston, 1975; Berman, O'Nan, & Floyd, 1981; Deutsch, Zalenski, & Clark, 1986; Wernick & Manaster, 1984) that asked participants to rate the attractiveness of photographs of people of varying ages found that although attractiveness ratings of both men and women decline with age, the rate of decline for women was greater. In one study (Deutsch, Zalenski, & Clark, 1986), participants were asked to rate the photographs for femininity and masculinity as well as attractiveness. The researchers found that both the attractiveness and femininity ratings of the female photographs diminished with age; the masculinity ratings were unaffected by the age or attractiveness of the photographs. Women are acutely aware of the double standard of attractiveness. At all ages women are more concerned than men about weight and physical appearance and have lower appearance self-esteem; women who define themselves as feminine are the most concerned about their appearance and have the lowest self-esteem (Pliner, Chaiken,

& Flett, 1990). In fact, women are so concerned about their body size that they typically overestimate it. Women who overestimate their size feel worse about themselves, whereas men's self-esteem is unrelated to their body size estimates (Thompson, 1986). In a review of research on the stigma of obesity, Esther Rothblum (1992) concluded that the dieting industry, combined with Western attitudes toward weight and attractiveness, causes more pain and problems for women than for men.

Thus, the emphasis on beauty has political as well as psychological consequences for women, as it results in oppression and disempowerment. It is important for women to examine the effects that the pursuit of the perfect female body has had on their lives, challenge their beliefs, and take a stand against continued enslavement to the elusive beauty ideal. Women would then be able to live life more freely and experience the world more genuinely. Each woman must decide for herself what beauty really is and the extent to which she is willing to go to look attractive. Only a more diverse view of beauty and a widespread rebellion against fashion extremes will save us from further physical and psychological tolls.

Imagine an American society where the quality and meaning of life for women are not dependent on the silence of bodily shame. Imagine a society where bodies are decorated for fun and to express creativity rather than for self-control and self-worth. Imagine what would happen if the world's women released and liberated all of the energy that had been absorbed in the beautification process. The result might be the positive, affirming, healthy version of a nuclear explosion!

NO

Elizabeth Fox-Genovese

GROWING UP FEMININE

Feminists might well be stunned to learn that Gloria Patterson's young friends think that feminism means that you must shave your legs and straighten your hair. Feminists regularly insist that they stand for freedom of choice in everything from abortion to personal style. Feminists have never promoted an image of traditional femininity, which many feminists deplore. And Brooke Mason, as a self-consciously feminine Southern woman, has some grounds for her belief that feminists do not approve of her personal style. Knowing more about feminism than Gloria's friends, Brooke believes that feminists do not approve of shaved legs or pink dresses. Brooke associates feminism with the feminist leaders of the late 1960s and early 1970s who encouraged women to burn their bras and give up high heels. In fact, leading feminists no longer lecture women about bra-burning, but even today it is sometimes hard to avoid the impression that their movement has declared war on much of what most women, especially young women, think of as typically feminine, namely style, appearance, and clothes.

Feminists have not had much patience with femininity, which they see as a trap that distracts women from the pursuit of power and independence. For what is femininity except a disguise that women adopt to appeal to men? As it happens, most women still do want to appeal to men, which may help to explain why they do not have much use for feminism. For centuries, women have shared a special interest in appearance and clothing. The femininity that feminists see as a trap, other women see as a bond to other women. And it is not difficult to understand that these women might resent feminists for trying to make them ashamed of the skills and pleasures in which they find satisfaction....

Notoriously, women spend a lot of time worrying about how they look and, especially, what to wear. Naomi Wolf savaged these preoccupations in *The Beauty Myth*, claiming that our media-led culture conspires to keep women permanently insecure and anxious because they do not measure up to some abstract and unattainable standard of beauty. Concern with looks, she warned, literally kills women, frequently through anorexia, sometimes through breast implants. Who could doubt that it is in men's interest to keep

From Elizabeth Fox-Genovese, *Feminism Is Not the Story of My Life: How Today's Feminist Elite Has Lost Touch With the Real Concerns of Women* (Doubleday, 1996). Copyright © 1996 by Elizabeth Fox-Genovese. Reprinted by permission of Doubleday, a division of Bantam Doubleday Dell Publishing Group, Inc.

women fixated on their looks? How better to keep them dependent and discourage them from competing with men for power and prestige?

Wolf echoes the complaints of generations of feminists who, from Mary Wollstonecraft to the present, have criticized the ways in which feminine fashion keeps women in thrall to men. Simone de Beauvoir, in her feminist classic, *The Second Sex*, especially deplored women's disadvantage in a culture in which they must always look beautiful and young, while men could grow old in the security that the character and power etched on their faces would only enhance their appeal to the opposite sex. Femininity emerges from these accounts as a mask that gullible women are forced to assume in order to pass in the world.

* * *

Women spend considerable, sometimes staggering, amounts of time and money on decorating or reshaping their bodies: nail polish, sculpted nails, hair color, perms, electrolysis, dieting programs, plastic surgery, breast implants, breast reductions—the list goes on. Many women spend their lives dieting. They try one, lose a few pounds, gain them back, and try another. All this even before we get to clothes. In extreme cases, women do jeopardize their health, and, although Wolf's statistics on deaths from anorexia have been disputed, the case of anorexia remains instructive.[1]

Like women's attempts to transform and decorate their bodies, anorexia reminds us that women, like men, develop a sense of self through their interactions with other people, especially those to whom they feel most closely connected. Women frequently display their sense of self on their own bodies. But the view

of anorexia as the result of a misogynist conspiracy will not wash. Anorexia is not about being slim. It is about control— more a revolt against becoming a woman than a pathological quest of femininity. It has nothing to do with appealing to men. In fact one of the more thoughtful if controversial psychoanalytic interpretations of anorexia regards it as a young woman's desperate attempt to separate from her mother.[2]

Many women do see clothes, dieting, and self-decoration as a way to attract men, but for most women, attracting men is only part of the story. Young women develop ideas of how they want to look long before they are especially interested in attracting men. In fact, other women are much more likely to shape young women's ideas of how they want to look than are men, and many young women develop what they like to think of as their own style as much in rebellion against women (usually their mothers) as in a desire to win acceptance from other women, usually their friends.

Susan Douglas, in her book about women's relations to the media, wryly notes how her young daughter sits transfixed in front of television images of young women in sparkling, garish dresses that simultaneously capture and caricature the ideal of femininity. But to Douglas's daughter the women in those dresses embody femininity and an irresistible magic. Somehow the little girl translates those glittering images into a vision of what she would like to be. Susan Douglas understands her daughter's fascination, and remembering the female idols of her own girlhood, she does not especially worry about the lasting harm it may cause, although her own dreams for her daughter focus on strength, independence, and accomplishment, not alluring femininity. A time may come when Douglas and her daughter, like other mothers and daughters, clash over clothes, especially if the daughter decides that clothes offer a self-definition. But the odds are good that by the time Douglas's daughter has a daughter of her own, her taste in clothes will resemble her mother's....

Talk to young women and you will find that the great majority have an acute and frequently whimsical sense of costume, and that they enjoy it to the hilt. The spirit of the game was captured by the young Emory undergraduate who arrived in my office to discuss what she, as a thoroughly independent young woman, thought was wrong with feminism. In a typical gesture of independence, Carla had made an appointment with me via E-mail. On the appointed day she arrived in my office in the ubiquitous undergraduate uniform of jeans, carrying a tape recorder, and with an electric head of bright fuchsia hair. After greeting me with a polite, professional handshake, she settled down to the business of the interview. And I, doing my best to respond in kind, refrained from staring at her hair. Just before leaving, she turned to me with a bright smile and said, "I suppose you have been wondering about my hair." Before I had time to gulp a polite "not at all," she continued, "It's simple. Pink for femininity, of course, but dark pink for strength and independence." "Of course," I responded. And since then she has continued to consult me, via E-mail, about whether "fuchsoid" would not be the appropriate term for a strong young woman who has no patience with mainstream feminism.

* * *

Little girls begin by trying on Mama's clothes, painting their faces with lipstick, draping their bodies with the finery that engulfs them. But at very young ages, most girls begin to want costumes that fit their bodies and meet the exacting codes of their friends. And as they struggle to understand and meet prevailing standards of what looks right, they embark on what may prove to be a long process of self-definition. We all know some women who seem to have an instinctive gift for rightness and who always look perfect for every occasion. Normally, they are the cautious ones who never risk their self-image on a flight of fancy. Other women always risk the flight of fancy, frequently turning it into a refined art. One of my graduate students, who is fair, willowy, a bit ethereal, and gifted with an exquisite sense of style, frequently turns up in clinging, diaphanous, long-sleeved black dresses that sway just above her black-stockinged ankles. At her neck, she wears an antique brooch on a velvet ribbon, or perhaps a long strand of jet or pearls. On her head, shading her eyes, sits a glamour hat, sometimes enhanced by a drooping veil. Looking for all the world like her great-grandmother as a young woman, she has turned retro-dressing into high style.

Most of us all fall between the extremes, searching in fits and starts for what we hope will be our "style." And as we search, we frequently turn to things that remind us of other women we love, as if, through clothes, we could share a piece of their identity. Only years later did I understand that throughout my late teens and twenties, when I was trying to find my place in the world, I frequently shopped as if I were buying for other people. These "mistakes" would have looked wonderful on my best friend, my sister, my mother, a favorite professor—just not on me.

Many of us, myself included, have raged against fashion and its abuse of the female body. Feminists especially protest the ways in which women have forced themselves into shoes, shirts, bras, girdles (now resurrected as "body-toners"), and other items that may endanger their health and constrict their mobility. Women emerge from these diatribes as the helpless victims of a vast plot to undermine their independence and self-respect. And we all know how often the concern with looking "right" may gnaw at our self-confidence. It is hard to match the fury of a twelve-year-old girl ripping off a pair of pants because "they make me look fat" or throwing her hair brush against a mirror in frustration.

No doubt there are more "constructive" things for girls and women to be doing with their time than agonizing about how they look. But no amount of righteous preaching is likely to dent the pattern, although a sense of competence and self-acceptance will significantly reduce the anxiety. Women see clothes as an extension of their identifies and a protection of their privacy. Clothes simultaneously expose them and encase them in armor. The concern to find clothes that "look like me" embodies both attitudes. For clothes permit women to create an image of themselves with which they are comfortable, and experienced women learn to look at themselves in clothes as if they were looking at a mannequin.

An interest in clothes binds women together, permitting them to share and even to talk about things they might usually be reluctant to mention. Nancy

Wilson and I, who as busy professional women have innumerable "important" things to talk about and never enough time to scratch the surface, frequently spend one of our rare days together shopping. As we wander the aisles of store after store, we talk disjointedly but meaningfully. The clothes and our possible relation to them ("Should I try this? How would that look on you?") act as props that evoke pieces of our lives ("I need a jacket to wear with the skirt I wear for my evening classes") or people ("Do you remember your mother's polka-dot dress?") that might never come up in one of our serious talks. The special quality of our shopping conversation captures a companionship that women have always shared. Many men also care about clothes and may even enjoy shopping for them. Many even enjoy shopping for or with women—up to a point. But if there are men who shop as women do, I do not know them.

In Atlanta, where I live, Loehmann's discount clothing store attracts women of all ages, shapes, colors, and backgrounds from all over the city. At Loehmann's, men are literally relegated to the margins of the serious business; Those who are brave enough to accompany a female friend or relative sit uncomfortably on the few chairs set against a wall near the entrance. Men never get anywhere near the real center of Loehmann's, the large, crowded dressing rooms, where each woman has a peg to hang the clothes she is trying on and a bit of bench for her own things. Everyone dresses and undresses in full view of everyone else: middle-class white mothers from the suburbs with teenage daughters in tow; well-to-do young black women, toting Vuitton bags; petite Asian-American women; anxious grandmothers; working and professional women of various classes and colors.

What the dressing rooms lack in privacy, they make up for in companionship. As you look uncertainly into the mirror, pulling at the dress and craning your neck to see if it wrinkles over your hips, wondering if it makes you look too fat, the friendly voice of a stranger invariably reassures you that it looks stunning or tentatively suggests that another color would be more flattering. Across lines of race, education, income, and taste, women understand other women's anxieties about their bodies and insecurities about clothes. Some of the most accomplished and devoted Loehmann's shoppers I know are professional African-American friends who frequently have a gift for elegance that puts their white colleagues to shame. One day I conveyed my admiration to one of my African-American feminist friends. Yes, she agreed, many black women do have a rare sense of style. But then, she said sadly, "I'm not sure it's always a good thing. You know, we have always cared too much about clothes in the black community. In the end it is a kind of control."

Through years of such conversations, I have discovered that the control of which my friend complained is exercised by women over younger women. All too familiar with the dangers of an inhospitable world, generations of African-American women have learned to cultivate what Sicilian-American men are wont to call "respect." The right clothing indeed provides a kind of armor, particularly against a white world that perennially doubts your respectability and taste, but also against other women in your own community. One evening, a colleague had a group of us in stitches, describing the way her grandmother would dress for church.

"Grandmama would finally get to the hat —of which she had scores. The hat had to be perfect, and she would try and retry it until it set on her head in the perfect gesture of superiority and defiance." My friend's grandmother was married to the minister, whom women found especially attractive. Her job, then, was to show by her dress and demeanor that those other women were "no 'count." "Grandmama was the minister's wife, and she knew just how to show all of them that nothing they did could touch her."

On another occasion, a college classmate, now a successful psychiatrist, and I fell into a conversation about shopping. The conversation had begun as a discussion of young women, especially her daughter, a freshman in college. As a rule, she and her daughter get on wonderfully well, but, as in any mother-daughter relation, there are moments of friction. You know, my friend confided, Gillian can be unbelievably stubborn. But, she added, "Even when things are most difficult, all I have to do is say, 'Let's go shopping.' We can always smooth things over by going shopping." No, mother and daughter did not usually agree about how Gillian wanted to look, but they could talk about clothes when they could not talk directly about other things.

It has taken years for most of the women I know well, including my sister and me, to get over dressing to please or displease our mothers. I know successful, independent women who can still be reduced to anxious girls—or even to tears—when their mothers disapprove of something they wear or, worse, suggest that maybe it does not do much for their figure. It is as if mothers unconsciously see clothes as a way of retaining control of their daughters—of keeping them girls rather than facing them as independent women. Certainly, I now believe that concern about my emerging sexuality motivated my own mother's hostility to my elegant—and revealing—straight skirt.

Who among us knows for sure what goes into all of that? Even those of us who deeply love our mothers have, at one time or another, experienced the tensions of trying to pull away—of trying to establish ourselves as independent people. For the young girls who are so determined to be "me," relations with mothers normally lie at the heart of the matter. Our mothers are the women we know best, even if we do not really know them at all. Seeing them both as extensions of ourselves and as powerful figures of authority, we search for ways to become adult women (like them) and a person in our own right (different from them).

Especially in these times, when women's roles and expectations are changing radically and rapidly, young women desperately seek to become a different kind of woman from their mothers. Today's young women enjoy opportunities from careers to sports to sexual freedom that most of their mothers never dreamed of. But no matter how successfully they prove themselves, most remain tied to their mothers and continue to pull against their authority—even when they do not entirely know what they are doing....

* * *

Women have always imposed dress codes on other women, especially to keep them in line. More often than not, women isolated the bold woman who knew how to be especially alluring to men and would not play by their rules. Was this not the case of Ellen Olenska of Edith Wharton's *Age of Innocence*, who, in Martin Scorsese's

film, captured the American imagination? If we may believe *Vogue*, working women still impose dress codes upon one another. The conventional suit... remains required dress in business and the professions.[3] Former Congresswoman Marjorie Margolies-Mezvinsky of Pennsylvania told the *Vogue* reporter, "I really do think there is something in us that says it's better if our clothes are not distracting." Others worry that a fashionable or, heaven forbid, revealing dress would invite sexual harassment. Margot Parker, a director of government relations for GM, believes that women should dress according to their rank in the company: "If you're staff, I think you should look the part." And she has been known to reprimand women who did not.

Women, who well understand the fine points of dressing to fit your rank, have been known to be less than charitable toward those who fail to notice. Professional women usually fall back on their intuitive knowledge of what "looks right" without stopping to think that what is supposed to "look right" for a secretary might not be what they would want for themselves. Hierarchies of dress codes reflect differences in economic status and income. Those differences and their significance were dramatically illustrated in the film *Working Girl*. The secretary, played by Melanie Griffith, wears the clothes of her boss, played by Sigourney Weaver, and in putting on her boss's clothes assumes her executive role as well. As *Working Girl* clearly illustrates, the tasteful clothes of professional women visibly define a female elite whose work justifies the expenditure on themselves. These are women who have joined the higher echelons of what was recently a man's world. Women who work in traditional female occupations as secretaries or beauticians, women who work for minimum wages, or women who do no paid work at all can rarely justify those expenditures. . . .

* * *

Why should we condemn everything associated with femininity as bad or oppressive? Those who most bitterly attack femininity assume that it has been imposed upon women by men. Yet women themselves clearly have done much to cultivate femininity and a vast number continue to value it today. It takes a breathtaking elitism, which is common among those who most vehemently denounce the presumed elitism of others, to charge that the mass of American women have let themselves be brainwashed—a charge that in effect reduces most women to "bimbos."

Elite professional women may feel especially conflicted about femininity because it stands in such sharp contrast to the masculine world they have entered. And usually, the women in that world who most clearly display femininity are secretaries and receptionists. Understandably, but not admirably, professional women recoil from the thought that their male coworkers confuse them with secretaries, and try to draw sharp lines. And because professional women may still feel uneasy about bossing or supervising other women, just as the women they boss or supervise often resent them, conflicts over status among women easily erupt.

These problems often plague relations among professional women themselves. The bonds of femininity do not offer a reliable guide for dealing with other professionals or with female employees, although they may still facilitate communication among women. From time to time,

when trying to observe the rules of professionalism in dealing with other professional women whom I do not know well, I have been surprised to find that if, however accidentally, the conversation slips to clothes, parents, children, or men, the ice is suddenly broken. For men the equivalent is often professional sports, which more and more women are also becoming fans of, and women who want an easy relation with male coworkers often find that learning the language of sports eases their way. Still, to break the ice for women there is nothing like a good exchange about the difficulty of finding attractive and comfortable clothes ("I won't buy a skirt without pockets") or about what to take on a business trip ("Will one jacket do for three days if you have two skirts to go with it?"). Suddenly, we are back in the familiar conversational world in which we grew up. We have found our bearings and can more comfortably return to the business that brought us together in the first place. . . . [We] recognize clothes as at once a uniform and a form of self-expression—as a way of expressing both our membership in a group and our individuality.

It is hard to imagine anything farther removed from [a] black-lace bodysuit than what one of my successful friends mockingly used to call her "lady lawyer" suits. And women of different groups have styles of dress that differ from both. If we are to believe the ads and the magazines, fashion gets "freer" by the day in response to women's growing sense of their own freedom. Yet most women continue to share an interest in how they dress, even when they continue to dress in very different ways. The bond is not that we all want to wear the same things, but that we all know that what we wear—how we put ourselves together—

will identify us in the eyes of others. Thus even as we choose different costumes, we share an interest in the craft of costume, for we implicitly acknowledge... that no matter what women wear, they are costuming.

The complexities of costuming were recently brought home when I was working as an expert witness in a legal case in which many of the litigants were highly accomplished young women. When I first met two of these lawyers in a series of depositions, their clothes immediately caught my attention. One, a lovely blonde, always appeared in a cautious, conservative tweed suit, which she wore buttoned up to her chin. The first time I met the other, a bolder strawberry blonde, she was wearing a low-cut, bright red dress with an oversized pearl choker and earrings to match.... The next time, she appeared in a long, flowing flowered print, again with a low neckline.... But when they appeared in court a few days later, both were wearing impeccable black suits and white blouses. Yet even then, their individual styles showed through the uniform, and to my amazement, the cautious blonde, if anything, overmatched her bolder colleague in both elegance and femininity.

Whatever the frustration and pain, most women clearly value the distinctly female core of their identities. It offers a connection to history and to all the women who have come before. It offers a connection to other women across lines of race, ethnicity, and class. It offers a foundation for coexistence with men, who express their own anxieties and disruptions in different ways.

NOTES

1. Christina Hoff Somners, *Who Stole Feminism? How Women Have Betrayed Women* (New York: Simon and Schuster, 1994). The debate about deaths from anorexia are inherently misleading, since anorexia is best understood as a symptom of deep psychological disorder, frequently conflicts about independence. Typically, anorectics are more concerned with asserting control over themselves than with looking beautiful. Most do not die of anorexia, although some who suffer from anorexia die through suicide.

2. Hilde Bruch, *The Golden Cage: The Enigma of Anorexia Nervosa* (Cambridge, MA: Harvard Univ. Press, 1978), and her *Eating Disorders: Obesity, Anorexia Nervosa, and the Person Within* (New York: Basic Books, 1973).

3. "Fashion Taboos at Work," *Vogue* (August 1993): 219–21.

POSTSCRIPT

Is the Quest for Beauty Necessarily Damaging to Women?

In "An Image to Heal," *The Humanist* (January/February 1997), Jill S. Zimmerman discusses weight control issues and eating disorders. She supports the feminist view that the portrayal of a certain image in supermodels promotes eating disorders. However, the models themselves do not tend to see this "standard of beauty," which they help to create, as intrinsically problematic. For example, when a group of college students asked supermodel Cindy Crawford whether or not she felt that the modeling industry promoted eating disorders, she was reported to have said, "Does looking at me make you want to puke?" In "How Does a Supermodel Do Feminism? An Interview With Veronica Webb," in Rebecca Walker, ed., *To Be Real* (Anchor Books, 1995), another model was asked if she felt a conflict between being a feminist and working in a profession that "objectifies" women. She stated, "I think all people are judged by their looks, especially women.... I'm not saying it's right or wrong." Webb also stated that she does not feel "objectifed" in her work because she controls the way her looks are used. She claims that the beauty industry is an influential and powerful entity that can and should be used to women's advantage.

Agreeing with Webb is Nancy Friday, in *The Power of Beauty* (HarperCollins, 1996). Friday suggests that when women do not elect to make the most of their beauty they do not know what they are losing. Women should not "focus on men as perverted voyeurs" but should use their beauty to their own advantage and profit. The only people who disagree with these ideas, says Friday, are jealous, unattractive, and older women who are "without a man." She believes that feminists oppose beauty as a woman's greatest bargaining chip because it reinforces a system in which men have all the economic power and women are their trophies. But Friday dismisses any notion that personal awareness and attention to appearance encourage dependence on men. Joining the libertarian ranks is Karen Lehrman. In *The Lipstick Proviso* (Anchor Books, 1997), she sees beauty as an invaluable personal asset. Naomi Wolf, on the other hand, criticizes the corporate world for subjecting women to a "professional beauty qualification" that keeps women focused on their appearance rather than on climbing the corporate ladder. See *Beauty Myth: How Images of Beauty Are Used Against Women* (Doubleday, 1992). In "Beauty Laid Bare: Aesthetics in the Ordinary," in Rebecca Walker, ed., *To Be Real* (Anchor Books, 1995), bell hooks argues that African American women have been socialized to consume in an unmindful manner and have been encouraged to value goods, especially luxury goods, over their own well-being and safety. Furthermore, many women remain in domestic situations where they are hurt and even abused by sexist men because of an attachment to material wealth and privilege. Danzy Senna, in "To Be Real," also in *To Be Real*, discusses how light skin for blacks can bring status within the black world. She also discusses how the new "power feminism" represents not a "new school" in feminism but rather a very old school imbedded in whiteness, privilege, "beauty," and consumerism, of which the mainstream media has always been in favor. Other African American women writers maintain that to be a white female is enough to satisfy those beauty standards that include long hair, fine features, and fair skin. For example, *Wild Women Don't Wear No Blues* edited by Marita Golden (Anchor Books, 1994) contains the thought-provoking quotes, "African American women have been damaged from years of white denigration of their dark full-featured beauty and more independent ways of moving" and "Aunt Jemima is built to serve, not to adore."

ISSUE 3

Is the Men's Movement "Promise Keepers" Socially Positive?

YES: Edward Gilbreath, from "Manhood's Great Awakening," *Christianity Today* (February 6, 1995)

NO: John Swomley, from "Promises We *Don't* Want Kept," *The Humanist* (January/February 1996)

ISSUE SUMMARY

YES: Edward Gilbreath, associate editor of *New Man* magazine, says that Promise Keepers (PK) is a socially positive organization that seeks to reconnect men to their roles as husbands, fathers, and moral leaders and to make them more accountable.

NO: John Swomley, a professor of theology, contends that Promise Keepers emphasizes the patriarchal family with no compromise and serves as a cover for a takeover by the fundamentalist religious right.

The first men's movement was introduced by Warren Farrell, the author of *The Liberated Man* (Random House, 1974). He organized hundreds of men's groups, which were intended to be counterparts to women's consciousness-raising groups. Within these sessions men were encouraged to listen to women rather than to dominate, to explore the political underpinnings of their marriages and relationships, and to explore the link between machismo and violence. Farrell also founded 60 "men's liberation" chapters under the aegis of the National Organization for Women (NOW) in the 1970s and was hailed in the *Chicago Tribune* as the "Gloria Steinem of men's liberation." By the mid-1980s, however, Farrell began referring to men as the "new downtrodden" and suggested that "slavish men had been reduced to sex objects by women."

A subsequent men's movement was introduced by Robert Bly, who suggested that "stereotypical sissies" had replaced "macho men." He began running "all-male workshops" and weekend wilderness retreats where men wore tribal masks, dressed in animal costumes, beat drums, and "rediscovered the beast within." This movement involved strict separatism, and by the mid-1980s many men were claiming that they were undergoing a "masculinity crisis." By the end of the decade, this men's movement was in full swing, complete with a lecture series, books, newsletters, radio shows, and brotherhood lodges.

The newest of the men's movements, Promise Keepers (PK), started in 1990 in the charismatic Vineyard Church. This all-male social movement was founded by Bill McCartney, a former football coach at the University of Colorado. Of current men's movements, PK is the strongest and the most pervasive. PK was ostensibly organized in response to men's failures to fulfill their roles as husbands, fathers, and moral leaders, failures that leaders say led to the breakdown of family values and of society. In the past seven years the movement has grown from a local fellowship of 72 men joining for prayer to a multidenominational national phenomenon with 4,200 members in 1991, 52,000 attendees at a national rally in Boulder, Colorado, in 1993, and 234,000 participants in national workshops in 1994. Currently, PK holds countless meetings of local men's groups all over the United States, and these small groups are all linked to the main organization via a key member, or "point man." PK has become a truly significant movement among Christian men.

Advocates of PK say that the organization provides healthy and useful activities for Christian men to do together while positively reinforcing the importance of being true to marriage and family obligations. PK claims to benefit society by focusing on its most pressing problems—violence, teenage pregnancy, and broken families—and by reducing these problems to their lowest common denominator: a lack of male leadership. PK supporters blame the sociological changes that followed the Industrial Revolution for separating men from their families and isolating them in offices and factories. With men out of the picture, women became the primary providers of moral and spiritual leadership in the home and the driving forces in the church, leading to a spiritual malaise among Christian men.

Critics, on the other hand, fear that PK is one of the most dangerous fundamentalist Christian political agents active in the United States today. They claim that this men's movement has emerged in protest to women's developing power: It calls for men to "take back the power"; it promotes a tough, take-charge image of men; and it carries the ultimate goal of undermining a socialization process that threatens men's power. Men's movements tend to be controlled by hegemonic masculinity, say opponents, and PK is the ultimate manifestation of this phenomenon. Composed as it is of white, married, heterosexual, patriarchal, privileged males and expressly prohibiting female membership or attendance, PK disavows the political, social, and economic gains that have been made by women, critics say. It is difficult to sort out the criticisms that are associated with fundamental Christian zealousness, however, from those associated with legitimate sociopolitical concerns.

In the selections that follow, Edward Gilbreath praises the PK movement as embodying "manhood's great awakening" and claims that the organization will remedy many of the social ills of our times. John Swomley sees PK as a dangerous organization with strong right-wing political backing and support. He accuses the PK movement of trying to derail gains by women and to reassert the mode of living that was popular in more oppressive times.

YES

Edward Gilbreath

MANHOOD'S GREAT AWAKENING

I'm among 52,000 men packed into gritty Folsom Stadium in Boulder, Colorado. I am not at a football game or Wrestlemania XVII. What is playing on this scorching July weekend is a meeting of Promise Keepers, and according to the advertising, the home team is the Father, Son, and Holy Ghost. I've been in huge crowds before, but not one made up entirely of hairy, sweaty, and emotionally uninhibited Christian males. The legion of masculine voices sings, shouts, chants, cries. Frisbees, footballs, and plastic-foam planes constantly zoom overhead. Amens, hallelujahs, and praise the Lords ring out to affirm the steady lineup of preachers and speakers. Periodically, swarms of bodies go up and down throughout the stadium to create a human wave. And between speakers, the stadium spontaneously breaks out into deafening macho chants: "We love Jesus; yes, we do! We love Jesus; how 'bout you?"

But Promise Keepers wants this to be more than a testosterone charged pep rally. They want to change men. And the men who come seem ready to be challenged. In fact, any man wanting to be a true Promise Keeper must pledge to embrace seven commitments:

1. Honor Jesus Christ through worship, prayer, and obedience to his Word.
2. Pursue vital relationships with a few other men, understanding that a man needs brothers to help him keep his promises.
3. Practice spiritual, moral, ethical, and sexual purity.
4. Build strong marriages and families.
5. Support the mission of the church by honoring and praying for one's pastor and by actively giving of one's time and resources.
6. Reach beyond racial and denominational barriers to demonstrate the power of biblical unity.
7. Influence the world by being obedient to the Great Commandment (Mark 12:30–31) and the Great Commission (Matt. 28: 19–20).

Almost everyone is willing to take the pledge—at least while on the mountaintop.

"This weekend has given me the desire to have a daily relationship with God again," said an attendee from Fayetteville, North Carolina.

"Man, that's the kind of stuff I can't take," remarked a choked-up Promise Keeper, referring to a young boy crying in his dad's arms after the boy had gone forward during an altar call.

"I'm divorced, and sometimes I feel like I'm alone in the church," confided another Promise Keeper from Polk, Nebraska. "This shows me that there are a lot of other men like me, struggling to get their lives together through Jesus."

"We've been too proud to cry out to God and to say we need help," declared Southern California evangelist Greg Laurie during a message that echoed the tone of the weekend. For the thousands of men attending its conferences, Promise Keepers is all about dropping their masks.

BIRTHING A MOVEMENT

We're looking for a few good men is no longer the exclusive claim of the U.S. Marines. Today, wives, children, churches, and communities have entered the search. More than ever, the estrangement of men from their roles as husbands, fathers, and moral leaders is being cited as reason for the breakdown of family and society.

For years, the evangelical response to male absenteeism has been through sermons, books, and sporadic workshops addressing the issue. Not until Promise Keepers has there been a large-scale mobilization of men to counter the problem.

In just five years, Promise Keepers has made it a summer ritual for churches large and small to ship busloads of men to its conference sites across the country. Once this would have been implausible: men assembling for something other than a sports event or Rotary meeting. Promise Keepers has changed that. As a result, the Christian male—a distant and, arguably, indifferent constituent of the twentieth-century church—is being challenged to assume a new level of spiritual leadership and vitality in his home, church, and community.

Founded in 1990 by Bill McCartney, who recently resigned as coach of the University of Colorado football team, Promise Keepers began as a local fellowship of men joining for prayer, fasting, and mutual encouragement. Though the original group was led by McCartney and other members of the charismatic Vineyard church, the men promptly sought to take the group across denominational borders.

The core group of 72 has since mushroomed into a national phenomenon, rocketing from 4,200 in 1991 to a national rally in Boulder of 52,000 in 1993 to a combined total of 234,000 during the summer of 1994, the first year of the conference's expansion to regional sites. (More than 60,000 assembled in Indianapolis alone.) Add to this the countless meetings of local men's small groups growing out of the larger meetings and you have a significant movement among Christian men.

This robust interest in men's issues has not gone unnoticed by publishers and marketers. A visit to your local Christian bookstore reveals that the shop's titles are no longer aimed primarily toward women; men now have a section of their own. Tapes, T-shirts, and hats are also available for the male willing to be parted from his money. Promise Keepers also has inspired the launch of *New Man*, a glossy, bimonthly magazine by Strang Communications; the publisher reports a current paid circulation of 100,000.

"Christian men have finally come out of hibernation and are seeing their need to come together," says Promise Keepers' president, Randy Phillips. "I think it's time to acknowledge that the Holy Spirit is igniting a flame in the hearts of men all over the nation."

MEN WILL BE BOYS

Being surrounded by 52,000 men takes some getting used to. Now and then one longs for a hint of soprano in the bass-heavy singing. The sounds and smells of the testosterone-drenched conference are reminiscent of a locker room. Although the messages emphasize love and sensitivity, speakers as genial as James Dobson and Charles Swindoll constantly employ sports and military metaphors (but so does the Bible). Even worship is occasionally framed as competition, such as when opposite sides of the stadium challenge each other to shout the loudest praise.

A few women volunteers are in evidence, working registration tables, selling refreshments, or providing first-aid support. But, by and large, this event is woman-free—and for good reason, say Promise Keepers' leaders. "We want to create an environment where men can let down and be real," says Phillips.

Being real, for these men, means unabashedly shedding tears, embracing one another during prayer and singing, huddling to confess their hidden sins and fears, and, very simply, being free to play.

The men erupt in laughter as preacher Charles Swindoll, clad in faded denim, rides into the arena atop a Harley-Davidson motorcycle, the savage vocals and scratchy chords of "Born to Be Wild" blaring in the background. Later in the evening, author and speaker Gary Smalley displays some wildness of his own, making his entrance on a kiddy-sized Big Wheel bike.

"Promise Keepers is a fun thing as well as a serious time for men to grow," says Nate Adams, author of *Nine Character Traits Separating the Men from the Boys*, who attended the regional rally in Indianapolis. "An important aspect of the conference is the chance men have to express their boyish and playful sides."

Notes Adams, beyond the challenging messages on marriage and accountability, much of the fascination with Promise Keepers lies in the fact that it is something Christian men can do together. Indeed, at times the Boulder crowd seems excited not so much by what is being said as by the opportunity to "hang" with other men—perhaps an indication that something is askew in the American church, which tends to provide an abundance of gathering options for men and women or women and women but few geared specifically for men.

NO WOMEN ALLOWED

One of the most dramatic moments of the 1994 Boulder conference occurred when a small airplane, pulling a long banner, began to circle Folsom Stadium. Soon thousands of heads were turned upward to read the message: "Only weak men are afraid of strong women." The words provoked a few jeers before the plane moved on. But several minutes later, the plane returned, this time with a new message: "Promise Keepers, losers and weepers." Already charged up from a sermon by San Diego pastor John Maxwell, with upraised fists and a building intensity, the men began to chant: "Je-sus, Je-sus, Je-sus," as if to praise the plane's banner out of the sky.

From the beginning, Promise Keepers has been an object of suspicion from many women—feminist and otherwise—who are certain a meeting of so many Christian men can only be about one thing: keeping women in their place.

Promise Keepers president Randy Phillips says he understands the distrust that many women have toward his organization. "I think there are a lot of women inside and outside the church who have been victims of the misuse of male authority, and it has brought a lot of pain and wariness."

According to Phillips, although women are not permitted to register for the conferences, it is not because men are conspiring against them. On the contrary, he says, women are the beneficiaries of the positive things that are happening at the meetings. "We're not asking men to go back with an iron fist. We're asking them to go back on their knees, with a spirit of service and respect for their wives and families."

Lois Rabey, a writer who covered the 1993 Boulder meeting for a Christian women's magazine, found the conference to be positive. "As a woman, I didn't hear anything particularly alarming from the speakers," she says. "Frankly, I felt the men were finally doing what Christian women have been doing for a long time."

Indeed, women have been shouldering much of the work of the church. Although men, in most cases, continue to hold the most visible leadership roles in the church, women are often the driving force behind church activities, Sunday-school programs, and getting the family to church in the first place.

"Let's face it," says psychologist Gary Oliver, a Promise Keepers board member, "if it weren't for women, there would be no prayer in many churches, missionaries would not get ongoing support, and there would be a lot fewer Bible studies. There has definitely been a vacuum of men doing what God has called them to do in the church."

This can be explained, in part, by sociological changes in the nineteenth-century. With the coming of the Industrial Revolution, men went from work that revolved around the home to factory and office jobs that physically removed them from their families. This ultimately spelled bad news for the spiritual lives of men and, consequently, society.

Notes historian E. Anthony Rotundo in his book *American Manhood*, the increasing absence of husbands and fathers from the home "entrusted women with the care and nurture of communal values—of personal morality, social bonds, and, ultimately, the level of virtue in the community." With men out of the picture, mothers became the primary providers of moral and spiritual leadership in the home and the most active persons in the church pew. This fallout can be seen Only in America's spiritual landscape today. Recent Gallup surveys report that, by a margin of 46 percent to 38 percent, women are more likely than men to have attended religious services in the past week. What's more, by a margin of 57 percent to 37 percent, women are more likely than men to say they give serious and consistent attention to the development of their faith.

This perception of a feminized church has contributed to a feeling of spiritual malaise among many Christian men. In his book *Uneasy Manhood*, Robert Hicks claims Christian men have developed a "deep-seated inferiority complex about spiritual things." When it comes to prayer, devotions, and attending Bible studies, men just don't see themselves as measuring up to their wives, Hicks suggests. "In most men's minds, the standard is whatever their wives are into, so that makes the standard feminine."

Perhaps that is why many Christian wives have been praising Promise Keepers for its work in bringing men back into the life of the church. In fact, in my Boulder encounters, many of the men admitted that their wives had made them come to the conference.

Nonetheless, while many women may celebrate the work of Promise Keepers, one still wonders if the tone of the conferences carries a subtle and generally unspoken promotion of male hierarchy in the church. Women are not allowed to attend, yet they can work booths; although a good number of the sessions deal with relating to women, never is a female voice heard. Says Rabey, who is herself a conference speaker and has sat in on her share of workshops led by men, "If Promise Keepers is really serious about better marriages, better communication, and all of those things, I think it would be helpful for the men to hear from a female perspective besides that of their wives."

"We actually had a woman address the men during our Anaheim [Calif.] conference," says Phillips. "But we've not made any real steps toward having regular women speakers. Most of what we're doing at the conferences depends on men opening up with other men."

Suggests one observer, "It really doesn't matter who you have speaking there. As long as they are solid Christians, God is going to bless."

WHERE'S DADDY?

Although the subjects of the Promise Keepers speakers range from God's holiness to racial reconciliation, the tone of all the addresses seems to presuppose married-with-children status. Unmarried Promise Keepers attendees quickly realize they are badly outnumbered. In fact, according to a representative survey, nearly 90 percent of the summer of '94's Promise Keepers were married.

Promise Keepers' heavy focus on marriage and family issues is no coincidence. The organization has emerged at a time when the American family is in shambles: millions of children are born out of wedlock, divorce has become routine, and fathers are becoming less of a presence in the home.

"Promise Keepers is strategic," says Steve Farrar, executive director of Point Man Leadership Ministries and a Promise Keepers speaker—suggesting that God's remedy for America's moral decay lies in a revival among husbands and fathers. "When you take the major pressing issues that are facing us—violence, teen pregnancy, broken families—and reduce them to their lowest common denominator, you're going to find a lack of male leadership at the root."

Indeed, to an unprecedented degree in our nation's history, the political Left and Right agree that something must be done about the male leadership crisis. Both Dan Quayle and Bill Clinton sing the praises of fathers in the home. And a high-powered profamily organization called the National Fatherhood Initiative (NFI) has joined the crusade with voices as diverse as William Bennett and Al Gore.

According to the NFI, approximately one out of every three American children does not live with his or her father. The problem crosses racial and economic lines: 22 percent of white children are born to unmarried mothers, as are 68 percent of black children. As a result of out-of-wedlock births, divorce, and premature death, 5.6 million children under the age of 15 are being raised without a dad in the house.

While the number of physically absent fathers is staggering, one can only guess at the gargantuan figures for *emotionally* absent fathers. According to Ken Canfield, executive director of the National Center for Fathering, fatherlessness can be more than the physical absence of dads. "When there's lack of attention, lack of emotional connection, or a subtle workaholism," he says, "this creates a situation of a father who's there but really isn't there."

Says Phillips, "There are times when I pursued work and ministry at the expense of my own home. Most of us have not lived up to God's design in our relationships with our wives and children."

The success of Promise Keepers, explains Phillips, is both proof of the problem's existence and the desire among Christian men to do something about it.

THE WOUNDED MALE SOUL

The work of Promise Keepers and other groups in the Christian men's movement has arisen against the backdrop of a waning *secular* men's movement. The late eighties and early nineties saw white baby boomers displaying a frenzy of interest over the perplexing puzzle of being a man in America. Sociologists and journalists were soon tracking the activity of a phenomenon that sought to get men in touch with themselves. The

movement's books shot high on the best-seller lists, and men lined up in droves to attend seminars and run around bare-chested during tribal-oriented "Wild Man" weekends. Some called it a reaction to the feminist establishment; others saw it as a way for men to be both vulnerable and aggressive without being lambasted for wimpiness or insensitivity.

In the long run, however, the secular men's movement turned out to be more effective at identifying problems—confusion over the meaning of masculinity, the disappearance of fathers, the need for older men to mentor boys as they grow into manhood—than at providing solutions.

"The Christian men's movement is not a spiritualized version of the secular men's movement; it is the men's movement," says Stu Weber, a pastor and author of the book *Tender Warrior*. "I think the secular movement has come and gone because it didn't have anywhere to go. You can only go so far with myths and tribal lore. Eventually, you've got to get to the Genesis spring, which is a Judeo-Christian foundation."

Many of the speakers refer to what is called the wounded male soul. This woundedness springs from the cultural estrangement of boys from their fathers and the emotional repression American culture has deemed necessary for true maleness.

Like Rotundo, Oliver, who wrote the book *Real Men Have Feelings Too*, believes the Industrial Revolution is at the heart of the present dilemma. "It changed the meaning of manhood in America," he explains. "Men left their homes and farms to work in factories and offices. Through much of our history, child rearing was shared by men and women. With industrialization, child rearing became a 'feminine thing.' Boys no longer had their father's physical presence as a model and a source for their ideals and identity."

Oliver adds that industrialization accelerated the pace of living, creating a major social shift from stability and community to insecurity and detachment. "I think this process caused men to lose touch with what it meant to be a husband, a father, a friend—and a person."

The results can be seen at every hand in our society. The expectation for men to be the prime breadwinners in our society has driven them to correlate their self-worth with their earnings. And cultural images of John Wayne and Arnold Schwarzeneger taint perceptions of what a "real man" is, often leading men to buy into the strong and silent approach to life. All of this has led to men who are disconnected from their families and themselves.

And yet, as men try to overcome this legacy of inexpressiveness and emotional distance, they are faced with conflicting expectations. On the one hand, men are told—whether directly or implicitly—to be gentle and compassionate. On the other hand, the message urges acting strong and taking responsibility. Men must somehow navigate between being lions and lambs.

Some observers, like Steve Farrar, would say that the church sometimes errs on the side of gentleness. "Traits like tenderness and sensitivity are very important, but I think we sometimes elevate those over other traits like courage and aggressiveness." True manhood, believes Farrar, should be gleaned from the example of Jesus. "Jesus could be tender and gentle, but Jesus could also walk in and clear out a corrupted temple."

But is there a real biblical model of gender for understanding what it means to be a *Christian* man or woman? According to theologian Lewis Smedes, probably not: "Men's and women's roles may be situationally different and have different forms of expression, but the Bible is mainly interested in the moral and spiritual qualities of a human being." Smedes, who recently retired from Fuller Theological Seminary, suggests that following Christ is a gender-neutral calling: "That which is important about Jesus being a model is not his modeling of maleness but his modeling of humanity."

Promise Keepers has already entered into the tricky task of showing that feminine virtues and masculine virtues need not be a conflict in the lives of Christian men. But in a day when many men buy into the idea that being active in the church means putting one's masculinity on hold in favor of characteristics associated with femininity (nurturing, servanthood, vulnerability), will men receive Promise Keepers' version of the story? The thousands of teary-eyed, hand-holding men gathered in Boulder seemed to.

THE COACH

The climax of many of the Promise Keepers meetings comes with the rallying address of founding Promise Keeper Bill McCartney. Most of the men refer to him as "Coach McCartney," which seems appropriate given the inspirational, locker-room brand of pep talk he delivers.

"We're calling men of God to battle—we will retreat no more," the coach declares. "We're going to contest anything that sets itself up against the name of Jesus Christ." The men respond with deafening cheers and standing ovations.

Although Coach McCartney can inspire thousands to stand up for Jesus, it does not take long to realize that these men are not flocking around him because of his charismatic oratory. After several minutes, his speeches begin to take on a rambling quality that makes one understand quickly why his first job was football. What gives McCartney such influence among thousands of men is his image as a championship-winning football coach who has taken a very public stand about his faith and about being a good husband and father.

Many, like Gary Oliver, see McCartney as the spark that has set the Christian men's movement ablaze. "This movement was beginning in churches across the country on a smaller scale throughout the eighties," says Oliver. "For years we've had Ed Cole, Gary Smalley, John Trent, and James Dobson writing and speaking on these issues. But the burden that God gave to Bill McCartney opened the whole thing up. It gave direction and clarity to it."

Observes Ken Canfield, "Bill McCartney has been honest about issues he has struggled with, and he has spoken very clearly about how the Lord can change a man's life."

Without question, Christian men are proud to claim such a strong man as one of their own. Suddenly, being a Christian is for tough guys, too. "If he can be outspoken about his faith, heck, so can I," exclaimed a fired-up Promise Keeper.

The coach is someone men can identify with. Indeed, the essence of many a Promise Keeper's experience can be found in McCartney's own story of how he allowed work to come between him and his family. He took over a football program that was going nowhere and produced a national championship; yet, in the midst of an the fanfare, at the very peak of success, he realized how he was failing to fulfill his roles as a husband and father—and chose to do something about it.

In the process, he has been very candid about his then-teenage daughter's pregnancy (the father was one of his star football players) and his own share of responsibility for her actions. When she needed him, he had not been there.

In a tragic, but triumphant story, McCartney eventually led that football star who fathered his grandchild to Christ just before the young man died from an inoperable stomach cancer.

Recently, McCartney made headlines again by unexpectedly resigning from his coaching position at the University of Colorado while still at the top of the game, explaining that it was presently the best thing for his family.

As a result of his very public spiritual pilgrimage, McCartney has taken beatings for his outspoken pro-life views and for his denunciation of the homosexual lifestyle—a daring stance in ultraliberal Boulder. Consequently, homosexual-rights groups have picketed the Boulder conferences for the past two years; during the 1994 meeting, poet Allen Ginsburg led a "diversity rally" targeting Promise Keepers' "anti-gay" and "anti-women" agenda.

Still, McCartney continues to lead the charge for a return to Christian values among men. "It's time for men who love Christ to stand up and make their presence felt," he says. And, because of his example, thousands and thousands of men are taking the call seriously.

KEEPING THE PROMISE

Building on five years of sustained growth, from a small local assembly to six regional conventions, Promise Keepers has bold ambitions. International conferences are being devised, and plans are in the works to assemble 1 million men in Washington, D.C., in 1996 to pray for the nation.

Every area of the Promise Keepers organization is expanding. The group has gone from 29 staff members in 1993 to 150 full-time employees in 1994, and in that same period, its annual budget has risen from $4 million to $22 million.

But Phillips is quick to explain that it is not Promise Keepers' purpose to grow big simply for the sake of numbers. "We do not want to build a monument. We want to serve this movement as a mission. It becomes a monument when the focus turns to personalities or the organization. It becomes a mission when it's focused on God's purpose to honor his Son through the church and bring millions to the person of Christ."

So far, Promise Keepers has maintained its commitment to build up the local church through empowering pastors. The last two Boulder conferences have concluded with all the clergy in attendance going to the front of the arena to be prayed for and applauded by the other men. McCartney has made it an ongoing aim to restore the office of the pastor to one of respect and authority. "Our leadership is wounded, beaten down, and beleaguered," he says, noting that too often congregations and committees have made pastors afraid to preach the gospel wholeheartedly.

The organization has also sought to strengthen local churches through encouraging the formation of men's small groups for fellowship and accountability. Says Promise Keepers' media director Steve Chavis, "All of our success here is contingent upon men taking part in small groups when they return home." Clearly,

the true measure of this present revival of Christian manhood is not the enthusiasm demonstrated during the summer rallies but rather the enduring commitment that win carry men through the year.

Can Promise Keepers make good on its promises? Demanding the establishment of home-grown discipleship and Christian-service groups is a good start, but, like other ministries before it, Promise Keepers could go even further.

If the problems Promise Keepers seeks to combat arise from the Industrial Revolution, a massive structural shift in our society, then ultimately, any solution to those problems must address structural as well as individual issues. The epidemic of fatherlessness is in part a consequence of massive social change. Racism is an institutional evil as well as a matter of individual wrongdoing. Will Promise Keepers itself eventually branch out to develop public-policy arms to support the goal of structural change? For instance, advocating flex-time programs for working fathers or racial-awareness initiatives for young men might be logical extensions of the organization's current objectives.

As a movement, Promise Keepers has promise: a flexible leadership not concerned with building an empire, a commitment to communicating the basics, a holistic vision for men—encouraging them to be servants at home, at church, and in their community—and a desire to see things happen at a grassroots level. Admirable goals for a still-fledgling ministry. Yet, after several winning summers, it is still being determined how well this game plan is working in the cold off-season months.

If our culture continues in its current state of moral chaos, and if Promise Keepers' ultimate promises of stable homes, unified communities, and stronger churches begin to be realized, America at large may find that promise-keeping is not just about evangelical religion or male leadership but about truth, responsibility, and agape love—concepts that find their true fruition in the Christian faith.

If Promise Keepers can accomplish this, it will prove itself as not only a men's movement but also a powerful move of God.

NO

John Swomley

PROMISES WE *DON'T* WANT KEPT

One of the most dangerous of the fundamentalist Christian political groups active in the United States today is the Promise Keepers. Led by Bill McCartney, the former football coach at the University of Colorado, Promise Keepers has been developing a mass macho appeal designed to provoke a backlash to the women's equality movement—part of the new strategy of Christian right leaders to build a mass male movement. The big guns of the fundamentalist right—from Pat Robertson of the Christian Coalition and James Dobson of Focus on the Family to Florida televangelist D. James Kennedy and Bill Bright of Campus Crusade for Christ—are all publicly promoting Promise Keepers.

Promise Keepers has been able to fill football stadiums recently in Detroit and Los Angeles, with numbers over 70,000 each. In September 1995, it also moved into mainline churches with chapters like the United Methodist Men of the Kansas East Conference in Camp Chippewa, Kansas.

A vivid illustration of the Promise Keepers' anti-women ideology appears in *Seven Promises of a Promise Keeper*, which is published by Dobson's Focus on the Family. An essay by evangelist Tony Evans tells men how to deal with women: "I can hear you saying, 'I want to be a spiritually pure man. Where do I start?'" The first thing you do, Evans says, "is sit down with your wife and say something like this: 'Honey, I've made a terrible mistake. I've given you my role. I gave up leading this family, and I forced you to take my place. Now I must reclaim that role.'"

Evans then tells his male readers: "Don't misunderstand what I'm saying here. I'm not suggesting that you ask for your role back. I'm urging you to *take it* back." This emphasis on the patriarchal family, Evans insists, must involve "no compromise." He tells women that they must submit for "the survival of our culture." As Evans puts it:

> I am convinced that the primary cause of this national crisis is the feminization of the American male.... I'm trying to describe a misunderstanding of manhood that has produced a nation of "sissified" men who abdicate their role as spiritually pure leaders, thus forcing women to fill the vacuum.

From John Swomley, "Promises We *Don't* Want Kept," *The Humanist* (January/February 1996). Copyright © 1996 by John Swomley. Reprinted by permission.

Evans's directive is reinforced and reiterated by other specimens of Promise Keepers literature, such as *Strategies for a Successful Marriage: A Study Guide for Men.* In it, author E. Glenn Wagner discusses "praying over your wife" and quotes Coach McCartney:

Almighty God is calling men to pray over their families in such a way that, if a man will pray daily, regularly, over his wife, praying for God's blessing upon her, Almighty God will restore her self-image.... Our women need a man providing the spiritual tempo and leadership in the home.

When McCartney prays over his wife, this is his "model" prayer:

Lord Jesus Christ, I invoke Your power and Your spirit upon Lindi. Lord, I pray righteousness and purity upon her. Lord, I pray that You will heal all of her scars, that You will mend up all those things that keep her from being the woman that she desires to be and that You call her to be.

Lord God, I pray that you will breathe excitement into her....

This and more is said with "his hand upon her." Tellingly, there is no reference to Lindi's being allowed or encouraged to lay her hand upon Bill and to pray over his "scars" or his "righteousness and purity." Men who dominate women don't seek equal treatment.

Bill McCartney and his right-wing allies intend to build a disciplined and authoritarian army. The key to this is the formation of "accountability" cells of no more than five members, each one of whom is expected to expose all aspects of his life to the others. Each cell member must answer any questions about his marriage, "his family,

his sexuality, his financial dealings, and his relationship to others." These cells usually operate within a church or other religious group. They are led by a "point man" who reports to an "ambassador," who, in turn, reports to headquarters in Boulder, Colorado. The staff there numbers 150.

Various chapters in Promise Keepers books stress the importance of "mentoring"—persuading men to form small cells or groups with other men. The "point man" for each cell is recruited by the "ambassador," who himself must be approved by the leaders of Promise Keepers. "Training is required for *all* Ambassadors," reports one book. Each ambassador must agree with the Promise Keepers' "Statement of Faith" and with the "Seven Promises," and each must be recommended by his pastor, who must also agree to the Promise Keepers' mission.

This is the way to build political power, which is precisely what Promise Keepers' leadership and sponsors intend. McCartney, for example, is a member of the board of Colorado for Family Values, which sponsored the infamous anti-gay-rights initiative known as Amendment Two. That amendment would permit the state to nullify local equal-protection ordinances that prevent discrimination against gays and lesbians in such areas as employment and housing. It was declared unconstitutional by the Colorado Supreme Court and is now before the Supreme Court for review.

Promise Keepers is particularly dangerous because of the divisions it seeks to create within mainline churches that do not accept the Promise Keepers' Statement of Faith, which is obviously fundamentalist. That statement includes the following sentence: "We believe that the

Bible is God's written revelation to man and that it is verbally inspired, authoritative, and without error in the original manuscripts." There is also a passage that speaks of the second coming of Jesus Christ "to earth in power and glory," which is a euphemism for a messianic leader who will triumph over the enemy.

Moreover, in the *Seven Promises of a Promise Keeper*, the question is asked: "Do you belong to a Bible-believing, Bible-teaching church?" That is another euphemism, this time for a fundamentalist church which requires an absolutist belief in the inerrancy of scripture (or, at least, those select verses of scripture that are emphasized in such churches). McCartney associates himself with the Word of God Community, which requires complete submission to a person called "the head." He also has links with the Vineyard Church, which has a branch in Boulder. One of the leaders of the Vineyard Church has described his work as "power evangelism" and his followers as "self-conscious members of God's army sent to do battle against the forces of the kingdom of darkness." If you are not in "God's kingdom" as he describes it, you are "in Satan's."

McCartney's pastor at the Boulder Valley Vineyard Church is the Reverend James Ryle, who is also a member of the Promise Keepers board. *Charisma* magazine of May 1995 reports that Promise Keepers' "top leaders are affiliated with Vineyard churches." According to an interview by Russ Bellant, an expert researcher on right-wing activity, Ryle says that Promise Keepers is the fulfillment of the end-time "day of Jehovah and the destruction from the Almighty," as described in chapter 21 of the Book of Joel. "Never have 300,000 men come together throughout human history," said Ryle, "except for the purpose of war."

McCartney also uses the language of war. In a rally reported in the *Boulder Daily Camera* on July 28, 1994, he said:

> What you are about to hear is God's word to the men of this nation. We are going to war as of tonight. We have divine power; that is our weapon. We will not compromise. Wherever truth is at risk, in the school or legislature, we are going to contend for it. We will win.

The war is against secularism, abortion, homosexuality, and other enemies of the far right.

This is not to suggest that the teachings of McCartney or others in the Promise Keepers leadership are totally misleading or bad; for example, McCartney has an excellent chapter opposing racism. On the other hand, in the Promise Keepers' study series is a section called "The Devil Made Me Do It," which insists that there must be no compromise with school board members who would "soften your stance on abstinence based sex education." Abstinence is fine, but it provides no precautionary education for those teens who are already sexually active and who know little about using contraceptives to prevent pregnancy and disease. And when laudable teachings on racism are mixed with reactionary teachings about women, gays, and sexuality, the result is less than laudable.

Promise Keepers is now a national phenomenon. In 1995, it held rallies in 12 major cities featuring right-wing religious leaders such as James Dobson as speakers. Even more ominously, Promise Keepers is related—through Dobson, Robertson, and others—to the secretive Council for National Policy, which seeks political power. Paul Weyrich, a key member of that council, said: "We are no longer working to preserve the status quo. We are radicals working to overturn the present power structure of this Country."

Promise Keepers is not a separate Christian fundamentalist movement. It functions within the context of both fundamentalist religion and the radical religious and political right.

POSTSCRIPT

Is the Men's Movement "Promise Keepers" Socially Positive?

Clearly, the goals stated by the PK leaders conflict sharply with the goals that their critics believe are at the organization's core. Can the PK goals be taken at face falue? Or could critics be correct in claiming that PK is really a political organization of the Right, which, in collaboration with fundamentalist Christians, seeks to assume leadership of America? Why should critics distrust an organization that professes such noble goals as renewed commitment to wives, family, and God? Is there an antireligious bias at work here? Or could this organization really be politically dangerous? A sample of writings in support of PK (and the related Million Man March on Washington, D.C., in October 1995, which was composed of African American males in support of their own men's movement) can be found in Debra Dickerson, "Queen for a Day?" *The New Republic* (November 6, 1995) and Steve Rabey, "Where Is the Christian Men's Movement Headed?" *Christianity Today* (April 1996).

The question of whether or not PK has a political agenda came up again in October 1997, when an estimated half million people arrived in Washington, D.C., for a religious gathering. PK insisted that the gathering was apolitical, and the majority of the men asserted that they had come to Washington solely to "confess and repent their sins." Critics, however, point to the presence of organizations such as the Family Research Council and Operation Rescue greeting people and distributing literature as well as poll results indicating that PK members are Republican and overwhelmingly conservative.

Critics against PK and similar religious organizations are quite outspoken. A sampling of their writing includes "The Appeal of Fundamentalism," *On the Issues* (Winter 1995); "The Virtuous Male," *Utne Reader* (January/February 1996); "One Man's March," *The New Republic* (November 6, 1995); and "Male Virgins, Blood Covenants and Family Values," *On The Issues* (Spring 1995).

In "God Squad," *The Progressive* (August 1996), Nancy Novosad refers to PK as a radical Christian patriarchy that claims, "By the year 2000, the strongest voice in America . . . is going to belong to the men of God." Do you see any contradictions between PK's stated organizational goals and its resolution for the year 2000? Novosad reports that when a family service worker criticized PK to the media, she immediately received a series of harassing phone calls and was eventually forced to retract her statement or risk losing her job along with the funding for her organization. This reveals PK's fanaticism and fascism, says Norosad. Why would such a flourishing organization as PK become so defensive in the face of one person's criticism? In "The Promise Keepers Are Coming: The Third Wave of the Religious Right," *The Nation*

(October 7, 1996), Joe Conason, Alfred Ross, and Lee Cokorinos suggest that PK as an "army of God" in the most literal sense has been articulated by the Reverend James Ryle, a PK director since its founding. Ryle refers to PK as the fulfillment of the Bible's prophecy of a great force that will destroy sinners and infidels in the period preceding Armageddon. PK functions within the context of both fundamentalist religion and the radical religious and political right. From the perspective of many of its critics, this is an ominous combination. Do you share their concerns? Or are these fears unwarranted? Do you agree with the theory that PK was actually *designed* to provoke a backlash?

In "A Match Made in Heaven: Lesbian Leftie Chats With a Promise Keeper," *The Progressive* (August 1996), Suzanne Phar articulates some questions following her conversation with a member of PK: "How do [progressive individuals] point out the differences between the generals of this [PK] army and their recruits? . . . Is there any hope for preventing the merger of church and state if we do not hold authentic conversations with those who believe firmly in the inerrancy of the Bible? How do we get closer to people's real needs and their values in our organizing for change? Finally, how do we carry on this conversation and organize as progressives committed to equal rights for everyone?"

ISSUE 4

Is the Sex Industry Harmful to Women?

YES: Sheila Jeffreys, from "How Orgasm Politics Has Hijacked the Women's Movement," *On the Issues* (Spring 1996)

NO: Camille Paglia, from *Vamps and Tramps: New Essays* (Vintage Books, 1994)

ISSUE SUMMARY

YES: Political science professor Sheila Jeffreys asserts that sex industry entrepreneurs have wrongly sought to discuss sex as if it were entirely separate from violence and had no connection with the oppression of women. She maintains that male ownership of female bodies via the sex industry provides an arena for male supremacy and oppression.

NO: Professor of humanities Camille Paglia dismisses the contention that women in the sex industry are victimized by men, arguing instead that prostitutes and women in pornography are powerful, autonomous, and in control.

The sex industry, including prostitution, pornography, and strip clubs, is a subject of heated debate among feminists, antifeminists, and other groups. The industry has a particularly high profile on New York City's 42nd Street; in New Orleans, Louisiana, during Mardi Gras; and in the city of Amsterdam, the Netherlands. While all components of the industry are debated, the issue of pornography is particularly controversial. Many agree with antipornography feminists who reject the concepts of obscenity and censorship as appropriate frameworks for judging pornography. That is, they view pornography as inherently evil, a position that overwhelms any attempt to apply "community standards" to its regulation. Opponents of pornography assert that government, for the good of its citizenry, must enact laws against its promulgation. But where should the line be drawn when it comes to First Amendment rights?

A possible link between pornography and violence is a key point within this controversy. Censorship is very difficult to justify, and conclusive evidence of a causal connection between violence and pornography has not been made. An August 1993 poll by the National Opinion Research Center found that 57 percent of Americans believe that pornography (defined as any collection of writings, photos, movies, or drawings that show sexual activities) leads to rape, 34 percent do not believe that it does, and 9 percent do not have an opinion on the subject. Moreover, a recent study reports that pornographic films depict less violence than commonly thought. Two other studies found nonsexual violence in 4 percent of the pornographic material studied, while sexual violence was found in another 4 percent of running themes. Although pornographic films became more sexually explicit in the 1970s, violence in pornography has declined since that time. In 1973 the Supreme Court determined that sexually explicit materials could be defined as obscene if an average citizen in the community finds them to be objectionable and offensive. Even with this vague definition, local governments have shown a tendency to find in favor of First Amendment rights and to fail to utilize this ruling to ban pornographic material.

A few feminists have put forth the radical argument that all heterosexual sex is a power struggle in which men assert their dominance over women. Catharine MacKinnon, a professor at the University of Michigan Law School, and essayist Andrea Dworkin have been the most vocal and visible advocates of this view. They say that because pornography harms women, it naturally violates women's civil rights. MacKinnon was instrumental in writing the bill that resulted in the Butler Act, which banned pornography in Canada in 1992. One unanticipated consequence of this legal ruling has been the confiscation of material that was not intended to be pornographic, such as material written by antipornography feminists such as Dworkin. Another unintended consequence has been the disproportionate seizure of gay male and lesbian writing, both pornographic and nonpornographic.

In 1992 Senator Mitch McConnell (R-Kentucky) sponsored the Pornography Victims Compensation Act, which would permit victims of sex crimes and other violence allegedly inspired by obscene materials to sue producers and distributors responsible for these materials. The act was referred to as the "Bundy Bill" because serial killer Ted Bundy blamed pornography for his crimes. Despite support from the religious right and from the feminist left, the act has not passed Congress. Many worry that the act's vague language would seriously impinge upon First Amendment rights.

In the following selections, Sheila Jeffreys argues that the sex industry perpetuates the notion of male ownership of women's bodies and helps to build a foundation for male supremacy and oppression. Camille Paglia contends that women derive tremendous benefits from the sex industry. She characterizes pornography as usually consensual and states that women are depicted in dominant positions as often as they are in submissive positions. Moreover, she views prostitutes as shrewd entrepreneurs and businesswomen.

YES

Sheila Jeffreys

HOW ORGASM POLITICS HAS HIJACKED THE WOMEN'S MOVEMENT

The November/December 1995 issue of *Ms.*, cover-lined HOT UNSCRIPTED SEX, showed a close-up of an African American woman licking her lipsticked lips. Despite all the feminist work that has been done in the last quarter-century to critique and challenge the male-supremacist construction of sex, none of the four articles inside made connections to the whole of the rest of women's lives and status. Set in display type above one was a line from Barbara Seaman's 1972 book, *Free and Female:* "The liberated orgasm is an orgasm you like, under any circumstances." To judge from this issue of *Ms.*, and from the shelves of women's "erotica" in feminist bookstores, an unreflective politics of orgasm seems to have won out.

In the late 1960s and early '70s, it was widely believed that the sexual revolution, by freeing up sexual energy, would make everyone free. I remember Maurice Girodias, whose Olympia Press in Paris published *Story of O*, saying that the solution to repressive political regimes was to post pornography through every letterbox. Better orgasms, proclaimed Austrian psychoanalyst Wilhelm Reich, would create the revolution. In those heady days, many feminists believed that the sexual revolution was intimately linked to women's liberation, and they wrote about how powerful orgasms would bring women power.

Dell Williams is quoted in *Ms.* as having set up a sex shop in 1974 with precisely this idea, to sell sex toys to women: "I wanted to turn women into powerful sexual beings.... I had a vision that orgasmic women could transform the world."

Ever since the '60s, sexologists, sexual liberals, and sex-industry entrepreneurs have sought to discuss sex as if it were entirely separate from sexual violence and had no connection with the oppression of women. Feminist theorists and anti-violence activists, meanwhile, have learned to look at sex politically. We have seen that male ownership of women's bodies, sexually and reproductively, provides the very foundation of male supremacy, and that oppression in and through sexuality differentiates the oppression of women from that of other groups.

If we are to have any chance of liberating women from the fear and reality of sexual abuse, feminist discussion of sexuality must integrate all that we can understand about sexual violence into the way we think about sex. But these days feminist conferences have separate workshops, in different parts of the building, on how to increase sexual "pleasure" and on how to survive sexual violence—as if these phenomena could be put into separate boxes. Women calling themselves feminists now argue that prostitution can be good for women, to express their "sexuality" and make empowering life choices. Others promote the practices and products of the sex industry to women to make a profit, in the form of lesbian striptease and the paraphernalia of sadomasochism. There are now whole areas of the women's, lesbian, and gay communities where any critical analysis of sexual practice is treated as sacrilege, stigmatized as "political correctness." Freedom is represented as the achievement of bigger and better orgasms by any means possible, including slave auctions, use of prostituted women and men, and forms of permanent physical damage such as branding. Traditional forms of male-supremacist sexuality based on dominance and submission and the exploitation and objectification of a slave class of women are being celebrated for their arousing and "transgressive" possibilities.

Well, the pornography is in the letterboxes, and the machinery for more and more powerful orgasms is readily available through the good offices of the international sex industry. And in the name of women's liberation, many feminists today are promoting sexual practices that— far from revolutionizing and transforming the world—are deeply implicated in the practices of the brothel and of pornography.

How could this have happened? How could the women's revolution have become so completely short-circuited? I suggest that there are four reasons.

REASON NO. 1

Victims of the Sex Industry Have Become "Sex Experts"

Sexual capitalism, which has found a way to commoditize nearly every imaginable act of sexual subordination, has even found a way to repackage and recycle some of its victims. As a result, a small number of women who have had lifetimes of abuse and learned their sexuality in the sex industry serving men are now able, often with backing from male sex industrialists, to promote themselves as sex educators in the lesbian and feminist communities. Some of these high-profile women—who are hardly representative of most victims of the sex industry—have managed to set up sex magazines such as *On Our Backs* (for practitioners of lesbian sadomasochism) and stripping and pornography businesses. Many women have mistakenly accepted these formerly prostituted women as "sex experts." Annie Sprinkle and Carol Leigh, for instance, have recirculated into women's communities the woman-hating practices of the sex industry. These women have led the derisive laughter directed at those of us who have said that sex can and must be different.

At the same time, a few women who have profited from free-market capitalism in the '80s have demanded sexual as well as economic equality with men. They have escaped, and now want to use women as men do, so they consume pornography and demand strip clubs and brothels in which women will service them. This is not a revolutionary strategy. There is no threat here to men's privilege, no chance of releasing other women from their subordinate sexual status. And once more, men have become the measure of all things sexual.

Formerly prostituted women who promote the sex of prostitution—but now get paid to lecture and publish—provide a message that even some feminists have found more palatable than all the visions and ideas we have shared about how to transform sex, how to love each other in passionate equality as the basis for a future in which women could really be free.

REASON NO. 2

The Sex of Prostitution Has Become Accepted as the Model for Sex

We cannot construct a sexuality that will enable women to live without sexual terrorism without ending men's abuse of women in prostitution. Within the women's movement, however, the sex of prostitution has been explicitly advocated and promoted. Shannon Bell in *Reading, Writing and Rewriting the Prostitute Body* (1994) argues that the prostituted woman should be seen as "worker, healer, sexual surrogate, teacher, therapist, educator, sexual minority, and political activist." In this book Prostitutes of New York spokesperson Veronica Vera is quoted as saying we should affirm sex workers as "practitioners of a sacred craft" while affirming sex (presumably any sex including the sex of prostitution) as a "nourishing, healing tool." But in fact the most powerful engine for the construction of male sexuality today is the sex industry.

Prostitution and its representation in pornography create an aggressive sexuality requiring the objectification of a woman. She is made into a thing not worthy of the respect due to another equal sentient individual. Prostitution fosters a sexuality in which it is acceptable for the client to take his "pleasure" on and in the body of a woman who dissociates to survive. This is the model for how sex is conceived in male-supremacist society, and sexologists have built careers upon it. Masters and Johnson, for instance, developed their sex-therapy techniques from the practices of prostituted women who were paid to get elderly, drunken, or just plain indifferent men to have erections and be able to penetrate them. As Kathleen Barry has noted in *The Prostitution of Sexuality*, prostitution constructs a male-dominant/female-submissive sexuality in which the personhood and comfort of the woman, let alone her pleasure, is seen as irrelevant.

Prostitution is very big business and rapidly becoming globalized and industrialized. More than half the prostituted women in Amsterdam, for instance, are trafficked, i.e. brought there, often by deception, from other countries and often kept in conditions of sexual slavery. Australian women are trafficked into Greece; Russian women, into tabletop dancing in Melbourne; Burmese women, into Thailand; and Nepali women, into India. Millions of women in the rich world and many more millions in the poor world are being subjected to the abuse of suffering unwanted male hands on their bodies and penises in their bodies. Prostituted women do not like to experience this sexual abuse any more than any other women do. They are not different.

Prostituted women and children are expected to endure many of the forms of sexual violence that feminists would consider unacceptable in the workplace and the home. Sexual harassment and unwanted sexual intercourse are the basis of the abuse, but prostituted women have to receive obscene phone-sex calls, too. They work topless in retailing, car washes, and restaurants. Even as other women workers are seeking to desexualize their work so that they may be seen as something more than sex objects, women in prostitution and sexual "entertainment" are increasingly in demand. Men's prostitution of women reduces the women they abuse and all women to the status of bodies to be sold and used. How can feminists ever expect to eliminate abusive practices from their bedrooms, workplaces, and childhoods if men can simply continue to buy the right to those practices on the street, or, as in Melbourne, in state-licensed brothels?

Tabletop dancing is a type of prostitution now being made acceptable in rich countries as "entertainment." (In poor countries dependent on sex tourism, all prostitution is called entertainment.) Along with other women from the Coalition Against Trafficking in Women, I recently visited a strip club in Melbourne called The Men's Gallery. Some 20 or 30 women were "dancing" on tables. A cross-section of men—teenagers from the suburbs, men who looked like college lecturers and teachers, grandfathers, tourists—sat with their knees under the tables. Often in twos, these men would ask a woman to strip. Doing so, she would place her legs over the men's shoulders, gymnastically showing them her shaved genitalia from front and back in different positions for 10 minutes as the men put money into her garter. The woman's genitals would be inches from the men's faces, and the men would

stare, their faces registering expressions of astonished and guilty delight as if they could not believe they are allowed such dominion. Were the men sexually aroused by the incitement of their dominant phallic status? Was this simple exhibition of female genitalia, which denotes women's subordinate status, in itself arousing? For us women observers, it was difficult to understand the men's excitement. Many must have had teenage daughters, not unlike the women, many of them students, whose genitals danced before their mesmerized eyes.

Tabletop "dancing" tells us something we must understand about "sex" as constructed under male supremacy: The men bond through shared degradation of women. The men who frequent such clubs learn to believe that women love their sex-object status and love to sexually tease as they are examined like slaves in a market. And the women, as they told us, just cut off from what they are doing.

REASON NO. 3

Lesbians Have Been Emulating Gay Men

The feminist challenge to the prostitution model of sexuality has been especially resisted by many gay men and by lesbians who emulate them. As Karla Jay writes, apparently uncritically, in *Dyke Life*:

Today, lesbians are on the cutting edge of sexual radicalism. . . . Some lesbians now claim the right to an erotic freedom that was once associated with gay men. A few large cities have sex clubs and S/M bars for lesbians, while pornographic magazines and videos produced by lesbians for other women have proliferated across the United States. Our sexuality has become as public as our tattoos and our pierced bodies.

In gay male culture we see the phenomenon of a sexuality of self-mutilation and slavery, of tattooing, piercing, and sadomasochism, turned into the very symbol of what gayness is. Commercial gay interests have invested powerfully in exploiting this sexuality of oppression as constitutive of gayness. Much of the power of the pink (gay) dollar developed from the provision of venues, bars and baths, in which the sexuality of prostitution could be exacted, though now mostly unpaid. The cultural influence of gay male resistance to feminist challenges to pornography and prostitution has been extensive, heavily financed in gay media by advertising from the gay sex industry.

Some gay men have challenged the dominant/submissive sexuality that prevails in the gay male community, but few so far have ventured into print lest they experience the ire of their brothers. Gay men, raised in male supremacy, taught to worship masculinity, also have to struggle to overcome their eroticization of dominant/submissive hierarchies if they are to become friends to feminism.

The sex of prostitution has been central to the construction of gayness because of the role of prostitution in gay history. Traditionally male homosexuality was expressed, for middle-class men, in the buying of poorer men or boys—as done by Oscar Wilde, Andre Gide, Christopher Isherwood. This was not the model for lesbian practice.

In the 1980s, as lesbians lost confidence in their own visions, strengths, and possibilities—as feminism came under attack and the sex industry went from strength to strength—many turned to gay men as their models and began to

define themselves as "sexual deviants." They developed an identity in total contradiction to that of lesbian-feminism. Lesbian-feminists celebrate lesbianism as the apogee of woman-loving, as a form of resistance to all the practices and values of male-supremacist culture, including pornography and prostitution. The libertarian lesbians who rose up to decry feminism in the '80s attacked lesbian-feminists for "desexualizing" lesbianism and chose to see themselves as "pro-sex." But the practices of this "pro-sex" stand turned out to replicate the version of lesbianism that had traditionally been offered by the sex industry. The brave new "transgressive" lesbians were the very sadomasochistic, butch/femme constructions that had long been staples of heterosexual men's pornography.

Such lesbians embraced sex-industry practices as constituting who they really were, the fount of their identity and their being. But all the time they felt deficient because their idea of radical, robust sexuality, that practiced by some gay men, seemed always out of reach. In publications such as *Wicked Women* magazine from Sydney, in the work of Cherry Smyth and Della Grace in the U.K. and Pat Califia in the U.S., these lesbians bewailed their inadequacies at toilet sex, at one-night stands, at managing to be sexually attracted to children. Lesbian sex therapists, such as Margaret Nicholls, became an important part of a new lesbian sex industry.

Now there is a tendency in feminist and mainstream women's magazines to represent this lesbian sexuality of prostitution as a tantalizing dish for heterosexual women to sample and consume. "Transgressive" lesbianism, derived from the sex industry and mimicking gay male culture, is now presented as a progressive "woman's" sexuality, a model for how heterosexual women could and should be.

REASON NO. 4

Being Subordinated Can Feel Sexual
There is no such thing as a "natural" sexual pleasure that can be liberated. What gives men or women sexual sensations is socially constructed out of the power relationship between men and women, and it can be changed. In "sex" the very difference between men and women, supposedly so "natural," is in fact created. In "sex" the very categories "men," persons with political power, and "women," persons of the subordinate class, are made flesh.

Nor is sex a mere private matter. In liberal male thought, sex has been shoved into the private sphere and seen as a realm of personal freedom where people can express their individual desires and fantasies. But the bedroom is far from private; it is an arena in which the power relationship between men and women is most revealingly played out. Freedom there is usually that of men to realize themselves on and in the bodies of women.

Sexual feelings are learned and can be unlearned. The construction of sexuality around dominance and submission has been assumed to be "natural" and inevitable because men learn to operate the symbol of their ruling-class status, the penis, in relation to the vagina in ways that ensure women's subordinate status. Our feelings and practices around sex cannot be immune from this political reality. And I suggest it is the affirmation of this power relation, the assertion of a distinction between "the sexes" by means of dominant/submissive behavior, that gives sex its salience and the tense excitement generally associated with it under male supremacy.

Since the early '70s, feminist theorists and researchers have uncovered the extent of sexual violence and how the experience and the fear of it curtail women's lives and opportunities. Child sexual abuse undermines women's ability to develop strong and loving relationships with their own bodies and with others, and confidence about acting upon the world. Rape in adulthood, including marital and date rape, has similar effects. Sexual harassment, voyeurism, flashing, and stalking undermine women's equal opportunities in education, at work, in their homes, on the street. Women who have been used in the sex industry develop techniques of dissociation to survive, an experience shared by victims of incest, and deal with damage to their sexuality and relationships. Awareness of the ultimate threat clouding women's lives, the possibility of sexual murder, is brought to us regularly by newspaper headlines about the deaths of women.

The cumulative effects of such violence create the fear that makes women limit where they go and what they do, be careful about looking in the backseat of the car, locking doors, wearing "safe" clothing, drawing the curtains. As feminist research such as that of Elizabeth Stanko in *Everyday Violence* (1990) shows, women are aware of the threat of men's violence and change their lives in response to that fear even though they may not have experienced serious assault. Against this everyday reality of ordinary women's lives, the notion that an orgasm "under any circumstances" could vanquish that fear and remembered vulnerability is perhaps pseudofeminism's cruelest hoax.

Men's sexual violence is not the work of psychotic individuals but the product of the normal construction of male sexuality in societies like the United States and Australia now—as a practice that defines their superior status and subordinates women. If we seriously want to end such violence, we must not accept this construction as the model for what "sex" really is.

Sexual pleasure for women is a political construction, too. Women's sexuality as well as men's has been forged within the dominant/submissive model, as an artifice to appease and service the sexuality constructed in and for men. Whereas boys and men have been encouraged to direct all feeling into the objectification of another and are rewarded with "pleasure" for dominance, women have learned their sexual feelings in a situation of subordination. Girls are trained through sexual abuse, sexual harassment, and early sexual encounters with boys and men in a sexual role that is reactive and submissive. We learn our sexual feelings as we learn other emotions, in male-dominant families and in situations in which we lack power, surrounded by images of women as objects in advertising and films.

Dee Graham's wonderful 1994 book *Loving to Survive* looks at female heterosexuality and femininity as symptoms of what she calls societal Stockholm Syndrome. In classic Stockholm Syndrome, hostages bond with their captors in terror and develop submissive cooperation in order to survive. Handbooks for those who might be taken hostage, such as I was once given when working in a prison, describe survival tactics that resemble the advice offered in women's magazines for how to win men. If you are ever taken hostage, say these handbooks,

you should talk about the man's interests and family to make him realize you are a person and to activate his humanity. Stockholm Syndrome develops among those who fear for their lives but are dependent upon their captors. If the captor shows any kindness, however small, a hostage is likely to bond even to the point of protecting the captor from harm and entirely adopting his point of view upon the world. Graham defines the sexual violence that women routinely face as "sexual terrorism." Against this background of terror, Graham explains, women develop Stockholm Syndrome and bond to men.

Because women's sexuality develops in this context of sexual terrorism, we can eroticize our fear, our terrified bonding. All sexual arousal and release is not necessarily positive. Women can experience orgasms while being sexually abused in childhood, in rape, or in prostitution. Our language has only words like pleasure and enjoyment to describe sexual feelings, no words to describe those feelings that are sexual but that we do not like, feelings that come from experience, dreams, or fantasies about degradation or rape and cause distress despite arousal.

The "sex" promoted by women's and even feminist magazines, as if it were quite separate from women's real-life subordinate status and experience of sexual violence, offers no hope of deconstructing and reconstructing either men's sexuality or women's. Sadomasochism and "fantasy" scenarios, for instance, in which women attempt to "lose" themselves, are often utilized by women who have been sexually abused. The orgasmic excitement experienced in these scenarios simply cannot be felt in these women's bodies if and when they remain grounded and conscious of who they actually are. The orgasm of inequality—far from encouraging women to seek to create a sexuality commensurate with the freedom feminists envision—merely rewards women with "pleasure" for dissociating.

So many women, including feminists, lowered their eyes from the vision of how to make women free and decided to get stuck into having more-powerful orgasms in any way that worked. The pursuit of the orgasm of oppression serves as a new "opium of the masses." It diverts our energies from the struggles that are needed now against sexual violence and the global sex industry. Questioning how those orgasms feel, what they mean politically, whether they are achieved through the prostitution of women in pornography, is not easy, but it is also not impossible. A sexuality of equality suited to our pursuit of freedom

has still to be forged and fought for if we are to release women from sexual subjection.

The ability of women to eroticize their own subordination and take "pleasure" from the degradation of themselves and other women to object status poses a serious obstacle. So long as women have a stake in the sexual system as it is—so long as they get their kicks that way— why will they want change?

I suggest that it is not possible to imagine a world in which women are free at the same time as protecting a sexuality based precisely upon their lack of freedom. Our sexual passions must match the passions of our political imagination for an end to a world based on all abusive hierarchies, including race and class. Only a sexuality of equality, and our ability to imagine and work for such a sexuality, makes the freedom of women thinkable.

NO

Camille Paglia

NO LAW IN THE ARENA

SEX POWER: PROSTITUTION, STRIPPING, PORNOGRAPHY

The bourgeois limitations in feminist theory are clearly demonstrated by its difficulty in dealing with prostitution, which is interpreted solely in outworn terms of victimization. That is, feminists profess solidarity with the "sex workers" themselves but denounce prostitution as a system of male exploitation and enslavement. I protest this trivializing of the world's oldest profession. I respect and honor the prostitute, ruler of the sexual realm, which men must pay to enter. In reducing prostitutes to pitiable charity cases in need of their help, middle-class feminists are guilty of arrogance, conceit, and prudery.

An early admirer of *Sexual Personae* who came to Philadelphia to interview me was Tracy Quan, a working prostitute and activist with P.O.N.Y. (Prostitutes of New York), who supported the stand I had taken and described her violent fights with the doctrinaire feminists overrunning the world prostitute movement. I maintained, and Quan agreed, that the popular portrait of the hapless single mother forced into prostitution by poverty or a vicious pimp was a sentimental exaggeration. Psychologists were ushering ex-prostitutes onto television programs to make tearful recantations of their former careers and to testify that prostitutes hated their work and were merely misguided victims of child abuse. Listening to the radio at home, I heard Dr. Joyce Brothers confidently proclaim, "There are no happy prostitutes"—to which I angrily blurted aloud, "Dr. Brothers, there are no happy therapists!"

Moralism and ignorance are responsible for the constant stereotyping of prostitutes by their lowest common denominator—the sick, strung-out addicts, crouched on city stoops, who turn tricks for drug money. Every profession (including the academic) has its bums, cheats, and ne'er-do-wells. The most successful prostitutes in history have been *invisible*. That invisibility was produced by their high intelligence, which gives them the power to perceive, and move freely but undetected within, the social frame. The prostitute is a superb analyst, not only in evading the law but in intuiting the unique constellation of convention and fantasy that produces a stranger's orgasm.

She lives by her wits as much as her body. She is psychologist, actor, and dancer, a performance artist of hyperdeveloped sexual imagination. And she is shrewd entrepreneur and businesswoman: the madams of brothels, along with medieval abbesses, were the first female managers.

The power of ancient harlots, ancestors of Renaissance courtesans and chic modern call-girls, is suggested in *The Egyptian* (1954), the film of Mika Waltari's novel about the reign of Akhnaten and Nefertiti. For assignations with a hypnotically beautiful Babylonian temptress, the brilliant young Egyptian doctor surrenders his wealth, his house, his precious medical instruments, and finally, most shockingly, the embalming of his parents' bodies for the afterlife. When he has nothing left, her servants slam the door in his face. *The Egyptian* shows the prostitute as a sexual adept of magical skill and accurately documents men's excruciating obsession with and subordination to women.

Temple prostitution seems to have occurred in the ancient Near East, in association with goddess cults. In the Christian era, typified by St. Augustine's condemnation of Cybele and her mutilating sacrificial rites, the prostitute remains our point of contact with repressed pagan nature. We completely lack the fusion of sexual and sacred found in Hinduism, notably the Tantric school, where initiation in erotic arts by a sexually experienced woman is considered a form of spiritual instruction. Christianity splits woman into divided halves: Mary, the Holy Mother, and Mary Magdalene, the whore. Maternity and sexuality don't mix well in our tradition, with its transcendent, earth-shunning deity. In the Madonna-whore complex, which particularly affects Latin Catholics (e.g., Frank Sinatra), a man loses sexual interest in his wife when she becomes pregnant, activating memories of his sainted mother. The home becomes a shrine, and the man seeks sexual satisfaction elsewhere with whores, "bimbos," defensively minimized to evade woman's hegemony.

When they posit prostitutes as lost souls to be saved from satanic male clutches, feminists are collaborating in the systematic denigration of a class of women who, under dangerous conditions, perform a necessary social service. Governments that try to ban prostitution never succeed for long. Prostitution is always reinvented and flourishes, underground or in light of day. During the Sixties sexual revolution, I believed that, in a reformed future, prostitution would be unnecessary, since emancipated female desire would expand to meet men's needs. However, over time, I realized that sexuality can never be fully contained within social forms and that the old double standard was no misogynous fiction: promiscuity is risky to the health of procreative woman and her fetus. Hence the prostitute has come to symbolize for me the ultimate liberated woman, who lives on the edge and whose sexuality belongs to no one.

Often over the past decade, as I arrive at 8 A.M. at my classroom building on South Broad Street in Center City, I have been stunned to encounter a working whore sashaying cheerfully along in full brazen regalia—red-leather bolero jacket and bulging halter, white leather or lavender-suede thigh-high boots, black-spangle or gold-lame micro-miniskirt with no underwear and bare buttocks. White, black, or Latina, she dominates the street for two blocks in every direction. You can see the stir, as people hurrying to work break step, turn, or furtively stare. Working-class men brashly hail her in humorous admiration; middle-class men are startled, embarrassed, but fascinated; middle-class women, uneasily clutching their attaché cases, are frozen, blank, hostile.

Of the great sexual personae I have seen in my lifetime, Philadelphia prostitutes rank very high. They are fearless and aggressive, waving down business-men in sedans or bringing traffic to a halt as they jaw with taxi drivers. They rule the street. "Pagan goddess!" I want to call out, as I sidle reverently by. Not only are these women not victims, they are among the strongest and most formidable women on the planet. They exist in the harshest reality, but they laugh and bring beauty out of it. For me, they are heroines of outlaw individualism.

Prostitution should be decriminalized. My libertarian position is that govern-ment may not under any circumstances intervene in consensual private behavior. Thus, despite their damage to my gener-ation, I support the legalization of drugs, consistent with current regulation of al-cohol. And I would argue for the abso-lute right to homosexual sodomy. It is reasonable, however, to ask that sex acts remain private and that they not *visibly* occur in shared public spaces like streets and parks—the latter a favorite haunt of gay men, to the despair of neighbors. Neither Judeo-Christian nor pagan may dominate common ground.

Solicitation for sex should be tolerated and treated exactly like the vending of any commercial product: that is, pedes-trians have the right not to be crowded, touched, or fondled by salesmen, ped-dlers, or whores. Police may keep build-ing entrances unobstructed, guarantee a clear zone around schools and churches, and control noisy late-night auto traf-fic cruising in residential neighborhoods.

But harassment of whores and their clients must cease. Government should concern itself only with public health matters: hence free testing and treatment of venereal disease, without censorious-ness, should be required of prostitutes working in licensed brothels.

Mainstream feminist propaganda claims that prostitutes must "do what-ever men want." This is true only of the amateurish and weak-willed. Most professional prostitutes are in complete charge of the erotic encounter and do nothing they don't want. Things can certainly go wrong, with painful or fa-tal results—as is also the experience of gay men, whose sexual adventurousness over the centuries has often cost them their lives. Stranger sex will never be risk-free; it is just as challenging an ex-ploration of hazardous nature as cliff-climbing, sailing, car racing, big-game hunting, bungee-jumping, hang-gliding, or parachuting. The thrill is partly due to the nearness of disaster or death.

The prostitutes on window display in Amsterdam's famous red-light dis-trict, with their opulent fleshiness, earthy practicality, and bawdy sang-froid, im-pressed me enormously when I first saw them in 1969, as a graduate student still optimistic about bringing sophisticated European sexual values to puritan Amer-ica. By 1993, when I visited Amster-dam again, the scene had changed: it is now less homey and, influenced by the dance revolution in stripping, more the-atrical. The whores are dazzlingly multi-cultural. A conventional feminist analy-sis would see these women writhing and beckoning in glass cubicles as degrad-ingly accessible cream pastries in a male automat. But I see, as always, pure fe-male power. The men shopping in the street cluster together to bolster their confidence; most are awkward, uncertain, abashed. The young, lithe Thai whores boldly flaunt their breasts and buttocks in skinny white bikinis, blazing under violet Day-glo light. They are a pagan epiphany, apparitions of supreme sexual beauty. Jerusalem has never vanquished Babylon.

A luminous moment of this kind occurred in Naples in 1984, when I was walking with family friends near the bay late at night. A tall, striking, raven-haired whore in a tight white dress, who may or may not have been a transvestite, was bantering with a truck driver, her long leg perched raffishly on the running board. Spotting the flowing red hair of a mature married woman in our party, she grinned wickedly and yelled out, in a rich, gravelly, flirtatious voice, "Ciao, rossa!" ("Hey, redhead!") Everyone stared stonily ahead and kept moving. The group as a whole, with its middle-class American propriety, was not as powerful as this one extraordinary being, whose perverse, worldly consciousness seemed to take in and dominate the entire waterfront. This was her territory; we were the intruders. Lagging behind, I smiled conspiratorially and nodded back in homage. She was my confederate. Her humor and vitality were like those of Caravaggio's lewd urchins. I had an eerie sense of the Neapolitan side of my heritage (my father's people were from the inland towns of Benevento, Avellino, and Caserta), the stream of sensuality and decadence going back to Pompeii and ancient Capri, where the emperor Tiberius had his villa.

Strippers are not prostitutes, as they firmly point out. I first became aware of their free-lance lifestyle while I was teaching at Bennington in the Seventies, when several of my women students earned tuition money by dancing in topless bars in metropolitan New York and New Jersey. I questioned them closely and read their research projects compiling interviews with their fellow workers. The other dancers were often enterprising single mothers whose experiences depended on the quality of the clubs, the best of which protected women employees by escorting them to their cars and squelching overeager customers. At worst, the dancers had to fight off the managers themselves, but this was usually considered an occupational hazard that plucky women could handle.

Why do so many men want to see women undress? I have written about the pagan origins of striptease, the ritual unveiling of a body that will always remain mysterious because of the inner darkness of the womb, from which we all came. Sexual exhibitionism plays a part in most nature cults, such as Hinduism. My interest in this subject dates from a New York State Fair in Syracuse in the late Fifties, when I was around ten. A midway barker introduced a belly dancer, who undulated from a tent and struck a pose at one end of the platform. A trance came over me. I bolted from my startled family and darted through the dense male crowd to stare up at her in stupefied wonder. My parents told the story for years, since the dancer, used to women giving her a wide berth, eyed me back with alarmed perplexity. I'm sure I looked like a moron, with mouth agape and eyes like saucers.

Sexual dancing, which handsome boys also do for gay men, is a great art form with ancient roots. I reject feminist cant about the "male gaze," which supposedly renders passive and inert everything it touches. As I maintained in my first book, sexual objectification is characteristically human and indistinguishable from the art impulse. There is nothing degrading in the display of any part of the human body. Those embarrassed or offended by erotic dancing are the ones with the problem: their natural responses have been curtailed by ideology, religious or feminist. The early Christian church forbade dancing because of its pagan associations and its very real incitement to lust.

In modern times, dance has become progressively more sexually explicit, as the performers of classical ballet, once aristocrats of the *ancien régime,* shed clothing from the nineteenth century on. The calf-length ballerina's skirt, for example, became the tutu, just a fringe of chiffon at the hips. The molded Renaissance tights of male dancers accent bulging genitals and buttocks. Half the appeal of today's classical ballet productions, I would argue, is their ravishing semi-nudity. It's striptease in the name of high art. Modern dance, from the Greek-inspired free movement and bare feet of Isadora Duncan to the tribal pelvic thrusts and spasmodic contractions of Martha Graham, has always been sexually revolutionary. Jazz dancing is also boldly erotic, thanks to Bob Fosse's appropriation of burlesque moves, which he witnessed as a child in the demimondaine.

Since the Twenties, popular dance has been sexualized by wave after wave of African and Latin (really Afro-Caribbean) influences. As Eldridge Cleaver said in *Soul on Ice,* the 1960 twist craze activated the dead white pelvis, in an early skirmish of the sexual revolution. Grinding, provocative wiggles and shimmies are now the everyday recreational language of the white middle class. The line between striptease and respectable social dancing has blurred. Hence the recent evolution toward total nudity in topless clubs. Today, straight or gay men, tucking tribute bills into a woman's garter belt or a guy's motorcycle boot, can inspect the sexual terrain at microscopic proximity. Unescorted female customers are still disappointingly rare, as I can report from my own midnight forays.

In virtually all venues, the nude dancer is in total control of the stage and audience. The feminist scenario of a meat rack of ribs and haunches priced and fingered by reeking buffoons is another hysterical projection. Hard as it may be to believe, men in strip clubs *admire* what they see and are even awed by it. They gather round the women to warm themselves, as if the stage were a bonfire on a medieval winter's night. The dancers exert a magnetic force. The men don't know exactly why they must come there, but they sense that their ordinary lives and official religion don't fulfill their longings or answer all their questions. To reduce these ritual visitations to a matter of mechanical masturbation is unintelligent and unimaginative. The nude dancer can never be captured or completely known. She teases and eludes, like the female principle itself.

Extreme forms of sexual expression can only be understood through a sympathetic study of pornography, one of the most controversial issues in feminism. For more than fifteen years, the syllabi and reserve reading shelves of women's studies courses have been dominated by two sex-killing styles, the anti-art puritanism of the Catharine MacKinnon school and the word-obsessed, labyrinthine abstraction of Lacanian analysis. The pro-sex wing of feminism was virtually invisible until very recently, for two reasons. First, its adherents outside academe wrote fiction or journalism and never produced major theoretical statements anywhere near MacKinnon's level of argument. Second, its adherents inside academe shut themselves off in jargon-spouting conferences, which had no cultural impact or purpose beyond personal careerism. Free-speech feminists mobilized to defeat MacKinnon-inspired anti-porn statutes in Minneapolis and Indianapolis but then fell back into torpor, abandoning academe to the virulent ideologues, who seized administrative power in campus-life issues.

The pro-sex feminists were never able to stop MacKinnon, whose reputation rose steadily until she was canonized in a disgracefully uncritical cover story of *The New York Times Magazine* in October 1991. During the Clarence Thomas hearings that year, she was everywhere in the media. Even public radio and television were hopelessly biased, trotting out dozens of radical and establishment feminists pushing one party line. The sexual harassment crisis was the Waterloo of the pro-sex feminists, who lost all perspective and collapsed into rampant MacKinnonism. Not one leading feminist voice but mine challenged the sentimental Anita Hill groupthink or the creeping fascism of the date-rape and sexual harassment hysteria. Nor did any critique of MacKinnon gain ground until I called her a "totalitarian" and exposed the drastically limited assumptions in her cultural worldview. In late 1993, the free-speech feminists finally—and far too late—launched a searing personal attack on MacKinnon (over her gross exploitation of the Bosnian rapes) in central feminist territory, *Ms.* magazine.

My skepticism about the courage and sincerity of the pro-sex feminists was confirmed by my own experience with them. The refusal or inability of the academic feminists to engage my work has eloquently demonstrated their insularity and hypocrisy. Of the best-known names outside academe, only film director Monika Treut and performance artist Annie Sprinkle took an interest in or publicly supported me and my views. Treut's avant-garde thinking was shaped by the greater cosmopolitanism of Europe, while Sprinkle's iconoclastic comedy draws on her intimate knowledge of the worlds of prostitution and stripping, which I celebrate. The parochialism and conventionalism in even the most ostensibly radical feminist views of sexuality were shown by Pat Califia's long silence about and then open attack on me, as well as by Susie Bright's catty impugning of my positions and right to speak. The latter's cliquish removal from the general culture was evident in her public dismissal of Dr. Ruth Westheimer, whose contributions to sex education of the American mass audience have been enormous.

A major problem with pro-sex feminism has been its failure to embrace the men's magazines, without which no theory of sexuality will ever be complete. I have gone out of my way to publish in and endorse *Playboy* and *Penthouse*, which have been vilified by both mainstream and anti-porn feminists, as well as by mainstream members of NOW [National Organization for Women]. I love the irony of bringing contemporary feminism full circle, back to where Gloria Steinem made her name by infiltrating a Playboy Club. In the Eighties, feminists and religious conservatives pressured convenience stores and drugstore chains to ban the men's magazines. This has led to a massive cultural ignorance on the part of feminists, inside and outside academe, about what is actually in those magazines.

Idiotic statements like "Pornography degrades women" or "Pornography is the subordination of women" are only credible if you never look at pornography. Preachers, senators, and feminist zealots carry on about materials they have no direct contact with. They usually rely on a few selectively culled inflammatory examples that bear little resemblance to the porn market as a whole. Most pornography shows women in as many dominant as subordinate postures, with the latter usually steamily consensual. Specialty mail services can provide nonconsensual sadomasochistic scenarios, but they are difficult to find, except in the vast underground of cartoon art, so subversively individualistic that it has thus far escaped the feminist thought police. Cartoons in R. Crumb's fabled Sixties style show the comic, raging id uncensored. Despite hundreds of studies, the cause-and-effect relationship between pornography and violence has never been satisfactorily proved. Pornography is a self-enclosed world of pure imagination. Feminist claims that porn actresses are coerced and abused are wildly exaggerated and usually based on one or two atypical tales.

Feminist anti-porn discourse virtually always ignores the gigantic gay male porn industry, since any mention of the latter would bring crashing to the ground the absurd argument that pornography is by definition the subordination of women. I have learned an enormous amount from gay porn, which a few lesbians have commendably tried to imitate but not with sterling success. The greatest erotic images of women remain those created by male artists and photographers, from Botticelli, Titian, Ingres, and Courbet to Richard Avedon and Helmut Newton. The advertising pages of gay newspapers are adorned with stunning icons of gorgeous male nudes, for which I have yet to see an impressive lesbian equivalent. Men, gay or straight, can get beauty and lewdness into one image. Women are forever softening, censoring, politicizing.

Unlike the art-illiterate anti-porn fanatics, gay men glory in every angle on the sexual body, no matter how contorted. A sleek, pretty boy in cowboy boots spreading his buttocks for an up-close glimpse of his pink anus is an alluring staple of gay magazines. In that world, everyone knows this splendid creature is victor, not slave. Sexual power defies or *reverses* rigid political categories. Feminists who see the bare-all, pubic "beaver shot" as a paradigm of women's historical oppression are cursed with the burden of their own pedestrian prejudices. Until we solve the mystery of sexuality, contemplation of our kaleidoscopic genitalia—from glossy and nubile to lank and withered—will remain an interesting and important exercise in human self-discovery.

Since paganism must give its due to Judeo-Christianity, we should respect the desire of the religious not to be assaulted with nude images in public spaces. Thus sex magazines should be freely available at newsstands but not necessarily displayed on them. Sealed plastic or paper sleeves don't seem unreasonable to me, though I would like opponents and proponents of pornography to be able to leaf through magazines to stay informed. Since television is also a public space, it is fair to ask, but not require, that stations schedule adult programming during late-night hours, when parents can best supervise their children. Unlike Frank Zappa, I feel that a ratings system is merely informational and infringes on no one's right to free speech. On the contrary, an "X" designation positively helps the lascivious to locate juicy material in every medium. The music industry must not confuse free speech rights with lucrative placement of product in suburban malls.

Far from poisoning the mind, pornography shows the deepest truth about sexuality, stripped of romantic veneer. No one can claim to be an expert in gender studies who is uncomfortable with pornography, which focuses on our primal identity, our rude and crude animality. Porn dreams of eternal fires of desire, without fatigue, incapacity, aging, or death. What feminists denounce as woman's humiliating total accessibility in porn is actually her elevation to high priestess of a pagan paradise garden, where the body has become a bountiful fruit tree and where growth and harvest are simultaneous. "Dirt" is contamination to the Christian but fertile loam to the pagan. The most squalid images in porn are shock devices to break down bourgeois norms of decorum, reserve, and tidiness. The Dionysian body fluids, fully released to coat every gleaming surface, return us to the full-body sensuality of the infant condition. In crowded orgy tableaux, like those on Hindu temples, matter and energy melt. In the cave spaces of porn, camera lights are torches of the Eleusinian Mysteries, giving us flashes of nature's secrets. Gay men appreciate pornography as I do because they accept the Hellenic principle that some people are born more beautiful than others. Generic granola feminists are likely to call this "lookism"—an offense against equality. I take the Wildean view that equality is a moral imperative in politics but that the arts will always be governed by the elitism of talent and the tyranny of appearance. Pornography's total exposure of ripe flesh, its dynamic of vigor and vitality, is animated by the cruel pre-Christian idolatry of beauty and strength.

Pornography *is* art, sometimes harmonious, sometimes dissonant. Its glut and glitter are a Babylonian excess. Modern middle-class women cannot bear the thought that their hard-won professional achievements can be outweighed in an instant by a young hussy flashing a little tits and ass. But the gods have given her power, and we must welcome it. Pornography forces a radical reassessment of sexual value, nature's bequest and our tarnished treasure.

POSTSCRIPT

Is the Sex Industry Harmful to Women?

Censorship, by its very nature, lends itself to discrimination. Lesbian bookstores have been disproportionately "regulated" since the passage of the Butler Act, and further censorship efforts are likely to result in more discrimination against disenfranchised groups, specifically, gay males and lesbians. Activist Pat Califia speaks out against censorship in any form as a threat to free speech and an infringement on First Amendment rights in *Public Sex: The Culture of Radical Sex* (Cleis Press, 1994). She believes that prostitution would always be in demand even in a "just society" because not everyone holds to an ideal of romantic and long-term relationships in association with their sex lives.

Additional interesting essays can be found in Paglia's book *Vamps and Tramps: New Essays* (Vintage Books, 1994), particularly "The Return of Carry Nation: Catharine MacKinnon and Andrea Dworkin." Another supporter of the sex industry, feminist Jocelyn Taylor, in "Testimony of a Naked Woman," in Rebecca Walker, ed., *To Be Real* (Anchor Books, 1995), attempts to combine responsibility for her body with her desire for political representation. She started a lesbian party club for women—"a place to unapologetically emphasize sexual pleasure for dykes in a club atmosphere." The club portrayed lesbian sexual images via videos, erotic slides, and nude dancers and held a "sex positive" vision. Taylor now makes videos that emphatically celebrate black lesbian sexuality.

A strong anticensorship advocate from a different camp, attorney Nadine Strossen, approaches the issue largely from a legal perspective in "The Perils of Pornophobia," *The Humanist* (May/June 1995). Her primary premise is that protective laws have the potential to bar women from full legal equality. She argues that such "paternalism" always leads to exclusion, discrimination, and loss of freedom and autonomy. In response to some of Strossen's writing, Dianna E. H. Russell, in "The Pornography Industry's Wet Dream," *On the Issues* (Summer 1995), faults Strossen for making no distinction between pornography and erotica and believes that Strossen ignores important scientific findings in her literature reviews—findings that suggest that pornography leads to rape. In nations saturated with pornography, such as the United States, scientific evidence shows that pornography predisposes some men to rape or undermines some men's internal or social inhibitions in acting out rape fantasies, according to Russell. She argues that scientific evidence that pornography can cause rape is as strong as evidence that smoking can cause cancer. Another who writes against the sex industry is Alice Leuchtag in "The Culture of Pornography," *The Humanist* (May/June 1995). She claims that under conditions of prostitution, feelings of empowerment are necessarily transitory and illusory, and that prostitution reinforces cultural assumptions that give legitimacy to women's social subordination. "Skepticism and liberalism need not hobble us in the face of pernicious social institutions," says Leuchtag.

On the Internet . . .

HandiLinks™ to Mothering
This Handilinks™ category provides links for women who choose to work, primarily or exclusively, as mothers. The links lead to support services, mothering and women's health resources, information on breast-feeding, housewife columns, and mothers' clubs.
http://www.ahandyguide.com/cat1/m/m1209.htm

Yahoo.com's Index to Women's Studies: History
This site provides information on women in history and links to associated resources, such as women's history magazines, collaborative encyclopedic projects, women of achievement in history and politics, women and slavery, and women's history in scholarly journals. It also provides reviews of national museums, university archives, and multimedia exhibits.
http://www.yahoo.com/Social_Science/Women_s_Studies/History/

The Glass Ceiling
This site provides information on the "glass ceiling." Resources include governmental publications, affirmative action programs, companies' breaking the glass ceiling, a glass ceiling interactive report, glass ceiling recommendations, news releases, mapping the glass ceiling, and related links for labor and women.
http://www.theglassceiling.com/

Feminist Internet Gateway
The Feminist Internet Gateway provides affirmative action links, resources from the Feminist Majority Foundation, information for empowering women in business, sexual harassment Internet resources, a sexual harassment hotline resource list, and a national feminist census on the 100 best companies for working women. It also includes links to the American Association for University Women, as well as other organizations.
http://www.feminist.org/gateway/sd_exec2.html

PART 2

Gender, Work, and School

Contemporary feminism has altered the structure of American society by promoting changes in traditional gender role expectations. In the interest of advancing the causes of women, feminism has supported women's expanded presence in a wide variety of work and educational settings. Numbers of women now match those of men in university enrollment and undergraduate degree attainment, and women are approaching men in their representation in postgraduate programs. Men and women also now work side by side in professions and trades that have traditionally been filled only by men. The six issues in this section have been highlighted by these feminist concerns: sexual harassment policies in the workplace, women's coverage in history textbooks, discrimination in the workplace, women's presence in the armed forces, religious discrimination, and women's needs versus children's needs.

■ Should Society Continue to Support Sexual Harassment Policies for the Workplace?

■ Should Women Receive More Coverage in History Textbooks?

■ Do Women Still Face Discrimination in the Workplace?

■ Do Women Belong in the Armed Forces?

■ Do Mainstream Religious Denominations Discriminate Against Women?

■ Should Women Put Their Children's Needs Above Their Own?

ISSUE 5

Should Society Continue to Support Sexual Harassment Policies for the Workplace?

YES: Robert L. Allen, from "Stopping Sexual Harassment: A Challenge for Community Education," in Anita Faye Hill and Emma Coleman Jordan, eds., *Race, Gender, and Power in America: The Legacy of the Hill-Thomas Hearings* (Oxford University Press, 1995)

NO: Jonathan Rauch, from "Offices and Gentlemen," *The New Republic* (June 23, 1997)

ISSUE SUMMARY

YES: Robert L. Allen, senior editor of the *Black Scholar*, argues that men do not understand the damaging impact of their own speech and behavior on women and that, while legal and punitive measures may be useful, prevention through community education should be utilized to reduce sexual harassment.

NO: Author Jonathan Rauch asserts that the hostile environment rule, which prohibits bigoted and offensive forms of speech in the workplace, is now the most virulent threat to free speech in the United States and that it directly violates the First Amendment of the U.S. Constitution.

The gap between men's perceptions and women's experience regarding workplace harassment emerged clearly during Judge Clarence Thomas's confirmation proceedings in 1991. During those proceedings, law professor Anita F. Hill charged that the U.S. Supreme Court nominee had sexually harassed her when she worked for him at the Equal Employment Opportunity Commission (EEOC). According to some writers, the outpouring of personal narratives and legal complaints following Hill's testimony reflected a substantial level of denial in the American population. Some of the following comments, made in response to the hearings, have been cited: "You can't legislate morality"; "It doesn't happen so much" or "It doesn't happen here"; "She provoked, enjoyed, accepted, or asked for it"; and "So what if it happened?" Although women as well as men engage in sexual harassment, the vast majority of reported cases (over 90 percent) involve males harassing females. Publications and training programs have reported that about two-thirds of surveyed women but fewer than 15 percent of surveyed men would find an unsolicited invitation for sex offensive.

American law currently bans two forms of conduct. One of these is "hostile environment harassment," which involves conduct that creates a hostile, intimidating, or offensive workplace. The other is "quid pro quo" harassment, which involves a supervisor's promising job benefits or opportunities in exchange for sexual favors. Hostile environment harassment is often motivated by a desire to exclude individuals and to remind them of their subordinate status. Quid pro quo harassment involves a situation where individuals with power abuse that status in order to impose a sexual relationship on someone who has less power.

Some Americans believe that sexual harassment is widely exaggerated and that most of those who report it are either hypersensitive, overzealous, or otherwise unstable. Some writers argue that women tend to invite or condone the behaviors they later report as harassment and that if women want equality, they should be able to tolerate the same type of workplace environment that men do. They also argue that the price that women pay for so-called harassment is trivial and that laws have become so strict that "men are being held liable for a look." However, the main objection to sexual harassment rulings in the workplace involves reluctance to utilize intrusive governmental regulation due to the free speech implications of monitoring offensive expression.

Those who argue on behalf of harassment laws and their enforcement claim that underreporting, not overreaction, is the norm. Only 5 to 10 percent of women who experience abuse make formal complaints, and even fewer can afford the costs of litigation. In response to those who minimize the extent of harassment, proponents of harassment laws point to innumerable court cases and judicial and arbitration decisions that prove (1) harassment is rampant, even though many laws prohibit it, and (2) decision makers often deny relief because the harassment was insufficiently "brutal" or "malicious." That is, in order to establish liability, plaintiffs must prove that there was pervasive and severe conduct that was injurious and unwelcome and that a reasonable person in their situation would have found offensive. One example of "trivialization of injuries" was reported in a highly publicized San Francisco lawsuit in 1994. The defense counsel of a leading law firm claimed that the harassment issue involves "current uncertainty" about acceptable workplace behavior. The "ambiguous" conduct in question involved 10 women over a six-year period who claimed that a law partner "put his hand down secretaries' blouses and grabbed their breasts." In a rare jury decision, a multimillion-dollar punitive damage award was given.

In the following selections, Robert L. Allen argues that sexual harassment laws play an important role in underscoring the power differential between men and women in society. Jonathan Rauch claims that workplace harassment and discriminatory speech laws violate First Amendment law.

YES
Robert L. Allen

STOPPING SEXUAL HARASSMENT: A CHALLENGE FOR COMMUNITY EDUCATION

There can be little doubt that an important outcome of the 1991 Senate Judiciary Committee hearings has been growing public recognition of sexual harassment as a major social problem. Virtually the entire nation has engaged in the public discourse around this issue, and this engagement is to be welcomed.

Like many men in the aftermath of Anita Hill's testimony, I found myself hearing harrowing reports of sexual harassment from women relatives and friends who had previously felt constrained to remain silent. They told me of awful things that had been said or done to them, on the job or in the streets, sometimes recently and sometimes years ago. They spoke of their anger and humiliation, of their shame and feelings of self-blame, of their fear of the consequences of speaking out or rebuking their harassers. They experienced sexual harassment—the imposition of unwanted sexual attention—as a violation of their human dignity.

I listened and shared their outrage—but I also found myself recalling things I had said or done to women in the recent or distant past, and the recollections were sometimes distinctly discomforting. I think an important value of these exchanges was the opportunity for men to learn from the personal testimony of women they love and respect how widespread sexual harassment is. At the same time, the self-reflection and discussions among men that were sometimes provoked by the women's stories offered an opportunity for men to recognize that harassing behavior is not simply an aberration, nor is it exclusively the province of macho males; on the contrary, harassing behavior is something that many of us men have engaged in at some point, if not on the job, then on the streets or on campus or even in our homes. We knew what we were doing, because we knew the women involved were made to feel uncomfortable or humiliated by our words or actions.

Why did we do it? Why do men harass women? Why, until recently, was such behavior generally acceptable in our culture—that is, acceptable to men? Aside from punishment, what can be done to stop harassing behavior?

In this essay I want to raise two points for consideration as part of the discourse on sexual harassment.

First, sexual harassment should not be dismissed as aberrant behavior, as the macho mentality gone wild, or as the result of male biology or uncontrollable sexual desire. Sexual harassment, like child abuse and domestic violence, is an outgrowth of socialization into male and female gender roles in a sexist society. It is learned behavior.

Second, if harassment, abuse, and violence are forms of learned behavior, they can also be unlearned. I therefore argue that in addition to legal or punitive approaches to sexual harassment, it is imperative to adopt a preventive approach through community education. We must create an environment, not only in the workplace but in our communities generally, in which harassment, abuse, and violence are no longer tolerated because men and women understand the damage such behavior does to all of us. That means adopting a social change perspective critical of the values of the dominant culture, a culture that is premised on inequality.

Gender roles are not foreordained by our biology or our genes. We learn gender roles as part of our socialization into the culture. When a child is born, the first question inevitably asked is "Boy or girl?" Our response to the child is then mediated by our knowledge of its genitals, and it is *our* actions that tell the child its gender identity and the behavior appropriate to that identity.

In California I work with an organization called the Oakland Men's Project (OMP). Formed in 1979, OMP is a nonprofit multiracial organization of men and women devoted to community education around issues of male violence, sexism, racism, and homophobia. Over the years we have worked with thousands of boys and men (and girls and women) in high schools, church groups, colleges, prisons, community groups, and rehabilitation programs. We conduct workshops that involve interactive role playing and discussions that allow men and women to examine gender roles and the social training we get in this culture.

In our workshops we ask young people what they think it means to be a man or a woman. It is remarkable how consistently they express the same set of expectations about appropriate male and female behavior. Men are expected to be in control, tough, aggressive, independent, competitive, and emotionally unexpressive (with the exception of anger and sexual desire, which are allowable emotions for men). Women, on the other hand, are expected to be polite, dependent, emotional, and sexy, to take care of others, and not to be too smart or pushy. In recent years we have noticed that sometimes girls will challenge these role expectations and occasionally even a boy will object, but for the most part they remain widely accepted. Paul Kivel, who has summed up the experience of the Oakland Men's Project in his *Men's Work: How to Stop the Violence That Tears Our Lives Apart*, refers to these as "core expectations" that we all have, especially men, regarding appropriate male and female behavior.

How do young men learn these expectations? At OMP to illustrate the socialization process, we use what we call role plays that dramatize common situations most boys and men have experienced. One of these involves an interaction between a father and his ten-year-old son, both played by facilitators. The son is sitting at home watching television when the father comes in from work, orders the boy to turn off the TV, and berates him for the messiness of the room. When the boy tries to explain that he was going to clean up later, the father tells him to shut up and stop making excuses. Then he shoves the son's report card in his face and demands to know why he got a D in math. The boy says he did the best he could. The father shames the son, telling him that he is stupid and that D stands for "dummy." The boy says that's not fair and begins to stand up. The father shoves him down, saying, "Don't you dare get up in my face, I didn't say you could go anyplace!" The boy is visibly upset and begins to cry. The father gets even more angry: "Now what? You're crying? You little mama's boy! You sissy! You make me sick. When are you going to grow up and start acting like a man?" The father storms out of the room.

When we do this role play, it gets the undivided attention of everyone in the room, especially the boys. Almost every young person has had the experience of being scolded and shamed by an adult. Most boys have had the experience of being humiliated by an older male and being told that they are not acting like men.

When we stop the role play, we ask the boys how it made them feel to witness this scene between the father and son. There may be a moment of embarrassed silence, but then the boys speak up and say it made them mad, upset, sad, etc. Often this is the first time they have articulated the feelings brought up by such an encounter, which sadly often replicates their own experience. Indeed, the power of this role play is that it is so familiar.

We ask the boys what messages such encounters send. They say things like, "A man is tough. A man is in control. A man doesn't cry. It's okay for a man to yell at someone. A man can take it. A man is responsible. A man is competent. A man doesn't take crap from anyone else." As they speak, we write their comments on a blackboard. Then we draw a box around the comments and label it the "Act Like a Man" box. Most males in this culture are socialized to stay in the box. We learn this from our fathers, older brothers, guys on the street, television, sports, movies, and so on. We may also learn it from our mothers and grandmothers, or from the reactions of girls in school. The fact is that this notion of manhood is so pervasive in our culture that everyone knows the role and anyone can teach it to a boy.

We ask the boys what happens if you step out of the box, if you stop acting tough enough or man enough. They reply that you get called names: sissy, wimp, nerd, fag, queer, mama's boy, punk, girl, loser, fairy. And what is the point of the name calling? The boys say that it is a challenge and you're expected to fight to prove that you're not what they called you. In other words, if challenged, boys are expected to fight to prove that they're in the box—that they're tough and not gay or effeminate. Homophobia and fear of being identified with women in any way are strong messages boys receive from an early age.

We also ask about expectations of female behavior. The young people say things like, "A girl should be polite and clean, she shouldn't argue, she's pretty, she doesn't fight or act too smart, she helps others, she's emotional." We ask what happens when a girl refuses to be submissive and dependent, when she's assertive and smart and doesn't kowtow to the boys. Again the reply is that she will be called names: bitch, tomboy, dyke, whore, ball-breaker.... And what is the point of the name calling? To tell the girl she'd better start "acting right." In other words, the name calling is like a slap in the face, reducing the girl to a despised sexual object, with the purpose of humiliating her and intimidating her into resuming "acceptable" behavior. If a girl fights when called names, she may emerge the victor, but her very success raises questions about her femininity.

Though our forays into junior highs and high schools hardly constitute systematic research, again and again we find the same core expectations of acceptable male and female behavior among young people. As I have said, there is a growing tendency to question these expectations, especially among young women, but the grip of traditional roles remains very strong.

Our work at OMP involves challenging role expectations by showing that male and female behaviors are neither biologically determined nor a function of "human nature" but are learned from our interactions with significant others and from the culture at large. Our workshops and role plays give boys and girls and men and women a way of analyzing social roles, not abstractly, but by drawing insights from their own experiences. Moreover, we show that social interactions involve making choices, and that we can break free of old roles by supporting each other in changing our choices.

An important component of our work is to look at structural relationships of power and inequality in our society. We ask workshop participants to think about their experiences with different social groups and to tell us which groups they think are more powerful and which are less powerful. Most often this elicits statements to the effect that men as a group are more powerful than women as a group, whites more powerful than people of color, parents more powerful than children, teachers more powerful than pupils, the rich more powerful than the poor, straights more powerful than gays, bosses more powerful than workers, and so on. If we ask how these inequalities are maintained, we are told that it is done through laws, through rules and regulations, through discrimination and stereotypes, and ultimately through force and violence. Thus, despite our country's rhetoric of equality, experience teaches us that people are not treated equally, that we all have assigned places in the social hierarchy, and that violence is used to keep less powerful groups "in their place."

This violence takes many forms and is often legitimized through the process of blaming the victim. Consider the Rodney King case, in which the jury was told that the police officers thought he was dangerous because he was high on drugs and "out of control," and at the same time was persuaded that he was actually "in control," deliberately taunting and manipulating the officers. Either way, the message of this incredible argument was that Rodney King "deserved" the brutal beating he received and the policemen could be acquitted. Blaming victims for their own victimization is a widely employed means of justifying abuse and violence of all kinds.

Sexual harassment plays a part in reinforcing the power differential between men and women in our society, and that distinguishes it from flirtation or a simple mistake in judgment. For example, a man may harass a woman when she steps out of the role he expects her to play. In the workplace, "uppity" women who hold jobs traditionally held by men, or who are regarded as "too" assertive, competent, competitive, or emotionally reserved, are likely targets of harassment. Men may also harass women who are not "uppity" as a kind of ritual that confirms male dominance and female submissiveness. Thus, the female secretary or domestic worker may be "teased" or pinched or subjected to sexual remarks that serve to remind her of her low status and her vulnerability to men. She is expected to acquiesce in this treatment by laughing or otherwise acting as if the harassment is okay, thereby reaffirming the male's superior status and power. A woman worker may also be harassed by a male worker who is angry at the boss but fearful of the boss's power, and seeks to regain a sense of his own power by humiliating her.

Whether in the workplace or on the street, the purpose of sexual harassment is to reduce women to objects sexually vulnerable to men, and to reestablish the traditional power relationship between men and women. Indeed, women's sexual vulnerability to men is a key locus of male power, something men learn to expect. As boys we learn it from stories of sexual "conquest" we hear from older males; we learn it from films, magazines, pornography, advertising. We live in a capitalist culture that promises women's sexual availability as a reward to the male consumer of everything from cars to cigarettes. It is not surprising, then, that men come to believe that every woman should be sexually available to any man. Sexual harassment is both a manifestation and a reinforcement of an exploitive system in which men are socialized collectively and individually to expect to have power over women collectively and individually.

Moreover, of the thousands of women who experience sexual harassment every day, a great many of them are women of color and poor women employed in the jobs that racist and sexist discrimination forces them to take—as domestics, clerical workers, farm workers, sweatshop and factory workers. Not only are these women especially vulnerable to sexual harassment, they also have less access to the levers of power needed to seek redress. Often they do not report harassment because they fear revenge from their employers or know their complaints will be dismissed. They are doubly oppressed: subjected to abuse and then constrained to remain silent about it.

The nature of sexual harassment is such that it is particularly easy to blame the victims. Often there is a suggestion that the woman somehow provoked or invited the objectionable behavior by something she said or did, or simply the way she was dressed. And if she did not protest the behavior immediately, it is insinuated that she must have enjoyed it, and any subsequent protests are suspect. In any case, the female victim's character is called into question and the male harasser is conveniently let off the hook, again reinforcing male dominance.

Of course, all men don't engage in sexual harassment, but we must ask why men who witness it often fail to intervene. One reason is obvious: male bonding to maintain male dominance. Men who would not engage in harassing behavior themselves may condone it in others because they agree that women must be "kept in their place." A second reason is more hidden: men's fear of being shamed or even attacked by other men.

As boys, most men learn that other men are dangerous. How many of us were called names or beaten up by other males when we were young? How many of us were ridiculed and humiliated by fathers or older brothers or coaches or teachers? How many were sexually assaulted by another male? We protected ourselves in various ways. Some of us withdrew into the private world of our fantasies. Some of us became bullies. Some of us became alcoholics and addicts so we wouldn't have to feel the pain and fear. Most of us learned to camouflage ourselves: we took on the coloration of the men we feared, and we hoped that no one would challenge us. We never talked about our fear because that in itself was dangerous and could mark us as targets of ridicule or violence from other men.

Instead we learned to keep our fear inside, a secret. In fact, we learned to keep most of our emotions bottled up inside because any sincere expression of emotion in front of other men was risky business that set you up to be put down. Only one emotion was considered manly: anger. Some of us learned to take other feelings—pain grief, sadness, shame, loneliness, depression, jealousy, helplessness, fearfulness—and translate them into anger, and then pass them on to someone weaker in the form of physical or psychological violence. The humiliation we experienced at work, the fear we experienced when hassled by cops, the grief we felt when a relationship ended, the helplessness we felt when we lost a job—we learned to take these feelings, roll them into a heavy fist of rage, and slam it into our wives, our children, our lovers, women on the job or on the streets, less powerful men.

Thus, women and children often live in fear of men, and men frequently live in fear of each other. Most of us men won't admit this, but deep inside we recognize that harassment, abuse, rape,

and violence are not simply "women's issues"—they're our issues as well. We know, but seldom admit, that if we didn't constantly protect ourselves, other men would do to us what we all too often do to women and children—as men who have been imprisoned can attest. So those of us who are not abusers or harassers sometimes wear the camouflage suits; we try to be "one of the boys." We present a front of manly power and control no matter what we may be feeling inside. We jostle and joke and push and shove, we make cracks about women and boast of our conquests, and we haze any guy who is different. We go along with harassers so as not to expose our own vulnerability, our fear of being shamed by other men— the weak point in our male armor.

Nevertheless, men have a stake in challenging sexual harassment, abuse, violence, and the sexist role training that underpins these behaviors. In the first place, men are not unconnected to women. We form a community of men and women—and children—together. A woman who suffers harassment might be my mother, my sister, my niece. She might be your daughter or your sister or your wife. A woman who is harassed, abused, or raped is part of a community that includes male relatives, lovers, and friends who are also hurt by the injury done to her. Men have a stake in stopping the abuse because it is directed against women we love and cherish.

I would argue that men have a further stake in challenging sexual abuse and the sexism on which it is based. Men are also damaged by sexism. A system that requires us to act as though we are always in control and to repress our emotions takes a heavy toll. It undermines our sense of authenticity. It results in a loss of intimacy with women and children.

It conceals but does not change our fear of other men. It produces stress that is hazardous to our health and shortens our life spans. It makes us sick in our souls and bodies, and it turns us into enemies of those we love and of ourselves.

Historically, Black men and women in America have been victims of especially brutal and systematic violence. In the past our community has been terrorized by the lynching (and castration) of thousands of Black men by white men, and the rape (and lynching) of thousands of Black women by white men. Today white mob violence and police brutality continue unabated. African American men know intimately the violent capabilities of other men. It is a tragedy that many of us have internalized the violence of this oppressive system and brought it into our communities and our homes. The injuries done by racism to Black men's self-esteem are sometimes devastating, but the expectations of manhood we have learned block us from revealing or acknowledging our pain. Instead, we too often transform it into rage and violence against those we love. This must stop. African American men, as frequent victims of white male violence, have a particular stake in standing with women and children against all forms of violence.

How can men of all races be brought into the struggle against harassment, abuse, and violence? That is the question we have been seeking to answer through our work at the Oakland Men's Project. We have learned that it is extremely important for men to begin talking with each other about these issues. In our experience we have seen that there are growing numbers of men who are critical of sexism. All too often, however, these men as individuals are isolated and fearful of raising their concerns with other men. It is time for men who want to stop the violence to reach out to other men and break through the barrier of fear that has silenced us.

This is not an easy task, but as we have learned at OMP, it can be done. The male sex role, with its insistence on emotional "coolness" and reserve, makes open and honest communication from the heart difficult between men. We can begin to break through this isolation by sharing the often painful and humiliating ways we were socialized into the male role as young boys. At OMP we have found that workshops using interactive role plays, like the father-son encounter described earlier, are an effective method of opening up communication between men. Such techniques enable us to examine how the male sex role often sets men up to be dominating, controlling, and abusive. In another role play we watch a bully harassing the new boy at school. We discuss what the bully gains or falls to gain by bullying. For example, the bully may be seeking to compel respect from the victim, but what the victim often feels is contempt. At the same time, the bully models abusive behavior for the victim. He fails to get what he wants, but he may teach the victim how to bully someone else.

Through role plays like these, we look at how men are trained to take the hurt that has been done to them, translate it into anger, and direct the anger at a weaker person in the form of violence. This is the cycle of violence. We see it, for example, in the fact that the great majority of child abusers were themselves abused as children.

Another role play we use recreates a high school dating scene in which a boy and his girlfriend are sitting in his car in a secluded spot at night. We recruit two students from the audience to play the roles. We tell them that the boy wants to have sex that night but the girl, although she likes him, does not. Then we ask them to play out the scene. Sometimes the two actors work out a resolution acceptable to both. Sometimes the girl gets out of the car and walks away. But often the tension simply builds as the boy attempts to dominate and get his way while the girl tries to be responsive without giving in to his demands. We stop the role play and talk with the actors about the pressures they felt to behave as they did in the situation. We relate these pressures to the male and female role expectations discussed earlier. We also talk about the risk of the situation escalating into violence and rape, and the need to recognize danger signs to prevent this from happening. (For other examples of role plays and antiviolence exercises for teens, see *Helping Teens Stop Violence*, by Allan Creighton and Paul Kivel.)

Interrupting the cycle of violence requires that we unlearn sex roles that set us up to be perpetrators and victims of abuse. I am not talking only about men who are harassers or batterers, or women who have been abused. I believe that in this culture most of us are at risk for abusive behavior because most of us have been socialized into traditional sex roles. The cycle of abuse and violence can be broken at its root by challenging those roles and the institutions that support them—that is, through a process of community education and social change.

It is important for men of all races to become involved in this process. Men can take responsibility for stopping the cycle of violence and offering alternatives to violence. Men working with boys can model supportive ways of interacting and constructive methods of using anger to bring about change. All of us constantly make choices about how we relate to others, and in the power of choice is the power of change, for we are not simply passive victims of our socialization. For African American men there is a special urgency to this work. Our sons are dying in record numbers, often at each other's hands in angry acts of violence whose goal is to prove their manhood. We need to be clear that anger itself is not the problem. In a racist society Black people and other people of color have good reason to be angry. The problem lies in how the anger is expressed. Turning the anger against ourselves or others in acts of abuse and violence is self-destructive. Using righteous anger to challenge racist and oppressive institutions empowers individuals and communities, creates the possibility of real change, and builds self-esteem. Black men's organizations such as Simba, the Omega Boys' Club, and 100 Black Men of America are helping to develop new models of manhood among teenage Black males. We need organizations like these in every city.

Equally important, men working together can model a new version of power —*power with* others to make change, as opposed to *power over* others to perpetuate domination. In our society power generally means the ability to control others directly, with violence as the ultimate means of control. Men are socialized to exercise this form of power in all their relationships. Women sometimes learn to do the same. But this kind of power necessarily sets up conflicts with others—those we seek to control—and is alienating and isolating for the individual power holder. Power *with* others breaks down the isolation we feel and makes it possible to relate as allies rather than as competitors or opponents. It allows us to recognize that we are a community of people—men, women, and children—who are interdependent.

All of us have had the experience of powerlessness, for all of us have been children. As children we learned what it meant to be controlled by others, and often we learned what it meant to be humiliated and shamed by others. Such experiences are painful, and we may prefer to forget them, but ironically, by "owning" them, we create the possibility of empowerment through establishing our connection with others who have had similar experiences. In this way it becomes possible for men to become allies of women and children, not out of guilt, but through insight into their own lives.

Harassment, abuse, and violence arise from a system of sexual and racial inequality. To stop them we must challenge the gender roles, institutions, and power structures upon which sexism and racism stand. This is a big task, but it is one each of us can undertake in small ways—in our homes, in our schools, in our communities. We can educate ourselves and offer our children new models of male and female behavior. We can support each other in finding healing responses to the pain and hurt we have suffered. We can insist that the schools educate young people about empowering ways to counter sexism and racism. We can confront institutionalized oppression and violence. We can support movements and organizations that work for progressive social change. In sum, working together with others as allies, we can build community responses to the system of inequality and the cycle of violence that blight our lives.

REFERENCES

Beneke, Timothy. *Men on Rape: What They Have to Say about Sexual Violence.* New York: St. Martin's Press, 1982.

Bravo, Ellen, and Ellen Cassedy. *The 9 to 5 Guide to Combatting Sexual Harassment.* New York: John Wiley and Sons, 1992.

Chrisman, Robert, and Robert L. Allen, eds. *Court of Appeal: The Black Community Speaks Out on the Racial and Sexual Politics of Thomas vs. Hill.* New York: Ballantine Books, 1992.

Creighton, Allan, with Paul Kivel. *Helping Teens Stop Violence: A Practical Guide for Parents, Counselors, and Educators.* Alameda, Calif.: Hunter House, 1992.

Hagan, Kay Leigh, ed. *Women Respond to the Men's Movement.* San Francisco: HarperCollins, 1992.

Hemphill, Essex, ed. *Brother to Brother: New Writings by Black Gay Men.* Boston: Alyson Publications, 1991.

Jackson, Walter H. *Sporting the Right Attitude: Surviving Family Violence.* Los Angeles: Self Expansion, 1992.

Kaufman, Michael, ed. *Beyond Patriarchy: Essays by Men on Pleasure, Power, and Change.* New York: Oxford University Press, 1987.

Kimmel, Michael S., ed. *Men Confront Pornography.* New York: Meridian, 1990.

Kivel, Paul. *Men's Work: How to Stop the Violence That Tears Our Lives Apart.* Center City, Minn.: Hazelden, 1992.

Kunjufu, Jawanza. *Countering the Conspiracy to Destroy Black Boys.* Chicago: African American Images, 1985.

Lewis, Michael. *Shame: The Exposed Self.* New York: Free Press, 1992.

Madhubuti, Haki. *Black Men: Obsolete, Single, Dangerous?* Chicago: Third World Press, 1990.

Majors, Richard, and Janet Mancini Billson. *Cool Pose: The Dilemmas of Black Manhood in America.* New York: Lexington Books, 1992.

McGill, Michael E. *The McGill Report on Male Intimacy.* New York: Harper and Row, 1985.

Miedzian, Myriam. *Boys Will Be Boys: Breaking the Link between Masculinity and Violence.* New York: Doubleday, 1991.

Staples, Robert, ed. *The Black Family: Essays and Studies.* 4th ed. Belmont, Calif.: Wadsworth, 1991.

Strauss, Susan, with Pamela Espeland. *Sexual Harassment and Teens: A Program for Positive Change.* Minneapolis: Free Spirit Publishing, 1992.

Wilkinson, Doris Y., and Ronald L. Taylor, eds. *The Black Male in America: Perspectives on His Status in Contemporary Society.* Chicago: Nelson-Hall, 1977.

NO

Jonathan Rauch

OFFICES AND GENTLEMEN

In 1995, the city of Murfreesboro, Tennessee, exhibited works by Maxine Henderson, a local artist, in the city hall rotunda. One painting—impressionistic, not remotely scatological—showed a partially clad female whose left nipple was partly exposed. An assistant school superintendent filed a workplace-harassment complaint, saying she had the right not to have "thrust in my face on my way into a meeting with my superiors, most of whom are men," art that she found "very offensive and degrading to me as a woman." The city attorney took the painting down and stashed it in his closet. You really can't be too cautious," he told reporters. "A sexual harassment judgment usually has six zeros behind it." (Henderson recently won a First Amendment case challenging the removal, but only because the court decided that the city hall rotunda was not actually a workplace.)

The country's most notorious sexual harassment case is that of Paula Jones against President Clinton, which the Supreme Court has unanimously ruled may proceed to trial. Most of the attention directed to Jones's case has, understandably, concerned itself with questions of effect on the Clinton presidency and on the presidency in general. But the case is also noteworthy as another milestone in the expansion of what constitutes a tortious sexual offense. As Jeffrey Rosen wrote in this magazine, assuming Jones's account of the facts is accurate, Clinton "made a pass at her, took no for an answer and reassured her that he meant her no harm." In the court of public opinion, Jones's case has already elevated an admittedly gross (alleged) sexual overture into a federal civil rights violation, and it may do this in a court of law as well. The case, Rosen notes, "shows how dramatically our increasingly amorphous conception of sexual harassment has expanded in the past decade." Indeed, in practice, virtually any sex-related expression involving employees and bosses of opposite sexes has become legally hazardous. President Clinton is merely the latest to discover that boorishness has become actionable under law.

Some of the cases of workplace behavior defined as sexual harassment are so ludicrous that they have become mildly famous. At the University of Nebraska at Lincoln, a harassment complaint was filed because a graduate student kept on his desk a snapshot of his wife in a bikini; the university ordered the photo removed. Penn State removed a painting by Goya from a classroom after a professor complained that it constituted sexual harassment. When a Minnesota public-library worker posted, in his own work area, a *New Yorker* cartoon making wry reference to the Bobbitt case (one fully dressed man says to another, "What's the big deal? I lopped off my own damn penis years ago"), coworkers lodged a harassment complaint, and supervisors ordered the cartoon removed....

No one denies that people sometimes say ugly things to each other at work, and that campaigns of vilification against women, blacks or other minorities (or nonminorities) sometimes happen. But in the workplace, where we spend more time than anywhere but our homes, the law has come to accept a doctrine that some minority activists have tried, but failed, to embody in college speech codes and First Amendment law outside the workplace: that purportedly bigoted or offensive speech is itself a form of illegal discrimination. So, to get rid of discrimination, you have to get rid of discriminatory speech—a project which is now under way. Walter K. Olson, in his new book *The Excuse Factory*, notes that just between 1989 and 1993 the number of harassment charges filed with the EEOC [Equal Employment Opportunity Commission] more than doubled, from 5,600 to 11,900. Only about 5 percent of the claims involved demands for sexual favors or the like; the rest alleged "hostile environments." Slippery slopes may be more common in rhetoric than in reality, but plainly the law is now on one.

Recently a few legal scholars, such as UCLA's Eugene Volokh (to whom I am indebted), have begun asking hard questions about discrimination law and free speech, and how to contain the corrosive effects of the one upon the other. But the hostile-environment rule is like an acid that eats through any container you put it into. A better idea is to repudiate it, since it is now the country's most virulent threat to free speech.

The most peculiar thing about workplace-harassment law is not that it has turned the First Amendment on its head, but that it has done so without even trying. Generations of would-be censors —opponents of pornography, sedition, evolutionism, hate-speech, flag-burning, Klan rallies—have charged the First Amendment head-on and broken their necks. But opponents of discriminatory speech, who never paid much attention to the First Amendment, have sleepwalked right past it. At no point, right up to the present, did the courts and government agencies step back and weigh the free-speech implications of what they were doing. They just went step by step.

They started from a sound intuition. If laws against job discrimination are a good thing, what about workplaces where racists or sexists use their mouths to drive minorities or women away? Employers should, of their own accord, demand civility on the job. Most of them do. But some don't. For instance, in a 1985 case, *Snell* v. *Suffolk County*, white corrections officers used demeaning epithets against their minority colleagues, posted vicious cartoons and images ("Official Runnin' Nigger Target"), mimicked minority stereotypes, and so on. When a Hispanic officer complained, his car was vandalized, he received vicious phone calls at home at all hours, and white officers were so slow reacting to his distress calls that he was assaulted.

Now, the first thing to notice here is that, as in most cases of pervasive harassment, speech was commingled with punishable conduct: threats (which are not constitutionally protected), discriminatory treatment, misfeasance, vandalism, and so on. But speech was unquestionably part of the problem; plainly, the place was full of racists. It seemed natural, then, for the judge to go further than, say, demanding a halt to discriminatory practices, or granting compensation to the abused officers. He imposed a speech code. The employer, he decreed, must forbid corrections officers from using racial epithets on county property, posting or distributing "derogatory bulletins, cartoons, and other written material," to mimic minority stereotypes, and using "any racial, ethnic, or religious slurs, whether in the form of 'jokes,' 'jests,' or otherwise." Even a single "joke, jest, or otherwise" would require "prompt and severe discipline."

* * *

But wait a minute. The *Snell* injunction traduces more or less every known principle of First Amendment law. It bars speech that is not libelous, obscene, threatening or otherwise outside First Amendment bounds. It uses prior restraints to do so. It engages in viewpoint discrimination, barring only speech deemed to bear a discriminatory message. Its terms are extremely vague ("other written material," "or otherwise"). It creates unbounded peril, so that even one private critical remark is hazardous. It doesn't even require that punishable jokes actually bother anybody....

As it turns out, Title VII of the 1964 Civil Rights Act says nothing about speech. It forbids employers "to discriminate against any individual with respect to his compensation, terms, conditions, or privileges of employment, because of such individual's race, color, religion, sex, or national origin." Much like affirmative action, hostile-environment law grew obliquely from a series of decisions by courts and administrative agencies in the 1970s and 1980s, each building on the last but none stepping back to view the bigger picture. As it has evolved, the standard holds employers accountable for preventing speech that is:

- "severe or pervasive" enough
- to create a "hostile or abusive work environment"
- based on minority status (race, sex, national origin, religion, age, disability, and so on)
- for the plaintiff and for a reasonable person.

From a common-sense point of view, that seems a fairly unalarming definition. Admittedly, "hostile or abusive" is vague, and "for the plaintiff and for a reasonable person" puts the listener and the public authorities in a position to veto speech that they don't like. But "severe or pervasive" seems comforting. Plainly, the definition isn't aimed at the odd racist joke, or the desktop picture of a bikini clad spouse, or an impressionistic painting hanging in city hall. So why are courts banning any and all "derogatory written material," pervasive or not? Why was Maxine Henderson's painting removed from the Murfreesboro city hall?

Here we encounter a nasty surprise. What looks like a clear limiting principle isn't. "Severe or pervasive" gives defendants a fighting chance in court. But it doesn't do something that is, in the real world, more important: tell them how to stay out of court.

* * *

Imagine that a stranger showed you a ticking box labeled "BOMB" and said it might or might not be a clock. Do you open it? Now suppose your lawyer told you that your employees' speech might or might not embroil you in a potentially debilitating lawsuit. "Employers are not interested in winning lawsuits," says Michael J. Lotito, an employment lawyer with the firm of Jackson Lewis in San Francisco. "They are interested in making sure that lawsuits are never filed." The only way to do that is to stay on the right side of the law's bright lines. But, in hostile-environment law, there are no bright lines. Sensitivity trainers and diversity consultants often encourage workers to be thin-skinned, and plaintiffs build their lawsuits from particular instances of "harassing" speech, each of which they can cite to establish a "hostile environment." And employers know it. As Volokh points out, employers can't tell workers, "Say nothing such that the cumulative effect of your and all other workers' comments rise to a level that is severe or pervasive." They have to tell the employees to say nothing that might look to a jury like a "hostile environment." And judges can't say, "From now on, forestall the first incremental Holocaust joke that creates a hostile environment for a reasonable Jew." They have to say: no more religious jokes. The policy is driven by its logic to say: when in doubt, shut up.

Which, as Volokh notes, is exactly what employment experts advise. "Suggestive joking of any kind simply must not be tolerated," writes one. Another writes, "To avoid liability, the prudent

employer will proscribe all speech and conduct that may constitute harassment. The possibility of creating a 'chilling effect' from prohibiting speech and conduct that may constitute harassment is outweighed by the risk of significant liability." The relevant authorities agree. In a pamphlet called "Preventing Sexual Harassment—A Fact Sheet for Employees," the Maryland Commission on Human Relations notes that a "sexually hostile work environment" can be created by discussing sexual activities, telling off-color jokes, using "demeaning or inappropriate terms" (whatever those are), or using crude and offensive language (whatever that is). And then, with admirable if creepy candor, it advises, "Because the legal boundaries are so poorly marked, the best course of action is to avoid all sexually offensive conduct in the workplace." Note that "conduct" has been stretched to cover pure speech of the sort that, outside the workplace, would enjoy unquestioned First Amendment protection.

So, when the Murfreesboro city attorney summarily took down Maxine Henderson's painting, he wasn't indulging paranoid fantasies or bluenose obsessions. He was doing the prudent thing. Dozens, maybe hundreds, of city workers walked past Henderson's semi-nude in the course of doing their jobs. Wasn't that "pervasive"?

Still, the doctrine includes what seems to be another sensible limit: it applies only to the "work environment." And maybe workplaces should be treated differently. After all, jobs are hard to come by, and most of us need to have one. Employees can't easily avoid colleagues' racist, sexist or otherwise offensive speech. In that respect, aren't workers a captive audience?

Maybe so. But if listeners are captive at work, then so are speakers, and they can hardly be asked to accept government gag orders by taking a job. Moreover, in the legal sense, which is narrower than the colloquial one, the workplace is not "captive" at all. The Supreme Court has consistently refused to extend the "captive audience" doctrine beyond the home, for the sound reason that life is full of places where we have little choice but to be, and full of speech we can't help but hear.... Times Square commuters can't avoid seeing a Calvin Klein underwear billboard, workers can't avoid hearing picketers every day calling them "scab" or "ugly bitch," and people with school-board business can't avoid hearing a speaker who uses the word "mother f—ker" at a school-board meeting. But all of that speech, including "ugly bitch," is protected. In fact, even where the listener really *is* captive (at home), the Supreme Court still won't allow speech restrictions that favor one viewpoint over another, as restrictions on "discriminatory" speech clearly do.

So the "captive audience" argument actually doesn't help much, at least not where the Supreme Court is concerned. Still, an intuition nags. Surely going to work five days a week, sitting or standing next to the same bigot every day, is at least somewhat different from passing a billboard or hearing a foulmouthed school-board harangue. So maybe the Supreme Court should make an exception for the workplace. Maybe the limiting principle should be: restrict offensive, discriminatory speech in the workplace, but only there. But here arises nasty surprise number two. Not only is the "workplace only" rule ineffective as a principle for limiting the hostile environment doctrine, it's actually a principle for transmitting it, in

concentric circles, all through American life.

After all, everywhere is somebody's workplace—restaurants, shops, churches, streets, parks, even many homes. In 1991, a waitress at a diner in Berkeley refused to serve a journalist who was reading *Playboy*, on the grounds that this was sexual harassment. Better not laugh at her. Suppose a restaurant's regular patron customarily wears a cap with a Confederate flag on it, and a black waitress objects. Or suppose he likes to declaim, both to and around the waitresses, about the stupidity of women, or the waitress's beautiful breasts, or whatever. That's a "hostile environment." What do you do if you're the restaurant owner? "You may not think it's a big deal, but it's a big deal to the employee," says Scott W. Kezman, an employment lawyer with Kaufman & Canoles in Norfolk, Virginia. "The safest thing you can do as an employer is to take some type of action." This may mean asking the customer not to wear the cap, or not to make sexist remarks. If all else fails, advise Kezman and two coauthors in a December article in a human-relations trade publication, "managers need to learn what they can do to stop offenders—remove them or permanently bar them from the premises."

This is not idle advice. A Las Vegas dealer filed a sexual harassment suit against her casino for failing to take action against customers who, she alleged, stared at her and yelled about her "great tits." Federal Express was sued by a courier for failing to act against a customer on her route who repeatedly demanded dates, stared and said she would look better with her clothes off. Under this theory (and application) of the law, employers become the state's agents for policing the speech not only of their workers but of their customers.

What about universities? They're workplaces, too. Federal courts have been fairly diligent about rejecting speech codes at public universities, on the grounds that the typically vague and overbroad codes violate students' First Amendment rights. But lately a new wrinkle has arisen: proponents are arguing that workplace harassment law *requires* speech codes. When the Kansas Board of Regents asked for an opinion last year on its racial and sexual harassment policies, the state attorney general noted, reasonably, that the courts routinely uphold—indeed require—broad speech codes in the workplace, so they ought, in the name of consistency, to uphold them in educational settings as well. And he went further: if a student commits a racially motivated crime, requiring him to "undergo racial sensitivity training in addition to the provided penalty" may be a good way "to avoid ... liability under the 'hostile environment' formulation." So mandatory re-education for racists (meaning, of course, for individuals accused of racism), far from being constitutionally suspect, may be the best protection from a federal lawsuit!

Forget, then, about limiting the hostile-environment doctrine "only" to the workplace. Yet common sense still tugs at our coat-sleeves. Isn't there some way to punish foulmouthed bigots in the office without giving a speech-veto to the most sensitive pair of ears on the premises? Instead of looking for firm limits where none exists—well, how about just reasonableness? But here is the third and biggest nasty surprise. However benign it looks on the outside, the hostile-environment doctrine contains a savage seed, one that undercuts the very legitimacy of the First Amendment.

* * *

This is an astonishing, profoundly radical, statement. It says that it is the proper work of the state to stamp out "unacceptable" attitudes privately held by citizens, and that workplace law is a wonderful tool for accomplishing this. It makes explicit what the hostile-environment doctrine implies: that silencing obnoxious racists and sexists and so on is not just a by-product of antidiscrimination policy, but a goal. There is just no way to square any such goal with the central premise of free speech, which is that the only legitimate way in which the state may seek to eliminate biases in society is to allow an environment where biases are pitted freely against each other.

The 1988 decision was not merely loose talk by one misguided court. It was an expression of a doctrine that is now being widely applied. In 1994, the Kentucky Commission on Human Rights wrote to South Central Bell, explaining that the company's "Men Working" signs were discriminatory. The company replied that the signs would be replaced as they were retired. No, retorted the commission's managing attorney—the law requires *prompt* remedial action. Not later—now. "I feel confident," she said, "that if your signs included any other protected class, such as 'Whites Working' or 'Women Working,' they would be immediately removed and not utilized or replaced. Since we have been unable to resolve this problem through informal means, I am recommending that a Commissioner-initiated complaint be filed." The company, understandably, caved.

Now, no one, neither workers nor passersby, had complained about the company's "sexist" signs. A Bell South Kentucky spokeswoman says that if anyone had complained, the company would have begun phasing out the signs of its own accord. "It's important to us that our employees feel comfortable at work, and that our customers not feel offended," she says. Replacing hundreds of signs immediately, under threat of legal action, cost upwards of $36,000.

Cost, of course, is the least of the issues here. The bigger problem is that the law has given up any pretense of viewpoint neutrality. Instead it is openly, indeed eagerly, suppressing incorrect thinking, not in confined quarters but in a public street. What a mess this makes of traditional free-speech protections. The First Amendment is supposed to require the government to tolerate the expression of all sorts of beliefs without coercively favoring one over another. The new approach to workplace harassment turns the state's role precisely upside down. Wherever people work—which is practically everywhere—the "hostile environment" rule places the state squarely in the role of judging and enforcing which beliefs or prejudices or even conventions of language are acceptable and which are not, and which may be uttered and which may not. No one even bothers to pretend that hostile-environment law is meant to give racists or sexists a fair shake. "Dozens of reported cases involve liability claims based on anti-feminist statements that are frequently not at all obscene but often highly political and analytic in content," writes Olson; "an exhaustive search fails to uncover a single case in which feminist assertions have been ruled to contribute to a hostile environment." One court has said that work-

ers' use of job titles like "foreman" and "draftsman" may constitute harassment. This is not about stopping "harassment," in any traditional sense; it is about suppressing speech to impose an egalitarian orthodoxy. In 1994, a jury slapped a $500,000 judgment on a Washington, D.C., television station because, as one juror told *The Washington Post*, managers "seemed to feel it was partly okay to make jokes about women" (for example, a production manager complained that "Nazi feminists" wouldn't let him smoke a cigar). A few years ago, when *The Los Angeles Times* proposed an internal speech code barring use of "offensive" terms such as "gyp" and "Dutch treat," the idea was hooted down in a barrage of ridicule. But when discrimination law does the same thing, no one laughs; increasingly, no one even notices.

For that matter, if the goal is to stamp out "hostile environments," why just the workplace? After all, a hostile educational environment is illegal under federal law; in 1994, the Education Department's civil-rights office concluded that some sexist remarks posted on a college-run electronic bulletin board created a "hostile environment on the basis of sex" (even though the complainants had not actually read them). The law also forbids discrimination in public accommodations. Are hotels creating "hostile public accommodations" for Muslims by putting Gideon Bibles in their drawers? Are public museums harassing women by displaying nudes? Nadine Strossen, president of the American Civil Liberties Union, points out that artwork has been removed from classrooms, city halls and public galleries on sex-harassment grounds—including art by female artists and with feminist themes. A Wisconsin state agency decided that an overheard, though loud, restaurant conversation using the word "nigger" created an illegal hostile public accommodation for black customers. Even the Internet may be a kind of public accommodation. Why not bar discriminatory speech there? Equating discriminatory speech with discrimination obliterates the very concept of an expressive zone where prosecutors, plaintiffs and equal-opportunity agencies can't try to censor whatever they regard as bigotry or sexism.

There aren't a lot of alternatives. One, of course, is to declare that ending discrimination is more important than the First Amendment, so there should be no right to expression deemed racist or sexist. That would end freedom of speech as we know it.

Another is to confess—as, for instance, the ACLU's Strossen does—that the First Amendment and the hostile-environment doctrine are in conflict with each other, but to say that nothing much can be done about this, so we'll just have to muddle ahead without any clear lines. "Protected expression can be distinguished from proscribable harassment only on a contextual basis, turning on the facts and circumstances of each particular case, writes Strossen. That, however, is exactly the current non-rule, and the whole problem is that employers, unsure what the judge or jury will decide, repress anything that looks dangerous if anybody complains.

A third alternative is more promising. The law should stipulate, argues UCLA's Volokh, that hostile-environment "harassment" occurs only when discriminatory speech is targeted at an individual in one-to-one conversation, when the individual has given notice that she objects, and when the speech is repeated often enough to rise to the level of pervasive-

ness. Overheard comments, group conversations and cartoons posted for general viewing wouldn't count.

Make no mistake, Volokh's rule would be an improvement over current law. By bringing the law into line with what most people mean when they use the word "harassment"—targeted vilification—it puts some sensible bounds on the reach of the hostile-environment doctrine. But the notion of a listener's veto, even if limited to one-on-one conversation, remains deeply troubling. What about cases where two employees work together: Does one get to shut up the other? And how would you confine Volokh's principle to the workplace, since, as he himself points out, the workplace is everywhere? Although Volokh's idea limits the listener's veto to groups of two, it nonetheless cedes the principle that individuals have a legal right to censor speech they find disagreeable, as they define disagreeable. It also cedes that the government can pick and choose which opinions to suppress. Those are awfully big concessions.

So another possibility remains: extend First Amendment protection to workplace speech. Just say that if the First Amendment is good enough for everywhere else, it's good enough for the workplace. The hostile-environment doctrine would be effectively abolished.

At first glance, this seems to leave minorities high and dry when surrounded by bigots at work. But that isn't so. Discriminatory actions—in hiring, firing, pay, promotion and so on—would still be illegal. So would quid-pro-quo harassment, in which supervisors demand, say, sexual favors or religious obeisances from employees. So would threats, obscenity and slander, which the First Amendment doesn't protect. Remember, most cases of genuinely pervasive verbal harassment directed at minorities, like the *Snell* case described at the beginning of this article, involve patterns of behavior, nor just speech. In fact, the more damaging objection to abolishing the hostile-environment doctrine is that doing so might not make enough of a difference. Since racist speech could still be used in court to establish discriminatory treatment, employers would still probably err on the side of squelching it. A boss who admires his assisant's legs would still need to worry about a jury's finding that he was trying to get sex from her.

Still, the principle would be established that the First Amendment does not crumble into dust at the office door. The courts would have to stop ordering speech codes. Employers could force judges and juries to weigh First Amendment concerns rather than just ignore them. Most important, the barrier between discriminatory speech and discriminatory action would be restored....

* * *

The argument I'm making here isn't a comforting one, but it's the argument that has underpinned free-speech theory for centuries. In a free society, everyone, male or female, white or black, has a positive responsibility to be thick-skinned. Activists who insist that personal offense is a cause for public action are a menace to the freedom of conscience that protects minorities above all. So if you care about freedom of expression, then you will have to put up with hearing some deeply objectionable, even monstrous things, sometimes on a daily basis. No doubt minorities will get more than their share. Jews will have to hear Holocaust deniers. Blacks will have to hear racists.

Women will have to hear their "hooters" praised. But the white heterosexual male population will come in for its share of insults, too; indeed, in many of today's diversified and minority-sensitive workplaces, white men may also get more than their share. And, anyway, it should not be illegal to be a jerk.

What I'm proposing isn't radical. I'm only asking that legally designated minorities live under the same free-speech principles that other people live with right now: fat people, short people, ugly people, unpopular people. And I do know something about this. I am homosexual, and, in most jurisdictions, homosexuals are not a protected class. We have no legal recourse against "faggot" or "queer" or other, more insidious forms of disparagement on the job. Gay people deal with it as people always have: by combining humor, stoicism, courage and appeals to the better nature of those around us. That is not always good enough, but is the law better? Where "sexual orientation" is a protected category, a complaining heterosexual might claim she was being "harassed" by a gay colleague who openly discussed his homosexuality. If that sounds far-fetched, please note: it has happened! In 1990, a plaintiff alleged that her supervisor harassed her by "repeatedly [speaking] to her about his alleged homosexuality and [trying] to draw her into conversation on the topic of sexual preference." That particular claim ran aground on a side issue. But there will be more like it.

I personally have never been vilified at work on grounds of homosexuality, or any other grounds. So perhaps the case I make is easier for me than for others. But I do not think that joke police and state-imposed speech codes can be the answer.

POSTSCRIPT

Should Society Continue to Support Sexual Harassment Policies for the Workplace?

Many claims of reverse discrimination have been introduced in the wake of a 1991 federal law that allowed women, for the first time, to sue under federal statutes for emotional damages resulting from employment discrimination. Hastily passed after the Thomas-Hill hearings and signed into law by President George Bush, this law was intended to fully compensate women who were victims of sexual harassment.

Hanna Rosin, in "Sleeping With the Enemy," *The New Republic* (June 23, 1997), contends that men are being mistreated by the new sexual harassment rulings. She believes that such rulings forced the military to "embrace a theory of sexual intercourse which belongs to far left feminism" when they defined rape as occurring when a man has sexual intercourse with a woman who is in a subordinate position to him. Rosin argues that the military took a "harsh, moralistic" view of the facts when Staff Sergeant Delmer Simpson was sentenced to 25 years in prison for "raping" six women. Rosin claims that Simpson was convicted on the basis of his authority over the women, as there was no physical force involved. Many find the idea that women are powerless to resist persons in authority untrue and offensive. For example, Camille Paglia, in "No Law in the Arena," from her book of essays *Vamps and Tramps* (Vintage Books, 1994), states that "objective research would likely show that incidence of sycophancy by subordinates far exceeds that of coercion by bosses." If someone offends you by speech, she says, you must learn to defend yourself by speech.

If it is true that sexual harassment rulings are unfair to men, it is also true that a war is being waged on their behalf. Andrea Bernstein, in "Sex Harassment Suits: The Fight for Damages Gets Uglier," *Ms.* (July/August 1996), notes that attorneys are utilizing what is known as an "alternative stressors" strategy in defending their clients. Alternative stressor theory posits that there is no probable causal relationship between sexual harassment and emotional stress. More likely, the plaintiff's stress is brought on by a difficult childhood or a troubled marriage. Attorneys are being allowed to ask questions unrelated to the case, just as they did in rape trials decades ago, and unrelated documents can be subpoenaed. However, some judges are beginning to bar irrelevant information, and the rape shield law has been applied to harassment cases at times. Currently, however, there is no limit on questions regarding the plaintiff's sexual history at discovery. For more from the military front, see Richard J. Newman, "Did We Say Zero Tolerance?" *U.S. News and World Report* (March 10, 1997), in which the author argues that men are hobbled by threats of sexual harassment accusations. He reports that military officials are being bulldozed into appeasing an irrational public and being forced to take an aggressive public stance against the mistreatment of military women. To make matters worse, he says, rape hotlines have been established, which circumvent the typical military chain of command. This potentially "hurts military leaders," especially junior officers and senior enlisted individuals, by depriving them of the opportunity to handle problem situations from within, says Newman.

In at least one instance, the judiciary did *not* send the message that sexual abuse is a deprivation of women's federal civil rights. Joy Ward, in "The Judge Who Got Off," *On the Issues* (Fall 1996), notes that the U.S. Sixth Circuit Court of Appeals returned a judge who had been convicted of multiple counts of sexual harassment and abuse to his home jurisdiction, effectively failing to send the message that sexual abuse is a deprivation of federal civil rights. Failure to use U.S. Code 242, which defines as criminal the deprivation of any rights protected by the Constitution by any person acting under "color of law," sets a jurisdictional precedent that could be harmful to many women.

ISSUE 6

Should Women Receive More Coverage in History Textbooks?

YES: Michelle Commeyras and Donna Alvermann, from "Reading About Women in World History Textbooks from One Feminist Perspective," *Gender and Education* (March 1996)

NO: Robert Lerner, Althea Nagai, and Stanley Rothman, from "Gendering American History," *The World and I* (April 1996)

ISSUE SUMMARY

YES: Michele Commeyras and Donna Alvermann, both associates at the University of Georgia, assert that when they analyzed history textbooks they found serious omissions and misrepresentations due to ideological and value differences, along with insensitivity in gender positioning.

NO: Historians Robert Lerner, Althea Nagai, and Stanley Rothman maintain that federal regulations calling for systematic recasting of American history in terms of content and process are unnecessary.

A number of people have recently observed that history texts had been essentially devoid of information about women until the last decade. Prior to that, history texts were typically written from the male perspective, primarily covering topics about men and their accomplishments. The contributions and influence of women were largely ignored, and schoolchildren were exposed almost exclusively to the actions of men in politics, economics, culture, and war. The controversy over what should be taught in history classes reveals a deep fissure between some of today's dominant and conservative historians and a new breed of historians who seek to change the presentation of the past.

Women's history began by challenging the claims of the traditional and accepted accounts of the past. It raised questions about how power is exercised and certified and how knowledge is restricted and produced. Some claim that the long-standing approaches of historians result in an "elitist history" that is "white, male-oriented, and hero worshiping," effectively eliminating the voices of people who significantly affected the course of America's historical development. This includes women, a group that many say was historically excluded, exploited, and enslaved within American society and in other societies around the world.

Within the past decade, the federally funded National Standards Project (NSP) called for a systematic recasting of American history texts in terms of process as well as content. Writers, editors, and publishers were charged with including historical events as they affected women, along with women's roles in these events. Sexism and oppression, of course, would need to be dealt with extensively in order to accomplish this goal.

Writers who contest the gender adaptation of history textbooks are concerned that such adaptation could result in the systematic insertion of even the most minor female figures presented exclusively in a positive light and with little complexity or ambivalence. Some say that this is already happening. They also fear that biases will favor individuals who were supportive of women's rights and level criticism toward those who did not support those rights. In addition, some worry that painting a picture of a sexist society, particularly in American history, could corrupt students' patriotic views of their society, erode the legitimacy of institutions, and diminish important documents such as the Declaration of Independence.

Many traditional "truths" as written in history have been challenged in order to construct new definitions of class and to reveal the meanings of customary ideas and metaphors about women. Writers have explored the seemingly devastating effects on women being excluded from the historical record and have argued that women's struggle to understand their own history lies at the heart of their ability to envision a world in which they are full participants. Recognition of women's historical relevance would ultimately unsettle historical narratives as they have been written, sometimes in radical ways, but to do otherwise may be to risk allowing the dominant groups in society to maintain their power by depriving the people they dominate of the knowledge of their own history.

In the selelctions that follow, Michelle Commeyras and Donna Alvermann argue on behalf of incorporating women into history texts, noting that once the notion of one "real" history is dropped, the awareness of many historical truths will emerge. Robert Lerner, Althea Nagai, and Stanley Rothman argue that current historians have swung too far to the left already, showing prejudice against "patriotic events of any kind."

YES

Michelle Commeyras and
Donna Alvermann

READING ABOUT WOMEN IN WORLD HISTORY TEXTBOOKS FROM ONE FEMINIST PERSPECTIVE

Studies in women's history have flourished in the past 30 years, in regard to feminist politics, specialized historical studies of women, and analyses of gender in the production of knowledge (Scott, 1993). The evolution of the contemporary women's history movement differs from earlier dispersed writings about women's history because it embraces the idea that there are many historical 'truths' and rejects the notion of one 'real' history waiting to be written (Zinsser, 1993). In effect, feminist historians have been engaged in rewriting history. To date, however, the women's history movement seems to have had little impact on secondary school textbooks. Joan Wallach Scott (1993) contends that publishers of the 1990s have done little more than add subsections on women in history to the standard fare found in most textbooks. Even those individuals who see advances in the representation of women in world history, textbooks acknowledge that insensitivity to gender positioning still abounds (e.g. Sleeter & Grant, 1991). Beyond insensitivity issues, there is evidence of serious omissions and misrepresentations in textbooks due to ideological differences and values. As Jean Anyon (1979) pointed out more than a decade ago, ideological perspectives that serve the interests of particular favored social groups at the expense of less favored social groups often find their way into history textbooks. When they do, they carry with them serious consequences. For example, textbooks that ideologically serve the interests of males over females to legitimate certain social 'realities' about women's place in history produce distortions that are harmful and impede the development of respect for all human beings. A consequence of reading and discussing texts that ideologically serve the interests of males over females is the legitimation of a social 'reality' that continues to be passed down, almost uninterrupted, through generations of readers and writers....

From Michelle Commeyras and Donna Alvermann, "Reading About Women in World History Textbooks from One Feminist Perspective," *Gender and Education*, vol. 8, no. 1 (March 1996), p. 31. Copyright © 1996 by Carfax Publishing Limited, P.O. Box 25, Abingdon, Oxfordshire OX14 3UE, United Kingdom. Reprinted by permission. Notes omitted.

TEXT ANALYSES: FROM CHRISTINE DE PISAN TO JANICE LAW TRECKER

Content analyses, such as the one undertaken in this paper, have a long history dating back at least to the Renaissance. In the late fourteenth and early fifteenth centuries, Christine de Pisan, who is considered the first professional woman writer in Western history (Gross, 1987), claimed her right to reread male-authored texts about women as a woman (not like a woman—a 'perjorative' comment made by her male contemporaries). Using her own experiences and knowledge about women's positioning in history texts, de Pisan wrote *City of Women* about 1405. According to Susan Schibanoff (1986), this book, which went out of print after its first edition, contains de Pisan's rewritten narratives of more than 120 famous women who lived between the time of the ancient poet Sappho and Queen Isabella of Bavaria.

Analyses of texts that address the positioning of women in society have varied widely in their focus in recent years. Sex bias has been studied by examining seventeenth-century English funeral sermons (Doebler & Warnicke, 1987), children's picture-books (Barnett, 1986; McDonald, 1989), high school chemistry textbooks (Bazler & Simonis, 1991), and teacher education textbooks (Titus, 1993). The findings from such studies reflect the many ways in which texts perpetuate social constructions of gender. For example, seventeenth-century funeral sermons were published for males more often than for females. When sermons were published for females, the laudatory comments emphasized the idealized characteristics of womanhood (Doebler & Warnicke, 1987). By the twentieth century, textbook analysts focused on examining trends toward greater equity in sex representation. In doing this, they relied primarily on analyses that involved comparisons between the number of male and female characters and illustrations. While useful in some ways (e.g. pointing out greater representation of females), these kinds of analyses have presented only a superficial view of gender equity. Moreover, they often led to the criticisms that Joan Wallach Scott (1993) and others have leveled against the additive nature of women's representation in textbooks.

Of all the textbook analyses we surveyed, two were most relevant for our project. We summarize the findings from Janice Law Trecker's (1971) analysis of women in US high school history textbooks and Audrey Osler's (1994) analysis of gender equity in UK history textbooks.

Trecker (1971) was concerned with whether or not the textbooks conveyed stereotypes that might limit girls' aspirations. After examining over a dozen of the most popular US history textbooks, Trecker concluded:

> Despite some promising attempts to supplement the scant amount of information devoted to women in American history texts, most works are marred by sins of omission and commission. Texts omit many women of importance, while simultaneously minimizing the legal, social and cultural disabilities which they faced. The authors tend to depict women in a passive role and to stress that their lives are determined by economic and political trends. Women are rarely shown fighting for anything; their rights have been 'given' to them. (p. 251)

Trecker also noted that publishers' efforts to improve coverage of black history minimized or omitted the achievements of African-American women. She called for changes in the construction of high school history texts that go beyond brief profiles or special sections on women. Before this could happen, Trecker concluded, those responsible for writing and publishing history textbooks would have to come to terms with 'the bias against women in our culture, a bias so smooth, seamless, and pervasive, that it is hard to even begin to take a hold of it and bring it into clear view' (Trecker, 1971, p. 260).

Osler's (1994) textbook analysis is particularly relevant because it was conducted in response to the publication in 1991 of the National Curriculum History Programmes of Study for primary and secondary schools in England. Osler's intent was to examine whether the representation of women in textbooks published in 1991–92 reflected equity initiatives promoted in the new National Curriculum. She did an exhaustive study of the visual images, the language of texts, and the exercises and activities in 36 textbooks. The results of her study showed that history textbooks were successfully avoiding sexist language but that they still had a long way to go to achieve a balanced historical record, one that promotes understanding of the lives of women in the past....

METHOD

We selected three high school world history textbooks (Beers, 1991; Krieger, et al., 1992; Perry et al., 1992) for analysis. The texts were chosen because of their recent publication dates and high visibility in the the market-place. In fact, all three textbooks are currently on the state-wide adoption lists for Texas and Florida (State Departments of Education, personal communication, 6 February 1995). Both states represent unusually large markets for textbook distribution. The multiphase analysis used in this study was also used to examine the history of peoples from 'Third World' countries (Commeyras & Alvermann, 1994) and a modified version of the analysis has been recommended as a way for teachers to engage students in critical examinations of textbooks (Alvermann & Commeyras, 1994b)....

MICROANALYSIS OF LANGUAGE

Women's Rights

The rights and status of women throughout history in different civilizations and eras is a recurring theme in the three textbooks we examined. Generally, women's status across the ages has been portrayed as being governed by whether or not they had the right to vote, to choose freely to marry or divorce, to own property or conduct business, to assume positions of leadership, and to protect their rights through the legal system.

Joan Wallach Scott's observation that the word *women* 'has no intrinsic definition; but only a contextual one that cannot be elaborated except through contrast, usually to "men"' (Scott, 1993, p. 249) seems relevant to a pattern we found in the portrayal of women's rights....

Generalized terms such as *people, most people,* and *Egyptians* implies either that these terms are synonymous with men; or else that women, who are people, believe themselves to be inferior. These implications dilute and obscure the identity of those who create and support a patriarchal world view. The use of language in these textbooks that obfuscates patriarchal control over women's lives and male agency may appear to some as feminist hypersensitivity, but there are parallels in studies of language in other settings that further illustrate our concern with how language can be used to mask patriarchal oppression. For example, consider the following quotation from a review of books recently published on violence against women:

> [A] Chicago study found the following phrases in emergency records filled out by doctors who had treated battered women: 'Hit by lead pipe.' 'Blow to head by stick with nail in it.' 'Hit on left wrist with jackhammer.' Or if instruments are not accused, abstractions are the villains: women are 'mutilated by spousal hostility and murdered by domestic incidents.' Or they 'undergo assault.' (Wesson, 1994, p. 33)

As Mimi Wesson (1994) argues in her review, the agency for battering women is attributed to anything but the batterer. Language usage that denies agency and social systems that produce conditions where, according to FBI statistics, a woman is beaten every 10 seconds in the USA is a concern to those who author, publish, and use textbooks.

Power, Fighters, and Mediators

One prominent feature of women in world history, at least as depicted in the three textbooks we examined, was their reliance on Eve-like characteristics in their climb to positions of influence and power. Whether in their ascendancy to powerful stations in life or in their fight to maintain those new-found positions, women were pictured as using what John Phillips (1984) referred to as Eve-like characteristics, such as insecurity, sensuality, beauty, willfulness, and cupidity, to get what they wanted....

TAKING STOCK: THE EDUCATIONAL SIGNIFICANCE

After completing our analysis of the positioning of women in three world history textbooks, we directed our thoughts toward the educational significance of our findings for literacy educators. As members of that community, we believe that helping others become literate involves focusing on all the ways people learn and engage in reading words and their worlds. Our analysis of how women are positioned in the three textbooks we examined has confirmed our belief that gender issues are central to the experience of reading words and worlds....

Engaging in reading subtexts as human artifact meets the challenge feminist scholars have posed to educators, namely to present gender as a problematic area of study rather than as the natural order of things. We see a need for literacy teacher educators, teachers, and students to engage in more reading of the subtexts when textbooks like those we analyzed are used to teach world history....

DISCUSSION OF SUBTEXTS BY RESISTANT READERS

Focusing classroom discussions on women in history, or at least on women as they are positioned in world history texts, is one way of challenging the differentiations textbook authors make between the sexes. It is also a way of exploring the potential for such differentiations to influence adversely students' interpretations of, and attitudes toward, women in general. Textbook authors who consistently and over time accord males the dominant role in their relationships with women effectively (though perhaps not intentionally) thwart any hope of creating respect for difference. When differences are respected and celebrated, practices that support exclusion, domination, and marginality become irrelevant.

Based on our analyses of the three textbooks in question, we believe there is a need for teachers to become proactive in the way they help students deal with age-old myths surrounding the dominance of men in relation to women. Because issues of dominance typically rest on one or more underlying (and usually unstated) presuppositions about the need to differentiate between men's and women's roles in history, it is important to engage students in critical discussions of what they have read in their assigned history texts. Teachers can facilitate these discussions by sharing with students how they, the teachers, read the subtext as resistant readers (see Commeyras & Alvermann, 1994)....

accounts for women's demeaning experiences and differential treatment throughout history.

The significance of our analysis for educators lies in our call for a focus on engaging students in reading the subtext. Given the continuing resistance to teaching history in ways that are more inclusive and critical, it is imperative that we find ways of teaching students to recognize unstated assumptions, subtleties of language, and why some individuals are championed while others are omitted from historical accounts. Too often, reading materials in the USA have encouraged assimilation and conformity more than difference and critical thinking (Kaestle, 1991). Our analysis suggests that reading these three textbooks in ways that focus simply on getting the 'facts' would further legitimate a patriarchial view of world history.

CONCLUSION

Our reading and subsequent analysis of the presentation of women in three secondary school world history textbooks used in the USA coincides with Zinsser's (1993) assessment that textbooks of the 1990s still present an androcentric view of history. Efforts to integrate women into a history divided into time periods that revolve around exploration, conquest, consolidation of power, and the politics of ruling expanding empires are accomplished by adding subsections on famous women, paragraphs about women's status and rights in these time periods, and sentences about their enabling contributions as wives and mothers of famous men. More subtle was our analysis of how language functions in these textbooks to position women in stereotypical ways or to obfuscate the patriarchal system that

REFERENCES

Alvermann, D. & Commeyras, M. (1994a) Gender, text, and discussion: expanding the possibilities, in R. Garner & P. Alexander (Eds), *Beliefs about Text and about Instruction with Text* (pp. 183–199). (Hillsdale, NJ: Lawrence Erlbaum).

Alvermann, D. E. & Commeyras, M. (1994b) Inviting multiple perspectives: creating opportunities for student talk about gender inequalities in texts, *Journal of Reading, 37*, pp. 566–571.

Anyon, J. (1979) Ideology and United States history textbooks, *Harvard Educational Review, 49*, pp. 361–386.

Barnett, M. A. (1986) Sex bias in the helping behavior presented in children's picture books, *Journal of Genetic Psychology, 147*, pp. 343–351.

Bazler, J. A. & SIMONIS, D. A. (1991) Are high school chemistry textbooks gender fair? *Journal of Research in Science Teaching, 28*, pp. 333–362.

Beers, B. F. (1991) *World History: Patterns of civilization* (Englewood Cliffs, NJ: Prentice Hall).

Commeyras, M. & Alvermann, D. E. (1994) Messages that high school world history textbooks convey: challenges for multicultural literacy, *The Social Studies, 85*, pp. 268–274.

Doebler, B. A. & Warnicke, R. M. (1987) Sex discrimination after death: a seventeenth-century English study, *Omega Journal of Death and Dying, 17*, pp. 309–320.

Gross, S. H. (1987) Women's history for global learning, *Social Education, 51*, pp. 194–198.

Kaestle, C. (1991) *Literacy in the United States: Readers and Reading Since 1880* (New Haven: Yale University Press).

Krieger, L. S., Jantzen, S. L. & Neill, K. (1992) *World History: Perspectives on the Past* (Lexington, MA: D.C. Heath).

McDonald, S. M. (1989) Sex bias in the representation of male and female characters in children's picture books, *Journal of Genetic Psychology, 150*, pp. 389–401.

Osler, A. (1994) Still hidden from history? the representation of women in recently published history textbooks, *Oxford Review of Education, 20*, pp. 219–235.

Perry, M., Scholl, A. H., Davis, D. F., Harris, J. G. & Von Laue, T. H. (1992) *History of the World* (Boston, MA: Houghton Mifflin).

Phillips, J. A. (1984) *Eve: the History of an Idea* (San Francisco, CA: Harper & Row).

Schibanoff, S. (1986) Taking the gold out of Egypt: the art of reading as a woman, in E. A. Flynn & P. P. Schweickart (Eds), *Gender and Reading* (Baltimore, MD: Johns Hopkins University Press).

Scott, J. W. (1993) Women's history, in L. S. Kaufmann (Ed) *American Feminist Thought: at Century's End* (Cambridge, MA: Blackwell).

Sleeter, C. E. & Grant, C. A. (1991) Race, class, gender, and disability in current textbooks, in M. W. Apple & L. K. Christian-Smith (Eds) *The Politics of the Textbook* (New York: Routledge).

Titus, J. J. (1993) Gender messages in education foundations textbooks, *Journal of Teacher Education, 44*, pp. 38–45.

Trecker, J. L. (1971) Women in U.S. history high school textbooks, *Social Education, 35*, pp. 249–260.

Wesson, M. (1994) Digging up the roots of violence, *The Women's Review of Books, 11*(6), pp. 1, 3.

Zinsser, J. (1993) *History and Feminism* (New York: Twayne).

NO

Robert Lerner, Althea Nagai, and Stanley Rothman

GENDERING AMERICAN HISTORY

The publication of federally funded national textbook standards raised a large hue and cry across the land. Lynne Cheney, the former head of the National Endowment of the Humanities, for example, bitterly criticized the tendentiousness and bias that, she argued, characterized them. The U.S. Senate voted 99–1 to repudiate the standards, with one senator voting nay because the denunciation was not, in his eyes, strong enough. Even the *New York Times* conceded that there were problems with the standards, but the editors argued that it was necessary to keep them nonetheless because they represented a good beginning.[1]

The controversy over what should be taught in American history classes reveals a deep fissure between today's dominant school of historians and mainstream public opinion. This is not entirely new. University historians have long disdained the study of great men and what one historian calls the "filiopietistic" history of popular imagination.[2]

The progressive historians of the early twentieth century who are the intellectual ancestors of today's historians of the academic Left, viewed American society quite critically.[3] Charles Beard, professor of history at Columbia University, popularized the economic determinist debunking of the Constitution and the Founding Fathers. V. L. Parrington, historian, literary critic, and author of the three-volume *Main Currents in American Thought*, romanticized American agrarianism and disdained industrial capitalism, all the while believing in an economic interpretation of American history. Despite his fear of state power, Parrington saw good use in taking the word *liberal* "and warping it to the left."[4]

Carl Becker, historian and author of the best-known study of the Declaration of Independence, believed that ultimately history is only a pack of tricks played on the dead for our own peace of mind.[5] Becker thought that history should be written in support of social reform, because American society needed less competition and more control. He contended that collectivism in modern society is in any case inevitable.[6]

By the 1950s, this liberal-progressive history dominated university departments. Samuel Elliot Morison, the then president of the American Historical Association, could thus comment that it would be almost impossible to find a good history of the United States that did not follow the Jefferson-Jackson-FDR line. Morison described himself as an adherent of that school but still warned that such imbalance in history was not good. To redress the imbalance, Morison recommended a revival of "Federalist-Whig-Republican" writing, which favored strong but limited central government, free competition, individualism, private property, American capitalism, and the inevitability of individual inequality.[7]

This did not happen.

Current historians have swung even further to the left. In his book on Paul Revere, historian David Hackett Fischer notes the prejudice of contemporary historians against "patriotic events of every kind" among multiculturalists and various proponents of political correctness. "The only creature less fashionable in academe than the stereotypical 'dead white male' is a dead white male on horseback," Fischer claims.[8] Gary Nash, professor of history at UCLA and codirector of the National Standards in History project, declared the traditional treatment of American history "white, male-oriented, [and] hero-worshiping."[9] Such treatments, says Nash, are "elitist history" and "render(s) voiceless and powerless people who deeply affected the course of our historical development, and the same can be said of the excluded, exploited, and enslaved in other societies around the world."[10]

The federally funded National Standards Project (NSP) called for the sys-tematic recasting of American history, in terms of content as well as process. "Standards for United States history," it asserted, "should reflect both the nation's diversity exemplified by race, ethnicity, social and economic status, gender, region, politics, and religion and the nation's commonalities. The contributions and struggles of specific groups and individuals should be included."[11]

The NSP divided American history into traditional historical periods such as the American Revolution, the Civil War, the period of industrialization, and World War II. Nonetheless the study notes, "In a nation of such diversity as the United States, no periodizing scheme will work for all groups. American Indian history has benchmarks and eras that sometimes but not always overlap with those of European settlers in the colonial period. Iroquois history would have to be periodized differently from Sioux or Zuni history. African American history would have its own watersheds.... So also with women's history and with Mexican American history."[12]

In *Molding the Good Citizen*, we—Robert Lerner, Althea Nagai, and Stanley Rothman—document the changes in American high-school history books and the intellectual and political movements that led to these changes.[13] We undertook a systematic quantitative content analysis of major historical figures in the most popular high-school American history textbooks from the 1940s to the 1980s.[14]

The book presents the results of a number of different content analyses. We analyze the coverage of women, minorities, the original conquest of America, the American presidency, and the so-called robber barons and capitalism.

Our findings regarding women and American history show that the history standards are largely supererogatory. The NSP contends that more attention should be paid to women, even though the books published in the 1980s already do so. In a radical break with past books, the NSP focused students' attention on women by adding more women, inserting sections on how historical events affected women, expanding coverage of significant feminist events, and reminding readers of how sexist America was.

We will now examine the multiple ways the contemporary books genderized American history. Where appropriate, we will include the most recent revision of a classic textbook, *Todd and Curti's The American Nation*, modified by a committee of historians and educationists headed by historian Paul Boyer.[15]

HOW TO GENDERIZE AMERICAN HISTORY BOOKS

First, add more women. The most visible way textbooks acceded to feminist demands was by adding more women.... The most popular textbooks of the 1940s featured roughly twenty women, and in the 1970s, fifty-five women. In the 1980s, popular books incorporated more women than the past forty years combined.

Moreover, in deference to girls' supposedly low self-esteem, women are depicted in one moral shade. The books make no negative comments about women, although there were eighty-two negative male characters in the 1980s books.

Second, put women in both words and pictures. Books have always accentuated important historical figures by using critically placed pictures to reinforce the text. Authors now consistently rely on this technique to focus attention on women. In the 1940s, only five women were important enough to rate a picture and some words. By the 1980s, the number had increased over tenfold.

A popular 1980s book included special portraits of thirty Americans who have, in the authors' view, contributed to American life. "Some are famous. Others are not."[16] The selections are biased against the native-born white Protestant male. Ten are women, seven are minority males, and eight are immigrants (two are Jewish immigrants but not identified as such). Only five are American-born white men, including one indicted for treason in North Carolina.

In the 1995 edition of *Todd and Curti's The American Nation*, the author systematically includes women in pictures in every chapter wherever possible. On the French Resistance during World War II, the caption to a picture notes, "This French girl was part of a patrol that hunted down German snipers in Paris late in 1944."[17] Later, on the Soviet front, we are taught that "more than 100,000 Soviet women earned military honors for their participation in the war. Here [in a photo on the left] two [women] snipers, E. Novikova (left) and O. Mokshina wait for hours in the snow to ambush German troops."[18]

Third, make all historic events address the woman question. The standards for American history called for systematically including the contributions of women, as a group and as individuals. Recent books already accomplish this. Take, for example, women and the military. In the 1940s, there were three important women in American wars, a figure remaining essentially unchanged until the 1980s. In the 1980s, sixteen women in

American wars were deemed important enough to include. They included such notables as Sybil Ludington, Rose O'Neal Greenhow, and Margaret Corbin. One prominent theme is how women managed farms and businesses while men went off to war.[19]

Recent books present isolated sections devoted to women within their chapters, such as "Women in the New England Colonies," "Women in the Civil War," "Women in the Industrial Revolution," "Women in World War I," "Women in World War II," and so on. Section reviews routinely have at least one question on women's contribution regarding a major historical event.

The NSP resorted to the same method. There is one question per era devoted to women. The First Era is "Three Worlds Meet," where students look at the pre-Columbus Americas, western Europe, and West Africa. According to the NSP, students should be able to look at gender roles and family organization among these cultures.[20]

In the Second Era, teachers are instructed to make students think about gender roles in the North American colonies,[21] while in the Civil War and Reconstruction section students are encouraged to examine the role of women —particularly that of Clara Barton, Belle Boyd, Rose Greenhow, and Harriet Tubman—at home and on the battlefields. Students are told to look at how war creates new roles for women and new relationships between the sexes.[22] The NSP followed a similar format for other periods.

Fourth, expand coverage of feminist events. Recent books expand discussions of feminists' favorite events: the early women's rights movements and Seneca Falls, the Nineteenth Amendment, and of course, the contemporary feminist movement. Before the 1980s, fewer than ten women associated with the feminist movement were deemed significant enough to feature in these books. During the 1980s, the number jumps to thirty-five, and almost all of them are positively portrayed. In contrast, women not associated with the women's rights movement are portrayed positively less than half the time in the 1980s books.

The 1980s books transform men who are considered to have negative attitudes toward women's rights into the real villains of American history. Half the men are described in negative terms, either some of the time or totally. Only 14 percent of men having nothing to do with women's rights receive either negative or mixed ratings.

The later books also link the abolitionist movement with the early feminists and proportionately downplay white males such as William Lloyd Garrison. The 1995 edition of *Todd and Curti's The American Nation* highlights the Grimke sisters but focuses on their work for women's rights rather than against slavery. Past editions of the book focused on their abolitionism.[23]

The suffragist movement also receives more attention over time. The 1960s edition by Todd and Curti briefly mentions the women activists in the larger context of expanding opportunities for women. It later describes women's suffrage in a single paragraph as one part of progressive activism.[24] The 1995 edition keeps this point but gives it considerably more space. The new book also adds that progressivism was an attempt by the conservative, white middle class to hold on to political and economic power.[25]

Recent textbooks naturally treat the ERA affirmatively. They briefly note its failure to pass and its lack of support among all women, but they still speak favorably of ERA proponents. Opponents are either ignored, as in the 1980s books, or mentioned for their most strident claims, such as the claim by some that the ERA amendment would lead to common public restrooms for men and women.[26]

The books treat the National Organization for Women (NOW) positively and consider its founding to be an important event. NOW's portrait ignores the prominent place of lesbian rights in modern feminist ideology. The books also ignore the results of public opinion surveys. These show that most women do not call themselves feminists and do not like to be called such.[27]

The negligible coverage of contemporary groups opposing feminism extends into the past. The books slight prominent women of the past who were not associated with earlier feminist movements. Thus, Alice Roosevelt Longworth and Clare Booth Luce receive little coverage.

Fifth, remind readers that America is a sexist society. No properly modern textbook would be complete without frequent reminders of America's sexist past. Current books are replete with such reminders. They assert without argument or evidence that the Declaration of Independence did not apply to women or blacks, because people at the time would not have regarded blacks, Indians, or women as having any rights.[28] No real effort is made to place American history in a comparative perspective by comparing the American record with that of other societies.

It is thus clear that the genderizing of books results in the systematic insertion of minor and inconsequential women characters, presented in one basic moral shade and with little ambivalence or complexity. Women active in the rights movement are always portrayed sympathetically, while the arguments and actions of their opponents are rarely taken seriously. The books are liberally sprinkled with ad hoc statements regarding prejudice and discrimination facing American women.

These books did not get this way by accident. They were created with the help of the federal government, paid for by the American taxpayer, promulgated by feminist and education interest groups, and supported wholeheartedly by textbook publishers.

ALTERING THE AMERICAN HISTORY CURRICULUM

An unintended consequence of the Cold War was federal government involvement in children's education, something heretofore left entirely to the states.[29] People of all ideological persuasions believed that increasing federal government control over science education was a price worth paying in the struggle against communism.

Congress passed the National Defense Education Act in 1958 to support the study of science, mathematics, and foreign languages. Groups of mathematicians and scientists joined together to develop new materials in mathematics and physics at the high school level. The major philanthropic foundations (Ford, Carnegie, Rockefeller) funded various programs seeking to improve public education. The Carnegie Corporation supported the famous Conant Report on public education, while the Ford Foundation funded model programs for education reform in big cities. The National Science Foundation created standards for the new physics, the new chemistry, the new biology, the new math, and the new social studies. School districts all over the nation experimented with new curricula and professional training and staffing, with significant foundation and government support.

Two decades of government and foundation support of national curricula, plus the radical egalitarian politics of the late 1960s, made possible the politicizing of history textbooks at a national level. Until the 1970s, most textbook controversies were local: between parents and the school system, between parent groups and state adoption boards, or between parent groups and publishers. Even today, media portrayals of textbook fights follow a standard script, dating as far back as H.L. Mencken's dispatches on the Scopes trials in 1925. Those who object to textbook content on religious grounds are routinely accused of assaulting free speech and the separation of church and state.

The feminist elite, however, have long demanded educational reform and have lobbied the federal government extensively toward this end.[30] In 1973, NOW demanded textbook publishers take action to reduce gender stereotypes. In 1974, NOW, the League of Women Voters, and other political groups formed the National Coalition for Women and Girls in Education, in support of a Women's Educational Equity Act (WEEA), claiming a need for federal assistance in combating sexism in the American classroom. The American Federation of Teachers (AFT) presented materials in support of the bill. The National Education Association

(NEA) created an "Edu-Pak" on gender stereotyping. The American Personnel and Guidance Association, the National Foundation for the Improvement of Education, and the National Council for Social Studies all came out in favor of eliminating supposed gender bias in education.

The political elite in the 1960s and '70s took for granted the expansionist role of the federal government, so there was little opposition to spending federal dollars to combat classroom sexism. Sen. Walter Mondale (D-Minnesota) introduced the WEEA legislation in Congress. With no opposition and little publicity, the bill became law in 1974. Through the WEEA, the federal government funded curricula for solving cutting-edge, feminist-defined problems of sexism.

The WEEA was qualitatively different from other government programs involved in school curricula. Other projects, such as the remolding of American science programs, had political implications but were not explicitly set up to change the values and attitudes of future citizens. The WEEA, however, sought to do just that.[31]

Educational interest groups also attacked the sexism problem with zeal. As early as 1975, the National Council for Social Studies devoted an entire issue of its official journal to sex balancing in social studies.[32] Edited by the head of their Committee on Social Justice for Women, the issue explicitly calls for consciousness raising and working for changing sexism in schools.

The education elite, of course, assumed that sexism was a problem in schools and that a program should be implemented from the top down. There was no public response and no local input. In the eyes of the activists, sexism was so pervasive and nonfeminist consciousness so rife that the process had to be controlled from the top down. Local schools and parents were precisely the reactionary forces that had to be defeated, not included.

Textbook publishers were eager to follow suit. As part of the liberal cultural elite, publishers had no problem quickly issuing textbook guidelines on dealing with gender issues. The problem, according to one publisher, was not that there weren't women in books; the problem was that they were mothers and sisters.[33] Scott-Foresman and Company, a major textbook publisher, testified in favor of the WEEA, pointing out how the company had already had in place guidelines for dealing with such issues since 1972. The spokesperson proudly noted that 80 percent of the editors at Scott-Foresman were women, so the guidelines were well received.[34]

By 1978, the NEA claimed victory, noting that all major publishers had adopted these gender guidelines.[35] Nor has this changed. As the recent well-known report by the American Association of University Women proudly points out, all textbook publishers use these guidelines for their books.[36]

And publishers adhere rigorously to these guidelines. One Holt, Rinehart, and Winston reading series was rejected because while the ratio of female to male characters was the politically correct 1:1, the counters forgot to include male and female animal characters in their tally. Another story was added, despite the editor's conclusion that it was "not great literature," because the leading character was female and other characters had Spanish surnames.[37]

WHAT DIFFERENCE DOES IT MAKE?

The ultimate question, nevertheless, is what difference it makes. Even though textbooks follow the feminist agenda, how much do teachers rely on these books, and, moreover, have not surveys shown that American students know little about American history anyway?

Textbooks are in fact the most widely used instructional medium in high-school history classes. Teachers not only rely heavily on books but generally believe in their accuracy. Most students will learn about American society and government through these classes. It is the only social studies course mandated by most states and local districts.[38] Few schools teach civics classes, and where it is taught, it is almost never required. Almost all students open their history textbooks at least twice a week, and 60 percent claim to read them every day.

The results of such genderized books can be seen in survey data. In a national study of what seventeen-year-olds know,[39] more can identify Harriet Tubman than can identify Winston Churchill or Joseph Stalin. More know that Tubman ran the Underground Railroad to free slaves than know that George Washington commanded the American army during the Revolution, or that Lincoln wrote the Emancipation Proclamation. Most teenagers know that women worked in the factories during World War II and that Susan B. Anthony was a leader for women's rights. A bare majority know about the Great Depression.

The lopsided nature of student knowledge is also found in a recent poll of Ivy League undergraduates. Ninety percent correctly identified Rosa Parks, while only 25 percent knew who wrote "government of the people, by the people, and for the people." Only 18 percent could name even a single Supreme Court justice, not even Clarence Thomas.[40]

PC [politically correct] textbooks erode respect for America's past. When the essentially feminist subtext becomes clear, many come to consider the texts as propaganda, not fact. History written to manipulate feelings ultimately leads to a rejection of all messages the books are trying to convey. The genderizing of books ultimately leads to a decline in respect for the discipline of history and contributes to a greater cynicism about learning more generally.

The charge that American society, then and now, is a sexist society erodes the legitimacy of our institutions. To "know" that the Declaration of Independence was written only for white males diminishes the document, its author, and the nation founded according to its principles.

Tocqueville wrote that historians are prone to ignore great men and assume a sort of determinism, or even fatalism, in democratic societies. They ignore men's character and will and attribute larger causes for even the smallest particular events.[41]

The vices of modern historians are thus especially apparent. American history is presented through the politically correct pantheon of race, class, and gender. The National Standards Project codified what has long been happening in the textbooks themselves. We have come to attribute all events to great causes and general trends, without any role given to independent free will and individual character. We have come to denigrate individual action and deny the influence of great individuals.

In their drift toward group determinism, contemporary historians remove from individuals the capacity to modify their own lot. If aristocratic historians taught only how to command, as Tocqueville wrote, those of our own time teach only how to obey "We need to raise men's souls, not complete their prostration."[42]

NOTES

1. "Maligning the History Standards," *New York Times*, 11 Feb. 1995, A–18.
2. David Hackett Fischer, *Paul Revere's Ride* (New York: Oxford University Press, 1994), iv.
3. Richard Hofstadter, *The Progressive Historians* (Chicago: University of Chicago Press, 1970); Gary Nash, "History for All People," in *Historical Literacy: The Case for History in American Education*, ed. Paul Gagnon and the Bradley Commission on History in Schools (New York: Macmillan, 1989), 234–48.
4. Hofstadter, *The Progressive Historians*, 430.
5. Carl Becker, *Everyman His Own Historian* (Chicago: Quadrangle Books, 1935), 253.
6. Becker, *Everyman*, 91–100.
7. Samuel Elliot Morison, "Faith of a Historian," *American Historical Review* 56:2 (January 1951): 261–75.
8. Fischer, *Paul Revere's Ride*, xiv.
9. Gary Nash, "History for a Democratic Society: The Work of All the People," in *Historical Literacy: The Case for History in American Education*, ed. Paul Gagnon and the Bradley Commission on History in Schools (New York: Macmillan, 1989), 241.
10. Nash, "History for a Democratic Society," 241.
11. Charlotte Crabtree and Gary Nash, *National Standards: United States History—Exploring the American Experience* (Los Angeles: National Center for History in the Schools, University of California, Los Angeles), 3.
12. Crabtree and Nash, *National Standards*, 4.
13. The study was sponsored by Smith College's Center for the Study of Social and Political Change, directed by Stanley Rothman.
14. Historical figures were included in the coding if they met certain criteria. They had to be identifiable in a picture, be the major subject of a paragraph, or occupy at least one column inch. For more details on the process of textbook selection and content coding, see Appendix 1 and 2 of Robert Lerner, Althea Nagai, and Stanley Rothman, *Molding the Good Citizen: The Politics of High School History Texts* (New York: Praeger Press, 1995).
15. Paul Boyer, *Todd and Curti's The American Nation* (Austin, Tex.: Holt, Rinehart and Winston, 1995).

16. Leonard Wood, Ralph Gabriel, and Edward Biller, *America, Its People and Values* (New York: Harcourt, Brace and Jovanovich, 1985), xxiv.

17. Boyer, *Todd and Curti's*, 737.

18. Boyer, *Todd and Curti's*, 749.

19. For example, see Daniel Boorstin and Brooks Kelley, *A History of the United States* (Lexington, Mass.: Ginn and Company 1986), 89. Julia Ward Howe is an exception that proves the rule about the antipatriotic bias found among historians. In the contemporary books she is ignored, even though she was a suffragist and abolitionist, and despite the popularity even to this day of the "Battle Hymn of the Republic." Perhaps it has something to do with the song's themes of God, liberty, and country.

20. Crabtree and Nash, *National Standards*, page 40 for Native Americans, page 43 on West Europeans, and page 44 on West African gender roles, family organization, religion, and relationship to the environment.

21. Crabtree and Nash, *National Standards*, 54.

22. Crabtree and Nash, *National Standards*, 126–27.

23. Boyer, *Todd and Curti's*, 297–98; Todd and Curti, *Rise of the American Nation* (New York: Harcourt, Brace and World, 1966), 341.

24. Todd and Curti, *Rise of the American Nation*, 504, 524.

25. Boyer, *Todd and Curti's*, 553.

26. Boyer, *Todd and Curti's*, 922.

27. Karlyn Keene, "Exploring American Society: Feminism vs. Women's Rights," *Public Perspective* (November–December 1991): 3.

28. Wood, *America, Its People, and Values*, 152; Boyer, *Todd and Curti's*, 118.

29. Diane Ravitch, *The Touble Crusade: American Education 1945–1980* (New York: Basic Books, 1983), 228–33.

30. The following account is taken from the *New York Times* (19 Feb. 1973, 23 March 1973, 12 June 1973, 5 Feb. 1974) as well as Ravitch, *The Troubled Crusade*, 298–300.

31. Title IX of the Education Act of 1972 banned sex discrimination in federally supported activity. Title IX said nothing about the content of the curriculum, however.

32. Carole Hahn, "Eliminating Sexism from the Schools: Implementing Change: A Special Section," *Social Education* 39 (1975): 133–47.

33. *New York Times*, 30 Apr. 1978.

34. U.S. Congress, *Women's Educational Equity Act of 1973: Hearings before the Subcommittee on Education of the Committee on Labor and Public Welfare*, 93rd Congress, 1st session (1973), 488–91.

35. *New York Times*, 30 Apr. 1978.

36. American Association of University Women, *Shortchanging Girls, Shortchanging America* (Washington, D.C.: American Association of University Women, 1991).

37. Stephen Bates, *Battleground: One Mother's Crusade, the Religious Right, and the Struggle for Control of Our Classrooms* (New York: Simon and Schuster, 1993), 216–23.

38. Diane Ravitch and Chester Finn, Jr., *What Do Our Seventeen-Year-Olds Know?* (New York: Harper and Row, 1987), 8.

39. Ravitch and Finn, *What Do Our Seventeen-Year-Olds Know?*, 263–77.

40. *U.S. News and World Report*, 12 Apr. 1993, 63.

41. Alex de Tocqueville, *Democracy in America*, ed. J. P. Mayer, trans. George Lawrence (Garden City, N.Y.: Anchor Books, 1969), 493–96.

42. Tocqueville, *Democracy in America*, 496.

POSTSCRIPT

Should Women Receive More Coverage in History Textbooks?

Linda K. Kerber and Jane Sherron De Hart, in *Women's America: Refocusing the Past* (Oxford University Press, 1995), assert that one of the most effective ways in which dominant groups maintain their power is by depriving the people they dominate of the knowledge of their own history. They believe that the historical experience of the two sexes, for all their similarities, are profoundly different. Along with Commeyras and Alvermann, Kerber and De Hart believe that it is important to become aware of women's history.

Commeyras and Alvermann state, "Feminist historians have been engaged in rewriting history." What does that mean to you? How is it possible to rewrite history? In doing so, is it likely that (as Lerner, Nagai, and Rothman suggest) feminists are rewriting history in ways that support their causes and their politics? Feminists and others believe that it is important to understand economic and social relationships that benefit one sex at the expense of another. Are history textbooks appropriate venues for promoting such a cause? Annette Van Howe founded the women's history coalition in 1968. In "Remembering the Women of History," *The Humanist* (September/October 1996), she reviews a 1979 survey conducted by the National Organization for Women (NOW) and finds that for every 700 pages about men in U.S. history texts, there were only 14 pages about women. Gerda Lerner, author of *The Creation of Patriarchy* (Oxford University Press, 1986) and *The Creation of Feminist Consciousness: From the Middle Ages to Eighteen-Seventy* (Oxford University Press, 1993), has challenged many traditional historical concepts, such as the emergence of slavery, to construct new definitions of class and thereby reveal the meanings of customary ideas and metaphors about women.

Walter A. McDougall, in "What Johnny Still Won't Know About History," *Commentary* (July 1996), notes that the National Standards Project (NSP), which presented a series of "lessons" on how history should be taught in schools, provoked scores of op-eds and letters and a 99–1 vote in the U.S. Senate condemning the NSP as anti-American. Lynne Cheney, originally head of the National Endowment for the Humanities and responsible for assigning the task, later denounced the two volumes of standards with their outlines for teaching as "a brazen exercise in political correctness." The standards were revised following severe criticism, resulting in the downplay of the judgmentalism that pervaded the original world history standards and a watering down of the language that made the struggle by women and minorities against the white patriarchy seem to be the central theme of American history.

ISSUE 7

Do Women Still Face Discrimination in the Workplace?

YES: Amy Oakes Wren, Roland E. Kidwell, Jr., and Linda Achey Kidwell, from "Managing Pregnancy in the Workplace," *Business Horizons* (November–December 1996)

NO: William A. Henry III, from *In Defense of Elitism* (Doubleday, 1994)

ISSUE SUMMARY

YES: Amy Oakes Wren, an assistant professor of business law, Roland E. Kidwell, Jr., an assistant professor of management, and Linda Achey Kidwell, an assistant professor of accounting, argue that workplace discrimination against pregnant women continues to be rampant in spite of pregnancy discrimination laws.

NO: The late cultural critic William A. Henry III states that while women are paid less and are disproportionately grouped on lower rungs of the economic ladder, prejudice is not to blame. He asserts that most women are less committed to their careers, as proven by their willingness to stay home or otherwise sacrifice work for family.

In "Why Do So Many Employers Put Part-Time People on the Slow Track?" *Glamour* (July 1997), the writer says she redesigned her job as a marketing director so that her work could be done competently in three, rather than five, days a week. This working mother wanted to have more time with her three children and believed that she could outperform others in terms of quality, even while putting in fewer hours. Subsequently, she was ridiculed when she asked for a promotion, left out of the communication network, passed over for better assignments, not taken seriously by her staff, and subjected to diminished performance evaluations. For most women who choose it, part-time work involves serious trade-offs, she says, including being viewed as unambitious and not promotable.

Despite gains made in the 1960s and 1970s, women are still treated as second-class citizens in the workplace, according to some writers. Although women have made strides in obtaining equality in education, they graduate into a workplace that pays them an average of 25 percent less than men for similar work. Studies have found that factors such as experience, education, and hours worked account for no more than 50 to 60 percent of all sex-based disparities. Women also continue to fill the majority of low-status positions.

Gender segregation in the labor force is pronounced, and, according to some writers, about 80 percent of female workers remain in traditional female occupations such as teaching, sales, waitressing, and clerical assistance. Sixty-two percent of women make only minimum wage, and two-thirds of America's poor adults are women. Fewer than 0.5 percent of top corporate managers and fewer than 8 percent of federal and state judges are women. Research suggests that while charges by women of workplace discrimination have risen considerably, monetary awards to plaintiffs decreased by two-thirds in the 1980s and in the first half of the 1990s.

However, many policy analysts maintain that it is not lack of opportunity or sex discrimination that keeps women from joining the ranks of men in terms of status and income. Rather, it is the choices women make that place them in lower-paying, lower-status occupations. These choices involve the types of jobs women select, childbearing and family issues, desired work hours, and level of time and energy commitment. One researcher notes that women tend to avoid the dirtiest, most dangerous, and most stressful occupations as well as positions with extended or inconvenient hours.

Furthermore, many commentators do not see women as having the same capabilities or the same priorities as men. Sociobiologists argue that the male drive for power and control of resources is partly the result of women's preference for successful, ambitious mates. Because women depend on men to support them during periods of pregnancy and breast-feeding, natural selection has been said to favor male development of characteristics that account for contemporary gender roles and their manifestation in the work setting. These characteristics include physical strength, aggression, and promiscuity in men and caretaking and fidelity in women.

Some critics say that women rarely encounter workplace discrimination and that they instead benefit from preferential treatment. In recent studies, only 15 to 25 percent of women reported experiencing workplace discrimination, and only about one-third perceived it as a major factor holding women workers back. Another argument suggests that gender discrimination cannot survive in a competitive market. By this logic, it is inefficient to exclude workers because of their sex, so it follows that if women are excluded, they must not be competent. Moreover, critics believe that society has done as much as it can to help women at the level of public policy. We now have laws requiring equal employment opportunities, equal pay, family leave policies, and tax-subsidized child-care assistance.

In the selections that follow, Amy Oakes Wren, Roland E. Kidwell, Jr., and Linda Achey Kidwell assert that many of the laws designed to ensure equitable treatment are ignored by employers and unenforced by the government. They elaborate on this point in their discussion of pregnancy discrimination. William A. Henry III argues that women have a lower rank and lower pay in the workplace because they have a general lack of career commitment, alternative priorities, and passive personalities.

YES

Amy Oakes Wren,
Roland E. Kidwell, Jr., and
Linda Achey Kidwell

MANAGING PREGNANCY IN THE WORKPLACE

Two months into her first pregnancy, Angela Anderson was called into the office of the president of a major Louisiana bank. The president was very complimentary of Angela's work in one of the bank's branch offices, where she had served as a teller for almost two years. As a result, he told her, he had decided to promote her. She would become his personal assistant, a position sought by many of the bank's employees.

In her excitement, Angela told him that the promotion was the second most exciting thing to happen to her that week. When her boss asked about the first exciting event, Angela said she had just discovered she was going to have a baby. The president's demeanor suddenly changed. He said he did not think he could rely on a pregnant personal assistant, and he was withdrawing the promotion. Devastated, Angela left the office and returned to her position as teller.

Although many managers and employees might be amazed at this blatant bias against Angela, her case is a fairly typical example of pregnancy discrimination. Most such actions toward pregnant women result from outdated beliefs that pregnant women are unproductive, sickly, and delicate. Yet these mistakes have cost employers millions of dollars because pregnancy discrimination violates federal laws.

Despite the laws designed to protect workers who become pregnant, female employees increasingly believe they are unfairly denied promotions, proper medical leave, and even their jobs because they have become pregnant, or because they *might* become pregnant. In fact, the Equal Employment Opportunity Commission reported that pregnancy discrimination complaints nationwide have increased 40 percent in the first half of this decade, from 3,000 in 1991 to 4,191 in 1995.

The issue of pregnancy discrimination has become even more focused as women of child-bearing age enter the work force at higher rates and corporate downsizing forces many managers to seek higher levels of productivity among remaining employees. Unfortunately, some managers have taken unlawful actions against pregnant workers because they perceive them as less productive, absent more often, or unable to perform their jobs. With two-thirds of the net additions to the U.S. work force in the remainder of the 1990s projected to be female, the treatment of women at work is a crucial issue for organizations.

FEDERAL LAWS RELATED TO PREGNANCY DISCRIMINATION

Three federal laws designed to protect workers relate to pregnancy: Title VII of the 1964 Civil Rights Act, the Pregnancy Discrimination Act of 1978, and the Family and Medical Leave Act of 1993. In addition, the Americans With Disabilities Act, or ADA, may provide some protection for pregnant employees.

The 1964 Civil Rights Act. Title VII of the 1964 Civil Rights Act prohibits employers of 15 or more employees from refusing to hire or discharge any person or otherwise discriminate in terms, conditions, or privileges of employment based on an individual's sex. Originally, the U.S. Supreme Court held in *General Electric v. Gilbert* that discrimination based on pregnancy was not the same as discrimination based on sex. In the Gilbert case, decided in 1976, GE provided a disability plan to all employees disabled because of sickness or accident, but excluded all disabilities from pregnancy.

The reasoning used in not finding discrimination was that the plan provided benefits to both men and non-pregnant women. The Court stated the disability plan was simply an insurance policy that covered some risks and not others. Pregnancy was a condition that was not covered. In addition, the Court said, "There is no risk from which men are protected and women are not. Likewise, there is no risk from which women are protected and men are not."

Pregnancy Discrimination Act of 1978. In the aftermath of the Gilbert case and others like it, Congress amended Title VII of the 1964 Civil Rights Act by passing the Pregnancy Discrimination Act (PDA) of 1978. This act essentially overruled the Gilbert decision by making it clear that all employers must treat pregnant and nonpregnant employees in the same manner. As a result, pregnant women must be given the same benefits as men and nonpregnant women. The act states that:

> The terms "because of sex" or "on the basis of sex" include, but are not limited to, because of or on the basis of pregnancy, childbirth, or related medical condition; and women affected by pregnancy, childbirth, or related medical condition, shall be treated the same for all employment-related purposes, including the receipt of benefits under fringe benefit programs, as other persons not so affected but similar in their ability or inability to work.

The Family and Medical Leave Act. The Family and Medical Leave Act (FMLA), which became law in 1993, is one of the most important federal laws dealing with pregnancy, childbirth, adoption, and placement for foster care for both men and women. Under the FMLA, men and women can take 12 weeks of unpaid leave per year for the birth or adoption of a child, placement for foster care, the care of a sick child, or chronic illnesses such as morning sickness. To be covered, the person must work for a company that employs at least 50 people within a 75-mile radius and must have worked there for at least 12 months or 1,250 hours. The employee must give 30 days' notice of an intent to take leave when possible. An example of this would be giving notice of intent to take leave 30 days before the due date of a birth.

Recent Court Rulings Provide Some Guidance

There are at least a dozen ways employers can illegally discriminate based on pregnancy. [The box entitled "Practices That Could Lead to a Pregnancy Discrimination Lawsuit"] summarizes these instances. Examples range from intentionally eliminating pregnant applicants from the labor pool to unintentionally discriminating against a pregnant woman because of an apparently sex-neutral insurance policy. Each of the following guidelines, based on the latest court rulings, reveals just how far application of the pregnancy discrimination laws can go:

1. An employer may not refuse to hire, refuse to promote, or fire a pregnant employee because of her pregnancy. On top of that, an employee does not have to prove that pregnancy was the only reason for her employer's decision not to hire, to fire, or not to promote her. Instead, she need only show it was considered in the decision.

2. An employer must provide the same benefits to all employees regardless of whether they are pregnant. However, an employer is not required to provide more benefits or special treatment for pregnant employees. Full benefits must be given to spouses of male employees if full coverage is given to spouses of female employees. This was not the situation recently at Newport News Shipbuilding and Dry Dock Company. The firm provided full benefits to the spouses of female employees but provided only limited benefits for pregnancy to spouses of male employees. In the ensuring court case, the U.S. Supreme Court ruled the company's plan discriminatory because protection given to married male employees was not as good as protection given to married female employees.

3. An employer may not refuse to provide light duty for a pregnant employee while doing so for a non-pregnant one. When Charlotte Adams, a patrol officer for the city of North Little Rock, Arkansas, was six months pregnant, she told her supervisor she needed to be placed on light work duty because of her doctor's recommendation. The North Little Rock Police Department denied Adams' request because of a recently implemented leave policy that had been passed in response to a "rash of pregnancies" in the department. According to the policy, employees who suffered non-work-related injuries or illness that included pregnancy, miscarriage, abortion, childbirth, and recovery thereof could not take light duty but must instead use accumulated sick leave, then vacation leave, and finally unpaid leave of absence. Adams continued to work as long as she could and then took an unpaid leave of absence for 26 weeks. Upon returning to the police department, she discovered she had been removed from the patrol officers' roster. At the same time Adams had requested and was denied light duty, the North Little Rock Police Department had given light duty to a male officer who had a non-work-related disability. This constituted unlawful discrimination.

PRACTICES THAT COULD LEAD TO A PREGNANCY DISCRIMINATION LAWSUIT

- Refusing to hire or promote a pregnant employee because of her pregnancy.
- Threatening to fire or terminating an employee because of her pregnancy or potential pregnancy.
- Failing to provide the same benefits to all employees regardless of pregnancy.
- Refusing to provide light duty for a pregnant employee while providing light duty for a non-pregnant employee.
- Discriminating against an employee based on a potential or intended pregnancy.
- Discriminating against an employee because she has had or is considering an abortion.
- Refusing to allow a pregnant employee to continue work if she is physically capable of continuing to work and wishes to do so.
- Evaluating a pregnant employee differently from a non-pregnant one when the employer has unilaterally lessened her work load in response to the pregnancy.
- Excluding or permitting exclusion of a pregnant employee from the normal office culture and social circles.
- Reassigning an employee to a lower-paying job because she is pregnant, or changing her job description and then eliminating the new job in restructuring.
- Discriminating against a male employee for his wife's pregnancy or pregnancy-related condition.
- Requiring a note from a pregnant woman's doctor concerning her ability to continue to work if the employer does not require a similar note from doctors of other employees with short-term disabilities.

By contrast, in *Elie v. K mart*, a U.S. district court in Louisiana dismissed a claim against K mart in which the plaintiff did not prove she had been treated differently from non-pregnant employees. The woman, who was 19 weeks pregnant, requested reassignment to a job not requiring heavy lifting. She refused the evening and weekend hours her new assignment required because they were incompatible with her child care needs, and she was subsequently fired. The court ruled that the plaintiff had failed to prove that other employees who objected to new assignments based on medical reasons had not been terminated. The statutes, it said, "protect against employment decisions which are unlawfully motivated by an intent to discriminate. The law does not guarantee that pregnant employees will not suffer any adverse employment decisions."

4. An employer may not discriminate against an employee based on potential or intended pregnancy. This occurred in the case of Charlene Pacourek, who went to work for Inland Steel in 1974. In 1986, Pacourek, who was infertile because of a disability called esophageal reflux, began an experimental in-vitro fertilization treatment to become pregnant. Until that time, she had worked in good standing for the company and had been promoted several times. When she informed her employer she intended to continue the treatments and become pregnant, problems began at work, resulting in Pacourek's termination in 1993. Among other things, evidence indicated that company managers attempted to apply a sick leave policy to Pacourek that they did not apply to other employees; supervisors verbally abused her by expressing doubts about her ability to conceive and be a working mother; and managers told her that her condition was a problem and eventually placed her on probation. A U.S. district court found that the PDA had been violated because the employer's actions discriminated against an employee with a "pregnancy-related condition" (infertility). The court stated that the PDA

... does not affirmatively instruct employers to treat pregnancy, childbirth, or related medical condition(s) in any particular way; rather, it instructs employers to treat those things in a neutral way....

The basic theory of the PDA may be simply stated: only women can become pregnant; stereotypes based on pregnancy and related medical conditions have been a barrier to women's economic advancement; and classification based on pregnancy and related medical conditions are never gender neutral. Discrimination against an employee because she intends to, is trying to, or simply has the potential to become pregnant is therefore illegal discrimination.

5. An employer may not discriminate against an employee because the latter has had or is considering an abortion. Kim Turic, a 17-year-old mother of one, was employed at a Holiday Inn to bus tables in the restaurant and as a member of the room service staff. Upon learning she was pregnant, Turic informed her supervisor that she was considering an abortion. When the other employees heard the news, the ensuing discussions resulted in an "uproar" and conflicts between Turic and the staff. Several days later, Turic was terminated under the pretext of poor work performance. In *Turic v. Holland Hospitality Inc.*, a Michigan court found that Turic was fired because she was considering an abortion, and her dismissal violated the PDA. In its finding, the court deferred to EEOC guidelines:

The basic principle of the PDA is that women affected by pregnancy and related medical conditions must be treated the same as other applicants and employees on the basis of their ability or inability to work. A woman is therefore protected against such practices as being fired ... merely because she is pregnant or has had an abortion.

6. An employer will also violate Title VII, and possibly the PDA and the ADA, by refusing to allow a pregnant employee to continue work if she is physically capable and wishes to do so.

7. An employer may not evaluate a pregnant employee differently from a non-pregnant one, especially when the employer has unilaterally lessened the

employee's work load in response to the pregnancy.

8. An employer may not exclude or permit the exclusion of a pregnant employee from the normal office culture and social circles because this may cause her to become, as Bennett-Alexander & Pincus (1995) have stated, "less aware of matters of importance to the office or current projects."

9. An employer may not threaten to fire or terminate an employee because of her pregnancy or potential pregnancy. In 1993, a jury awarded $2.7 million to Lana Ambruster because she had been fired from her job upon revealing that she was pregnant. Ambruster was a claims adjuster for California Casualty Insurance Company when she became pregnant. On several occasions her boss had threatened to fire anyone who became pregnant because the firm had no budget for maternity leave. Although the boss claimed during the trial that such statements were made in jest and that the firing was for poor job performance, the jury found that the firm's actions violated pregnancy discrimination laws.

10. An employer may not reassign an employee to a lower-paying job because of her pregnancy. Nor may an employer change a worker's job description and then eliminate the new job in restructuring. Both of these actions violate the PDA. For example, Sundstrand Corporation recently settled a federal lawsuit brought by the EEOC on behalf of present and former Sundstrand workers that alleged such conduct. In June 1995, the company agreed to open jobs to pregnant workers that had originally been off limits to them.

11. Just as an employer cannot discriminate against a woman for pregnancy or a pregnancy-related condition, it cannot discriminate against a man for the same reasons. In the late 1980s, after Judy Nicols announced she was pregnant, she and her husband Scott were subsequently fired from the company where they worked. Managers explained that the dismissals were caused by declining sales and company cash flow problems. But the Nicolses filed complaints with the EEOC alleging pregnancy discrimination. A federal judge in Virginia agreed that the couple was protected by the PDA and could claim discrimination, so the company settled the lawsuit out of court for an undisclosed sum. The judge's ruling indicates that a man can sue for discrimination based on his wife's pregnancy. In states where martial status—or lack thereof—is protected under discrimination laws, this ruling may apply to pregnancies involving unmarried couples.

12. An employer may not require a note from a pregnant woman's doctor concerning her ability to continue work if the employer does not require similar notes from doctors of other employees with short-term disabilities. Such an action violates the PDA because the employer would be treating a pregnant person differently than a non-pregnant person. The PDA does not require an employer to offer maternity leave or take other steps to make it easier for pregnant women to work. However, it does require that the employer ignore the pregnancy and treat both pregnant and other employees in the same manner.

Pregnant Employees and the ADA

The Americans with Disabilities Act is another important law that may affect the rights of pregnant employees. This Act, which applies to companies that employ 15 or more people, requires reasonable accommodations for disabled employees or job applicants if they are qualified for a position. It also requires that an employer disregard a person's disability.

The EEOC recently published its "Compliance Manual Section 902: Definition of the Term Disability" specifically excluding pregnancy as a disability. However, this does not mean the decision is necessarily binding on the courts. Although courts generally give great weight to EEOC regulations, they have been known to disregard these guidelines if they are believed inconsistent with Congress's intent or are unreasonable.

One case illustrates the right of the court to rule in opposition to the EEOC Compliance Manual. In *Chapsky v. Baxter Healthcare*, decided in 1995, the plaintiff was fired for a single violation of the company's no-smoking policy the day before she was scheduled to undergo surgery for pregnancy complications. A male employee had received progressive disciplinary action, including 23 warnings and probation, before being discharged for violating the policy. Chapsky had consistently received outstanding ratings by her supervisors until her dismissal. So the court found that sex discrimination had occurred. Notably with regard to ADA applications, the court also ruled that she had established a case for disability discrimination, recognizing pregnancy as a disability under the ADA.

The final status of this case is unclear. The court based the disability finding on *Pacourek v. Inland Steel*, which relied on the PDA, not the ADA, and did not address pregnancy from the standpoint of a disability. However, the most recent U.S. district court rulings have refused to extend the ADA to pregnancy and related temporary medical conditions. These courts based their findings on the EEOC regulations stating that conditions such as pregnancy that are not the result of a physiological disorder should not be considered impairments, and that temporary, non-chronic conditions with little or no long-term impact are usually not disabilities. In these rulings—*Johnson v. A. P. Products, Ltd.*, for example, decided in August 1996—the courts noted that plaintiffs' complaints of employment discrimination based on pregnancy are already specifically covered by Title VII in the PDA.

Even in light of these rulings and the EEOC determination that pregnancy is not a disability, EEOC guidelines recognize that pregnancy complications may be a disability under the ADA. As a result, gestational diabetes, toxemia, chronic morning sickness, and other potential long-term complications of pregnancy may require that an employer reasonably accommodate a pregnant employee. For example, she may have to take light or desk duty if she has high blood pressure. If the accommodation is reasonable and does not impose an undue hardship on the employer, the ADA may require such an action on the part of the employer.

IMPLICATIONS FOR MANAGERS

The laws and court cases reviewed here indicate that some managers have engaged in and been held liable for actions that discriminate against pregnant women, women who have announced an intention to become pregnant, women who might become pregnant, women who have had an abortion or plan to have an abortion, and even men whose wives have become pregnant. Companies can avoid the difficulties and costs associated with improper and illegal treatment of female employees by following the suggestions listed in [the box entitled

"Guidelines for Organizations"]. Most large corporations have taken the following steps to avoid being held liable for discrimination; smaller companies may want to consider similar actions.

Employment policies. One important step for companies is establishing, amending, and enforcing policies to meet the legal requirements outlined earlier. Policies should reflect the firm's position on other temporary physical conditions involving its employees, not just pregnancy. Evenhanded treatment of pregnant and non-pregnant employees is crucial to the legality of such policies. It is important not to restrict employees from working as long as they are able to perform job duties effectively and safely. Workers and their doctors should be encouraged to notify the employer in writing when the job cannot be performed without risking health and safety; again, this applies to *all* employees, not just those who are pregnant.

Some organizations, such as police departments, trucking companies, and airlines, have different requirements regarding public health and safety. In these cases, the employer should provide alternative light duty job assignments for pregnant workers if similar assignments are provided for other employees who are unable to perform their jobs because of a temporary physical condition. The key is a policy that does not demote, harm, or malign an employee because of pregnancy.

Employee selection. It is important to ensure that interviewers do not ask questions of applicants regarding their families or their intentions to have a family. Focusing the questions around the duties and requirements of the job on the employment application and during the interview protects the manager and the employer from future allegations of illegal discrimination. If a firm's managers attempt to avoid pregnancy discrimination by hiring only men, the managers will be violating Title VII for discriminating against women.

Bona fide occupational qualification (BFOQ) is often used as a defense in discrimination cases. However, managers who treat married and unmarried pregnant employees differently—arguing that unmarried pregnant women are negative role models under the BFOQ discrimination exception—would be violating current law unless they fall within very narrow exceptions, such as religious organizations that counsel young women.

Benefits. Whereas federal law does not require health benefits to be offered to employees, several states mandate that they be provided by many employers. The key for employers who offer health care, disability, sick leave and other benefits—mandated or voluntary—is to treat women affected by pregnancy, childbirth, and related medical conditions the same as other employees. For example, if an employer offers 12 weeks paid disability leave as a benefit for all illnesses, this benefit should apply to pregnancies as well. However, the U.S. Supreme Court has ruled that even if an employer does not offer disability leave to employees, it can (but does not have to) provide pregnancy leave even though male employees do not receive similar benefits.

Alternative work arrangements. Various options have been instituted to enable women to succeed and thrive in companies. These include alternative career

---

GUIDELINES FOR ORGANIZATIONS

Employment Policies

Establish company policies that reflect the firm's position on all temporary physical conditions involving employees, not just pregnancies.

Employee Selection

Focus interview questions and employment applications around the duties and responsibilities of the job. Treat all applicants similarly.

Benefits

In designing benefit programs, treat women affected by pregnancy, childbirth, and related medical conditions the same as other employees.

Alternative Work Arrangements

If alternative arrangements are offered, they should be provided to all employees.

Performance Appraisal

Carefully document *all* employee performance; disciplinary actions for excessive absences and low productivity should begin when performance problems occur.

---

paths, extended leave, flexible scheduling, job sharing, and telecommuting. Some firms adopted such policies to attract and retain talented women. However, these policies must be applied to all employees to avoid problems with discrimination. Obviously, fathers could also take advantage of such programs, so excluding men would constitute sex discrimination and perhaps pregnancy-related discrimination as well.

Performance appraisal. Several organizations have fired pregnant workers who were said to be unproductive or incompetent and then lost court cases after discrimination was charged by the fired worker. These decisions raise the question of whether poor performers who are pregnant can ever be fired. Obviously, it is easier to terminate incompetent employees who happen to be pregnant in states that have retained a strong employment-at-will doctrine, particularly during an employee's probationary period. However, in many states the employment-at-will doctrine has deteriorated, and often organizations want to demote or fire employees who have been with the company past their probationary period.

Managers are advised to document employee performance carefully and write accurate employee evaluations. If an employee has been having work-related problems, these should be documented and disciplinary action begun immediately, not after the employee has become pregnant. It may appear to a jury that a pregnant worker was unfairly dismissed if her performance appraisals indicate that she did not become "a problem" until after announcing her pregnancy.

* * *

Ignoring the issue of pregnancy discrimination carries a high price tag for employers. Costs borne to defend and settle lawsuits are the most obvious result of engaging in discriminatory actions. Another cost is the potential loss of skills if those affected by pregnancy are not accommodated when they are in need. As the labor pool contracts and certain skills become difficult to obtain, companies that have gone an extra mile to oblige employees by instituting family-friendly policies regarding leave and work arrangements will retain those highly skilled employees. They will avoid costs associated with high turnover: training and development of new workers and the performance lapse that occurs while employees of less experience learn how to perform their jobs.

Despite the federal laws, job bias against pregnant women remains an underlying problem. There is a concern that although discrimination laws have aided employees who have faced blatant bias, these protections will negatively affect the hiring and advancement of women in some organizations. Requiring companies to obey law related to the treatment of pregnant workers may result in subtle discrimination against hiring women of childbearing age. This type of discrimination usually offers no "smoking gun." However, the realities of work force demographics will increase a firm's long-term costs of discrimination against women, pregnant or not.

REFERENCES

Adams v. Nolan, 962 F.2d 791 (8th Cir. 1992).
D. Bencivenga, "ADA Coverage For Pregnancy Bias Rejected; But Federal Judge Says Other Laws May Be Used," *New York Law Journal*, August 15, 1996, p. 1.
D. D. Bennett-Alexander and L. B. Pincus, *Employment Law for Business* (Chicago: Irwin, 1995).
Chapsky v. Baxter Healthcare, Mueller Div, 66 EPD ¶ 43,573 (1995).
Civil Rights Act of 1964, 42 U.S.C., 2000e2(a)(1964).
Cleveland Board of Education v. LaFleur, 414 U.S. 632 (1974).
Doe v. First National Bank of Chicago, 668 F. Supp. 10 (N. D. II 1. 1987), affd. 865 F.2d.
Elie v. K mart Corp., No. 93-1077 (E.D.La., filed February 11, 1996). .
General Electric v. Gilbert, 429 U.S. 125 (1976).
H. R. Conference Report, No. 95-1786, 95th Congress, 2d Sess. 4, reprinted in 1978 U.S. Code Cong. & Admin. News, pp. 4765–4766.
International Union, *UAW v. Johnson Controls, Inc.*, 499 U.S. 187 (1991).
W. Johnston, "Global Work Force 2000: The New World Labor Market," *Harvard Business Review*, March-April 1991, pp. 115–127.
C. Kleiman, "Man Allowed To Sue For Pregnancy Discrimination," *Chicago Tribune*, June 15, 1992, Busn. Sec., p. 5.
M. Lord, "Pregnant—And Now Without A Job," *U.S. News & World Report*, January 23, 1995, p. 66.
Newport News Shipbuilding and Dry Dock Company v. EEOC, 462 U.S. 669 (1983).
Pacourek v. Inland Steel Company, 858 F. Supp. 1393 (D.C. 111, 1994).
Pregnancy Discrimination Act, 42 U.S.C., 2000e(k)(I 978).
F. N. Schwartz, *Breaking With Tradition: Women And Work, The New Facts Of Life* (New York: Warner, 1992).
Shafer v. Board of Public Education of the Pittsburgh School District, 903 F.2d, 243 (3d Cir. 1990).
"Sundstrand Settles Pregnancy Suit," *Chicago Tribune*, June 27, 1995, Busn. Sec., p. 1.
Troupe v. May Department Stores Company, d.b.a. Lord & Taylor, F.3d (7th Cir. 1994).
Turic v. Holland Hospitality, Inc., 858 F. Supp. 759 (W.D. Mich. 1994).
"Woman Wins Suit Over Her Pregnancy," *Chicago Tribune*, November 21, 1993, p. 27.
D.C. Wyld, "Is There A Dan Quayle (Or Role Model) Exception To The Pregnancy Discrimination Act? An Analysis," in C. Boyd, ed., *Southwest Academy of Management Proceedings* (Springfield, MO: Southwest Missouri State University 1995), pp. 81–85.
Zaken v. Boerer, 964 F.2d 1319 (2d Cir. 1992).

NO

William A. Henry III

WHY CAN'T A MAN BE
MORE LIKE A WOMAN?

"Woman: the female of man. See Homo.*"*

— Complete Encyclopaedia Britannica entry
for *woman*, first edition, 1771

The moral rationale for affirmative action on behalf of women is even weaker than the political and economic one. When blacks point to the cumulative effects of slavery and racial discrimination as a basis for giving them special advantage, they are speaking as an identifiable community. Both they themselves and the larger society around them have viewed them as a collective entity. In every generation up to the present one, and to a distressing extent even today, blacks have been born into families apt to be disadvantaged socially, educationally, and economically, have grown up in neighborhoods where similar disadvantages were the norm, and have entered schools and workplaces prone to perceive them as automatically inferior. It does not take much imagination to trace a clear hereditary line from the injustices of the past to the inadequacies of the present. Even so, the time must come when affirmative action gives way to open competition.... [W]hen it comes to elite jobs, that time is already here.

Women, by contrast, can claim no such hereditary burden. Their sense of historical grievance is largely irrelevant and almost entirely self-imposed. Whatever happened to women in the past, it is only minimally visited upon women of today. Feminist anger is primarily a theoretical and ideological, not a practical, construct. Novelist Michael Crichton summed up the absurdity of much such posturing by privileged women in his latest socially astute best seller *Disclosure*. A careworn husband whose wife starts running a feminist guilt trip on him says in reply, "You're a partner in a law firm, for Christ's sake. You're about as oppressed as Leona Helmsley."

Yes, women are descended from a long line of thwarted women. They are equally descended from a long line of admittedly unthwarted men. The spiritual connection with female forebears may seem stronger, but the biological link is exactly the same. The distribution of children by gender remains roughly fifty-fifty no matter the social class of the parents, so women cannot claim, as blacks can, to have been born into comparative economic privation.

It is true that adult women tend to be paid less than men and to be grouped disproportionately on the lower rungs of the economic ladder. Susan Faludi's *Backlash* and its ideological kin notwithstanding, that variance is attributable to many other factors besides overt prejudice. Women are often less educated or credentialed. They tend to be employed in fields that society rewards less extravagantly (some women, ill versed in the workings of the free market or temperamentally inclined to the folly of Marxism, see that fact of life as some sort of conspiracy). In no-nonsense economic terms, women tend to be less committed to their careers. They take time away to have children. They are ready to stay home or leave work abruptly when one of those children is sick or when an aging parent is in trouble. They often object on family grounds to long and irregular hours or abruptly scheduled travel and other normal, male-accepted demands of a job. All these outside concerns are socially valid, but they get in the way of work. Many women who also see themselves as caregivers want the rules of the workplace rewritten to suit their personal needs. Indeed, they want their relative lack of commitment (or, as they would phrase it, alternative set of priorities) treated as something

admirable and reward-worthy in a business setting. That attitude almost never wins appreciation from an employer and has rarely if ever led men to success; still, women argue that past and proven ways of doing business are irredeemably commingled with "sexism." In personal style, moreover, women tend to be less aggressive and confrontational than men while performing in an economy that seeks and compensates those go-getter qualities.

The real goal of many in the women's movement, I have come to feel, is not to change the way women think about themselves—breaking psychological fetters so they can maximize their potential —but to change the way men think, both about women and about themselves....

* * *

But at a deeper level the aim of many feminists is to debunk the most basic fact of history—that the civilized and cultured world was built almost entirely by men, pursuing such male-defined aims as conquest and fulfilling such male urges as competition and aggression. Many feminist scholars squander their careers on attempts to assert that the world owes its shape to those who cooked and cleaned, or alternatively to unsung geniuses whose memories men conspired to erase (a not entirely incidental parallel to the more exaggerated claims of Afrocentrists).

Even among women prepared to accept the reality of the past, one finds a widespread yearning to rewrite the rules of the present so that women may enjoy a more glorious future.

The overt goal of these feminists is to change ground rules of working life so that wives and mothers can, as the boast runs, "have it all." They argue that society benefits by giving special privileges to mothers in the marketplace. Is that so? Let me admit here that I think children are better off when their mothers (or fathers) stay home full-time, at least until the children enter school. I believe that much of the perceived educational decline of children has very little to do with the favorite whipping boy, television, and a great deal to do with a phenomenon that more closely fits the time frame of the decline— the two-income household, which in practice generally means employment for the mothers of young children. If this causal relationship holds true (and I readily concede that it is opinion rather than fact—if shared, albeit reluctantly, by virtually every working mother I know), then any benefit to society from the mother's working has to be weighed against the developmental loss to the next generation. Day care, the common solution, is usually merely custodial. The yuppie alternative, a live-in nanny, clearly represents an intellectual step down for the child. Of the ten parental couples to whom my wife and I are closest, eight have used live-ins, of whom not one had attended college (although the biological parents were mostly Ivy Leaguers) and only three were native speakers of English.

If we have swamped the schools by asking them to carry too many social burdens, might we not do the same to the economy? We have already made our business less free, and perhaps less competitive, by imposing the obligations of affirmative action for blacks, women, and assorted other minorities. If we add the necessity of being flexible in scheduling, pay, and promotion on behalf of mothers—plus the inevitable ill will that this is bound to cause among at least some nonmothers, male and female

—the likely result is less efficiency, not more. There is, further, a question of fairness. Changing rules to accommodate those who try to combine parenthood and the workplace inevitably imposes a disadvantage—if only by taking away a competitive advantage—on those who don't. Why, pray, *should* an employee with divided loyalties be treated the same as one who will give his or her all to the job? And on the philosophical plane, how can the very people most apt to say that childbearing is a private matter when the subject is abortion then reverse themselves and insist that it is a societal matter when the subject is their personal need and convenience in the workplace?

Even so, such changes are ardently sought. They have become almost dogma in the mainstream of my Democratic party. The ideological push is coming from some highly influential places. In April 1992 the Yale Graduate School marked the centenary of its admission of women with a three-day symposium. The capstone was a speech by Wellesley College president Nannerl Keohane, a recipient of a 1967 doctorate in political science from Yale. She complained with some legitimacy, that the very word *admit* suggests that women's participation at Yale was a benefice conferred by men (for which women presumably ought to be grateful) rather than a basic human right. This is a significant perception. Blacks feel much the same ambivalence about Lincoln and the Emancipation Proclamation, for it, too, suggests that they were "given" something to which they feel entitled as a matter of elemental dignity. It must be added, however, that the "right" of any or all women to be enrolled at a particular private university is much less evident in the language of the Constitution than the rights to work, vote, and enjoy other civil liberties made implicit in the Fourteenth Amendment.

Keohane asserted the existence of a glass ceiling throughout society, but based her evidence almost entirely on statistics concerning top universities. Those numbers are compelling at first glance. Women constitute half the enrollment at Yale College, for example, and almost half the student body of the Yale Graduate School, yet they are only twenty-two percent of the faculty and just eleven percent of those with tenure. Those statistics are misleading, however, not only about the rest of America but also about the good intentions and accessibility of the ostensibly discriminatory universities. At the junior level of assistant professor, some forty-two percent of Yale's faculty are women. The combined effects of life tenure, a later average retirement age than in other fields, and a drastic shrinkage in senior staff positions (because of declining enrollment and straitened finances) have kept schools like Yale from moving women along into the senior ranks. While Keohane advocated one-for-one promotion, moreover, there are still a few elitists left who think that tenure and full professorship ought to go to the most distinguished scholars, regardless of race or gender. Does this concern for standards make them sexist bigots?

In truth, as Keohane acknowledged, bigotry and sexism are not the real problems. "The most primitive explanations for the glass ceiling are sociobiological. In our instinctual constitutions, women most of all want to have babies, and when the biological clock begins ticking in our thirties, our bodies realize this. No matter how ambitious or energetic we have been about our jobs, we inevitably resort back to nature."

Those years of ticking, it might be added, tend to coincide with the pivotal years in most careers—the tenure decision in universities, the partnership decision at law firms, the point where corporate or media comers move onto the fast track to the very top. To want it all is to want too much.

For Keohane, the solution is obvious, and the people who are to pay for it should be anyone but the direct beneficiaries:

> There will need to be more flexibility in our expectations for how one performs in high-powered jobs at different stages of one's life, and also in the support systems for working parents. More flexible timetables for coming up for tenure, or the chance to attain tenure as a part-time professor, as well as more generous child-care and leave provisions and other policies that recognize the actual circumstances of people's lives, could make a big difference in opening those blockages in the pipeline. Changes will occur only if people press for them, if desirable young working couples insist on such arrangements before they will accept employment [Does she mean a husband should use himself as a bargaining chip to sweeten his wife's career, another easy way to breed workplace resentment?] and if citizens press for changes in our laws and tax structures.... I spoke earlier of the "admitting" mind-set that dominated our thinking from 1892 until quite recently. The "incorporation" mind-set, by comparison, acknowledges and celebrates the fact that including women as full partners makes a difference in the tone and temper of any human community or enterprise.

This airy claim to competitive advantages, special bargaining rights, and unspecified tax benefits for those who make the private decision to have children is a blatant form of special pleading. The last two sentences of the speech, moreover, underscore the inherent illogic and inconsistency of Keohane's position, and by extension that of the countless feminists who side with her on this issue (or, as they see it, nonissue already beyond debate). To claim the right to admission, or rather "incorporation," women are purporting to be equivalent to men. But they do not want to play by the same rules as men; instead, they demand that the rules be rewritten solely to benefit working mothers (and, ostensibly, their husbands). Further, these women claim to be different from men in tone or temperament—and, by implication, better. While Keohane is prudent enough not to articulate the words directly, this smacks of the "communal" and "nurturing" claims made for women, black "sun people," and other minorities seeking an instantaneous moral basis on which to redistribute power and remake the very dynamics of public life.

In fairness to Keohane, there is a solid elitist argument to be made for reintegrating mothers into the work force as soon as possible. Educated women are an asset to society—"human capital," in the phrase Bill Clinton likes to toss around—and they ought, all things being equal, to be utilized as thoroughly as possible. This is the rationale for the "mommy track," the alternative career path (with admittedly lower expectations) that was widely being urged a few years ago until zealots renewed the call for having it all. It is also the rationale for the family leave bill, vetoed by President Bush but signed by Clinton, that compels employers to rehire staff who take extended leaves to fulfill emergency family responsibilities. While there is a more airtight case to be made for the optional mommy track than for the obligatory preservation of jobs during family leave, both are premised on the real world in which we live—a world in which women voluntarily take on a disproportionate share of domestic worries.

Feminists object to such arrangements on three grounds. First, they do not wish to validate what they see as an unequal sharing of the household burden, based on what they reject as stereotypical views of the roles of the sexes. Second, they see compromise as a betrayal of feminism's promise of unlimited options. Third, they see it as both possible and preferable to compel the public world to make compromises rather than expect individual families (meaning, in practice, just the women) to do so.

The choice between career and family is so painful that women would rather not make it—and feminist activists are offering the illusory promise that they will not have to. The truth is, however, that in our culture most of the jobs truly worth having, those that are stimulating and demanding and full of intellectual peril, cannot be confined to forty hours a week or anything remotely like it. Working mothers of young children can hardly accommodate themselves to the minimum demands, let alone the maximum and erratically scheduled demands of the best jobs. The ancillary mommy track is not a dismissal; it merely describes reality.

* * *

By this point, any woman still reading is probably wishing she could puncture my bombastic carcass with whatever is the contemporary equivalent of a hatpin. I freely confess to having paid no attention here, let alone obeisance, to the very real problem of sexual harassment (accompanied, it must be pointed out, by some surreal claims seeking to extend the definitional boundaries of that sin). I have paid little attention to the troubles of women who can't get into the most lucrative unions or who are paid, as secretaries, a mere fraction of what men get for driving buses or hauling garbage. The first concern of this [selection] is the elite. Blue-collar jobs are outside its purview.

I strongly support the concept of equal pay for equal work. I do not join in the feminist campaign for *equivalent* pay for *equivalent* work (as if it could be defined in a neutral, objective way). This "refinement" is meant to overturn the judging process of the free market because some people don't like its outcomes. There undoubtedly are elements of historical prejudice in the lower pay scales for jobs customarily taken by women. But in the world of today, no one obliges a woman to take any particular job—she can slop hogs, chase crooks, or peddle commodities options if she likes and can qualify—and the rest of us should not be penalized for a woman's free choice to do something that traditionally has been done mostly by women.

Is Susan Faludi right that a lot of men continue to resent the women's movement and to thwart the progress of particular women? Do some other men behave with less conscious, but sometimes just as destructive, insensitivity or ignorance? Absolutely. But the point is not any individual lapses from perfection. The point is whether the upper reaches of American society are functioning effectively and, if not, whether a communal, nurturing, and infinitely flexible management structure is the best way to fix things. For many feminists, tribalists, Marxists, and new

agers, it is self-evident that such a structure is best. To them, that is the way the world ought to be. But in my experience of corporate life, executives and professionals already spend far too much time in meetings, feel-good sessions, and public relations exercises and far too little in actually turning out the product and getting it sold. "Human resources," issues, from alcohol treatment to affirmative action, already consume an immense amount of time and preclude many decisions, particularly on hiring and firing, that would get made swiftly and surely in a truly free market. I welcome women into the workplace—and they are there in their millions, with or without my welcome. But the last thing the country needs is to further encumber the economy with social burdens likely to raise costs and reduce competitiveness.

* * *

Wrongheaded as it may be when applied to remaking the American workplace, there is something attractive and even noble in women's global sense of sisterhood. One need not accept the argument that the world would be a better place if women ran it to concede that the spirit of humanism and compassion seems to run deeper among the female of the species than the male. This may simply be the converse of women's lesser ardor for competition and conquest. But a plausible case can be made that the aggressive qualities needed to build the modern world are rather less helpful in sustaining it....

There are other, arguably more cynical motives for the feminist campaign. The very existence of women's studies departments provides both a rationale for feminist ideology and a place to develop and refine it. Administratively, the existence of such departments offers chair-manships, full professorships, and other career-advancing appointments that will automatically be set aside for women. In addition, the growth of such courses creates a guaranteed market for textbooks, which will again perforce be written by (and bring a resounding royalty income to) feminist women.

Without overstating the impact of universities, which are as much mirrors as makers of the larger society, one must recognize that the scholarly questions surrounding women's studies and feminist critiques are outshouted by politics. Lest you think I am overinterpreting, consider such ostensibly cultural works as *The Reenchantment of Art,* in which author Suzi Gablik writes: "The calculating, dominating male intelligence is opposed to the visionary, empathetic female principle, bound to the core of the universe." Or the "scholarly" conference topics cited scornfully by Camille Paglia in *Sex, Art and American Culture,* including an analysis of the significant pink and blue "genderized" disposable diapers, the gender roles of shell collectors within the Philadelphia Concological Society, and the assessment of sexism in the layout of the New Jersey Turnpike, with its ramps and tollbooths, breakdown lanes and emergency phone system—"a man's road . . . constructed with no thought to the feminine view of reality." Or a review by Mary Jo Weaver in which she praises essayist Mary Daly's *Outercourse* for its "confrontations with rapacious patriarchy and her demanding calling to create a meta-patriarchal language." Weaver hails Daly as "intrepid . . . in the face of an exponentially increasing list of atrocities against women and the planet"—a list she does not bother to explicate. She refers to present-day life as "a

world on the brink of self-destruction," although she does not explain how. The most shocking thing about this polemic masquerading as analysis is not that its author is a professor of religious studies and women's studies at Indiana University, but that it was published in the January 24, 1993, edition of that barometer of the mainstream, the Sunday *New York Times Book Review.*

Women trained in such programs as Weaver's, and arguably men trained at universities that have women's studies departments, are apt to go out into the world expecting to see opportunities specifically earmarked for the advancement of women. And they will find them aplenty.

Of these, affirmative action targets are the most obvious and pervasive but by no means the only examples. PBS now offers the weekly half-hour talk show *To The Contrary,* aired on more than two hundred stations, in which analysis of news and national affairs is conducted by an all-women panel. Women are not exactly invisible elsewhere in television news and public affairs, and no one would dream of offering an officially all-male show. But this series is sponsored by the mainstream-to-conservative Toyota USA and Sun Company and has aired virtually without objection to its exclusionary casting. Elsewhere, on cable, one finds the women-only talk show of Jane Wallace and Mary Matalin, even though the need for a gender-identified talkfest is not so clear in a form dominated by Oprah, Joan, Sally Jessy, et al.

Jeopardy!, the only television game show that is premised on knowledge rather than gambling, guesswork, or holding opinions resembling the statistical norm, has been shuffling its selection of topics and questions to ensure that more women succeed. This may be merely the free market at work rather than reverse sexism; the show has more female than male viewers, and its producers want to be sure the audience can empathize with the winners. On the other hand, anyone interested in a game based on knowledge is presumably prepared to accept that a fact is a fact rather than a "masculinist" principle at work.

In Britain, the Labour party has voted to exclude male candidates from about forty parliamentary seats in an attempt to double the party's female share in the House of Commons. Under a decision adopted by the party's National Executive Committee in June 1993, half of all constituencies where a sitting member is retiring or where a seat held by another party is considered attainable will be instructed to have women-only shortlists. Explained Clare Short, who chairs the Executive's women's committee: "The number of women will gradually increase every Parliament until eventually there is fifty percent women." She predicted a future "psychological breakthrough where it becomes normal to have women MPs and people like women candidates." Apart from the rigidity of the scheme, one might question its timing, coming nearly fifteen years after Margaret Hilda Thatcher began to make herself the most successful British prime minister of the postwar era. The American electoral system precludes such quota setting. But in our elections—where, as California legislator Jesse Unruh famously observed, "Money is the mother's milk of politics"—the for-women-only Emily's List is now widely viewed as the most effective fund-raising and targeting organization. The National Organization for Women, which used to judge candidates on their ideology, bolted toward gender-based endorsements in 1993 when its New Jersey chapter backed moderate-to-conservative Republican Christine Todd Whitman rather than her much more liberal Democratic opponent, incumbent James Florio, almost entirely on the basis that she was a woman. (The sole additional proviso, it seemed, was that she take the "correct," i.e., pro-choice, position on abortion.)

* * *

"What do women want?" Freud asked in a letter to Marie Bonaparte in 1931. The answer, of course, depends on which women and in what country one does the asking. In China, women probably want an end to the prejudice that leads to vastly more abortions and infant deaths of girls than of boys. In India, they probably want an end to the dowry scams that treat daughters of marriageable age as burdens that families must buy their way out of. In Muslim Africa, some of them surely want an end to the genital mutilation of small girls to ensure their lack of interest in sex and consequent marital fidelity—and, of course, an end to the kind of patronizingly pro–third world scholarship that attempts to explain this butchery as a mere cultural custom, not to be meddled with by outsiders. In the Philippines and Thailand, women may want economic growth that will challenge prostitution as the only viably lucrative job open to them.

In America, women laudably want an end to all the indignities and injustices visited on their sisters around the world, and they want equality for themselves. But feminist rage masquerading as scholarship here won't do anything to change inhumanity elsewhere. Rejection of "rationalism" and its social and political fruits will make the American economy weaker, not stronger, and hence diminish women's benefits from it. Revamping the rules to give special opportunity to working mothers will heighten, not diminish, any residual male resistance.

And mistaking equality of opportunity for equality of outcomes will amount to binding ourselves to the very real ways in which women's lives are different— in which they are, if not more, certainly other than just "the female of man."

POSTSCRIPT

Do Women Still Face Discrimination in the Workplace?

While Henry believes that women carve their own career paths via the decisions that they make, Wren, Kidwell, and Kidwell assert that workplace discrimination is widely present, even in the face of federal laws that prohibit it. According to Wren et al., women have been fired, passed over for promotion, or not hired at all because they are pregnant or because they openly express their intent to have children. Henry contends that the choice between career and family can be painful and that feminist activists offer illusory promises when they suggest that such a choice need not be made. The most intellectually challenging jobs, he says, could never be confined to "forty hours per week." He maintains that working mothers can hardly accommodate themselves to meet minimal demands, and he views as ludicrous the idea that women can achieve at the same rates as males or as their childless female peers. Henry concludes that the only alternative is reduced status for mothers in the workplace.

Do women entering the workforce today encounter the same obstacles that their mothers did? In "Glass Ceiling? So What?" *Chief Executive* (April 1996), Sally Pipes says no. She believes that, regardless of gender, success depends on hard work. Complaints about a glass ceiling—a metaphor for the invisible barrier that some feel corporate leaders erect to prevent women from advancing beyond middle levels—ignore smaller companies in compiling statistics, Pipes says, and she suggests that women do not reach parity at the highest levels of corporate America because they do not want to. The glass ceiling myth has finally been debunked, say Diana Furchgott-Roth and Christine Stolba in *Women's Figures: The Economic Progress of Women in America* (Independent Women's Forum, 1997). When there is a gap, they contend, it is accounted for by "sensible refusal to place work above personal life." Furthermore, they argue that the wage gap is narrowing—especially for young women—and is about to narrow further as more women are earning Ph.D.s and professional degrees. However, in "Women and Academia," *Working Woman* (June 1997), the writer asserts that men with Ph.D.s consistently achieve more professional success than their female equivalents. The presence of the glass ceiling is stronger than ever, according to "Through a Glass Darkly," *The Economist* (August 10–16, 1996), causing women to leave employers and to start their own businesses. See also "Glass Ceiling Cracks but the Wall Is Holding Firm," *Business Journal Serving Greater Sacramento* (September 1996). For a review of challenges for feminism in the business world, see "Cracks in the Glass Ceiling," *World Press Review* (September 1996).

ISSUE 8

Do Women Belong in the Armed Forces?

YES: Rene Denfeld, from *Kill the Body, the Head Will Fall: A Closer Look at Women, Violence, and Aggression* (Warner Books, 1997)

NO: Stephanie Gutmann, from "Sex and the Soldier," *The New Republic* (February 24, 1997)

ISSUE SUMMARY

YES: Author Rene Denfeld asserts that women have shown themselves to be capable of the fiercest fighting and claims that their presence in all areas of the military is supported by most Americans. Furthermore, since combat helps to form a soldier's identity, women in the military should not be relegated to minor roles.

NO: Writer Stephanie Gutmann maintains that the integration of women into the military leads to gender differences becoming a disruptive force and compromises the integrity of the American national security system.

Women have never constituted more than 13 percent of the U.S. armed forces, partly because their involvement in many areas has been banned throughout much of history and partly because many women have been wary of, or uninterested in, joining the military. Historically, women have been recruited for service or placed into positions of military leadership only when men were in short supply. Barring extreme circumstances, most societies have, in fact, restricted women from serving in the military. Society's perception of appropriate roles for men and women together with concerns about national security have traditionally provided the rationale for these restrictions.

Although women have long served as nurses and in supportive roles, they were not officially enrolled in the U.S. armed forces until World War I. Thirteen thousand women served in World War I, mostly in support positions, but they were denied military rank or benefits and prohibited from remaining in the military after the war. Women's roles changed abruptly with the onset of World War II. While American involvement in World War I lasted just over a year, the four-year-long World War II proved to be a severe drain on the nation's resources. Women began to fill men's positions in factories and workplaces, were recruited for noncombat military service, and, by the end of the war, were granted military rank and benefits. More than 350,000 women served in World War II in clerical and support positions.

After the war the nation quickly returned to its original definition of male and female roles. Women were organized into their own institutions, such as the Women's Army Corps, rather than being integrated with men. In the mid-1970s the military reflected social changes consistent with the times when it abolished all-female service organizations and integrated men and women. The first women generals in U.S. history were appointed in 1970, and the service academies were opened to women by 1976. Although positions for women were limited at first, they gradually expanded so that by 1990, women composed 11 percent of the U.S. armed forces and were allowed to serve in nearly all noncombat positions. In 1991 Congress passed a bill that allowed U.S. Air Force servicewomen to fly in combat missions. Also, since there is no longer a draft, many see women as saviors in the all-volunteer forces (AVF). The AVF still depends on women to fill its ranks.

Despite the increasing recognition of women's importance in the military, the controversy over this issue has not diminished. In fact, with their increasing visibility in the military, the debate seems to have intensified. With regard to combat, a 1991 poll found the U.S. population to be split roughly in half, with a very slight majority of participants saying that women should be assigned to ground combat positions. However, many Americans remain unprepared to acknowledge females as warriors—brutal, aggressive, and capable of killing. The debate over women in the military is unique because it concerns both the issue of national defense and the issue of equal opportunity for women.

In the selections that follow, Rene Denfeld asserts that women have shown themselves to be capable of the fierceness and intensity that combat inevitably entails. Technology, she says, neutralizes any reasonable concern over effectiveness. Denfeld believes that women can and want to fight. Stephanie Gutmann finds that gender differences, which can largely be masked by technology in the civilian world, stand out in high relief in the unremittingly physical world of the military. She expresses concern about the cost of "regulating sex" in terms of money, labor, and morale, and she concludes that women's presence in the military exacts a price that is not prudent for society to pay.

YES   Rene Denfeld

WOMEN IN THE MILITARY

Sometimes sparring comes infrequently. One summer, the gym was nearly empty, tranquil.

Other times, sparring can occur often, like a gift. For a few weeks, I was able to work with Miguel, a fighter preparing to turn pro. Miguel weighs about 130 pounds and has a solid, muscled frame.

The more I get into the ring, the more I feel at ease and eager for more. Slowly, I lose my fear. It makes me exultant. At the same time, constancy blurs sparring, making it common. Time after time, I crawl through those ropes; time after time, I face a partner and touch gloves. Time after time, the bell rings, until I feel the emotional importance of all that is happening is becoming ordinary—although never deadened by frequency.

Each day is magically different, because the same opponent can change dramatically round to round, minute to minute. And at the same time, you are changing, with practice and training. It explains why the public so often wants to believe there is a fix when a boxer once beaten badly triumphs, or when one once unbeatable is sent to the canvas.

The eccentricities of the human body, and the human spirit, are encapsulated in boxing. The opponent you face right now, in this ring, is never the same as he was the month or day—or even the moment—before.

This is a truly frightening thing about boxing. It can be so accidental. Whether you win or lose sometimes has as much to do with pure chance as with training: a slip a referee counts as a knockdown; a bad case of nerves; a bad case of judges. No matter how hard you train, part of you places your hope not in your strengths but in your opponent's weaknesses, and also on whatever charm or religion you may have, because there is never a guarantee.

I learned this with Miguel, the way we surprised each other. Boxers learn one another's styles. You discover if they have a strong jab or devastating body punches, as Miguel does. He learned I like to come in full-bore, but at the same time I still forget to tuck my chin in, making myself vulnerable. But no matter how much you learn, the opponent will always be unpredictable. A tiny change in stance, a lateral movement here, an uppercut there—each can change the entire tone of a fight.

One day, sparring with Miguel was like hot wires downed by a storm. I got in the ring and a packed gym found reason to come around. A sense of anticipation filled the air, though I didn't know why—Miguel and I had been sparring together often. It may have had to do with several new fighters in the gym. They gawked at me: a woman. I was wearing my new headgear and gloves, which Jess had finally talked me into buying. They are Reyes, a popular brand. Both helmet and gloves are candy apple red leather, the headgear light and cushiony over my skull, leaving my face open, the gloves Mexican-style, which means less padding over the knuckles and a heavier, firmer wrist, which Jess laced tightly on my arms.

Miguel had just finished two rounds with another fighter, and as I climbed through the ropes, I wondered if he would be tired. When the bell rang, however, there was a sudden explosion. Jess and Chuck snorted and laughed at the side of the ring, as suddenly, with the final sound of that bell ringing across the gym, Miguel and I were at each other's throats, feathers fluttering to the ground.

I didn't plan on that coming, and I didn't have time to figure it out.

Everything was a blur of action. Miguel cornered me and threw a beautiful combination—a set of blows to the body, and then suddenly that crushing left hook to the chin. I wondered if I threw anything before—you can never quite remember who threw the first punch—but that doesn't matter, because I was on top of him, he was on top of me, and the fight was on.

We raced around the ring, cutting each other off, squaring off, and throwing hard, fast punches. Not a second was spared—not a moment passed when we considered, or reconsidered—just these fast combinations, constant and unrelenting.

The round was going by faster and faster. Jess was giving advice to Miguel. Chuck was talking to me. "Where is your jab?" he asked. And I responded by moving quickly left to right, forking that puppy out and tapping Miguel in the face with it, keeping him off. Miguel only bored in tight and unleashed body shots. He drove me against the ropes and I dipped slightly, using my forearms to block the blows as I bobbed and weaved, then came back swinging. My hands were talking before I could tell them what to do, and I threw a blurringly fast combination: a right to the body, a series of left hooks to the head, followed by a chopping straight right to the chin. Miguel was dazed, backed off quickly.

The crowd around the gym made a little sound of appreciation. A few of the boys laughed, an exuberant sound. Miguel responded. I responded. We didn't stop. I was throwing furiously to his dipping, bobbing head—angry, I let go—and the bell suddenly rang.

We stopped, smashed gloves. Jess and Chuck warned me not to stand up so straight, to keep my chin down. Chuck popped out my mouthpiece and rinsed it and my mouth with a strong spray of warm water from a bottle, then pushed the mouthpiece back in.

The next round started.

It was almost as furious, and twice as fast. Miguel, now on his fourth round of sparring, was in full flower. He drove, bobbed, and weaved. I could sense strength in his body. When we got in close, he pushed. From the side of the ring, Chuck said, "I know he's stronger than you, but push back." I tried, but my strength was slipping. He was bigger, and stronger. He kept driving at me with those body punches, and I was open for them: hard, punishing shots.

Punches to the head don't really hurt —at least in a sharp, painful sense—but blows to the body can take the starch out of you. Getting hit in the midsection sends the most horrible paralyzing, burning sensation up and down you before it turns your legs rubbery and soft. Every fighter knows that if you want to take out your opponent, go to the body.

Jess stopped me suddenly. He signaled me to the side of the ring, told me to duck in with Miguel, to work on the inside, punching close in. I was standing too erect again, which is why I was getting hit easily. Miguel and I touched gloves and began fighting once more, midway into the round. The action was so fast, the sweat was already pouring down me. I dropped to drive a straight right into his stomach, right above the waistband of his trunks, then returned to the head. He didn't wilt under my pressure, but returned. In close, in the middle of the ring, he chanted under his breath, "*come on, come on.*" I could hear him, feel the hot powdery scent of his breath on my cheek. But my hands at this point were dulling; my reflexes were off because of those body blows.

I summoned the energy to strike back. Miguel drove me into a corner with a sharp jab, cut me off. It was the corner where Jess, Chuck, and some of the fighters stood nearby. I could feel the spongy rubber of the corner mat behind my back. Miguel began really unleashing his strength. One body punch sunk in so deeply, right under my rib cage over the liver—that I let out this half-involuntary grunt: *uuummph.*

The sound, as soft as it is, was caught in the air. Everyone heard it.

Miguel instantly apologized, under his breath. Before I could even think about it, I used the opportunity to dodge out of the corner and send a straight left his way. I was laughing. His chin crumpled. Of course he returned the favor. The moment passed, and we were shifting, tired but still as fast, across the ring.

Later, after the sparring session, Jess pointed to my midsection. He was worried about the body shots I took. I tried to make a joke out of it, saying that *that* should teach me about defense. I know he doesn't worry with the guys. It's my internal female organs that concern him. I said that Miguel throws a good punch to the belly. Jess looked pleased at this compliment to Miguel, but he was still disquieted by worries about my midsection, the land of strange female parts.

Miguel, who was standing nearby, suddenly dashed off. I worried instantly that he felt ill at ease with me and upset.

I was suddenly struck by how discordant I can feel, here in this gym full of male fighters. There are times when I feel accepted, and this acceptance is genuine, and yet there are other times when my presence is as painful and sharp as a knife.

I know how disruptive I am in this gym. I know the disruption is like a deep fault that keeps the splintered parts of Jess's team from forming into a whole.

* * *

I know I am the girl whom the boys have to fight.

Women fighting men. What is a strong taboo actually has a long history, from Queen Boadicea, the Celtic leader who took her troops against the Romans, to the esteemed pilot Rufina Gasheva, a hero of the Soviet Union who flew 850 missions in World War II.

Their lives have been largely glossed over, and lost, but women have been involved in militaries and revolutions since before recorded history.

Sometimes we have been directly involved in fighting. It was a nearly all-female mob of thousands that stormed Versailles in 1789, looting and murdering in revolutionary anger. In India, lower-caste hero Phoolan Devi was the female leader of an all-male revolutionary gang that killed at least twenty during the early 1980s. In Zimbabwe, Parliament member Margaret Dongo was one of many women guerrilla warriors who fought to overthrow the white government; today, she is still as feared as she is respected.

Other times, our role has been peripheral, or behind the lines: the women of Nazi Germany who sent Hitler adoring love letters; the nurses and technicians of American wars. Women have shown themselves to be capable of the fiercest warmongering, and they are generally just as supportive of war efforts as men.

It's only been in the past few decades, as women have moved from the rear of the battlefield toward the front—and, importantly, from taking orders to giving them—that our role in war has suddenly ignited intense controversy.

The female soldier confronts society with an aggression as real and as controlled as a man's. She is not hysterical, a fishwife, an irrational shrew. She is calm and confident. She causes deep discomfort not just because she is aggressive but also because she breaks the rules against combat between the sexes.

* * *

The 1991 Gulf War woke America to women's role in the military. Over 41,000 women served. Fourteen died.

Never before had so many women fought in an American war. Overwrought articles on the "mommie war" appeared, complete with photos of military mothers kissing their babies good-bye. As usual, pollsters raced to capture what the public made of all this.

But just as the Gulf War demonstrated a positive move toward allowing women the same opportunities as men, it also brought old fears tumbling out of the closet. Some worried that the women wouldn't be able to stand up to the job physically. Others fretted that the troops would engage in sexual shenanigans, or that women would be captured by the enemy and raped. A lot of people couldn't quite figure out just *what* women were doing over there. What was the difference, they asked, between direct and indirect combat, and why were women dying if prohibited from the former?

Politicians convened hearings and created commissions to discuss women in combat. What started with gravity reverted to exclamation points. The opposition was reduced to alarmism. They were puzzled as to why the country didn't balk when women started coming home in body bags. Instead, the families mourned privately, for sons and daughters alike. No one could figure out the mood of the country, if there ever is one mood.

The polls came back. Most Americans now support women being allowed into at least some areas of direct combat.

* * *

"I would take the ten best," Capt. Chris Lemay with the Canadian Forces Office of Public Affairs answers. I have asked him who he would rather have under his command, men or women. "It's not a matter of gender," Lemay says, "but a matter of who's the best person for the job."

Lemay speaks with a strong French-Canadian accent, a heady mixture of lilting vowels and thick English. He seems intent to convince me that the 1989 ruling allowing Canadian women into all combat posts—including the infantry, armor, and artillery—has been successful. But his eagerness to persuade does not seem like the hand-wringing of an administrator hiding faults as much as it does a commander speaking from a deep affection for his troops.

Lemay has trained these new women combat soldiers. His firsthand experience has convinced him that women are capable of the punishing life of a foot soldier.

In the United States, women are still barred from direct-combat posts in the infantry, armor, and field artillery units. More combat positions, such as fighter pilots and some artillery positions, are being opened to women. But the major routes for advancement are in the small percentage of posts that remain closed.

Several lessons from Canada are now clear. Some women are physically capable of being foot soldiers. Others are not —and neither are all men. Lemay points out that quite a few men are physically weak and unfit.

During the first few years combat posts were opened, Canadian women did well in artillery and armor, but many failed infantry training. Part of the reason is that large numbers of women were recruited, and not many had an idea of what they were getting into.

Now less women try out for the posts, but those who do seem better prepared. In 1994–1995, for example, only five women tried for Canada's small infantry force, compared with 672 men. Three of the women graduated, making the female success rate 60 percent. Comparatively, 82 percent of the men made it. In artillery, four women entered the course and three of them graduated, for a 75 percent success rate, compared with a 96 percent success rate for men. Only one woman trained as an infantry officer, and she passed.

These numbers are too small to be used to draw conclusions about attrition rates. Just a few additional women each year could raise or lower the success rates dramatically. It's obvious, however, that of those women interested in combat, enough are capable of meeting the requirements to allow them to try.

Lemay dismisses the oft-heard concern that standards have been lowered to make room for women. "The standards are set by what's needed in the field," he says. "It's not an issue to say, 'The standards are set for the guys or for the women.'... In armor and artillery, for example, they have to be able to lift these heavy shells." He hasn't found women's presence hurts troop cohesion or damages military effectiveness.

Near the end of our interview, Lemay mentions with pride that one of his women infantry soldiers was serving with the United Nation's forces in Bosnia. Put to the test, women prove they, too, can go successfully to battle.

* * *

Technology has changed the face of war. As the United States found in Iraq, there are no solid front lines anymore. Combat can mean manning advanced weaponry far from the enemy or firing from offshore. It also can mean that women supposedly prohibited from direct combat end up under long-range enemy fire, which is how women died in the Gulf. Army captain Mimi Finch says that modern battle is "much more confused. Everyone is at risk."

Because of these advances, combat policies that sound workable on paper are somewhat inane in practice. Retired Maj. Gen. Jeanne Holm points out in her book *Women in the Military* that women in the Gulf were allowed to serve on tactical air bases targeted by Iraqi Scud missile attacks but were banned from better-protected aircraft carriers offshore. They were shot down while flying supply helicopters but were barred from piloting combat aircraft.

Combat policies tend to be driven more by politics and moral concerns than by objective research. Put a man and a woman in a trench together and supposedly you'll have trouble.

There have been some problems with sexual relationships in the military. Thirty-six women got pregnant on one American ship during the Gulf War, leading some to call it the "Love Boat," signaling a dire need for leadership and control, or at least birth control. This ship was unusual, though.

Sexual relationships developed in the armed forces when women were confined to supportive posts such as secretaries, and they will continue to develop regardless of whether women are allowed equal opportunities. The question is whether such relationships endanger the forces, and so far the answer is no.

The Love Boat aside, pregnancy did not turn out to be a hindrance in the Gulf War. Even when pregnancies are included, men tend to miss more days on duty than do women, due to sports injuries, alcohol abuse, and disciplinary causes.

A 1995 navy policy shows that the inevitable pregnancies that come with a co-ed volunteer force seem best addressed by a reasonable policy. The policy gives pregnant soldiers full natal care, and returns them to their former or equivalent duties without professional downgrading. Pregnancy, the navy concluded, does not seem to be having any effect on military readiness.

Despite House Speaker Newt Gingrich's comment that women soldiers are prone to "infections" every thirty days, menstrual periods also do not create the hindrance some worry over. As English journalist Kate Muir discusses in her book *Arms and the Woman*, women in the Gulf found that menstrual periods turned out to be minor annoyances at most. Muir spent days in the field with women soldiers, and she writes eloquently about the heat and discomfort of the battlefield, where "soldiers of either sex hated the dust storms, the stinking chemical latrines, the constant stress of Scud attacks and the boiling hot, charcoal-lined, chemical warfare suits that turned their skin black.... 'the separate toilets and shower problems' also dissipated in the desert, when creating a ladies meant no more than digging an extra hole in the sand...."

Yet another fear also dissipated in the desert of the Persian Gulf—the fear that the sexual assault of women prisoners of war would damage troop morale.

Incidents of women POWs being sexually assaulted are uncommon. A woman flight surgeon was sexually molested after her helicopter was downed in Iraq. She later stood before a presidential commission to assert that while the assault was unpleasant, it was also an "occupational hazard" of war. It was clear she did not want her trauma to be used against other women.

In all the papers, reports, and military documents I've read that concern themselves with the rape of women POWs, few deal with male sexual victimization. There are cases of male soldiers being sodomized and assaulted, by the enemy and their comrades, but such incidents appear seldom reported by the victims, and when they are, they get little attention. During the time the Tailhook sexual harassment scandal was front-page news, for instance, two different cases of American male sailors raping other male sailors came to light.

* * *

When examining the arguments marshaled by critics of women in combat, it's easy to lose sight of what is happening within the forces themselves. Looking into this topic, I initially found soldiers like Chris Lemay surprising. The last thing I had expected to hear from a male officer was his spirited praise of women combat soldiers.

Like so many women, my opinion of the armed forces has been shaped by highly publicized stories, such as Shannon Faulkner's rough treatment at the hands of the Citadel, the private all-male military school she fought for years to enter but soon left, exhausted and despairing.

I was pulling for Faulkner. I admired what the Mexican guys refer to as *cojones*.

And I felt for her when she dropped out. The attack from other women was merciless. Women columnists—many not exactly svelte themselves—criticized her weight and savaged her appearance. How many of us could cope with such pressure and publicity, and at that young age? And how could the commanders at the Citadel be so obtuse not to recognize this young woman's incredible courage? You would think they would welcome such a fighting spirit with open arms.

The Citadel, like Tailhook, is the kind of story that makes the news. But it does not reflect the attitudes of the military as a whole. At the same time Faulkner left the Citadel, in August of 1995, a record sixty-five women quietly took their places in Norwich University's military college, which has admitted women since the early 1970s.

Most military academies accept women, and new zero-tolerance policies are making headway fighting sexual harassment. The Undersecretary of Defense for Personnel and Readiness, Edwin Dorn, believes that as women "begin to occupy more of the war-fighting roles" and so achieve leadership positions, sexual harassment will decline just as racial harassment did following the integration of the forces.

While there is still a great deal of sexism in the military, there are many commanders who are genuinely committed to equality. Curiously, it is the military's functional approach to aggression that allows this. Having seen that women can perform, some officers waste no time changing their mind about allowing them to. It is those distanced from the field who remain most ensconced in sexism.

It is pragmatism, rather than the pie-in-the-sky idealism some politicians claim, that drives efforts to open all military posts to women. Rear Adm. Philip Quast, Assistant Chief of Naval Operations, asserts that the policies against women in combat are actually hurting the navy. "I have personally seen mixed-gender ships turned around, broken off from an engagement or an evolution simply because they were reaching an invisible line that, if they crossed it, would put them into a combat zone," he said. "These lines are artificialities. They are counterproductive, they are wasteful and, frankly, they are dumb."

The issue of effectiveness is a good one. At the same time the percentage of women increases in the armed forces, technological advances demand specialized training. Removing a female specialist from a ship or troop when fighting breaks out has the potential to undermine the forces.

Policies against allowing women into combat worked in the past, when men were drafted into the armed forces and when technological skills were less crucial. Today, these policies are no longer functional. The military has recognized that women are a better "buy," with the average female recruit better educated than her male peers. This is why we so often see commercials for the army appealing directly to women. In an all-volunteer force, women have not just become indispensable; they've become highly desirable.

Women continue to find themselves cut out of good-paying career paths because of the combat policies that remain. This is not a minor issue: Over 28,000 American women enlist in the armed forces every year. It is especially pertinent to black women, who are now one out of every fourteen army sergeants, and who have found in the armed services a solid career often not available to them in civilian life.

But there is also a symbolic loss. Combat is the reason we have armed forces. It is the point of soldiers, their identity. Whether we endorse that or not, allowing men to develop this identity but refusing it to women has meaning for our society far beyond war and conflict.

Even when she is in reality near the front of the battlefield, facing danger and taking responsibility equally with men, the woman soldier is symbolically relegated to the rear. No matter how you try to get around it, the perception remains that her skills are inferior.

* * *

The female soldier puts us face-to-face with the fact that women can fight—not just in passion or anger but for a cause—or for the excitement of combat, the personal challenge of pitting oneself against another. What's more, they want to, thousands upon thousands of them.

Women's military service is one of the more frank examples of women's aggression. Most will not relish violence, although some will take joy in it. But all find in themselves a capacity to compete —against men and against one another.

NO

Stephanie Gutmann

SEX AND THE SOLDIER

February 4, 1997, and an all-too-familiar looking headline—"TOP ENLISTED
MAN IN THE ARMY STANDS ACCUSED OF SEX ASSAULT"—occupies a
prime corner of the front page of *The New York Times*. Just a few weeks
earlier, the papers had been reporting charges of inappropriate hazing of
female cadets at the Citadel. And just a few months before that, several
female recruits at the Army's Aberdeen Proving Ground had accused drill
instructors of rape and sexual harassment, unleashing a torrent of similar
accusations from female soldiers around the country. In this latest case, as in
so many of the others, blame will be difficult to affix. Once more it will come
down to "he said, she said." Once more there will be op-eds, hand-wringing
and counselors; once more the Army will have to deploy its investigatory
troops. This, just as the Army digs out from Aberdeen—where there are
still over 200 criminal charges to investigate, and a hot-line brings in new
complaints every day.

What no one is publicly saying (but what everyone in the military knows)
is that incidents like these are bound to recur. In a military that is dedicated
to the full integration of women, and to papering over the implications of
that integration as best it can, sex and sexual difference will continue to be
a disruptive force. And regulating sex will become an ever more important
military sideline, one whose full costs in money, labor and morale we will
not really know until the forces are called on to do what they are assembled
to do: fight.

* * *

The military's sex problems begin with the simple anatomical differences between men and women. Racial integration, to which the integration of women
is ceaselessly compared, took the military about a century to achieve (quite
successfully in the end) and that involved differences that are only skin deep.
An effective fighting force depends on a steady supply of known quantities;
it needs "units" made up of interchangeable elements called soldiers. Once
one got over skin color, racial integration was still about integrating the same
body.

From Stephanie Gutmann, "Sex and the Soldier," *The New Republic* (February 24, 1997). Copyright
© 1997 by The New Republic, Inc. Reprinted by permission.

But what happens when you try to absorb a population that is not, in unit terms, interchangeable? What happens when you try to integrate into a cohesive whole two populations with radically different bodies? In the elemental, unremittingly physical world of the soldier, sex differences—masked by technology in the civilian world—stand out in high relief. Consider the female soldier not in political terms, but in the real, inescapable terms of physical structure. She is, on average, about five inches shorter than the male soldier, has half the upper body strength, lower aerobic capacity and 37 percent less muscle mass. She has a lighter skeleton, which may mean, for instance, that she won't be able to "pull G forces" as reliably in a fighter plane. She cannot pee standing up, a problem that may seem trivial, but whose impact on long marches was the subject of an entire Army research study; under investigation was a device called the "Freshette Complete System," which would allow women to pee standing up in places where foliage doesn't supply ample cover. She tends, particularly if she is under the age of 30 (as are 60 percent of military personnel) to get pregnant.

One would expect that such a sweeping social experiment (and one so expensive—just refitting the *USS Eisenhower* to accommodate 400 new female sailors cost $1 million, for example) would hit some rough patches. But don't expect to hear about them from the military brass. Afflicted by a kind of "Vietnam syndrome" about the possibility of winning an ideological battle against the civilians who increasingly influence military policy, the brass now seem mostly concerned with trying to prove how well, as one officer put it, they "get it" where women are concerned. This week, when Army Chief of Staff General Dennis J. Reimer said he thought the service should reexamine whether the advantages of jointly training men and women outweigh the drawbacks, it was something of a bombshell. In general, the military has maintained a virtual silence about problems with the new influx of female soldiers, and, in the ranks, negative comments about integration are considered "career killers." Those who don't "get it" talk about it in the barracks and on the Internet, which has become a haven for military samizdat about sex and other dicey matters. As one soldier wrote in a typical online exchange, "examples of these latest 'revelations' [about sex between subordinates and their immediate superiors] are known to nearly everyone who has served. But we were never allowed to discuss... our concerns openly because it would raise issues about the efficacy of mixing girls and boys and that was politically incorrect, a career-ending taboo."

In general, the military's response to the problems of gender integration has been to recruit more women. The more women, the more feminized the culture, the fewer problems with sex, goes the thinking. (One corollary of this may be the recent decline in male enlistment. In focus groups, young men tend to cite, among other reasons for not joining up, fear of purges like the one after Tailhook and the increased presence of females in the ranks.)

The big recruitment drive has brought the percentage of women in the force to 14 percent, which may not seem like much but is up from 2 percent at the close of the Vietnam War. Women now make up 20 percent of new recruits—compared to 12 percent a decade ago. And the effort to recruit still more women is relentless.

In 1991, when the Marines replaced their slogan "A FEW GOOD MEN" with "THE FEW, THE PROUD, THE MARINES," the idea was to sound more female-friendly. Nowadays, much of a military recruiter's time is consumed with trying to cajole women to enlist. And in practice, unfortunately, this often means adapting —which is to say, lowering—standards without exactly admitting to doing so.

The goal for a young Marine recruiter named C. J. Chivers, for example, became just " 'Get 'em on the plane.' If there were any problems, boot camp could sort it out." Chivers, whose stint as a recruiter lasted from 1992–94, adds that "invariably we would fill up the white male quotas almost immediately. So it became any woman that came in there that met the minimums, we gotta hire. What that did was take all the subjectivity out of it, an enormous part of the evaluation process. I couldn't say 'I got a bad vibe' the way I could with a guy." A recruiter also had to work hard to maintain what Chivers calls an "informal double standard" on strength differences: "Invariably the guys went down to Officer Candidate School with a near-perfect physical score while the women just cleared the minimum" —even using what military brass call "gender-normed" test results and "dual," i.e. lower, standards: for example, in the Marines, fitness for women is tested with a flexed arm hang instead of pull-ups, half the number of sit-ups and a slower run.

Women have also been lured into the service with the promise of a more important role. Since 1994 more than 80,000 new jobs have been opened in positions that were formerly off-limits. Rescinding the combat exclusion law and the risk rule has allowed women to qualify to fly combat planes and to serve on combat ships. Women are still not allowed to serve on submarines, but *Navy Times* reports that "a review underway to examine future submarine designs may include a study on including women crew members."

And ever since the Gulf war, when women served in combat support roles, the possibility of taking that last step—of knocking down barriers to the infantry— has been very much in the air. Ground combat, considered the most potentially brutal, the most physically demanding and certainly the grubbiest form of combat, is seen as a crucial piece of turf by the Old Guard and plenty of the young old guard, too. Opponents of integrating ground combat tend to argue that mixed-sex units won't achieve the right kind of "cohesion," that women on the whole aren't strong enough to, say, effectively lob grenades or load tanks, and that there is, at bottom, something repugnant about a male officer ordering women barely out of their teens into harm's way. The opposing argument has been pointedly made by N.O.W. President Patricia Ireland, who maintains that exclusion promotes the view that women are weak, inferior and in need of protection. (With Patricia Schroeder, the great pro-combat warrior, in retirement, the next pro-combat push may come from a commission appointed by Army Secretary Togo D. West Jr. after the rape charges surfaced at Aberdeen. The commission's official mandate is to look at causes of sexual harassment, but the many pro-women-in-combat appointees are expected to argue the familiar exclusion-equals-lower-status-equals-harassment line when they make their recommendations.)

* * *

To understand why gender integration became such an unquestionable in the military culture, we have to return to 1992, the year of the Clarence Thomas hearings, the trial of Mike Tyson, "They Just Don't Get It"—and the Tailhook investigations. Tailhook was officially declared a symptom of a larger problem—not an isolated event involving at most about six men—when investigators were ordered to scrutinize the "cultural" context. Through the prism of Tailhook and of sexual harassment, the culture that had long prepared men for battle suddenly looked, as then-acting Navy Secretary J. Daniel Howard put it, "diseased and decaying." "What happened at Tailhook," he told reporters, "was not just a problem with the integration of men and women in our ranks. It was just as much a problem with the toleration of Stone Age attitudes about warriors returning from the sea...."

Somewhere in the committees and hearings charged with studying this "cultural problem" a remedy swam into focus: men harassed women because they did not see them as equals. If women were brought in in great numbers, "the warrior culture" would be diluted. After Tailhook, the military made recruitment of women a top priority; barriers toppled, policies changed, promotions were spirited through the pipelines.

The new thinking also held that, if you got to them early enough, all kinds of "sexist attitudes" could be nipped in the bud. And early enough meant starting with boot camp. Enter Gender Integrated Basic Training. In 1992 the Navy began training all new female recruits at one of three integrated boot camps—a way, as Captain Kathleen Bruyere put it, to give recruits "a chance to make mistakes, say stupid things, and tell them we don't do that here." At Bruyere's camp in Orlando, Florida, recruits did "everything but sleep together in the same compartment"—including physical training and bunk and dress inspections. They also spent a good deal of time watching films about sexual harassment, while questionnaires like the one that stated "The Navy is a man's world. True? or False?" gave the new troops ample opportunity to "say stupid things."

By the end of 1993, and into 1994, the Army followed suit with its own gender-integrated training. The Army may have been slower on the uptake because it had already experimented with the process in the early '80s and found that when the sexes, say, ran obstacle courses together, the women tended to have a high injury rate from trying to keep up, and the men complained that they weren't challenged.

To avoid dealing with the problems posed by differences in physical strength between men and women, the proponents of sexual integration have increasingly favored a movement to "reevaluate" the way soldiers are trained. As Barbara Pope, then assistant secretary of the Navy for manpower and reserve affairs, put it in the early '90s, "We are in the process of weeding out the white male as norm. We're about changing the culture." And so, in some boot camps, the fundamental character of training is changing. Fort Jackson, the camp where gender-integrated training was thought to have failed in the early '80s, began to evaluate "soldierization skills" by putting more emphasis on skills like "map-making and first aid" at which female recruits excel. The result has been a kind of feel-good feminization of boot camp culture, with the old (male) ethos of competition and survival giving at least partial way to a new (female) spirit of cooperation and esteem-building.

At the instigation of a Navy weekly called *Soundings*, a group of middle-aged officers revisited their old basic training camp last fall to see how "the kinder, gentler Navy" was doing things. The oldsters were greeted by a commander—one Captain Cornelia de Groot Whitehead—who used her opening briefing to inform them that 40 percent of new recruits have at some time been victims of serious physical or sexual abuse, while 26 percent have contemplated suicide. Accordingly, de Groot Whitehead said, "We've decided we needed to do something different." The tourists from the "Old Navy" were bemused to learn that the infamous obstacle course of yore had been renamed the "confidence course" and moved indoors to comprise "an indoor labyrinth of pipes to crawl through, monkey bars to swing from, ladders to climb up and balance beams to sidestep over."

And at Fort Jackson, South Carolina—where, in 1995, boys and girls shared barracks—an *Army Times* reporter recently found that grunts no longer have to do pushups to a count. Instead, they are asked to perform "a timed exercise in which soldiers do the best they can in a set period." One drill instructor has solved the male/female strength discrepancy problem by putting young recruits in "ability groups" for their morning run. "You're not competing with the rest of the company," Colonel Byron D. Greene, the director of Plans, Training and Mobilization, told *Army Times*. "You are competing against yourself and your own abilities."

But life—especially military life—does not ignore physical differences. When young soldiers leave training, they are as-

signed jobs (called Military Occupational Specialities or MOSs), and the physical requirements of these jobs are not nearly as forgiving as a "New Army" drill instructor. A typical Army MOS, the kind of combat support MOS a young woman might request, could involve lots of lifting and loading, of shell casings, for instance. Pat Schroeder can say what she likes, but "a shell casing," groused an Army physiologist, "is always gonna weigh ninety pounds. There's nothing we can do about that."

Female soldiers themselves know this. A 1987 Army Research Institute survey found that women are more likely than men to report that insufficient upper body strength interferes with their job performance. Twenty-six percent of female light wheel vehicle mechanics, for example, said they found it "very difficult" to do their job, as opposed to 9 percent of the men in that speciality who were polled.

And, according to Army physiologist Everett Harman, "[Command Reports] have indicated that many soldiers are not physically capable of meeting the demands of their military occupational specialities. Unfortunately women fall disproportionately into this category." Attrition is particularly high, Harman said, in "heavy" (requiring, 100-pound lifting) and "very heavy" (over 100 pounds) MOSs like Food Service Specialist, Motor Transport Operator and Unit Supply Specialist. Retraining and reassigning a soldier has been estimated to cost about $16,000, but advising a female soldier that she may have trouble with an MOS she is considering is, sources say, one of those "career-killing" statements that bureaucratically wise officers have learned to avoid.

There have been two attempts made in the past fifteen years to establish "gender-neutral" strength standards and a qualifying pre-test for each MOS, but as *Army Times* reported, "on both occasions, the requirements were eventually abandoned when studies showed most women couldn't meet the standards proposed for nearly 70 percent of the Army specialities." In 1995, a group of military researchers were set to try again, but this time the project didn't even reach the partial implementation stage because funding was denied. Funding was also recently denied to Harman, who had applied for a grant to do a second study of "remedial strength training for women," after his first had shown promising results. Harman believes the brass do not like his approach because it admits that female soldiers are not strong enough to perform basic military tasks, which is contrary to the military's line. "At the highest level, I think they feel that if we show that women can get stronger, then the onus would be on the women to get stronger," he says, "while it is the jobs that should be made easier."

But can the jobs be made easier? Can weapons get lighter (as some advisers are urging)—without reducing lethality? Proponents of the change-the-equipment-not-the-people view point to the highly automated Air Force. But the Air Force is not the Army, and it is not the Marines. "If you have a plane sitting on the runway and you have to load it with supplies—bombs, whatever, you can have machines that drive out there, that raise the stuff on a little elevator," Harman points out. "But out in the woods and fields a lot has to get done by hand. Even in the kitchen there are big pots weighing about 100 pounds or so. It would take a tremendous amount of research to make certain jobs lighter, because you're talking about reengineering the whole thing. Carrying a tool box, changing a truck tire; there are certain jobs, for instance, where you have to carry a toolbox that might weigh a few hundred pounds and put it up on the wing of a plane."

Online, where military folk often say impolitic things, there is a sense of foreboding about the danger of ignoring the strength issue: "Nothing is more demoralizing," wrote one Marine, "than to have to turn your formation around to go pick up the females. This is only training. I can even put the females on remedial training and they still hold up my formations. I would hate to see how many Marines I would lose if we were in combat and had to be somewhere fast."

* * *

There is one respect, though, in which the stubborn physical realities of integrating women cannot be easily denied —and that is their capacity for childbearing. A recent article in *Stars and Stripes* reported that a woman had to be evacuated for pregnancy approximately every three days in the Bosnian theater from December 20, 1995, when the deployment began, until July 19, 1996. Army public relations people in Bosnia don't dispute that claim, but they also say pregnancy is no particular problem for the Army, "no different than appendicitis."

It is clearly not a problem anymore in a career sense. All branches and some of the service academies have softened policies on pregnancies and made it clear that their official stance is now completely accepting. Unfurling one such policy in February, 1995, Navy Secretary John H. Dalton told reporters that "Navy leadership recognize that pregnancy is a natural event that can occur in the lives of Navy servicewomen... and is not a presumption of medical incapacity." The Army has followed suit, stating that "Pregnancy does not normally adversely affect the career of a soldier."

In fact, pregnancy is now so "non-adverse" that soldiers say it's sometimes used to get out of "hell tours" like Bosnia, to go home. "I know other females that have done things... probably to get out of going somewhere," Specialist Carrie Lambertus told *Army Times*. "It happens all the time."

A woman who turns up pregnant in Bosnia is shipped in short order to the U.S. or Germany. Then, according to an Army spokesman, "female soldiers have the option of either staying on active duty or applying for release [with an honorable discharge] from active duty." Those who decide to stay in the military get six weeks maternity leave. The new Navy policy also provides for help in locating a runaway dad and in establishing paternity.

In the Navy, pregnancy rates run about 8 percent of the force at any given time. A pregnant woman is allowed to stay onboard ship up to her fifth month; then she gets reassigned to shore duty to avoid the heavy lifting that is a sailor's lot, not to mention the hazardous chemicals in engine rooms. Of the 400 women on the first gender-integrated warship, the *U.S.S. Eisenhower*, twenty-four were "non-deployable" due to pregnancy at the start of a Persian Gulf tour and another fifteen were evacuated once on the water. On the *U.S.S. Acadia*—dubbed "the Love Boat" by the press—thirty-six out of a total 360 female sailors aboard had to be evacuated during a Gulf tour.

And no matter how determinedly the military defines pregnancy as a non-issue, the facts of pregnancy cannot be altered. A pregnant soldier is—or soon will be—a non-deployable soldier. A General Accounting Office study of soldiers called up to go to the Persian Gulf showed that women were four times more non-deployable than men—because of the pregnancy and recovery numbers. As Lambertus puts it, "If you're in a platoon where they're moving equipment or digging, setting up tents, [pregnant soldiers] are not going to be doing anything, except maybe sitting there and answering the phone all day. That really does cause some resentment." If her commanders had wanted to make sure the unit was truly deployable "they'll have to reclassify me and send me somewhere else, which would take more money, more time. So actually, it would be cheaper for them just to wait and keep me [here]."

* * *

Then there is the matter of how one gets pregnant in the first place—the matter of what happens when you take men and women, aged on average 18 to 25, away from what are generally small-town homes, ship them to exotic ports of call, house them in the catacomb-like berthing areas of ships, in coed tents or in crowded barracks and then subject them to loneliness, boredom and high stress. The fantasy of civilian activists like Pat Schroeder is that the result will look something like the bustling, efficient bridge of the *Starship Enterprise*. The reality is apt to look more like "a big high school"—which is the way a sailor named Elizabeth Rugh described her ship, the newly integrated *U.S.S. Samuel Gompers*.

Troops in Bosnia and Herzegovina (there were 1,500 female troops in the first deployment) generally live in coed tents with eight to ten people. Ranks are mixed, privates bedded down next to superiors. Troops are not allowed to drink alcohol or eat in restaurants, but they *are* allowed to have sex—as long as they are single and not doing it with a subordinate (or superior) in their chain of command. In a solemn statement provided to *Stars and Stripes*, Army spokesman Captain Ken Clifton wrote that "the Army does not prohibit heterosexual relations among consenting single soldiers ... but it does not provide facilities for sexual relations."

Lack of official facilities does not seem to be a great obstacle. "Where there's a will there's a way!" Captain Chris Scholl told *Stars and Stripes*. Favorite locations, he said, include the backs of Humvees parked on a deserted air strip, tents, latrines, even underground bunkers—if you can hack standing up to your ankles in icy water. "It's going on all over the place," said Scholl. "They've locked us down so what else is there to do?"

And there is, of course, the problem of nonconsensual sex. A Defense Department spokesman says "there is no way to get a good number" on the frequency of rapes and sexual assaults in the armed forces, because each service keeps its own numbers and defines things slightly differently. Still, it is clear that the Aberdeen case was not an isolated incident. The Army recorded twenty-four incidents it categorized as "sexual assaults" involving U.S. soldiers in the Gulf war; these cases range from that of a 24-year-old specialist who had been on overnight guard duty in the desert with a male soldier and awoke to find him fondling her under the blanket they had shared for warmth to that of a 21-year-old private who was raped at knifepoint by a sergeant.

* * *

The making of a soldier is a rough, hands-on, invasive process—a preparation for what may be a very rough end. "[T]he training, the discipline, the daily humiliations, the privileges of 'brutish' sergeants, the living en masse like schools of fish," wrote James Jones in his essay "The Evolution of a Soldier," "are all directed toward breaking down the sense of sanctity of the physical person, and toward hardening the awareness that a soldier is the chattel (hopefully the proud chattel but a chattel all the same) of the society he serves."

Soldiers abuse each other—in training, in command, in hazing rituals. It is a self-regulating mechanism; finding the weak links, then shaming them or bullying them to come up to par, is one way a unit ensures, or tries to ensure, its own survival, since on the battlefield one's life depends on one's buddies' performance.

Meanwhile, the brass attempt to operate on both tracks, to honor the standards of both the civilian and the military world. They know they must encourage "cohesion" in their mixed-gender units, but they know, too, that they must avoid the wrong kind of cohesion—the kind that could stimulate jealousies, lovers' spats and ... babies. So they end up sending a rather scrambled message, something like "Women are different but they're not different"; "We have the same expectations for women but you cannot treat them the same."

"Cry havoc and let slip the dogs of war," roared Shakespeare's Marc Antony. Something tells me he wasn't talking about 19-year-old girls. "Let the dogs loose," read a piece of locker-room samizdat (observed by writer Kathy Dobie) at a coed basic training program in

Florida. Men ache to unleash their dogs of war. Women generally have to be exhorted or trained to—then, good students and employees that they are, they can probably manage a semblance of dogginess at least for a while. But do we really want them to? Can a man of say, 35, be trained not to stay his hand when he needs to send a 20-year old girl onto a mortar-strafed field? Can the impulse which, still, impels men to try to protect women be overridden? Do we want it to be? Won't sex always gum up the works? Would we really prefer if it didn't?

POSTSCRIPT

Do Women Belong in the Armed Forces?

Supporters of women in the military believe that service benefits women, strengthens the nation's defense, and bolsters the family. Military service also provides career and educational opportunities for women and creates positive role models for children by showing them women's strength and competence as soldiers. Critics of women in the military are concerned about women's performance as soldiers, and they question the wisdom of having them serve with men. Critics contend that women not only strip themselves of femininity when playing the role of soldier but that they can also seriously compromise the national defense system if they cannot adequately serve in physically demanding positions. Critics also believe that a mother's departure for military duty threatens family stability and negatively affects children. For a summary of competing arguments, see Carol Wekesser and Matthew Polesetsky, eds., *Women in the Military* (Greenhaven Press, 1991), which addresses this controversy from a variety of perspectives, and "Women in Combat: A Quick Summary of the Arguments on Both Sides," *Minerva: Quarterly Report* (Spring 1990).

Denfeld claims that women have symbolically been relegated to the rear even when they are in the front. What does she mean by this? She states that combat forms the soldier's identity and that to deny women this right is to compromise their self-esteem. Other sources in support of women in the service include Linda Bird Francke, *Ground Zero: The Gender Wars in the Military* (Simon & Schuster, 1997) and Judith Hicks Stiehm, ed., *It's Our Military Too!* (Temple University Press, 1996). Francke is convinced that civilian and military service leaders in the Pentagon know that the U.S. military cannot perform without a female presence but have not been able to break down their resistance to the idea. She believes that the post–Persian Gulf War move in the 1990s to open combat positions to women has threatened the last intact all-male domain.

Articles supporting Gutmann's position include "Dames at Sea," *American Spectator* (August 1996); "Babes in Arms," *Men's Health* (June 1996); and "Girls With Guns," *National Review* (July 14, 1997). How would Gutmann respond to Denfeld's criticism that lines demarcating the combat zone are arbitrary, artificial, and counterproductive, resulting in high risk for women without the corresponding recognition? How does having women in America's armed forces affect women and the nation? Why has gender integration become so inevitable in the military culture? Or has it? Can weapons be made lighter— and therefore easier for women to handle— without reducing their lethality?

ISSUE 9

Do Mainstream Religious Denominations Discriminate Against Women?

YES: M. T. Stepaniants, from "The Image of Woman in Religious Consciousness: Past, Present, and Future," *Philosophy East and West* (April 1992)

NO: Kenneth L. Woodward, from "Gender and Religion: Who's Really Running the Show?" *Commonweal* (November 22, 1996)

ISSUE SUMMARY

YES: M. T. Stepaniants, a professor of philosophy, maintains that patriarchal religious denominations have overtly discriminated against women from the beginning and that they continue to do so.

NO: Writer Kenneth L. Woodward asserts that sociological aspects of American religious life privilege the feminine over the masculine and that this "feminization" has not been restricted to mainstream denominations that ordain women.

Religion has been a prominent force in American culture, defining notions of the universal and of the particular and establishing rules and guidelines for behavior. Gender asymmetry has been predominant in the mainstream religious denominations, and changes in this asymmetry have been associated with their widely perceived decline. Although women outnumbered men in membership roles as early as colonial times, only in the second half of the twentieth century have they begun to take their place in the governing councils of most Protestant denominations, and only recently have they become ordained ministers in most mainstream churches. In January 1977 the passage of the canon allowing women into the priesthood took effect in the Episcopal Church.

Throughout the nineteenth century women acted as "permanent" volunteers for their churches. This permitted men to work in their specialized spheres with the knowledge that the agencies of social control and social service needed for social order would be maintained by a staff of dedicated, unpaid, female workers. Despite their service and devotion, the Catholic Church still does not ordain women. In 1976 the Vatican Declaration rejected the ordination of women on the grounds that women did not bear a natural resemblance to Christ. In May 1994, in the Apostolic Letter of Pope John Paul

II, *Ordinatio Sacerdotalis*, the pope wrote on reserving priestly ordination to men alone. Women religious (nuns) have traditionally composed the arm of volunteerism for the Catholic Church, providing the church with a version of the dedicated, unpaid worker: necessary but largely unacknowledged. Conservative Catholics despair that the women religious have begun to concern themselves more with liberating the poor and oppressed and have developed an ecological agenda along with an interest in consolidating power for women in their churches and in society. In 1996 Pope John Paul II invited these women to "return religious life to the norms outlined by the church." Without the support of women religious, some are worried that a number of Catholic institutions may not survive into the 2000s.

Along with abdicating their volunteer roles in the Catholic Church, some Catholics believe that women have actually taken over the church. Every aspect of American religious life, they say, has begun to privilege the feminine over the masculine. Critics claim that disproportionate numbers of women fill congregations and that there is a local predominance of women, arguing that this "feminization" is not restricted to mainline "liberal" denominations that ordain women. Although pastors are exclusively male, says Kenneth L. Woodward, "the altar and the pulpit represent the last bastions of male presence within American Christianity." Seminary statistics suggest that the future belongs to women.

Feminist thinkers assert that the Catholic Church, along with most other religious dominations, invariably sanctifies the unequal status of women in society. Furthermore, religious rules and institutions act as guardians and guarantors of the patriarchal world organization. Some believe that male domination should be renounced for a new "spiritual feminism." The idea of reform in institutions that discriminate against women in such a pronounced way, however, may be unrealistic. The goal, though, is to erase the dichotomous worldview of patriarchal religion and replace it with integrity and holism, which implies a harmony between body and reason.

In the following selections, M. T. Stepaniants argues that as humankind moves toward new forms of religious consciousness, we will be able to free ourselves from limitations of patriarchal religious domination. In contrast, Woodward contends that American Christianity has already been "feminized," and he seeks a return to an equal balance between the genders in religion.

YES

M. T. Stepaniants

THE IMAGE OF WOMAN IN RELIGIOUS CONSCIOUSNESS

According to the Hindu *Code of Manu*, "In childhood a woman must be subject to her father, in youth, to her husband, [and] after the husband's death, to her sons. A woman must never be free of subjugation." In the orthodox Jewish prayer that a male repeats daily, there are the words, "I thank Thee, O Lord, that thou hast not created me a woman!" The New Testament instructs, "Wives, submit yourselves unto your own husbands, as unto the Lord. For the husband is the head of the wife, even as Christ is the head of the church. ... Therefore as the church is subject unto Christ, so let the wives be to their own husbands in every thing" (Ephesians 5: 22–24). The Koran admonishes, "Men are in charge of women, because Allah hath made the one of them to excel the other..." (Sura 4, *āyah* 34).

It is needless to go on, for the injunctions above vividly show that major religious doctrines invariably sanctify the unequal status of women in society; hence the quite appropriate assertion that "religion, it would seem, is not sexless; it is a man."[1]

The Holy Scriptures reflect "the world historical defeat of the fair sex"[2] which led to the overthrow of maternity rights and the dismissal of women from social production, predetermined in its turn by crucial socioeconomic transformations, for it is an established fact that "the most important clue to woman's status anywhere is her degree of participation in economic life and her control over property and that which she produces, both of which factors appear to be related to the kinship system of a society."[3]

Over many centuries the patriarchal character of social relations went virtually unquestioned. The religious rules and institutions acted as the inexorable guardians and guarantors of the patriarchal world organization. It was not until the sixteenth century that the Reformation, which brought forth radical changes in Christianity as a result of the emergence and development of new bourgeois relationships from out of the depths of feudalism, gave a fresh impetus to the "feminist Renaissance." A brief moment of freedom was enjoyed by women in the years between Luther and Calvin. Women, "... like long-deprived plants brought out of the darkness into the sunshine, responded to

From M. T. Stepaniants, "The Image of Woman in Religious Consciousness: Past, Present, and Future," *Philosophy East and West*, vol. 42, no. 2 (April 1992). Copyright © 1992 by University of Hawaii Press. Reprinted by permission.

the unaccustomed light and warmth in a way that can be described only as miraculous."[4] Mention should be made at least of a few women who made themselves prominent during the initial stage of the Reformation, among them Beatrix Galindo, Francesca da Lebrixa, Catherine of Aragon, Queen Mary, Anna Bacon, Jane Grey, Margaret Roper, and Mary Sidney. By the end of the sixteenth century, however, this brief interlude which had offered the promise of liberation came to a close. The advent of puritanism in the Protestant world led to the consolidation of the unequal status of women. Moreover, the "witch-hunt" initiated by the Protestant church resulted in the deaths of thousands of women.[5] But perhaps the most oppressive development of the time proved to be the appearance of the Calvinist doctrine concerning divine predestination, which left no hope for any changes in the status of Eve's progeny, cursed for the sin of the mother of the human race.

The winds of enlightened change, although very weak and short-lived, came to be felt again in the eighteenth century. During the revolutions in France and America, which proclaimed the slogans of "Liberty, Equality, and Justice," women's political activity grew immeasurably. But as soon as the revolutionary storms passed, society immediately consigned to oblivion women's contribution to the victory: each and every seat in the legislative and executive bodies of the state came to be occupied by men, while women were deprived, as before, of elementary political and economic rights.

Only in the twentieth century did the movement to counter discrimination against women take on an irreversible character. With each decade, beginning especially with the 1960s, this movement gained in strength as it involved representatives of the most varied components of modern society.

The steady growth of women's participation in social production is convincing proof of the *objective* necessity of revising the social status of women. The realization of this tendency depends, however, not only on material development but also on ideological factors. The latter include, among other things, stereotypes which were introduced and reinforced in the public consciousness and which, to a great extent, depend on religion and its institutions.

Can the world and the so-called "national" religions be revised in such a way as to promote social progress and to do away with discrimination against women? There are different approaches to this matter. The most conservative thinkers believe that such revision is hopeless and in fact contradictory to the very spirit of religion.

Others in the majority have been ready and willing somehow to reform conventional religion. Thus, Hindu reformers succeeded in getting the revocation of a number of religious precepts and even legislative bans on some of them. For example, in 1829, the Prevention of Sati Act was adopted, which banned the self-immolation of widows; in 1856, the Widow Remarriage Act officially permitted widows to remarry (though to date very few women make use of this right); in 1929, the Child Marriage Restraint Act forbade the marriage of girls younger than fourteen. Finally, in the 1950 Constitution of the Indian Republic, Articles 14 and 15 on "Fundamental Rights" proclaimed the equality of citizens irrespective of sex. All of these overt legislative acts, and even the fact that the Indian government was for a long time headed by

Indira Gandhi, have nevertheless failed to ensure actual equality between women and men. As before, there are numerous appalling evidences of discrimination against women, among them the still prevailing practices of *satī*, the mounting of ransom (*"dauri"*) bridegrooms, and so on. It is noteworthy that all of the customs involving the disparagement of women are grounded in religious dogmas.

The women's question turned out to be "a dead horse" with the reformers of Islam. Even those reformers (Sayyid Ahmad-Khan, Jamāl al-Dīn al-Afghānī, Muhammad 'Abdūh, and Muhammad Iqbāl) who were most radical in reinterpreting the basic Islamic notions of being, of Allah's omnipotence and man's free will, of the correlation between faith and knowledge, religion and science, and who urged for a revision of the Shari'ā as it pertained to the political and socioeconomic domains, failed to engage in a more outspoken protest against the "patriarchal" orientation of Islam. The most that Muslim reformers have ventured to do has been to "soften" the most appallingly unfair Islamic precepts concerning women, such as legalized polygamy, men's unilateral right to divorce, and the wearing of traditional veils (*khijab*) by women as a sign of their seclusion.

The weakness or even the nonexistence of any movement for women's emancipation in the Muslim world is evidenced by the legislation currently in force in the majority of Islamic countries, which are still in full conformity to the medieval Shari'ā laws. Moreover, the upsurge of fundamentalism, or the so-called Islamic Renaissance, over the last two decades has had a reverse effect: the rejection of certain advances and a revival of the most rigid observance of Muslim prescriptions

with regard to women (Iran is the most graphic example in this respect).

Reforms aimed at eliminating discrimination against women gained their widest scope in the Christian world, and this is undoubtedly due to the advances made by most Western countries in the general course of social progress.

One of the undisputable achievements of this general movement is the admittance of women into the church hierarchy, although the small number of women priests is out of proportion to their representation in the confessional community, and they are still prevented from attaining the highest ecclesiastic offices. Feminists are fully justified in their observation that Christianity remains a "men's religion" that upholds stereotypes against women. This is borne out in the following concepts. First, there is "the male image" of God. Although in the Old Testament God is sexless, the church, throughout the course of its history, has invariably been headed by men; men alone have acted as the interpreters of the Holy Scriptures, and wherever God is mentioned, masculine nouns and pronouns are used exclusively for the Christian Holy Trinity. It is the "male terms" that are reinforced (God the Father, God the Son, and God the Holy Spirit), and inculcated in the public consciousness is the concept of God as a man.

Second, there is the divine predestination of women to be subordinated to men, the proof of which can be found in the creation story (Genesis 2:18–23), according to which God created a woman (Eve) from one of Adam's ribs for the purpose of being Adam's "helper."[6]

Third, in Christianity woman is symbolically represented by two persons: Eve and the Virgin Mary. In the first case woman is a personification of Evil, for the responsibility for man's Fall is borne by Eve, while Mary personifies absolute chastity and "eternal femininity." Feminist leaders believe that Christian theology promotes those symbols that reflect men's ideas about sex: whore as sexual evil, Virgin as sexual purity, and Mother as sexual reproductivity.[7] According to Mary Daly, "The description of woman in the categories of Virgin, Bride and Mother implies her treatment exclusively in terms of sex,"[8] whereas it has apparently never occurred to anyone to reduce man's characteristics to the categories of "Virgin, Husband and Father."[9] And, last but not least, the "divine proof" of woman's inferior nature (which justifies her subordination to man) is made manifest for the Christian clergy in the Epistles of Paul the Apostle. The most commonly used Pauline statements, taken from the First Epistle to the Corinthians, forbid a woman to pray with her head uncovered, while "a man indeed ought not to cover his head, forasmuch as he is the image and glory of God: but the woman is the glory of the man. For the man is not of the woman; but the woman of the man. Neither was the man created for the woman; but the woman for the man" (11:7–9). There are other examples in the Epistle to the Ephesians (5:22–24) and in the divine precepts from the First Epistle to Timothy: "Let the woman learn in silence with all subjection. But I suffer not a woman to teach, nor to usurp authority over the man, but to be in silence. For Adam was first formed, then Eve. And Adam was not deceived, but the woman being deceived was in the transgression" (1 Timothy 2:11–14).

Reform-minded theologians and church authorities, under the pressure of the feminist movement and taking into consideration the changes unfolding in modern society, resort in some cases to reinterpreting the Holy Scriptures and the Christian traditions with a view to abstaining from the precepts which discriminate against women in the most pronounced way. However, some feminists regard such reforms as unpromising and, therefore, put forward the idea of creating their own "feminist religion" or "women's spirituality." "Spiritual feminism" is not a uniform movement; it embraces the theorists of matriarchal futurism, the worshippers of the Goddess, the adherents of witchcraft, and so on. For all the varieties of the phenomenon tentatively defined as "feminist religion," however, we can identify some of its general, intrinsic characteristics. In the first place, the dichotomous world view of patriarchal religions is counterposed against the integrity and holism inherent in women's perception of the world.[10] This holism implies a harmony between body and reason, flesh and spirit, theory and practice, word and deed."[11] Holism means also the unity of nature and the human being, which is experienced by women fully and with particular intensity. Speaking about women, Susan Griffin points out: "And we are nature. We are nature seeing nature."[12] Hence, it is concluded that in contrast to the patriarchal mentality, which comes into conflict with nature and "rapes" it with its thoughtless interference, the feminist mentality brings harmony into the world and salvation from our ecological crisis.

The theorists of "feminist religion" set off the Goddess against God as a transcendental force. According to Naomi Goldenberg, the God of Judaism and Christianity is inadequate for modern women and, therefore, will be rejected and replaced by new feminine forms of religious expressiveness.[13] In "spiritual feminism" the Goddess is not opposed to nature, is not transcendental in relation to it, but, on the contrary, she, "as part of nature and interactive with natural forces, recognizes nature not as other to be conquered, but as another dimension of Self.,... Feminist spirituality is seen as an inherently ecological mode of worship."[14]

The holistic nature of "feminist religion" infers not the Goddess' transcendence but her interiorization, especially with the cultivation of witchcraft. Naomi Goldenberg says: "Modern witchcraft represents a profound shift in the human tendency to imagine gods, goddesses and divine beings as forces outside human selves and to conceive of these beings as interior experiences."[15]

Though the adherents of "spiritual feminism" believe that the philosophical basis of their religion is holism, they nonetheless fail to overcome the dichotomy that they criticize. In fact, they proceed along the same dichotomous lines which they identify with the "male culture." In the final analysis, the difference lies only in the choice of priorities. If, say, patriarchal culture focuses on such values as Reason and Culture, "feminist" religion glorifies Intuition and Nature. The patriarchal myths are replaced by a matriarchy-oriented mythology which idealizes a system based, in fact, on the supremacy of women. Elizabeth Davis writes:

> We are on the threshold of the new Age of Aquarius, whom the Greeks called Hydrochoos, the water-bearer, the renewer, the reviver.... It was at the dawn of another aquarian age, fifty-two thousand years ago, that Basilea, the great queen, brought order and justice to a chaotic world aflame with lawlessness and strife, a world similar to our own of the twentieth century. Today, as then, women are in the vanguard of the aborning civilization; and it is to the women that we look for salvation in the healing and restorative waters of Aquarius.... The ages of masculism are now drawing to a close.... Only the overthrow of the three-thousand-year old beast of masculist materialism will save the race. In the new science of the twenty-first century not physical force but spiritual force will lead the way.... Extrasensory perception will take precedence over sensory perception, and in this sphere woman will again predominate.[16]

This lengthy paragraph is cited to show most graphically the intentions of "feminist religion." Such extreme opposition to "patriarchal religions" is, no doubt, positive in the sense of awakening women to their self-awareness and expanding the range of the parties involved in the process of improving public life by challenging discrimination. Nevertheless, the mythology of "spiritual feminism" with its idealization of the "Golden Age" of matriarchy is fraught with many dangers. A movement based on the quicksand of mythology is vulnerable to various political orientations, the most reactionary example being the Nazi myth of Aryan supremacy. To quote Susan Walters' most fitting remark: "A movement that immerses itself in organic society mythology becomes easily enraptured of its own fantasies and soon believes its own fictions. These movements either evaporate from true content, or reify their mythology, creating an isolated, alternative way of life. Interestingly enough, the creation of this type of an alternative women's community often leads to the end of the much vaunted 'nurturance' through an antagonism, towards those who don't follow the 'correct cultural line'."[17]

To all appearances, none of the existing movements to lay the religious groundwork for the fundamentally new social status of women seems either satisfying or promising. Reforms within the framework of "patriarchal religions" can only proceed to a certain limit, otherwise they will demolish the fundamental concepts on which the religious dogmas have been founded. "Feminist religion" builds unrealistic myths around those things that can hardly find support from the majority of women themselves, since the reversal of the status of rulers and subordinates will not make humankind either free or happy.

Perhaps the way out lies in the search for a new, truly universal type of religiosity. As is known, the current processes of integration have resulted in a world market, a closer convergence of sociopolitical systems, a synthesis of cultures, and, in the religious world, an ecumenical movement. We are witnessing the hard, tortuous, but vitally important working out of a new type of thinking which becomes conscious of the common destiny, in certain respects, of all the inhabitants of this planet.

There are grounds to believe that one of the constituent elements of the new world perception will be a religious consciousness prevailing not only over the confessional but also over sex differences. (The goal is not to set aside all differences, but only those which are antagonistic in character.) The road to such a "universal religion" may be found in a religious trend inherent in all belief systems—in mysticism.

We do not want to treat mysticism idealistically. Acknowledging its negative aspects and the invariably controversial role it has played in human history, we nevertheless would like to under-

line those elements which might have a wholesome effect on the formation of a "universal" religious consciousness. In ontological terms, what is most important is the pantheistic coloring of the mystical concepts of human existence, with God being treated simultaneously as a transcendental and as an immanent force in relation to humankind and the world.

> There is nothing else besides me,
>   Arjuna.
> Like clusters of yarn-beads
> formed by knots on a thread,
> all this threaded on Me.
>
> Arjuna, I am the sapidity in water
> and the light of the moon and the sun;
> I am the sacred syllable OM in all the
>   Vedas,
> sound in ether, and manliness in men.
>
> I am pure odour in the earth
> and pure brilliance in fire;
> nay I am life in all beings
> and austerity in ascetics.
>
> Arjuna, know Me as the eternal seed
> of all beings.
> I am the intelligence of the intelligent;
> the glory of the glorious am I.
>
> —*Bhagavad-Gītā*, VII:7–10

In epistemological terms, of particular importance is the intrinsic skepticism and even mistrust of mysticism toward the comprehensive and absolute nature of rational knowledge; hence, its refutation of the unconditional authority of the dogmas, on the one hand, and its inclination to a constant search for Truth, on the other. "The incapacity of complete comprehension is comprehension; glory be to Him who has created for men the way of comprehending Him only by their incapacity of comprehending Him."[18]

In axiological terms, mysticism believes in the "perfect personality" of the individual who orients himself not toward the rigid normative rules of society, the church, and so on, but toward the realization of the "divine principle" inherent in *each* human being.

> I am a house, but a house forsaken
>   since time immemorial.
> To be exonerated from the curse
> It must be cleansed, restored, and
>   renovated.
> And plastered over with the clay of
>   God's Grace.[19]

These four lines from the *Lamentations* by the Armenian poet Grigor Narekatsi (A.D. 950–1003), a Christian mystic, are consonant with the following verses from *Mathnawi*, written two centuries later, by the Persian Sufist poet Jalāl al-Dīn Rūmi (1207–1273):

> ... Ruined the house for the sake of the
>   golden treasure, and with that same
>   treasure builds it better than before;
> Cut off the water and cleansed the
>   river-bed, then caused
>   drinking-water to flow in the
>   river-bed.[20]

What is most essential is that "perfection" is treated here as the achievement of one's *personal* efforts, irrespective of one's social status, holy order, or sex. It is no accident that despite the fact of women's interdiction from the church hierarchy, they have held a worthy place among the sacred mystics, either Christian, Hindu, or Muslim.

Of course, humankind may come to other forms of religious consciousness in the future. In all cases we can only hope and believe that it will be able to get free from the limitations of its patriarchal and matriarchal past.

NOTES

1. Barbara Gelpy, Chief Editor of *Signs* magazine, used as an epigraph to a special issue on "Women and Religion" this paraphrase of a statement by Virginia Woolf. The original reads: "Science it would seem is not sexless; she is a man, a father and infected too" (*Signs* 9, no. 1 (1983)).

2. F. Engles, *The Origins of the Family, Private Property and the State*, in K. Marx, F. Engles, *Works*, vol. 21; p. 60.

3. Ruby R. Levitt, "Women in Other Cultures," in *Woman in Sexist Society: A Study in Power and Powerlessness*, ed. V. Gornick and B. K. Moran (New York: New American Library, 1971), p. 396.

4. Elizabeth Gould Davis, *The First Sex*, (Baltimore: Penguin Books, Inc., 1971), p. 283.

5. Ibid., p. 287.

6. Meanwhile, a historical tradition came into being which consciously ignored the other (chronologically later) version of the creation story, according to which man and woman were created simultaneously and on equal grounds: "So God created man in his own image, in the image of God created he him; male and female created he them" (Genesis 1:27).

7. Judith Hole and Ellen Levine, *Rebirth of Feminism* (New York: Quadrangle Books, 1971), p. 381.

8. Mary Daly, *The Church and the Second Sex* (New York and Evanston: Harper and Row, 1968), p. 111.

9. Ibid.

10. Charlene Spretnak characterizes women's spirituality as "the inner unity of all forms of being." See Charlene Spretnak, "Introduction," in *The Politics of Women's Spirituality*, ed. C. Spretnak (Garden City, New York: Anchor Press (Doubleday), 1982), p. xvi.

11. Barbara Starret, "The Metaphors of Power," in *The Politics of Women's Spirituality*, p. 187.

12. Susan Griffin, *Woman and Nature* (New York: Harper Colophon Books, 1978), p. 226.

13. Naomi R. Goldenberg, *Changing of the Gods: Feminism and the End of Traditional Religions* (Boston: Beacon Press, 1979).

14. S. D. Walters, "Caught in the Web: A Critique of Spiritual Feminism," *Berkeley Journal of Sociology* 30 (1985); p. 21.

15. Goldenberg, *Changing of the Gods*, p. 109.

16. Davis, *The First Sex*, pp. 337–339.

17. Walters, "Caught in the Web," p. 29.

18. Abu Hamid al-Ghazali, *The Revival of Theologies*. (Moscow, 1980), p. 248.

19. *Armenian Medieval Lyrical Poetry* (Leningrad, 1972), p. 148.

20. Jalāl al-Dīn Rumi, *Mathnawi*, bk 1, pp. 306–308.

NO

Kenneth L. Woodward

GENDER AND RELIGION: WHO'S REALLY RUNNING THE SHOW?

> Annul me in my manhood, Lord, and
> Make me woman-sexed and weak,
> If by that total transformation
> I might know Thee more.

The poet William Everson died in 1994 at the age of eighty-one, a wispy, Whitmanesque figure from the Beat Generation. Known as Brother Antoninus, Everson spent thirteen years as a member of the Dominican order where he published the poem whose opening lines I quote above. The poem was inspired by a passage from Teresa of Avila, in which the redoubtable doctor of the church reports that, in her judgment and that of a holy priest of her acquaintance, women are more receptive than men to divine initiative. Can this be right? Is male sexuality a barrier to whole-hearted surrender to God?

One finds in this poem, as in the entire body of Everson's work, echoes of the psalms, the Song of Songs, of Augustine's *Confessions*, among other cornerstone texts of the Christian tradition that yoke the erotic with the mystical. And in much of that tradition, it is male—not female—sexuality which is problematic for those who would open themselves to the divine embrace.

The issues surrounding the relationships between gender—both genders —and religion are complex, deep, and of long standing. These concerns were salient long before the advent of gender studies. One has only to consult such fine works of historical retrieval as Caroline Walker Bynum's *Jesus as Mother: Studies in the Spirituality of the High Middle Ages* (University of California, 1982) to see that the relationship of the masculine and the feminine in religion is such that stark polarities do not do justice to the facts. Isn't it possible, for instance, that in the realm of religious experience maleness is at least as problematic as femaleness? Moreover, I would argue that in the everyday life of most Americans today it is the female, not the male, presence that is most noticeable—and, in ways that feminist scholars choose not to notice—also the most powerful.

From Kenneth L. Woodward, "Gender and Religion: Who's Really Running the Show?" *Commonweal* (November 22, 1996). Copyright © 1996 by The Commonweal Foundation. Reprinted by permission.

Nearly 90 percent of Americans claim at least nominal allegiance to Christianity. Most American Christians, of course, are Protestants. Too often, when Roman Catholics—including bishops—discuss issues like the ordination of women, they fail to look at the Protestant experience. I will focus mostly on that experience. Catholics, I think, can gain some perspective on their own experience by looking at Protestantism, and especially at what I call the feminization of American Christianity.

What I mean by "feminization" is not simple. Essentially, I want to call attention to those aspects of American religious life that privilege the feminine rather than the masculine. Most of these observations are sociological. But sociological change has deep psychological impact.

What I mean by the terms "masculine" and "feminine" will, I hope, become apparent as I go along. But to be clear I want to state at the outset that I do assume that there *are* differences between men and women, rooted in biology, and that, as a consequence of these differences, every culture makes distinctions between what is masculine and what is feminine, including the cultures of churches. The distinctions may be more or less arbitrary, but they are no less significant for being so. It is hard to imagine a culture that is not gender inflected. When Saint Paul wrote that "in Christ there is neither male nor female," he was not suggesting thereby that gender differences do not exist. Indeed, much of Christian tradition can be read as a continuing conversation about the meaning of male and female as it relates to God, who is beyond gender.

Today, much of that conversation is confined to women and to "women's studies." Like its counterparts in other disciplines, feminist theology places gen-

der at the center of inquiry, employing a hermeneutics of suspicion toward religious texts, and a strategy of retrieval to uncover the experiences and roles women really played in, say, the early Jesus movement. The goal is not female domination, but the liberation of men and women from androcentrism and its attendant evils. In short, the original sin was not pride but patriarchy, and from it has come all manner of evil: sexism, racism, clericalism, ageism, classism, conflict, leadership by hierarchy—even the rape of the environment.

Whatever the merits of this approach to theology and religion, what interests me is whether this hermeneutic of suspicion aligns with what I see of gender and gender relations among ordinary church folk.

* * *

For most Americans, religion is rooted in the local congregation. Particularly for the Protestant majority, the local congregation *is* the church. It is there that the word is heard, sacraments celebrated, connections made, marriages blessed, children baptized, loved ones buried. And if we look inside Protestant churches on Sunday, we find that most of the people in the pews are women. Although there are no hard-and-fast statistics, pastors I talk to say that women usually outnumber the men three-to-one. Congregations that are 80 percent women are not unusual, particularly an aging congregation, since women live longer than men. And that's just the weekend.

During the week, pastors live in women's world. Like the suburbs in a John Updike novel, the weekday world of American religion is a world without men. Women dominate the church committees, the prayer groups, the Bible study groups, the Sunday schools. You're much more likely to find a women's spirituality group than a men's spirituality group. "No one told me when I left the seminary," says William Willimon, a longtime Methodist minister, now dean of the chapel at Duke University, "that most of my time would be spent with women." From Monday to Friday, much of a Protestant pastor's time is spent in counseling. Many of the counselors are couples, but most are women. Indeed, in all the focus on pedophilia in the Catholic priesthood, attention has been diverted from the virtual explosion of sexual seductions involving male Protestant clergy.

The pastoral challenge facing most clergy is to find ways to draw men into active participation. Jews traditionally manage the problem by allowing only men to form a minyan. It used to be, of course, that in both Protestant and Catholic congregations certain roles were reserved for men. Only men could serve on the vestry, for example. Men were heavily recruited, though not always successfully, to teach adolescent boys in Sunday school. There were single-sex choirs. And among Lutherans there were the brotherhoods. But today exclusively male roles have virtually disappeared, while the sisterhoods, as at Jewish temples, are thriving. Among Catholics, the men were encouraged to make retreats with other men. But I myself have seen little movement among women to break up the brotherhood of ushers.

These are the homely facts of American religious life, far removed from robust themes of liberation and empowerment. But they well describe the environment of religion as it is experienced by the majority of Protestants. And that environment is perceived, at least by males, as essentially female. Which brings me to another level of observation: most of what goes on within church buildings is related to the nurturing of the young. And, fair or not, nurture is perceived as something feminine.

Synagogues, for instance, fairly bustle with women preparing the young for their bar or bat mitzvah. Sunday school is perhaps the major enterprise one finds under the roof of a Southern Baptist church. Those Catholic churches which most resemble the "community" that Catholics always talk about but seldom achieve are ones with parochial schools attached. Indeed, you don't have to be a sociologist to recognize the basic rhythm of American church membership. Americans are most likely to turn to church—usually after a long period of drift—when they become parents. Especially in the African-American community, which is the most "churched" community in the United States outside of Mormon Utah, adults use the church to help them in the rearing of their children. And it is through the children, I would argue, that churches reach most adults. That is, churches address adults essentially as parents.

In short, religion in American life is not only privatized; it is also domesticated, identified with the side of life away from work, from the civic and the public; away from the side which, rightly or wrongly, is identified with the masculine.

* * *

This is not a new phenomenon. As sociologist Rodney Stark demonstrates in *The Rise of Christianity* (Princeton University Press, 1996), early Christian communities were disproportionately female. In a pagan society that disparaged women, undervalued marriage, and regularly resorted to abortion and infanticide, Christianity extolled marriage and family life, protected and enfranchised women as members of the community, denounced abortion as murder, and readily encouraged their surplus of women to take (and domesticate) pagan husbands, who were notoriously inhospitable to both marital fidelity and family creation.

In American religion, women have always made up the bulk of Christian congregations. And churches, as cultural historian Ann Douglas has demonstrated, played the central role, from the middle of the nineteenth century on, in what she calls "the feminization of culture." In her book by that title (Alfred A. Knopf, 1977), Douglas examined how the liberal Protestant clergy, in league with women, sentimentalized American culture and transformed women into the exemplars of virtue. But there was little that was virile in the virtues upheld. Arguing from what she calls a "feminist" perspective, Douglas deplores the effects of all this on women, but she is curiously silent on its effect on lay men.

I was reminded of this prior "feminization" while doing an article for *Newsweek* on the rapid growth of the "Christian Men's Movement" among Evangelicals. I've long observed that Evangelicals are quick to recognize new markets and to exploit them. For example, the major reason why the liberal, mainline Protestant denominations are in deep decline is their failure to raise their own children in the faith. Evangelicals have noticed this, too, and for the last fifty years, through parachurch agencies like Youth for Christ, the Fellowship of Christian Athletes, and a whole Vatican-full of similar organizations, Evangelicals have focused on recruiting, organizing, and catechizing the young outside of congregational structures. So it pays a journalist to watch where these Evangelicals put their time, money, and effort. And their latest enterprise is the Christian Men's Movement. It is, I believe, a genuine response to the alienation of men from the feminization of Evangelical church life.

Keep in mind that Evangelical Protestants constitute the largest religious group in the United States—and the most committed. Remember, too, that most of them do not ordain women and take seriously the Pauline statements [of the apostle St. Paul] about male leadership in the church and in the home. I can only conclude that if these churches are having difficulty attracting men, then the feminization of American religion is by no means confined to those liberal mainline denominations that ordain women.

The first thing to notice about the Christian Men's Movement is its connection with sports. The movement's primary organization, Promise Keepers, was founded five years ago by Bill McCartney, a former Catholic who was the coach of the University of Colorado football team. The Promise Keepers meet in stadiums, where tens of thousands of men shout "Jesus, Jesus, Jesus" while doing the wave and chanting "we are the brotherhood, we are connected."

The second thing to notice is the promises they make: to be responsible to God, to their wives and children, to the church, and to each other, in that order. In other words, to be a man is to take charge, lead, protect. Leaders of the movement expect men to exhibit manly virtues and recognize these virtues as Christian. In short, these Evangelicals are responding in their own time and way to the feminization of religion that scholar Ann Douglas described.

The third feature is key. Jesus, the movement insists, is a man's man. He is not the androgynous Christ of sentimental Protestant iconography, but a mighty king and warrior, a leader of men and a willing Savior, a wild man with a redeeming purpose—and also the best buddy a guy could ever have.

Fourth, the movement is, in keeping with much of contemporary church life, highly therapeutic. Men are urged to confess their sins in small groups of strangers, to weep, emote, and show their vulnerability. Clearly, Promise Keepers has been listening to contemporary pop psychology which holds an article of faith that what is wrong with men is that they do not show their emotions as easily as women do.

Finally, following the model of all twelve-step programs, these men are expected to find a male faith partner with whom they share their temptations and weaknesses. Further, they form small male-bonding groups in order to spread the men's movement in local churches. Already, 260,000 local congregations have tapped Promise Keepers as a way of encouraging greater male participation in congregational life.

As I read it, the message of the Christian Men's Movement is this: Following Jesus is not for women only, nor is it merely a spectator sport, which it tends to become for men in our domesticated, mostly female congregations. Consciously or unconsciously, the movement also validates an insight which sociologists confirm: The best predictor of whether a child will remain religious as an adult is not the religiosity of the mother—for children tend to take that for granted—but of the father, because he is not expected to be religious. That is, if the father demonstrates that religion is not foreign to what a man is and does, the child—especially the male child—is much more likely to be religious upon reaching adulthood.

Let me sum up: On the local level, women predominate, and what takes place inside churches is mainly though not exclusively focused on the nurturing of the young and the support of family life and relationships. Americans, when they get religion, get it primarily through the aegis of women: mom, most of all, but also the Sunday school teacher, who is usually a woman, or in the case of Catholic parochial schools, Sister Mary or her female lay alternative.

The pastor, usually a man, may exercise authority in the congregation, but to the young he is like the principal of the local elementary school: a remote authority figure. In religion, those who do the formation are in fact more significant than those who run the show. And the hand that rocks this cradle is, invariably, a woman's.

But, Ah, you might say: It is the pastor who has the authority and therefore wields the power, and since most pastors are male—all of them in the case of Roman Catholicism—that is what is important and unjust about American religion. Never mind, in other words, that the two acolytes, two readers, and four eucharistic ministers up there in the sanctuary at Saint Mary's Catholic Church are women. What's important is that the single male among them is the presiding priest.

I think the reality of congregational life is more complex than that. Let's look, for example, at the black church in America, which, in terms of numbers essentially means the black Baptist tradition. Here we see that the black pastor is a powerful figure, not only in the pulpit but in politics and in the wider African-American community. There are very few female clergy in the black church—about 5 percent—and most of those are in the Pentecostal tradition. If we look closer, through the eyes of a leading black scholar like C. Eric Lincoln of Duke Divinity School, we see that "the well-organized black church is an organization of subgroups in which women predominate and wield their own power. Women raise the money and, though men dominate the church boards of trustees, it is their wives who effectively determine how it is spent. Among black Baptists, power belongs to "the Mothers," a group of older women who have been in their congregations for decades and constitute the heart and soul of the church. On Sundays, the Mothers dress distinctively in white and preside from a special section of the church—opposite the 'Amen corner' where the male trustees sit." Says Lincoln: "The minister who has the Mothers on his side is virtually unassailable, and woe be it to the minister who doesn't."

Because of their power, and because of the importance of the Old Testament in black religion, the Mothers oppose women preachers. Another reason for this opposition is that so many black families lack fathers that the women want their children to see in the minister a disciplined father figure. In the inner-city, where most black churches are, the priority is wooing young males to the church. Scholars estimate that 60 percent of young African-American males have no contact with church—up from 20 percent just a generation ago.

* * *

Obviously, space does not permit analysis of gender and power in every American denomination. But I want to note in passing that within the United Methodist church, second only to the Southern Baptists in terms of numbers, women exercised enormous power long before ordination was open to them. The organization United Methodist Women is, arguably, the most powerful single group among the denomination's various boards and agencies. It raises and spends millions every year with no interference from the hierarchy. Indeed, it constitutes a female hierarchy within the church.

From this brief survey of congregational life, I think it not at all an exaggeration to say that the altar and the pulpit represent the last bastions of male presence within American Christianity. But that too, is changing rapidly. Indeed, within the liberal mainline Protestant denominations, we are witnessing the rapid feminization of the clergy. Let's look at the figures.

Although men still outnumber women three-to-one in the mainline clergy, seminary statistics suggest that the future belongs to women. Among Universalist-Unitarians more than half of the clergy are women. According to the 1994 figures from the Association of Theological Schools, 37 percent of all the students now studying for the Master of Divinity degree—the ordination track—are women. That's up from 10 percent in 1972. Meanwhile, the number of men studying for the M. Div. degree has risen by less than 5 percent over the same twenty-one-year period. And that does not include those studying for degrees in Christian education, in which women also predominate.

In the United Church of Christ, there are 535 male seminarians and 531 female. Among Presbyterians, United Methodists, and Episcopalians, men out-

. In that overwhelming feminine ̶ment, he believes, the all-male ̶function as a countervailing force. ̶y be that Ong's reflections apply ̶ Catholics, or perhaps only to ̶hristian traditions whose high ̶entalism involves deep structures ̶masculine and the feminine. And ̶rom the dialectical relationship ̶sculine and feminine, he argues, ̶e church receives much of its ̶ism and energy.

̶ve spent time on the Protestant ̶ence because I want to indicate ̶ly what is happening among our ̶ian brethren but also to suggest ̶the loosening of this dynamic ̶n may be one reason why mainline ̶inations are in such dire straits.

̶ church as a profession is not like ̶w, medicine, or finance. Women who enter these professions do not change them; they are changed by the professions, and if they do not perform well they are out.

But religion is different. Whatever else it is, religion is a symbol system and to change the symbols is to change the meaning that religion expresses. Surely there is need to incorporate, expand, and deepen what is feminine in religion. But there are limits. And as we can see in the exponents of post-Christian feminism, those limits have already been breached. My concern is not with theory or theology but with the atmosphere of ordinary American churches as I find them. And what I find in them is the gradual disappearance of anything that might adequately be described as masculine, no matter who in the hierarchy is calling the shots.

number the women, but not by much. The Episcopalians, for example, have 248 women studying for the priesthood, and 323 men. Among the Disciples of Christ it is much the same: 237 women and 351 men.

If we consider only the prestigious, national, nondenominational divinity schools such as Harvard and Yale, women outnumber male students. And even though ordination is forbidden to women in the Catholic church, there are already more women than men working as professionals in the ministry of the Catholic church in the United States.

But statistics alone do not tell us very much. They do not tell us anything about the quality of today's seminarians, their attitudes toward ministry, or about the culture of divinity schools. Hence they do not tell us much about the feminization of the ministry.

A generation ago, the Protestant ministry rivaled the law and medicine as attractive options for young men. That is not the case today. A good indication of this change is that admission standards are lower than in the past. According to psychologist Joseph P. O'Neil, principal research scientist at the Educational Testing Service in Princeton, New Jersey, "Most theological schools are 'open admission' institutions that rarely reject anyone who is of sound mind and with a bachelor's degree." And not surprisingly, women entering seminaries are on average better educated than the men. They are also apt to be older and to have children. The average age of all seminarians has increased dramatically—at Yale Divinity, it is thirty-four—but that doesn't always mean they are more mature. Many are entering second careers, often after failing to find either success or fulfillment in their first choices. Many

of the women, in particular, are divorced, quite a few are middle-aged, and many are single mothers.

Now I'm sure you've heard that despite all this women in the clergy still face a "glass ceiling," as Joan Brown Campbell, the general secretary of the National Council of Churches, recently put it. She blames sexism for the fact that too few women are accepted as head pastors, and almost none at prestige churches. But is sexism the only or even the major reason?

Unlike Catholics, Protestants prefer that their pastors not only be married but that they set an example of married fidelity and virtue. Although Protestants accept divorce for themselves, they'd rather not have it in their ministers. Divorce and single motherhood are major factors working against acceptance of women as pastors.

But the difference between male and female seminarians that I find most interesting is in their attitudes toward authority and its exercise. Here I want to draw on a very illuminating research paper by O'Neil. In it, he reviews several studies of seminaries and seminarians, both Protestant and Catholic, and combines these with his own research. One study compared students at a Protestant seminary in Chicago with students preparing for careers as doctors and nurses. The study found that early on the students in medicine adopted "a cloak of professionalism" while the seminary students did not. Seminarians were less interested in displaying the knowledge and skills of their own profession than in being "the right kind of person." And they did that by relying on their "gut feelings," that is, by displaying their personal rather than professional skills. In short, the study finds the ministry becoming an oxymoron, a "profession without authority," a profession bent on erasing the distance between clergy and laity. The pastor as buddy, the minister as mom, are the models.

O'Neil candidly speculates that this deprofessionalization of the clergy, as he calls it, is "the effect of the huge increase of women candidates on the culture of Protestant seminaries." Women, he argues, are much more likely than men to create community by sharing personal information. And he adds that, by the sheer weight of numbers, "[women] are socializing the male seminarians to do the same."

Rebecca Chopp, dean of the faculty at Emory University's Candler School of Theology, draws remarkably parallel conclusions in her *Saving Work: Feminist Practices of Theological Education* (Westminster/John Knox Press, 1995). Women, she observes, enter seminaries for different reasons than men. They "come to theological education out of deep changes in their lives and cultures," she asserts. "Women... come for the space and time it gives them, and to gain valuable resources for living their lives." In those denominations where women take an active role, Chopp goes on, they have helped reshape the church's image as a "community of local belonging, of friends." In sum, "women bring what they know to a situation and it becomes transformed. The transformation is already occurring in many mainline denominations." Indeed it is.

But running a parish or congregation is not the same as sustaining a family. Like it or not, congregations are also institutions that require the exercise of authority and demand that some distance be observed between those who stand in the pulpit and those who sit in the pews. So it is

not at all surprising that O'Neil finds that women seminarians, far more often than men, opt to go into pastoral counseling and chaplaincies where small-group or face-to-face encounters make up a large portion of the work day. In sum, the glass ceiling may in fact be a glass door which women choose not to open because of the way in which they prefer to operate as clergy.

Not only is feminist theology widely taught in seminaries, but the informal curriculum is also frankly and ideologically feminist. Not surprisingly, Protestant seminaries are also home to large numbers of lesbians and gay men. Anyone acquainted with Episcopal seminaries, for example, can tell you which ones cater to lesbians and gays. Some seminaries have housing especially for homosexuals. Catholics who fear the celibate priesthood is attracting too high a proportion of gay men should look at what is happening—what in fact has been institutionalized—at interdenominational and mainline Protestant seminaries. None of this augurs well for the masculine presence in the ministry—if by masculine we also mean heterosexual.

* * *

My aim has been to keep an eye on what is going on. In this context, I was struck by a passage in Elizabeth Johnson's widely acclaimed *She Who Is* (Crossroad, 1991). I recognize that in her very interesting exercise in reconciling feminism with Catholic tradition, Johnson is pursuing a conservative, not liberal, much less a radical strategy, as feminists construe these terms. But I was struck by her negative references to the male images of God one finds in Christian art and churches: especially of Jesus as "the visible image of the invisible God" who

"is used to tie the knot between maleness and divinity very tightly."

I stopped and asked myself: What male imagery? In those Protestant churches that accept the iconic, one typically encounters—especially in Methodist churches—a very androgynous if not altogether feminized Jesus. The Good Shepherd and the Good Samaritan predominate with Jesus looking for all the world as if he were a permanent-wave advertisement.

But Johnson is a Catholic and I assume it is Catholic churches she has in mind. Yet what we find in Catholic churches is usually a suffering Jesus on the cross, though without the barely covered phallus that we find in Renaissance paintings. And when you look again at Catholic iconography, what do you see? Everywhere and always you will see a Madonna. Surely Johnson cannot be objecting to that. When Joseph shows up, he is usually depicted as an old, sexless man. And what of the much maligned God the Father? He gets no pictorial representation at all. One has to travel far, to the Uffizi Museum in Florence, to the Cathedral in Prague, or to the Franciscan church in Cracow, to find the most prominent Western images of the Father. And it is the same image: of an old man holding up the hands of a crucified Christ with a dove flying above the crown of thorns.

Now what is remarkable about this ancient image of the Father is that he reminds us not of a man, but by his posture of receiving the Christ on his lap, he is in the spitting image of that far more prevalent figure, the Pietà.

No, what seems to bother feminist theologians is the masculine language and verbal icons used in reference to God. These, they say, exclude, deny, and

oppress women. Do   really reinforce a mal and church? Are sy than reflections of a privileges the men women?

To turn one final Walker Bynum, this t book of essays, *Gender* con Press, 1986). There gious symbols are inh that is, they have "th fer to many levels of hu and also "the capacity symbols to appropriate symbols point." She cit as an example of wha points out that to Christ Europe, "God was som bridegroom to whom all what sort of sexual body related as a bride." That Everson was struggling

What Bynum also fir women's symbols and build from social and bi ences; men's symbols a to invert them. Women's symbols seems given to th position, while men's mo ized by emphasis on oppo diction, and conversion.

Much the same point h by Walter Ong, surely on Catholic intellects of our penetrating book *Fighting* nell University Press, 198 siders masculine and fem man contraries, finding in a need for agonistic exper sition, and "ritual contest" maleness from "its biologica human heights." To the psy marks, the church is alway whelmingly feminine—Holy

Church enviror clergy

It m only t those sacram of the it is of ma that t dynam

I ha experi not or Christ that tensio denom

The the la

POSTSCRIPT

Do Mainstream Religious Denominations Discriminate Against Women?

In *Sisters in Crisis: The Tragic Unraveling of Women's Religious Communities* (Our Sunday Visitor Publishing Division, 1997), Ann Carey reports that Catholic conservatives are upset that women religious have abdicated their volunteer positions in running the church and have moved in the direction of working for social change. Do you think that the situation would be improved in the Catholic Church if women were allowed to become priests? Have other churches become less patriarchal since they have begun to ordain women? Or do you agree that the Catholic Church and other religious bodies have swung too far in the direction of becoming feminine? Do you think that the "feminization" of churches has led to their decline?

Feminist spiritual thinkers have noticed that monotheistic religions such as Catholicism and Protestantism are among the few worldviews that envision the deity in predominantly male terms, using masculine pronouns and images. While a majority of believers see God as transcending gender, some see an uncritical, unreflective, literalistic insistence upon the traditional male images for deity as idolatry.

Some feminists are calling for a complete restructuring of religious institutions with regard to male and female roles. No scholar or theologian who uses feminist definitions of humanity would pronounce a clean bill of health on any of the world's major religious traditions. There are many objectionable common practices, including sexist institutions and teachings, seeing men as spiritually superior, preferring the birth of males, giving most or all of the roles of authority and prestige to males, allowing men to control and dictate norms, not allowing women to interpret or construct tradition, limiting women's ability to participate in key rituals, and rarely putting women in leadership positions.

For feminist writings on spirituality, see Mary Daly, *Beyond God the Father: Toward a Philosophy of Women's Liberation* (Beacon Press, 1985); Carol P. Christ and Judith Plaskow, eds., *Womanspirit Rising: A Feminist Reader in Religion* (HarperSanFrancisco, 1972); Elizabeth A. Johnson, *She Who Is: The Mystery of God in Feminist Theological Discourse* (Crossroad, 1992); Elisabeth Scheussler Fiorenza, *But She Said: Feminist Practices of Biblical Interpretation* (Beacon Press, 1992); Julie M. Hopkins, *Towards a Feminist Christology* (William B. Eerdmans, 1995); and Rosemary Radford Ruether, *Womanguides: Readings Toward a Feminist Theology* (Beacon Press, 1996).

ISSUE 10

Should Women Put Their Children's Needs Above Their Own?

YES: David Gelernter, from "Why Mothers Should Stay Home," *Commentary* (February 1996)

NO: Sharon Hays, from *The Cultural Contradictions of Motherhood* (Yale University Press, 1996)

ISSUE SUMMARY

YES: David Gelernter, a professor of computer science, argues that the "motherhood revolution," which was grounded on the assumption that paid employment would make women happier, has failed. He maintains that women are pulled in too many different directions to be happy and that their absence from the home is a disaster for their children.

NO: Sociologist Sharon Hays contends that "intensive mothering" is neither natural nor desirable and that mothers would be better served by utilizing child-rearing methods that consume less time, energy, and money.

Between 1983 and 1991 the number of professionals who chose to work part-time grew by almost 30 percent, even though the workforce grew by only half of that. The majority of part-time workers were, and continue to be, women, one-third of whom have children aged 13 or younger. The gradual transition from the role of full-time mother toward the multiple roles of wage earner and mother is the cause of much debate. Why, in the face of the political, social, economic, and demographic changes that have occurred over the past two centuries, do mothers remain primarily responsible for childrearing? Traditional answers tend to focus on biology (i.e., natural maternal instincts). Other theories point to the importance of sex role socialization—whereby girls are both taught, and expected to be, mothers—and to political agendas that reinforce this socialization.

Research tends to suggest that having a consistent and reliable person in a child's life is important. Conservatives who have recourse to the biological argument of natural motherhood conclude that the sacrifices that must be made to provide this constant presence are appropriately made by the female parent (in two-parent heterosexual homes). They claim that women's departure from full-time motherhood has led to a variety of social ills, some of which include teen pregnancy, high crime rates, drug abuse and addiction, and broken homes. Many Americans believe that the only remedy for current social problems is a return to traditional family structures and the values that sustain them. This family crisis, thought to have been engendered by the women's movement, is worsened by women who seek to expand their self-definition beyond that of mother and homemaker. These women are seen by some as career-driven and neglectful of their families.

Liberals believe that conservative accounts of domestic social ills misidentify their causes and misjudge their solutions. Gender inequality in family issues is a major problem, they say, and Americans tend to hold individual women far too responsible for social problems and solutions. It is simplistic to believe that a mass return of women to full-time mother status would ease these problems, even if such a return were desirable for women. Another concern is that the economic hardships, time demands and difficulties, and emotional strains associated with childrearing create anxieties and stressors, which are disproportionately borne by women and which may emerge in damaging forms, such as anger, depression, and anxiety.

Women who do not initially believe that their goals of personal fulfillment will sometimes dictate a choice between what is best for their children and what is best for themselves rapidly discover that motherhood does, indeed, cause such conflicts. People who advocate for women's development outside of the mothering role suggest that even these difficult choices may indirectly penalize children. A depressed, angry, or agitated mother who feels imprisoned by her role, especially one in an intensive mothering relationship, is likely to have a negative impact on the children with whom she is so intensely involved. Conservatives assert that if women have unique and natural roles as mothers, then they have a special responsibility to perform in that role. Feminists argue that taking this position effectively diminishes a woman's chances for success in other areas of life.

In the following selections, David Gelernter argues that the "motherhood revolution," which allegedly benefits women, is in fact a complete disaster. Sharon Hays suggests that the ideology of "intensive mothering" does not benefit women and is utilized by capitalists and the patriarchy to keep women oppressed.

YES
David Gelernter

WHY MOTHERS SHOULD STAY HOME

American children are doing badly. From drug use to suicide rates, from academic performance to the perpetration of violence, the numbers tell us that they are failing. "Practically all the indicators of youth health and behavior," notes the education expert William Damon in his recent book, *Greater Expectations*, "have declined year by year for well over a generation. None has improved."

There is little disagreement about one major cause of this general failure. "American parents," writes Elizabeth Fox-Genovese in her judicious and thoughtful *Feminism Is Not the Story of My Life*, "spend 40-percent less time with their children than they did only a few decades ago—down from 30 hours a week to seventeen." And Karl Zinsmeister, a researcher at the American Enterprise Institute, elaborates:

> We have kicked out a lot of the social supports that used to undergird child-raising in this country: decent public schools in the cities, strong "backdoor" networks among parents, extended families and relatives nearby to help out, a safe public environment that allowed children to play outdoors without supervision.

The decline that so many have noticed did not happen overnight. It coincided, roughly speaking, with the surge-tide of a Motherhood Revolution. Over two decades, the proportion of married women aged 24 to 35 in the labor force rose steeply: from 32 percent in 1965 to 39 percent in 1970, 48 percent in 1975, 59 percent in 1980, and 65 percent in 1985.

* * *

Could there be a connection between these two sets of facts? A substantial body of research suggests that, on the whole, it is better for children if their mothers stay home to care for them full time when they are small, and after school as they get bigger, than if mothers work and consign children to day care or nannies. As Todd Risley and Betty Hart point out in *Meaningful Differences*, a child's intellectual development depends crucially on the amount of attention he gets from adults during the first three or four years, and one would be "hard-pressed" (Risley says) to locate a day-care center where attention is paid to children on anything like the level a full-time mother provides. Worse, the child psychologist Jay Belsky, once a leading defender of day care, conceded in 1986 that "a slow, steady trickle" of accumulating evidence showed that day care can do actual damage. Children in day care can develop weaker than desirable attachments to their mothers; and, according to a 1988 article in the *Journal of the American Medical Association*, they can also show "heightened aggressiveness and noncompliance."

These findings are no surprise. They merely confirm what we already know: that, as Zinsmeister puts it, "someone caring for a child out of love will do a better job than someone doing it for pay." What is surprising is that virtually no one is willing to say out loud something else we know intuitively: that the Motherhood Revolution has been a disaster for our children.

Nowhere, for example, in William Damon's exhaustive catalogue of children's problems and their possible causes does the Motherhood Revolution arise as a possible contributing factor. On the *Wall Street Journal* editorial page, Andrew Thomas, assistant attorney general of Arizona, discusses ominous behavioral trends; he warns that "if we care about our children as much as we say we do, then we must at least acknowledge that" —what? That white illegitimacy rates are high and growing, and divorce rates are high. As usual, the Motherhood Revolution is conspicuous by its absence. Even conservatives seem to believe that, to cite an article in the *Public Interest*, "the career of full-time wife, mother, and homemaker has simply ceased to be an adequate life project." End of discussion.

* * *

And yet as a society we are plainly unsatisfied with this assertion. A vein of sad, desperate defensiveness runs through attempts to explain the Revolution. The main justification used to center on freedom and fairness: if men could have careers and families, women should too. "Most feminists," reports Elizabeth Fox-Genovese, "see paid employment as the bedrock of women's new freedom." Women, after all, are just as capable as men. "I had not spent all those days in classrooms and all those nights with John Donne," writes Mary Cantwell of the *New York Times* in her book, *Manhattan, When I Was Young*, "so that I could spend my time washing [my daughter] Kate's little shirts and nightgowns."

But recently this argument has lost ground. If the Revolution's goal was to produce happier mothers, modern mothers ought to be a reasonably cheerful lot. Some indeed *are* happier on the job than they would have been at home. Many others however, will recognize their own stories in Mary Cantwell's:

> I have never been there when Katie rushed home from school... nor have I ever seen Margaret flushed and sleepy after an hour on her little cot. I do not even know which blanket she took from home.... I am stuffed with memories.... But I do not have these.

Fox-Genovese summarizes her extensive conversations with working mothers:

> Even when things go well, the pull between family and work can drive working mothers to distraction. When they go badly, the pressures and, above all, the feelings of guilt may become almost too much too bear.

In post-revolutionary America, happiness (it seems) does not abound.

And so our most-cited justification has changed; nowadays it centers not on freedom or the sanctity of careers, but on money. Here is Ann Hulbert in the *New Republic*: "the two-pay-check family, as even its detractors increasingly admit, is largely the product of economic necessity." "Only the cruel or the ignorant," writes Fox-Genovese, "would charge working women with selfishly choosing careers and self-realization over the interests of their families." And elsewhere: "the global economy has left most men unable to support a family without a second wage earner."

* * *

The economic-necessity argument hits home with a nice solid thunk. Yet ultimately it makes no sense: as a nation we used to be a lot poorer, and women used to stay home. Of course there are many working mothers who labor to put bread on the table or provide a minimal living standard for their families. But the United States is an awfully rich country, and cases of true economic necessity cannot possibly account for so vast a social change as the Motherhood Revolution.

We are far wealthier than we were in 1965, when far fewer of our mothers worked; and the Revolution itself got under way during boom years—the late 60's and early 70's. True, from the mid-70's through the early 80's, and again from the late 80's through today, average wages stagnated or declined. But stagnation of averages does not mean that individuals fail to make gains as they work their way up. In absolute terms, moreover, Americans throughout the post–1965 years have been significantly richer than ever before in history.

In practice, the argument from economic necessity probably means not that American families must have more money but that they could *use* more—to stave off decline or slower than desired improvement in their living standards. In decades past, families coped with hard (or hardish) times in other ways, or made do with less. In 1935, average per-capita incomes were less than half today's, and food, clothing, and shelter accounted for almost 80 percent of the average American family's income; yet the proportion of working mothers was under a third what it is now. (Yes, there were fewer opportunities for women back then, but there were fewer opportunities for Jews as well, and for blacks—which did not prevent male Jews and blacks from joining the labor force as best they could.) From the end of World War II through the early 1950's, real wages fell as prices exploded. But the proportion of working mothers merely crept upward; there was no surge of the sort that began in the late 60's.

The economic gain when mothers work can be important to modern families. And possessions have value, too, not just in themselves but in relation to what everyone else has. It would be far more painful for a family to live 1935-style today than it was then. Still: the Motherhood Revolution represents a new American ethic, a clear-cut change in direction.

* * *

A generation ago, the same woman who now spends her days processing claims (say) in an insurance office would have spent them rearing her children instead —and would have lived in a smaller home than she occupies today, or rented a smaller apartment, or shared a car with her husband, or taken her washing to the laundromat, or never visited Disney World. Notwithstanding the financial sacrifice, many of today's mothers might well choose to stay home, too. What exactly has changed? Once, mothers were expected to stay home. Today they are expected to work.

Feminists like to argue that in 1935 mothers stayed home partly or mostly because of social pressure. If that argument is valid, it applies with equal and opposite force to working mothers today. Except for a few benighted precincts (the Mormon church, parts of the Orthodox Jewish community, parts of the Christian Right), society from Left to Right is lined up in force behind the idea of mothers taking jobs.

How this happened is a long and complicated story, but we can identify one big factor by asking simply who has benefited most from our present arrangements. After all, the woman's movement might have pursued a very different set of goals. It might have struggled to open fields that had been closed to working women, and simultaneously sought to imbue with dignity the position of full-time mother. It might have championed a national corps of full-time mothers as the mainstay of community and civil society. It might have lobbied for mothers to take over central roles in running the schools and local government. No nation in history ever had the luxury of full-time, well-educated mothers; if we had put them in central roles, a cultural and civic renaissance might have ensued.

Sounds quaint today. In the event, feminists took inspiration instead from Clara's song in Goethe's *Egmont: "Welch Glück sondergleichen, ein Mannsbild zu* sein!" "What matchless luck, to be a man!" To be worthy of respect is to do what men do.

Notice here that the Motherhood Revolution has followed the same basic pattern as the sexual revolution—and no pattern is more important in understanding modern America. The sexual revolution erased a traditional social constraint against unmarried sex. Men were on the whole delighted with the removal of this constraint, and quick to benefit. Women have become increasingly open about their unhappiness. An implicit message of (for example) the anti-"date rape" campaign is that where sex is concerned, the level playing field is a myth.

In the heyday of liberation, it used to seem as if the old social rule prohibiting unmarried sex were like the airport barrier that separates arriving passengers from the long-lost relatives who have come to greet them. Remove the barrier and a joyful rushing together would follow. It has now dawned on many people that the prohibition was no airport barrier after all; it was more like a cage at the zoo. Men were fenced in. Women were protected.

The social rule decreeing that mothers stay home functioned in much the same way. Some women were indeed constrained; many others were protected. Most mothers, my guess is, have always valued the best interests of their children above money or power or prestige, and still do. ("In general," writes Fox-Genovese, mustering Harris and Roper polls and expert opinion to back up her assertion, "women still feel bound to children in a way most men do not.") And I would claim, too, that the typical husband would *always* have been happy to pack his wife off to work; he had no need of Betty Friedan to convince him that better income in exchange for worse child care was a deal he could live with. Society used to restrain husbands from pressuring their wives (overtly or subtly) to leave the children and get a job. No more.

Lifting the barrier produced basically the same effect on the labor market as it did on the sexual scene. The loudest revolutionaries went on doing exactly what they had been doing: casual sex goes way back, and working mothers do, too. But millions of others were left unprotected, without the barricade that used to shelter the typical woman from the predatory interests of the typical man.

* * *

I am a beneficiary of the Motherhood Revolution myself. It is a rare day when I do not gain directly from the presence of talented working mothers all around me (not to mention my large indirect gains from living in a wealthier country). In science and engineering, where women are especially rare, they are especially welcome. I would be in bad shape without my female colleagues—who are, as a group, significantly more interesting than the men. The scientist in her lab, the stock analyst making millions, the lawyer leading her team: do I want all those working mothers to quit and go home? Of course not. Neither do their bosses; neither do their subordinates; neither do their husbands.

Do their children? Should their children? We cannot quite bring ourselves to answer; so we never ask.

NO

Sharon Hays

WHY CAN'T A MOTHER BE MORE LIKE A BUSINESSMAN?

THE TROUBLE WITH RACHEL

Rachel is a successful professional woman with a demanding, well-paying job, a marriage she considers egalitarian, and a two-year-old daughter. She told me the following story with measured rage. When her daughter was so ill as to be hospitalized, Rachel felt compelled to stay at her bedside "every second." The child's life was not in danger, Rachel explained, but she needed her mother's love and reassurance. Rachel's boss, on the other hand, needed Rachel for an important assignment and simply could not understand why Rachel had to be at the hospital all the time. Although Rachel's boss is a woman and therefore, Rachel implied, should have been sensitive to this situation, she is also a childless woman. Lacking empathy for Rachel's position, her boss was, as Rachel put it, "resentful and angry." Still Rachel refused to leave the hospital room. Her daughter was sick; she needed her mother—no one else would do.

It is clear to Rachel that her child is far more important than any work assignment, and she believes that everyone *should* understand that. People like her boss are simply ignorant and selfish, she tells me: "They have no conception at all of what it means to raise children; they just don't understand." To Rachel, the point of view of her boss is wholly unreasonable; the requirements of appropriate child rearing are self-evident, sacred, and untouchable.

But her boss's point of view might also be described as a sensible and rational one. Didn't Rachel understand that this assignment had to be completed right away? Couldn't Rachel's husband, sister, or mother stay with the child? Surely there were nurses as well. Or, even more cynically, this workplace manager might have inquired, "Is the child worth the cost?" Given that the child is neither a productive family member nor one bringing money into the household, from a certain point of view it would appear unclear what Rachel had to gain by maintaining her bedside vigil. Weren't the returns on Rachel's job much more tangible? And didn't she risk losing the next possible promotion by failing to follow through on her professional responsibilities?

Certainly any self-respecting business-man would know better than to spend so much of *his* time comforting a sick child.

Rachel's unsympathetic portrait of her boss, and my cynical extension of it, may or may not be accurate, but the self-interested, calculating, cold-hearted behavior attributed to her is not that far-fetched. Though her attitude may seem strange with reference to children and family life, in the larger world her attitude does not seem strange at all: not only does it correspond to a scholarly portrait of a "rational actor," it also matches a commonly held view of human behavior in general. According to this widely shared logic, any rational individual would seek to maximize her own interests (particularly her interests in material gain) without regard to the interests of others. Rachel's boss, then, would naturally attempt to manage her employees in the most efficient and profitable manner, since her own salary and career advancement depend upon it. And since Rachel is also clearly committed to pursuing a career, she does seem to be acting irrationally by devoting herself to her child at the expense of her paid work. From a hard-nosed outsider's point of view, Rachel appears morally and emotionally overinvested in her daughter and, without major changes, it seems that she will be facing the "mommy-track," her career permanently sidetracked by her commitment to mothering (Schwartz 1989). Given the higher status and greater material gain associated with career success, why does she choose to dedicate herself to a notion of appropriate child rearing that seems to put the child's needs above her own?

The contradiction Rachel faces between her commitment to her work and her commitment to her child is not just an individual problem; it is part of a larger cultural contradiction. In C. Wright Mill's terms, what Rachel experiences as the "personal troubles of milieu" are in fact closely connected to the "public issues of social structure" (1959:8). Rachel experiences these troubles, in part, because she is one of many mothers now in the paid labor force who must meet the dual demands of paid work and child care. More important, Rachel experiences these troubles because she shares with others a particular *perception* of those demands, one that is linked to contradictory cultural images of mothers who selflessly nurture their children and businessmen who selfishly compete in the paid labor force. To put it another way, Rachel's understanding of the logic of child rearing is connected to the cultural conception of women's private sphere in the home, and her boss's understanding of the logic of paid work is connected to the cultural conception of men's public sphere in the larger world. As an individual, Rachel is pulled between these two spheres.

The cultural contradiction between home and world has a long history, while the personal contradiction Rachel confronts as a mother and a career woman is a relatively recent historical phenomenon. Over the past two hundred years, Western society has been juggling the contradictory logics of appropriate behavior at home and appropriate behavior in the outside world. This tension, however, has been partially managed by attempts to maintain a clear ideological and practical separation between life at home and life in the outside world, with women responsible for one sphere and men responsible for the other. In accordance with this, the public ideology of appropriate child rearing has urged mothers to stay at home with their children, thereby ostensibly maintaining consistency in women's nurturing and selfless behavior. But in reality the wall between home and world has always been structurally unstable and insufficiently high, and over the past fifty years the integrity of its construction has been increasingly threatened by the ever-greater number of women who have climbed over it to participate in the paid labor force.

The paradoxical nature of the situation this creates comes out most clearly against the contrast of the 1950s, the era of suburban life, domestic bliss, the "feminine mystique," Dr. Spock, and "momism." At a time when there were far fewer mothers of young children in the paid labor force than there are now, and when more American families than ever before were able to realize the middle-class family ideal, mothers' intense emotional attachment and moral commitment to their children seemed less contradictory. Today, however, when well over half of all mothers are in the paid labor force, when the image of a career woman is that of a competitive go-getter, and when the image of the family is one of disintegrating values and relationships, one would expect a deemphasis on the ideology of child rearing as labor-intensive, emotionally absorbing women's work.

Since 1950, the number of employed women with young children has more than quadrupled: 58 percent of mothers with children under six years of age worked in the paid labor force in 1993 as compared to 12 percent in 1950. While no social consensus has been reached regarding the desirability of women with young children working outside the home, there has been a general acceptance of this trend (Greenberger and O'Neil 1990; Weiner 1985). In this social context, white, middle-class women in particular have become more and more committed to pursuing careers. Many of these women are entering the paid labor force not just reluctantly, or out of necessity, but because they *want* to. And when they choose a career over a job, they make a long-term commitment to a path that does not allow them to come and go at will but instead requires ongoing dedication to life in the world outside the home.

Under these conditions one might expect that women would fully assimilate the logic of the marketplace, that the barrier between home and world would completely crumble, and that the rational calculation of self-interest would lead all of us to perceive child rearing as a fairly simple task. Yet the commitment to emotionally demanding, financially draining, labor-consuming child rearing seems to be thriving. Like many other women faced with this burdensome contradiction, Rachel does not choose to give up one commitment for the other; she juggles both. For Rachel, appropriate child rearing is not an ideology but a given, a matter of what is natural and necessary —there is simply no question of ignoring the child's multifaceted needs.

However, this form of mothering is neither self-evidently natural nor, in any absolute sense, necessary; it is a social construction. Child-rearing ideologies vary widely, both historically and cross-culturally. In other times and places, simpler, less time- and energy-consuming methods have been considered appropriate, and the child's mother has not always and everywhere been the primary caregiver. The idea that correct child rearing requires not only large quantities of money but also professional-level skills and copious amounts of physical, moral, mental, and emotional energy on the part of the individual mother is a relatively recent historical phenomenon. Why, then, does Rachel persist in her commitment to intensive mothering?

Arlie Hochschild (1989) provides another version of this question in her book on two-career families, *The Second Shift*. She asks: Why has the cultural revolution that matches women's economic revolution stalled? When rapid industrialization took men out of the home and placed them in the factory, shop, or office, a corresponding ideological revolution encouraged women (middle-class white women, especially) to *want* to tend the home and care for the children. Hochschild argues that we now need a new ideological revolution encouraging men to want to cook, clean, and nurture children, and encouraging employers and the state to want to provide for child care, job sharing, and parental leave.

But what Hochschild suggests—that we shift the focus from intensive mothering to intensive *parenting*—is only a partial solution to the contradiction between the demands of home and work, and one that does not begin to address the larger cultural contradictions. If men and women shared the burden that Rachel now bears primarily, the larger social paradox would continue to haunt both of them and would grow even stronger for men. Given the power of the ideology of the marketplace, a more logical (and cynical) solution would be an ideological revolution that makes tending home and children a purely commercial, rationalized enterprise, one in which neither mother nor father need be highly involved. Why don't we convince ourselves that children need neither a quantity of time nor "quality time" with their mothers *or* their fathers?

After all, from a cold and calculating point of view, the ideology of intensive mothering seems to contradict the interests of almost everyone. Paid working women might like to avoid the extra work on the "second shift," stay-at-home mothers might enjoy a bit more free time, capitalists surely want all of their paid laborers' energy and attention, and husbands might prefer the career promotions of a woman who dedicates herself to bringing home the bacon. Such propositions are not so outlandish when we think about how powerful utility-maximizing assumptions are in modern society. If I were a Martian who had just landed in the United States, I might notice that the primary activity of the society seemed to be the instrumentally rational pursuit of self-interested material gain in a situation of limited resources. Most of the humans appear to be engaged in attempts to buy low and sell high, calculating the best possible gain and systematically pursuing it in the most efficient manner, individualistically competing with others for available resources all the while. Nurturing, moral mothers, constantly attentive to the needs and desires of another who has little tangible to offer them in return, seem quite out of place.

Of course human infants require a certain amount of physical care. Cultures around the globe and throughout time seem to have taken into account that children are not prepared to enter the adult world until at least age six or seven (Rogoff et al. 1976; Weisner and Gallimore 1977). But modern American mothers do much more than simply feed, change, and shelter the child until age six. It is that "more" with which I am here concerned.

Why do many professional-class employed women seem to find it necessary to take the kids to swimming and judo and dancing and tumbling classes, not to mention orthodontists and psychiatrists and attention-deficit specialists? Why is the human bonding that accompanies breast-feeding considered so important that elaborate contraptions are now manufactured to allow children to suckle on mothers who cannot produce milk? Why are there aerobics courses for babies, training sessions in infant massage, sibling-preparedness workshops, and designer fashions for two-year-olds? Why must a "good" mother be careful to "negotiate" with her child, refraining from demands for obedience to an absolute set of rules? Why must she avoid spanking a disobedient child and instead feel the need to explain, in detail, the issues at hand? Why does she consider it important to be consciously and constantly attentive to the child's wishes? Why does she find it necessary to apologize to the child if she somehow deviates from the code of appropriate mothering? Why is it important to have all possible information on the latest child-rearing techniques? Why must she assure herself that prospective child-care providers are well-versed in psychological and cognitive development? Surely all these activities consume massive amounts of time and energy. Why would a woman who has the opportunity to gain so much more from focusing on her professional responsibilities choose to believe in the need for these intensive methods?

INTENSIVE MOTHERING

Rachel is, without a doubt, a dedicated mother. Although she considers herself a feminist and has a fine, well-paying career with much room for advancement, a career that would be understood as meaningful and enriching by any standard, and one that consistently demands a good deal of her time and intellectual energy, she remains committed to what I call intensive mothering. She has juggled her schedule and cut back her hours so she can spend the maximum amount of time with her daughter, Kristin. And Rachel is very careful to choose the correct "alternate mothers" to care for Kristin while she is at work. Kristin now attends a preschool three mornings a week where cognitive and physical development is stressed but not, Rachel explains, at the expense of playtime. For the remaining hours that Rachel is at work, Kristin is cared for at home by highly qualified, credentialed, female child-care providers.

Rachel is active in La Leche League and for twelve months breast-fed Kristin on demand (against the advice of her pediatrician and friends). She also participates in a mothers' play group, made up of professional-class women who first met at an exercise class in which mothers and their babies jointly worked to strengthen their physiques. These women now collectively take their same-aged children on regular outings.

Rachel reads to Kristin daily. She takes her to ballet class and swimming lessons weekly. Every Thursday (the one weekday that Rachel is not working for pay) is designated "Kristin's day": Rachel works until midnight once a week in order to make this special day possible. And this day is just for Kristin: all activities are centered around Kristin and Kristin's desires.

Rachel's self-conscious commitment to intensive child rearing also appears in her belief that there is no such thing as a bad child: "If you love your child, your child is good. If a child acts badly, it's probably the parents who are to blame." It is crucial to avoid corruption of the child's goodness and the child's innocence, and parental love is the primary ingredient for the maintenance of these virtues. Appropriate parental love, Rachel reminds me repeatedly, includes the conviction that a mother should be, as Rachel is, ready to "kill and die" for her child.

Rachel has "smacked" Kristin only once. It was a particularly bad day, she explains, and Kristin was terribly fussy and demanding. Rachel hit her "once on the butt" when her behavior became too much to bear. However, she emphasizes, "I know I didn't hit her hard because I was *so* in control." Control is important to Rachel since every action of mothering is understood to have potentially damaging consequences. And Rachel is clearly sorry she hit her child. The incident required numerous subsequent discussions with the two-year-old: "We talked about it a lot afterwards," she continues, "you know, how mommy lost it, she was stressed. And I've never done it since."

Rachel tells me that her husband is just as concerned with Kristin's happiness and development as she is. They regularly discuss the stages Kristin is going through, he reads and plays with Kristin frequently, and, in Rachel's account, he shares equally in housekeeping and child-rearing tasks. He is, Rachel says, "protective and possessive" of Kristin. But the person Rachel most often talks to about child rearing is a female friend, and it is Rachel, not her husband, who takes Kristin to her lessons, chooses her caregivers, participates in the play group, and cuts back on her paid work hours to make time for "Kristin's day." Further, Rachel stresses that "the money from my salary goes to vacations and things for the house and Kristin's education and that

sort of stuff." In Rachel's rendition, then, a mother's salary (not a father's) pays for the enhancement of family life and the requirements of socially appropriate child rearing.

Rachel's love for her home and her child is so powerful that it frequently spills over into her paid working life. At the office, she tells me, "our desks are shrines to our children and our marriages." Nonetheless, Rachel strives to retain a clear sense of the distinction between home and work: "I try to separate the two as much as I can. They're two different worlds." She continues: "My home is my private life, my child, my soul-mate. My nurturing side is there." Life on the job is public, cold, and uncaring; one needs to bring pictures and mementos from home as reminders of the warm and nurturing private side of life.

Does Rachel consider her child more important than her career? Absolutely.

> I think human beings all have the desire just to bring another human being into the world, and raise another human being that's ours. To see a part of ourselves live on ... I think that we all have that desire. Most of us do. And that desire is more enriching [than a career] for most people, to share our lives with another human being.

Rachel's ideas of appropriate child rearing can be understood as a combination of three elements—all of them interfering with her commitment to her job, and all of them in contradiction to the ideology of the workplace and the dominant ethos of modern society.

First, in Rachel's image of appropriate child rearing it is critical that she, as the *mother*, be the central caregiver. It is Rachel who must be at her child's bedside throughout the hospital stay; her husband is not even mentioned in this context. It is Rachel who must make room for Kristin's day. And it is Rachel who is ultimately responsible for Kristin's development. Men, apparently, cannot be relied upon to provide the same level of care. There is an underlying assumption that the child absolutely requires consistent nurture by a single primary caretaker and that the mother is the best person for the job. When the mother is unavailable, it is other women who should serve as temporary substitutes.

Second, the logic that applies to appropriate child rearing, for Rachel, includes lavishing copious amounts of time, energy, and material resources on the child. A mother must put her child's needs above her own. A mother must recognize and conscientiously respond to all the child's needs and desires, and to every stage of the child's emotional and intellectual development. This means that a mother must acquire detailed knowledge of what the experts consider proper child development, and then spend a good deal of time and money attempting to foster it. Rachel understands that this is an emotionally taxing job as well, since the essential foundation for proper child development is love and affection. In sum, the methods of appropriate child rearing are construed as *child-centered, expert-guided, emotionally absorbing, labor-intensive,* and *financially expensive.*

Finally, Rachel believes that a comparison of her paid work and her child-rearing activities is ludicrous. Not only is the child clearly more important, but a completely different logic applies to child rearing than to paid work. While Rachel's daughter may be a net financial drain, she is emotionally and morally outside the scope of market valuation: she is, in Zelizer's (1985) phrase, a "priceless child." Innocent and pure, children have a special value; they therefore deserve special treatment.

It is this fully elaborated, logically cohesive combination of beliefs that I call the ideology of intensive mothering. Although Rachel is a unique individual and her status as a white, middle-class career woman places her in a particular social category, I will show that this constellation of beliefs is held in common by many American mothers today. These ideas are certainly not followed in practice by every mother, but they are, implicitly or explicitly, understood as the *proper* approach to the raising of a child by the majority of mothers. In other words, the ideology of intensive mothering is, I maintain, the dominant ideology of socially appropriate child rearing in the contemporary United States.

THE CULTURAL CONTRADICTIONS

From the point of view of Rachel's boss and any self-respecting businessman—that is, from the point of view of self-interested, profit-maximizing utility—women's commitment to intensive mothering seems mysterious. While some might argue that the competitive, self-interested, efficiency-minded, and materialistically oriented logic of Rachel's boss is likewise mysterious to Rachel and other mothers, the fact is that the two ideologies do not hold equal status in today's society. For instance, many Americans would assume that it is human nature to be self-interested; almost none would claim that it is human nature to give priority to the needs and desires of others. The logic of Rachel's boss is thus far more powerful, and Rachel and other mothers are fully aware of this. On the other hand, some might argue that the two logics are benignly complementary when they are clearly separated and functioning smoothly in distinct contexts. In these terms, Rachel's emphasis on intensive child rearing makes sense in the context of her life at home or the context of a hospital room where her sick daughter lies, whereas her boss's logic makes sense in the context of a busy office and an important work assignment that is not yet completed. But this analysis neglects the unequal status of the two logics, ignores the fact that these logics cannot always be neatly compartmentalized and, most crucially, implicitly denies the fact that these are *opposing* logics. In fact, Rachel and other paid working mothers are faced with the power of both logics simultaneously and are forced to make choices between them. In today's society, then, the strength and persistence of the ideology of intensive mothering seems mysterious for two related reasons—the first from the standpoint of paid working mothers, the second in terms of certain important trends in society as a whole.

Practically speaking, mothers who work in the paid labor force seem to be acting irrationally when they dedicate so much time and energy to child rearing, because this strategy is physically and emotionally draining—wearing them down with added demands on the second shift. At the same time, they face the contradiction of engaging in the self-interested pursuit of financial gain at work while simultaneously pumping vast resources into the appropriate rearing of their children. Many women find their take-home pay nearly wiped out by the costs of day care; others, like Rachel, regard their salaries as the means of ensuring their children's education and happiness. In those societies where chil-

dren offer some return on this investment —serving, for instance, as the providers of social security in their parents' old age —this outlay of time, energy, and capital might make more sense. But in this society most children are, in fact, a net financial loss (Huber and Spitze 1988).

Furthermore, an employed woman faces the possibility of losing out on job promotions, endangering her current position, and decreasing her material returns because of all those days spent at home comforting sick children, all those hours spent arranging for day care, dental appointments, birthday parties, shopping for new shoes and toys, and all those mornings when she arrives with less than her whole "body and soul" to dedicate to the job. Additionally, there is the strain of maintaining the two roles that these women experience as they attempt to be cool-headed and competitive at work but warm-hearted and nurturing at home. Finally, for those women with careers (rather than simply jobs), we know that professional success offers far more status in American society than success as a mother. Why pursue the latter at the expense of the former?

These practical contradictions faced by individual mothers are all related to a larger contradiction in society as a whole. The strength of the ideology of intensive, nurturing, moral motherhood is in tension with what many have identified as the central trends in modern Western culture. The classical sociological literature portrays our society as one that values the efficient, impersonal, competitive pursuit of self-interested gain above all else. For Max Weber, the impersonality and efficiency of the modern West are constituted by the rationalization of social life. For Marx and Engels, the competitive pursuit of private gain is the result of the extension and intensification of capitalist market relations. And for Ferdinand Tönnies, both impersonal and competitive relations are a part of the larger historical shift from the gemeinschaft system of beliefs and relationships, grounded in custom, tradition, and particularistic ties of mutual obligation and commitment, to the gesellschaft system, grounded in commodification, bureaucratization, and impersonal ties of competitive exchange and contract....

The argument between Rachel and her boss, then, is symptomatic of a larger struggle in modern society. Although this struggle was not initiated by present-day mothers, they have become some of the primary persons who must cope with the problems it engenders. Given its deeply rooted nature, it is also certain that this conflict will not be won or lost in battles waged by individual mothers. In the final analysis, the argument between Rachel and her boss is indicative of a fundamental and irreducible ambivalence about a society based solely on the competitive pursuit of self-interest. Motherhood, I argue, is one of the central terrains on which this ambivalence is played out.

POSTSCRIPT

Should Women Put Their Children's Needs Above Their Own?

Although Gelernter quotes from Elizabeth Fox-Genovese's *Feminism Is Not the Story of My Life* (Anchor Books, 1996) extensively in his selection, Fox-Genovese makes some points in her book that contradict his ideas. Women often do not have the choice of staying home with their children, she says. Gelernter believes that women could afford to stay home if they would simply cut back on "luxury" items such as a second car, sacrifices that people made in poorer days. Fox-Genovese states that for many parents, "being there" remains an unattainable luxury, and those who preach family values and women's responsibility to their children are rarely talking about most middle-class—much less impoverished—mothers' lives. The plight of children is not eased by condemning their working mothers as selfish. Fox-Genovese writes, "The feminist response, which even many nonfeminist women echo in their hearts, is why should it always be the woman? Why do we not condemn working men as selfish for not staying home with the kids? Scapegoating of mothers is neither fair nor helpful."

In addition to Fox-Genovese's contention that staying home and practicing "intensive mothering" is simply not an option for many women, other writers suggest that a mother's employment does not place children at risk anyway. For example, according to "Children of Working Mothers: What Research Tells Us," *Young Children* (vol. 38, no. 2, 1983), a review of research found no consistent adverse effect due to out-of-home child day care. This conclusion is based on the data of over a dozen child development investigators. In "Child-Proofing the World," *Reason* (June 1997), Nick Gillespie states that by most standards, the vast majority of American children are doing better than ever. With few exceptions, mortality and morbidity rates and educational attainment all suggest that children are flourishing, yet the air remains thick with stories of how children must be protected from a malevolent world.

Some writers take positions that are even more extreme than that taken by Hays in her discussion of the negative aspects of "intensive mothering" for women; they believe that intensive mothering is quite likely to be harmful to the mother. In "Gender, Parenthood, and Anger," *Journal of Marriage and the Family* (August 1996), Catherine E. Ross and Marieke Van Willigen report a study of over 2,000 families showing that women have higher levels of anger than men and that each additional child in the home increases that anger level. Such anger is found to be associated with the anxieties relating to child care and the economic hardships that childrearing often entails. Women are not more *vulnerable* to the stresses of parenthood, say the authors of this study, but rather more *exposed*. Given this analysis, it would seem that a balance could be achieved between mothers' and children's best interests by involving fathers more directly and more consistently. "Where Have All the Fathers Gone?" *Ms.* (January/February 1993) discusses the "network" of women who have always been expected to fill in when a family crisis occurs. The father is still seen as less amenable to changing or interrupting his work, and the "all-female network," which tends to substitute for other mothers in emergencies, reaffirms men's belief that interrupting their work is not a possible solution to child-care problems.

Child-care expert Penelope Leach suggests that women should not have children until they are prepared to forgo their sense of self. Children deserve the undivided attention of their mothers and should share in all decision-making processes, she argues. Joining in this view is Robert Bork, who, in *Slouching Towards Gomorrah: Modern Liberalism and American Decline* (Regan Books, 1996), asserts that although women are best served by retaining their traditional position in the family, feminism has attempted to subvert this status by presenting incorrect or inadequate theories of happiness.

On the Internet . . .

Divorce Resources on the Internet
This site offers information on divorce and related links. Links include the Divorce Institute, the Divorce Source, the Centers for Disease Control and Prevention, DivorceNet, Divorce Online, the ABA Homepage, and LawInfo. *http://www.iimagers.com/divorce-resources.html*

Lesbian.org
This site professes to contain the largest Internet collection of annotated lesbian-specific links. It promotes lesbian visibility on the Internet and provides links to resources and information for "cyberdykes," the National Lesbian Political Action Committee, the June Mazer Lesbian Collection, the Sappho Project, and the Lesbian Mother's Support Society. It also offers a mailing list, an interactive message board system, and information on local events and marches. *http://www.lesbian.org*

The World Wide Web Virtual Library: Custody
This site provides essays and commentary on issues of joint custody, sample cases, clippings, personal testimonies, legislation, studies and statistics, samples of court bias in awarding custody, and links to other sources on the Internet.
http://www.vix.com/men/custody-divorce/custody.html

Today's Black Woman
This site, featuring talk show host Jennifer Keitt, provides information and links related to black women today. It offers messages of inspiration and hope, encouragement, and instruction, as well as information and links on African American women and romance, health, beauty, and inspiration, a radio show, a newsletter, and a women's resource center. *http://www.jktbw.com/*

United Fathers of America
United Fathers of America is a nonprofit organization that provides low-cost alternatives for legal disputes. This page describes the organization and provides related resources, including comprehensive listings for information, legal research, and family law topics. The information on and links to family law topics includes attorneys, child support services, divorce, family law, fathers' and children's rights, federal government, and parental kidnapping.
http://www.ufa.org/

PART 3

Gender and Relationships

A variety of themes runs through gender controversies with regard to the appropriate construction of social relationships. Some groups believe that traditional relationships and social values are important and in the best interests of men and women. Other groups believe that these traditional arrangements are inappropriate in a progressive, modern world. To complicate matters further, certain governmental policies may reinforce or alter existing patterns involving gender, which often sparks debates over what constitutes appropriate intervention. The four issues included in this section discuss the effects of divorce, the importance of husbands for African American women, whether or not discrimination occurs against fathers in child custody hearings, and whether or not lesbian couples naturally adopt distinct gender roles.

■ Is Divorce Necessarily Bad for You?

■ Is Finding a Husband a Major Concern for African American Women?

■ Do Family Courts Discriminate Against Fathers in Custody Hearings?

■ Do Lesbian Couples Naturally Adopt Separate Gender Roles?

ISSUE 11

Is Divorce Necessarily Bad for You?

YES: John J. DiIulio, Jr., from "Deadly Divorce," *National Review* (April 7, 1997)

NO: John Taylor, from "Divorce Is Good for You," *Esquire* (May 1997)

ISSUE SUMMARY

YES: John J. DiIulio, Jr., a professor of politics, asserts that the institution of marriage is cheapened and detraditionalized by divorce. He views those seeking divorce as socially and morally irresponsible.

NO: John Taylor, senior writer for *Esquire*, contends that divorce may be the necessary choice in some instances. He feels that it may serve to lift an intellectual and emotional fog and may lead to increased energy and reduced self-doubt.

Divorce has become an American institution. From 1970 to the early 1990s the rate of divorce rose from 16 percent to 23 percent. In the 1970s the rate nearly doubled. Whereas prior to the 1960s women had trouble escaping from constraining or abusive marriages, it is now reasonably easy to obtain a divorce in most U.S. states. Most scholars acknowledge that health may be affected by a combination of economic, social, and behavioral factors, and a variety of works have emphasized the effect of family relations on physical well-being. According to some studies, married couples tend to enjoy greater health and well-being than nonmarried couples. However, investigators disagree about whether this is related to the quality of the marriage or to participation in the socially accepted role of marriage. Furthermore, the effects of marriage on physical and mental health may vary depending on gender.

Although researchers have found that married adults possess lower mortality and lower morbidity rates than unmarrieds, some have proposed that this marital status differential is due to better income, an increase in social support, and a decrease in risk-taking behaviors. In other words, it may not be marriage or divorce *per se* that influence health status but the variables that are often positively and negatively associated with being married.

Other researchers have postulated that marriage has no effect on health at all, despite positive findings. Their explanation for the findings lies in the assumption that healthier individuals are more likely to get, and perhaps stay, married.

Supporters of the theory that marriage is good for your health and that divorce is bad point without qualification to the higher morbidity and mortality rates for single and newly divorced men, the increased rates of premature death in divorced women, the higher levels of substance abuse in divorced individuals, and the higher death rates for divorced people in countries other than the United States. The most frequently and widely cited harmful effect of divorce is the damage it does to children; inevitably parents pay a price for lifestyle decisions they make that result in emotional trauma and injury to their children. All of these findings are used by this group to make the case that divorce is frequently a very bad choice, whether it is marriage or the lifestyle factors associated with being married that make the positive differences in health.

Critics of the theory that marriage is good for health claim that there are inherent problems with the cross-sectional studies that have typically been conducted. They cite methodological flaws and false assumptions that lead to the conclusion that a causal relationship is present. Critics are far more convinced by the argument that healthier people are more likely to get married in the first place. They add that proclaiming the health benefits of marriage in the media is harmful because marriage may actually be quite damaging for individuals whose relationships are largely characterized by negative interactions.

In the selections that follow, John J. DiIulio, Jr., provides a variety of data to support his assertion that people who get married and stay married to the same partner live longer and happier lives. He sees divorce as representing cowardice, failure, and moral deficiency. John Taylor asserts that a bad marriage is intellectually, emotionally, and physically damaging and that, in many circumstances, divorce leads to sharpened cognitive skills, increased energy, and a feeling of serene vindication.

YES

John J. DiIulio, Jr.

DEADLY DIVORCE

One day a middle-aged married male relative of mine paid an unexpected mid-week visit to the family matriarch, my old Italian grandmother. He had nervously come to beg her blessings on his decision to divorce his wife of many years, the mother of his several children. Instead of blessings, he got the back of her hand and some folksy but stern advice delivered in the mother tongue. Translated, she warned him that to divorce was "against God, against children, against health." He protested that he had found a "new life," and, besides, he fully intended to pay alimony and child support. "Hard head," my grandmother scolded him, "you stay married, you stay well!" As the cautionary family tale goes, he got his divorce, but in time he also got a heart attack, got deeply into debt, got depressed, contracted a deadly disease, and lost not only his "new life" but life itself.

I had always understood and respected my grandmother's views on divorce as morally Catholic and traditionally Italian, but hardly scientific. But according to Dr. David B. Larson, both Dan Quayle and my grandmother were right. An impressive mass of scientific evidence assembled by Larson and others indicates that getting married and staying married "for better or for worse" substantially raises one's chances, and one's children's chances, of doing better and avoiding the worst throughout life.

Larson, an MD who has taught at several major universities, won numerous research awards, and served as a senior analyst with the Federal Government's National Institutes of Health, is the president of the National Institute for Healthcare Research (NIHR) in Rockville, Maryland. A tall, lanky, all-American-boy-faced man who looks much younger than his fifty years, Larson founded the NIHR in 1992. He is best known as the incredibly prolific intellectual powerhouse behind the recent outpouring of empirical data on how the "faith factor" (church attendance, spirituality, and religious commitment variously measured) influences physical, mental, social, and economic well-being.

Take a look, for example, at the footnotes in Patrick Langan's fine January 1996 Heritage Foundation report on "Why Religion Matters: The Impact of Religious Practice on Social Stability." It's Larson, Larson, Larson. Likewise,

Larson's findings punctuate *Christianity Today*'s January 6 cover story, "God, MD: How Physicians and Scientists Are Discovering the Healing Power of Prayer." Larson and his colleague Dr. Byron Johnson recently completed the best study yet done of how Charles Colson's Prison Fellowship Ministries and similar faith-based programs cut inmate recidivism.

It was not, however, until I met the happily married Larson and his scholarly wife, Susan, at a research conference earlier this year that I learned that divorce was another one of his research conquests. One of his most user-friendly studies of the subject is the 1995 NIHR report entitled "The Costly Consequences of Divorce: Assessing Clinical, Economic, and Public Health Impact of Marital Disruption in the United States." I've since read for myself all of Larson's work in this field and much of the rest of the relevant divorce research literature—a literature with well over 130 serious studies to its credit. One of the biggest conclusions is as plain as the gold wedding band on the good doctor's finger: Don't part till death, for it's death if you part.

Getting a divorce is only slightly less harmful to your health than smoking a pack or more of cigarettes per day. Divorced men who smoke have a 71 per cent greater risk of premature death from cancer than married men who puff as much. The premature death rate from cardiovascular disease for divorced men is twice that of married men. The premature death rates due to pneumonia and suicide for white divorced men are four and seven times, respectively, those of their married counterparts.

Women, too, who want to stay alive and well ought to stay married. Divorced women die prematurely at higher rates than married women, and are more prone to acute conditions such as infectious and parasitic diseases, respiratory illnesses, digestive-system illnesses, and severe injuries and accidents. Indeed, divorced women lose 50 per cent more time to illness and injury each year than married women.

Both men and women who divorce are more likely to succumb to substance abuse. For example, adults who are separated or divorced are 4.5 times more likely to become alcohol dependent than comparable married persons. And divorce-escalated mortality and illness rates are not just an American phenomenon. In countries as diverse as Taiwan, Sweden, Canada, and Germany, divorced men had the highest death rates, higher even than other unmarried (single, widowed) men.

But as costly—even deadly—as the consequences of divorce are for the adults who untie the knot, the biggest victims of divorce are the children. The research shows that children of divorce have an increased likelihood of dropping out of school; suffering depression and other mental and emotional problems; engaging in precocious sexuality; getting hooked on alcohol or drugs; procreating out of wedlock; slipping economically below the poverty line; committing suicide; and, last but not least, getting divorced. As one 1993 study made plain, "the answer to the question of whether long-term effects of marital disruption can be seen in your adulthood is a clear yes."

Where youth crime and delinquency are concerned, make that a double yes. Parents who divorce are a conspicuously close criminogenic second to parents who never marry. For example, a 1994 report on two Wisconsin juvenile correctional facilities found that only 13 per cent of delinquents came from families in which the "biological mother and father are married," while 44 per cent came from "never married" households, and 29 per cent came from homes broken by divorce.

In 1996, George Mitchell and I reconstructed the records of a representative sample of Wisconsin prisoners. We found that the vast majority of adult convicts came from single-parent or broken homes. Divorce often takes fathers out of boys' lives and so reduces the amount of positive consistent adult-male discipline they receive. But it's not only boys who exhibit divorce-bred delinquency. A 1985 study of teenage girls found that girls in divorced families consumed more drugs, committed more petty thefts, and skipped school more often than did their peers in intact families.

Of course, as Larson himself is quick to emphasize, "there are bad marriages and good divorces." Not every gay divorcee stops laughing and starts dying. Just look at Liz Taylor, who has withstood two dozen operations and survived a number of life-threatening illnesses even as she married, then divorced, enough guys to field a basketball team. (That's true even if you don't count Richard Burton twice.) Still, the research is as clear as clear gets in the social sciences that, *ceteris paribus*, the institution of divorce is a definite personal, familial, and social loser.

And make no mistake: Divorce *is* now an American institution. From 1970 to the early 1990s, the fraction of all adults 18 and over who were never married more than doubled, to 9 per cent, and the fraction who were divorced rose from about 16 per cent to nearly 23 per cent. Since 1972 more than one million children each year have experienced the breakup of their families.

Cohabitation has largely supplanted marriage in the lives of the young and hormonally hyperactive. One 1991 study found that nearly half of women ages 25 to 34 had cohabited. Most women who live with men to whom they are not married expect their "significant other" to be significantly married to them sooner or later.

Better make that later or never, ladies. Only about half of cohabitations end in marriage, and, you guessed it, many of those marriages end in divorce. Too bad America's growing army of coughing, wheezing, whining, divorced, and never-married feminists didn't hear my grandmother on the subject of men and how they'll behave toward work, sex, and parental responsibility—even the "unmanly skinny ones," as she used to say—given half a chance.

And too bad so many women have bought into an "enlightened" view of society in which men are free to wink at such old-fashioned conventions as being and staying married to the first woman you impregnate, taking full responsibility for the children you have fathered (being there, not just sending checks or "doing weekends"), and staying by your wife "in sickness and in health" and all the rest of modern life's sweets and bitters. The dial-a-divorce culture, like such kindred "progressive" innovations as the widespread availability of wham-bam contraceptive technologies and the proliferation since *Roe* of drop-in, kill-for-convenience abortion clinics, has been a great bargain for sex-seeking, social-responsibility-shirking guys, and a near-total disaster for women. It accounts for the relentless rise in births to unmarried teenagers (about 75 per cent of births to teenagers occur outside of marriage, up from 30 per cent in 1970). And it accounts for what liberals like to call the "feminization of poverty," but what is really a direct result of the divorce-led social and sexual "liberation of men."

In 1989, divorce researchers Judith Wallerstein and Sandra Blakeslee wrote:

> Even though the divorce rate began to rise in the early 1970s and has remained high for a full generation, there is an extraordinary reluctance to acknowledge its seriousness and its enormous impact on our lives. We have been afraid to look at what is happening in our midst.

That was eight years ago. Since then Larson's work and other studies have added more compelling evidence to the anti-divorce pile. And today there are ever more elite social commentators, pundits, and politicians, left, right, and center, who are willing to say (almost) that two-parent families (as in mother female, father male) are best and that no-fault divorce is no good.

* * *

Why, then, do most states still have Vegas-style divorce laws on the books? And why do even most dyed-in-the-wool cultural conservatives stop far short of attacking divorce with their usual fervor? Mainly, it would seem, because they have not faced the evidence. So let me offer three prescriptions, the last two of which could cost me a divorced or divorcing friend or two.

First, announce the negative research verdict on divorce, but in a positive way. Most people still don't know that divorce is so risky, either for themselves, for their children, or for the society at large. "I don't think," says Larson, "that the public would be so ready to accept divorce if they knew more about the clinical health and other problems so clearly associated with it." The media have paid less attention to the "divorce factor" than they have to almost any other similarly documented cause of physical and socioeconomic ills.

Perhaps journalists and the rest of us would pay more attention if the focus were on the flip side of the Larson findings—that is, not on the costly consequences of divorce, but on the wonderful benefits of monogamous, no-quits marriage. More researchers, I suggest, should "spin" the divorce story à la the unpublished (and hitherto unpublicized) 1995 presidential address to the Population Association of America by Linda J. Waite of the University of Chicago, "Does Marriage Matter?":

> How does marriage reduce the risk of dying and lengthen life?... marriage increases material well-being—income, assets, and wealth—which can be used to purchase better medical care, better diet, safer surroundings... this is especially important for women. Also, marriage provides individuals with a network of help and support, with others who rely on them and [on] whom they can rely, which seems especially important for men.

Professor Waite also noted that marriage "provides adults with an on-site, readily available sex partner." If you think that's trivial or something that the cohab crowd gets with extra thrills, guess again. Most of the recent surveys indicate that marrieds enjoy sex (with their spouse, that is) more than bar-hopping singles or co-habbing doubles do.

Second, let's start to hold each other accountable for divorce. No, I'm not suggesting that we follow the example of my grandmother by giving the back of our hand to anyone who gets divorced.

But, in the spirit of a speech that William Bennett gave a year or so ago to a Christian Coalition convention, let's criticize selfish divorce-seeking and divorce-getting behavior with real moral gusto.

No one, least of all any self-described cultural conservative, should smile politely when a friend callously breaks the matrimonial bonds and hurts both spouse and children. And those who look the other way on divorce weaken their right to feel morally exercised when the institution of marriage is so cheapened and detraditionalized by divorce that same-sex "marriages" become something against which one actually needs to formulate a coherent rational/legal argument. Especially where vulnerable youngsters are involved, divorce is socially and morally irresponsible, period. Say so, and mean it, eyeball to eyeball with divorcing barbers, colleagues, and (ahem) fellow conservative editors and writers.

Third and finally, trumpet the science and stigmatize the act, but also dare to declare that marriage is sacred, divorce profane. The post-Vatican II Catholic Church in America has become something of a sieve on divorce, in let-it-slide practice if not in unchanged doctrine. But a recent Catholic catechism still catches the sacred spirit of marriage, defined as a union between a "single man and a single woman who are of age free to marry and capable of sexual intercourse, who intend to live together and be faithful to each other until death, intend to raise a family, and who are, in no way, prohibited by the law of God from marrying." Divorce and remarriage is unholy, forbidden, a mortal sin: "Everyone who puts away his wife and marries another commits adultery; and he who marries a woman who has been put away from her husband commits adultery" (Luke 16:18).

To secularize (and Kantianize) my point about the sacredness of marriage and the profanity of divorce, people who wed are morally obliged to act as eternal romantics. The spiritual beauty, social utility, and innate goodness of the traditional marriage is derived from its capacity to tether a man to a woman in a lifelong ritual of unconditional love, and to prepare them to offer themselves as one in unconditional love to any children, either procreated or adopted, with whom they are blessed. To say "I do" is to say that there is on this planet at least one person apart from blood relatives whom you view as an end in himself or herself; a "marriage of convenience" —or "being married" only so long as it's fun, profitable, or convenient—is a moral contradiction in terms. Unfettered divorce undermines a free society's one certain source of unconditional love and thereby gradually unleashes a host of unlovely consequences, individual, familial and social.

So, whatever your religion (or lack of same), try marriage, you'll like it. And, if Dr. Larson is even half right, you'll probably live longer, too.

NO

John Taylor

DIVORCE IS GOOD FOR YOU

"We have to separate," my wife told me. It was a late-summer evening two years ago. We were drinking gin and tonics and smoking cigarettes, an entitlement of marital stress, and watching the setting sun cast rose-colored shadows across the Victorian elementary school we could see from the back of our house. A straggling bumblebee drowsed in the geraniums. The noise of a basketball game—pre-adolescent shouts, the tripping thump of the dribbled ball and its rattled smack against the metal back-board—drifted across the intervening gardens.

"We do?" I asked. After all, my marriage wasn't hellish; it was simply dispiriting. My wife, Maureen, and I didn't hate each other; we simply got on each other's nerves. We had just, over the years, each accumulated a store of minor unresolved grievances. Our marriage was a mechanism so encrusted with small disappointments and petty grudges that its parts no longer fit together.

My wife exhaled impatiently—she is English and has that hurried European way of smoking—and tapped her cigarette into a flowerpot.

"What about the money?" I asked.

In the three years during which we had struggled toward, floundered against, and pulled back from the idea of separating, I had played the accountant. I had computed the cost of supporting two households, the tax disadvantages of filing separately—what I made, what I'd need, what my wife and our daughter would need. Eighteen years after finishing college, I was finally earning a decent though hardly spectacular salary. If we separated I'd end up living like an undergraduate again. My wife had no job, and her medical condition would make it difficult for her to find one.

"We can't stay together just for the money."

I thought about the phrase "irretrievable breakdown of the marriage." There is something deceptive about it. The passive, impersonal structure, the dry legalities, conceal a lie. It suggests that the marriage has an independent organic existence. It exonerates us by portraying us as merely the clinicians pronouncing the body dead.

But at what precise point does the breakdown of a marriage become irretrievable? The moment we declare it so and no sooner. And the marriage doesn't just break-down. We disconnect the life support. While it requires will to make a marriage work, it also requires a horrifying act of will to bring one to an end.

My wife put her cigarette out and looked at me. There was nothing insistent or demanding in her eyes, the pale hazel eyes of her Russian grandparents. She was, I realized, making an appeal to me. We had to help each other bring it to an end. I felt, at that moment, an exultingly pure sense of complicity and understanding. To summon the strength to proceed, we would need to reassure each other, to depend on and trust each other. We would have to work together to dissolve the marriage in a way we had never been able to do to sustain it. I saw all this with piercing clarity, and then I thought, But if we are capable of such a delicate and complicated collaboration, maybe we should stay together.

* * *

My wife and I were falling through the darkness. We had been for years. Our impending separation rushed toward us, but, spinning in the black air, unable to see, we had no idea when the moment of impact would actually arrive.

During that time, the national debate over divorce had grown louder and increasingly fatuous. Getting divorced had come to be regarded as an act of cowardice, a failure of character, a moral abandonment of responsibility

At one point or another, virtually every critic of divorce connects its existence to the supposedly pernicious spread of "moral relativism." Instead of faithfully adhering to codes—of duty, honor, family

—the critics complain, people these days continually improvise their ethics to justify the indulgence of their desires. But no one I know who has decided on divorce undertakes it lightly. It is a wrenching decision, fraught with remorse and heartache, imperiled by moments of genuine terror, and it has almost invariably been postponed for years. Who has the right to moralize about these choices, to add the weight of public censure to the private anguish they already entail?

Most of the couples I knew who had divorced, particularly those with children, seemed irreparably altered. Defeat haunted them. Their futures had been sapped of meaning. Other couples treated them gingerly, like convalescing soldiers, but also with caution, as if their misfortune might be contagious.

Divorce struck like some force of nature, a tornado ravaging one house and leaving the next intact. Our daughter's nursery-school teacher, a vivacious woman with dark eyes and plump legs, was the first person my wife and I knew, the first of our age, to get divorced; she and her husband simply didn't get along. An actor and a legal clerk, the parents of one of our daughter's school-mates, split up next. So did an editor and a press agent known for their nightmarish, relentless quarreling.

As time passed, the breakups became increasingly spectacular and baroque. The longer the marriage, the more deranged the couple seemed to become. One man, afraid to confront his domineering wife, moved out with no warning and lived in his office for the next three years. Another man, whom I had met when we brought our wives to the same Lamaze class years ago, moved into the basement of his house when his wife refused to go off Prozac. It cost them $1,000 in legal fees just to decide what type of door would separate the basement from the main house.

I ran into a man on the subway whose daughter played on my daughter's baseball team. I had seen him at games, a slight fellow with sad, watery eyes and a gray mustache yellowing at the corners of his mouth. He was divorced, he said. His wife had become a lesbian. She used to beat him, he said, but she had acquired sole custody of their daughter by falsely claiming that he had beaten her. I looked at him speechlessly. He shrugged and, as the train pulled into his station, touched me on the shoulder and said, "See you at the game."

These stories belied the notion that, as the social conservatives liked to maintain, divorce had become a casual, guilt-free enterprise pursued by the irresponsible with the encouragement of a licentious society. They frightened me. But the stories also aroused a voyeuristic excitement. It was not simply the display of psychic wounds, the blood and pain of lives in collision, that attracted me; I wanted to know how these people knew when they had reached an irretrievable breakdown. How did they know they had arrived? I sought the points of demarcation.

* * *

Over the years. when women have asked me, in vexed, slightly irritated voices, why my wife and I ever got married, the only halting explanation I could offer was "It seemed like a good idea at the time."

And it did. Not that I gave it much thought, however. I got married when I was twenty-eight. I was utterly unaware of what course my life might take. I had no idea of what consolations and confinements marriage offered. I never thought to ask myself what type of woman —compliant, independent, provocative, driven, nurturing, passionate—would be best for me. Who does? The question can be answered only in retrospect. My parents got married when my mother was nineteen, my father twenty-one, after a six-week courtship conducted while he was stationed at the Pensacola naval base and she studied nursing in New Orleans. Immediately after their wedding, my father was shipped off to Japan, and my mother blithely followed. What could they possibly have known about themselves, much less each other, at that point? Yet theirs has been a stable, productive marriage, and the family they raised a happy one—though two years before I got married, a psychologist spent nine months trying to convince me that this was a delusion.

They got lucky. A good marriage— since people cannot know what awaits them in life, how they'll react to it, and what they'll need from the person they've married—is largely a matter of luck. But at the time I got married, I believed you made your own luck. I had been moderately lucky so far. I gave myself credit for it, and I assumed that my luck would continue to hold. My wife was pretty and slight, with curling, sun-streaked hair she kept in an off-center ponytail. She had a quiet manner, a sense of humor that was dry but forgiving. When I first met her, I thought she was French; years of living in Paris had softened her English accent. "You're British?" exclaimed a real estate agent who was showing us a Manhattan apartment shortly before our wedding. "I thought you were just cultured."

What drew me to my wife, aside from her looks and her gentle voice, was her freedom of spirit. A freelance journalist, she had lived in Manila, Hong Kong, Jerusalem, and London as well as Paris and had come to New York on impulse, with no job, because she wanted to see what it was like. She expected to return to Paris after a year. I met her when that year was almost up. She stayed on. Eighteen months later, we were married in the back parlor of a candlelit townhouse before a glistening crowd of friends and relatives who without exception wished us well. In one photograph, a close-up, my wife and I are talking as we dance. She wears a slender garland of apple blossoms. Her small hands, extending from the lace sleeves of her cream-colored dress, cup the back of my head, her hazel eyes, in which you can see faintly reflected candlelight, hold mine, and she is laughing at whatever it is I am saying. That evening, we drove through falling snow to the Berkshires and made love in front of the fire the innkeeper had laid in our room.

At the time, it seemed, in fact, like a very good idea.

Historically, divorce rates have risen during periods of prosperity. Social reactionaries attribute this to the godlessness and self indulgence that affluence supposedly breeds; the decline of organized religion, they argue, corresponds to the rise in divorce. But another explanation is that prosperity frees people from their financial dependence on each other. Miserable couples who would previously have remained together only because they were forced to—either by circumstance or religious stricture—no longer do. Isn't it possible to view divorce, for all its attendant trauma, as a progressive, even healthy, development?

Even so, only the rich plan for divorce even as they get married. The rest of us, like criminals who refuse to think about prison in the midst of their felonies, never do. It would incapacitate us.

* * *

My wife and I had three or four, maybe even five, good years together. I enjoyed being married. I was proud of my wife and liked the idea that we formed a permanent couple. For the first time in my life, I truly felt like an adult.

My wife, who is several years older than I, taught me to enjoy caviar and raw fish, to cook with garlic, to appreciate a good Brouilly and Schubert's *A Quatre Mains* pieces. But her sophistication never felt daunting; we all learn from those we love. I edited her articles, taught her how to ski, drove the car, read the maps. I was also the more opinionated and forceful. I tended to set the agenda and make the decisions.

Our daughter was born fifteen months after my wife and I were married. We were living on the Upper West Side in an apartment so small that you could almost touch two opposing walls at once. We planned for the baby to sleep in the bottom drawer of our pine dresser, but three weeks before she was due, we recognized the insanity of this idea and moved to a larger apartment in Brooklyn.

It was, in its heedlessness and impetuosity, characteristic of the way we approached our marriage. We thought of ourselves as eminently flexible; even after our daughter was born, we entertained vague and improbable notions of moving to New Delhi or Beirut or Paris. What that turned out to mean was that we were unprepared for the inflexibility that marriage and children impose. My wife never quite reconciled herself to Brooklyn. Her life there contradicted her idea of herself. She was no longer the romantic nomad. A tremor in her left hand that was diagnosed as Parkinson's syndrome seemed to reinforce a sense of confinement and exile. She felt isolated, trapped, unappreciated, and unchic, and she resented my freedom—my job in Manhattan, my expense-account dinners, my business travel.

I sympathized. In bed at night, while my wife was asleep, I would enumerate the things I would give up in exchange for her health, and I wished I believed in an interventionist God with whom I could make the swap. But I also withdrew. I had an entirely separate life. It sometimes seemed like my real life, although of course it wasn't. There were women who were attracted to me, agents who wanted to represent me, editors who wanted to publish me. It was a period of deceptive flattery, of dangerously disproportionate self-regard. And so, like my wife, only for diametrically opposed reasons, I began to find our marriage a disappointment.

In those first few years, we tried to talk. But the conversations almost invariably degenerated into bouts of complaining, and after a certain point—the point at which decorum was satisfied—neither of us was interested in the other's complaints. And so we talked less and less. We fell into the habit of withholding our feelings. While that ensured a surface civility, it also initiated the deceptiveness that eventually penetrated the very heart of the marriage.

*　*　*

Is life the pursuit of a moral definition of the self? Or is that just a literary device, the motive for the modern protagonist? I had always had my suspicions, especially since the people who proclaim that pursuit to be our one authentic existential undertaking—Philip Roth, if you believe Claire Bloom's memoir; Sigmund

Freud, if you accept Jeffrey Masson's scholarship; Bruno Bettelheim, according to a new biography—prove to be the most dishonest, manipulative, and deluded among us.

I never developed the habit of honesty. Honesty requires hard work. It is easier just to tell people what pleases them. As complications branched out in my life, as my approach to my marriage became more dutiful and formal, I decided that the theory of the unified personality was a fiction. I subscribed instead to the Japanese view of the masks of life: the mask of the father, the mask of the husband, the mask of the employee. I didn't see the need to lead an integrated life. It was a self-serving approach; it allowed me to treat my dishonesty as functional, an adaptive strategy devoid of a moral dimension.

But I also felt that it was truer to human experience. Our real life is our interior one. We're imprisoned in a subjectivity that even the most articulate among us can never fully express. No one is completely open with anyone else. We would destroy one another if we were. We all determine not only the degree of personal dishonesty we can tolerate but the degree of candor those around us can stand. I was not faithful to my wife. At the time, armored in my oriental stoicism, I felt very little guilt about this. I considered adultery rakish, even glamorous. It infused one's life with drama. I also had a rationalization so convenient, so reassuring—I was unappreciated at home—that it essentially served as a license to cheat.

I first saw her on a street corner in midtown Manhattan. She had one hand raised, her beckoning fingers both graceful and peremptory, to hail a taxi. Her other hand clutched an oversize black portfolio case so thin it seemed two-dimensional. Her elegant raincoat billowed in the March wind. She was a striking woman, in advertising, as I discovered when we met. She was also a woman with an agenda. She'd had an impoverished childhood and a wild youth, and now that she had made a professional success of herself, she wanted a child. She was married to a divorced man. He was considerate, gentle, accomplished in his chosen field, socially connected—a man, in other words, with a number of desirable traits —but he had one child from his previous marriage and felt disinclined to have another. In addition, the woman found him emotionally inarticulate. He did not, she said, touch her soul. For some reason so profoundly intuitive she had difficulty expressing it, she could no longer bear sleeping with him.

The affair seemed to present her with a way, if not of punishing the man, at least of precipitating a crisis in their relationship, forcing her life in a new direction. Like all affairs, it had the intensified eroticism of the illicit, an intensification that was heightened further by a doomed quality. A foreshortened horizon, a sense of impossibility, hung over it. She wanted us to leave our marriages, but I felt responsible for my wife and daughter— particularly in light of my wife's medical condition—and had made it clear I was never going to leave them. The tremendous guilt I knew I would feel at abandoning them would have obliterated any measure of happiness I might have achieved in a new life. At first, the woman didn't believe me, then she thought she could change my mind, and for a while after that she consoled herself with the idea that only circumstance kept us apart.

But she couldn't sustain the contradictions the affair created in her life. She left her husband. This introduced an asymmetry into our relationship. The adulterous fires dwindled, sputtered fitfully; then, so that she would be free to pursue her agenda, we stopped seeing each other.

* * *

By that time, my wife and I had, at her urging, begun to see a series of marriage counselors. Although I have always been a skeptic of therapy, I liked these people. We eventually saw four, but our sessions yielded little insight. More often, they produced only mutual recriminations. In a misapplication of the causal logic that the therapeutic process encourages, we each sought to invalidate the other's grievances by establishing prior grievances of our own, as if all subsequent wrongs could be traced to some mythic first wrong, and whoever committed it could be held responsible for everything that had transpired since.

As my wife and I thrashed through the early days of our marriage, trying to isolate the turning point, I realized that there were many things about our relationship that I couldn't remember. Who had proposed? Where? What had our first argument been about? When had it taken place? I couldn't say. I slowly became aware that a fog, a sodden, occluding vapor, had settled over my mind. I felt dull and inadequate. My intellectual responses were slow to flare. I wondered whether I was drinking too much. I liked to have a stiff drink, and maybe a second, at the end of the day, and since my arguments with my wife usually occurred in the evening, she attributed them to my drinking. She became convinced that I had a drinking problem. Our arguments, it was true, coincided with my having a drink, but since I was gone all day, when else were we supposed to argue?

* * *

As it turned out, I was unable to adapt to the masks of life. Although not scrupulously honest, I had nonetheless been acculturated with the ideals of honesty to an extent I had not appreciated. The masks were rigid, stultifying. I tried to abandon them, but by then it was too late for honesty. Honesty, if applied selectively, at one's convenience, is dishonest. It is self-serving. The opportunistic confession, I came to understand, buys a very cheap form of peace. "Why are you telling me this?" my wife cried that time several years ago when, as a way of justifying a temporary separation, I admitted my infidelity. I had just, I realized then, compounded the betrayal.

As time passed, my ability to tolerate annoyances diminished radically. Any small disturbance could provoke a flooding sense of panic. Once, in the middle of the night, when the shrieking alarm in a maroon Volvo parked outside our house would not shut off, I attacked the car with a baseball bat. Another time, when I was driving down a narrow street and a man behind me began honking at me for not going fast enough, I stopped the car, ran back, and started kicking in his door. One night, I assaulted a cabdriver on Forty-second Street when he refused to take me to Brooklyn.

I was aware at the time of the stupidity and danger of this behavior—people were murdered during such inane confrontations—but I couldn't control myself. Minor frustrations—the stuck storm window, snarled traffic—enraged me so often that my daughter learned to judge the circumstances that could provoke me and would warn, in the tone of an adult admonishing an unruly child, "Patience, Dad."

* * *

Despite these alarming symptoms. I remained committed to my marriage. As the social reactionaries wanted, I was prepared to sacrifice my own happiness to fulfill my responsibilities. That was the noblest reason. There were others. "We thought you liked being miserable," one of my sisters told me. And it was true. The freedom to luxuriate in self-pity is one of the consolations of a marriage gone wrong. Failure can be gratifying, even liberating; it relieves you of the need to aspire.

Also, in some primordial layer of my cortex, I was superstitious, afraid that if I abdicated my responsibilities, I would bring even greater misfortune on myself. After all, if you make your own luck, you also make your own misfortune. That was what had happened, I couldn't help feeling, to the woman with whom I had had the affair.

We had kept in touch. I knew how her life was progressing. At first, she dated constantly. There were men who took her to the opera in the park, men who invited her out for dinners of lobster and champagne, men who asked her to accompany them on vacations to the nude beaches on Martinique. A wealthy older man wanted to marry her, but he, too, she felt, failed to touch her soul. Instead, she fell in love with a thoracic surgeon, but after four months he decided to return to his former girlfriend.

She had always been an optimistic woman, and with every adversity she encountered, her optimism grew increasingly insistent. The year after her divorce became final, while she was on vacation in Guadalajara, a balcony she was leaning against gave way. She fell three stories, broke her back, experienced temporary amnesia, and spent ten months in rehabilitation. The following year, her company closed its New York office. She lasted only six weeks in a new job for which she was unsuited, and she was unable to find another. But she remained optimistic. She worked at sustaining faith in herself even when she exhausted her large severance package and faced the prospect of leaving the city and returning to live with her retired parents.

I tried to remain encouraging—all her friends did—but the truth was we also watched with a kind of mesmerized horror as one disappointment unfolded into another with the logic of a grim parable. Had she, we wondered, in some way brought it on herself? Was this the price she paid for leaving her kind, successful, emotionally inarticulate husband to find a man who touched her soul? People choose divorce assuming their lives will in some fashion improve, but that assumption, it seemed, could be disastrous. It seemed, in fact, to contain within the marble purity of its motive a vein of the very arrogance that provokes the wrath of the gods.

* * *

"We have to separate." my wife said again.

She had swept us forward to a moment I had both dreaded and longed for. The plunge through the darkness had stopped; the encrusted mechanism of our marriage had finally sprung apart.

"You're right, I guess," I said. I looked across our yard. The sun had slid behind the mansard roof of the elementary school, veiling the surrounding gardens, with their birch trees and weeping cherry trees and tangled rosebushes, in a dusty golden light. The basketball game had stopped. The ensuing tranquillity felt dense, almost palpable. From deep within it could be heard the city's faint, incessant rumble.

I rattled the ice in my second gin and lit another cigarette. My senses felt constricted by the weight of the moment. I could see my daughter through the screen door, her head in profile, an image of innocent absorption as she sat at the dining table, finishing her homework and humming in a loud, tuneless voice. She was eleven at the time, blond, with my wife's almond eyes and my sudden moods.

It's been said that to stay together for the sake of the children, which has been the choice of many couples, burdens those children with the responsibility for their parents' unhappiness. It's been said, too, that to separate for the sake of the children, a less frequent rationalization but one that has also been used, makes them responsible for their own abandonment. It's been said that parents avoid taking responsibility for their own lives by claiming to act "for the sake of the children." And, of course, it's been said that to ignore the interests of the children is the height of immorality.

For years, my wife and I had talked—between ourselves, with therapists, with friends, with family—about what would "be best" for our daughter. We were sure our separation would be traumatic for her, less sure how enduring the trauma would be, and even less sure how healthy it would be for her to grow up in a household shaped by a lifeless marriage.

My wife worried more than I did about the effect of our unhappiness on our daughter, who, it was true, had become exquisitely attuned to intimations of discord. At the first note of tension tightening in our voices, she would warn, "Don't fight! Don't fight!" But if we separated, my daughter would stay with my wife. The thought of living without her paralyzed me. What role could I play in her life if I saw her only on Wednesday nights and alternate weekends? To be a real father, I was convinced, you had to be there when the moments of crisis or discovery occurred: when she asked how fish live underwater, when the math problem stymied her, when her finger got caught in the car door.

"I don't think I can go through with it," I said.

"We *have* to."

Why? I wondered. For all our problems, we managed the logistics of our lives: brought our daughter to the dentist, paid the bills, planned the holiday travel schedule. We had evolved a complex avoidance system. The morning, always a rush, provided little opportunity for confrontation. I took my daughter to school, returned in the evening, had my stiff drink, helped my daughter with her homework, washed the dishes after dinner while my wife watched TV in our bedroom, then read and nursed another drink until she turned off the lights. Often, I slept in the living room, a development my daughter accepted with mild, easily appeased curiosity. ("I don't want to catch Mommy's cold.") On weekends, we went our separate ways, with me taking my daughter skiing, skating, or swimming one day, then spending the long afternoon of the next at the gym while she and my wife went to the movies or a museum.

What this meant was that we had already separated, with an unacknowl-edged joint-custody arrangement, but just happened to be occupying the same household. I was involved with someone else and had begun to accept the fact that I was destined to have what I thought of as a European marriage: one wife, serial mistresses. But the prospect was demoralizing. I no longer found adultery so glamorous.

Is this it? I often asked myself lying on my makeshift bed on the living-room floor. Upstairs, my wife was asking herself the same question. And this *was* it. My wife and I both lacked the will to improve our marriage. We could either endure it or end it.

Facing divorce means answering this question: I have one life, and it's extremely short; how do I want to live it? My wife, with fewer options than I had outside our marriage, with an incurable medical condition, felt more urgently than I did the need to free herself from its confines. She was stronger than I was, I realized that summer evening, more self-reliant. I had believed I was staying married, in large part, out of a sense of duty to my wife, an obligation to stay with her in sickness and in health. But I saw, as the twilight settled over our neighborhood, that despite her medical condition, she did not need me as much as I had thought she did. She was prepared to absolve me of my guilt if I would leave.

* * *

Three months later, on a wintry afternoon, my wife and I called our daughter into our bedroom. She could tell by our expressions, the forced composure, that what was about to transpire carried a tragic gravity, a frightening emotional bottomlessness unlike anything she had ever experienced. We were leading her, she instinctively knew, out into water that was over her head.

Our bedroom never had good light. It faced north, into the branches of an oak tree the city had planted in the sidewalk almost a hundred years ago, and on that late afternoon—a Friday, chosen so my daughter could have the weekend to adjust to the new situation—snow clouds obscured the sun and the room was steeped in shadow. The gloom eased things, I now realize. It dulled the edge. My wife and I had both been struggling with a very real horror of this moment, dreading it the way you would dread an impending amputation. Bright light would have made it unbearable.

Sitting on our bed, our daughter between us, we started to proceed through the inevitable, overrehearsed, overrationalized points: We argued too much; it created tension; we would all be happier; it was no one's fault, certainly not our daughter's. She nodded at first. Tears welled in her eyes, but she was absorbing the information, and then she blurted out, in a tone of piercing fearfulness, "You're not getting divorced, are you?"

It was not the mere fact of my physical departure that disturbed her the most; it was the prospect of irrevocability. She wanted to know: Was the small world she inhabited, the one collapsing around her at that minute, ever to be restored?

My wife was crying; my daughter was crying; we were all crying, mourners grieving at the death of the family we had been. "Everything's going to be all right," I said. "We'll all be a lot happier. Everything will be all right."

I looked at my wife. She nodded. And then my daughter nodded, too. She couldn't quite comprehend how that might come about, how everything would work out for the best and we'd all be happier, but despite what we had just inflicted on her, her trust in our ability to protect her remained so ingrained, so instinctive, that she seemed to believe it.

At the same time, we all felt strangely, even perversely, relieved to have this particular hurdle behind us and to be able, after so many years of holding back our feelings, finally to air them. The catharsis left us light-headed. We took our daughter over to see my new apartment, in a converted factory only ten minutes away; the neighborhood lacked charm, but the parking was easier. She brought stuffed animals to put on what was to be her bed. And then we all went out to dinner to celebrate.

The months that followed were far from painless. For a while, I felt even more brittle and snappish than before. Waking up in the silent emptiness of my apartment could fill me with a loneliness so intense and bleak that it was frightening. My wife and I had exasperating fights over money. When we tried to talk to our daughter, she insisted everything was fine. At first, her most pressing concern seemed social: She was humiliated when one girl told the rest of her class that my wife and I had split up. But I began to notice that she had a quiet, stricken look those evenings I picked her up to spend the night at my place. Finally, I asked what was wrong.

"I don't like sleeping over. I never have all my stuff. My friends never know where to call me."

My heart froze. I launched into the standard blather about how lucky she was to have two houses.

"I don't *want* two houses," she said in a jagged voice. "I want one house."

* * *

Moments like this made me wonder whether the decision to leave had been a dreadful mistake. I had thought I was acting with moral clarity that I had in the end, unexpectedly and unintentionally, achieved a sort of moral self-definition: I was doing not what I wanted to do but what was right for everyone. But maybe, moments like this made me think, what I had been engaged in was an elaborate ruse, an act of self-justification. Had the breakdown become irretrievable only because I wanted it to be? Had I in fact willed that way?

But all of us have to learn to live with uncertainty. Uncertainty itself indicates the authenticity of the enterprise. Only the absolutists, blindly adhering to their codes of duty, and the narcissists, who lack any sense of obligation altogether, are free from doubt. The rest of us, struggling for moral coherence in a world that no longer imposes it, are not so lucky.

My wife and I counted on each other to get through these moments; she had more than her share. Separating, it surprised us to discover, left us freer to express ourselves than we had been before. We were no longer paralyzed by the need to preserve the artificial peace. Less afraid that the doubts and insecurities we revealed would be used against us, we became more open about them. We respected each other's frailties. Separating seemed to bring out the best in both of us.

Time passed; the seasons ebbed and flowed; the pages flew from the calendar. I received a bulky letter from my landlord with my lease renewal. I found it hard to believe that a year had elapsed. The brevity of life, a proposition I had dismissed when young as hopelessly banal and patently false, now seemed to be perhaps the one profound truth we all eventually confront. You did not have the opportunity to experiment with endless versions of yourself, to reinvent, to explore and retreat, to fail and start over.

That's not necessarily a disheartening discovery. It's a form of progress. The sense of limitation that overtakes you as you enter middle age forces you to sharpen your focus. Which was what I found I was doing. I also found, after a while, that the fog was lifting. I felt more alert, more energetic; my associative powers improved; I had greater recall. Eventually my daughter started wanting to sleep over again. One night, I came home from the gym and poured myself a Scotch. The silence of the apartment had by then lost its desolate quality; at times, it seemed almost serene. I called my daughter; she was jubilant over an A she had scored on a history test and a party she had planned for the weekend. My wife got on the phone. She had received the check. She was, as usual, reserved. I knew that from time to time, she enteriained second thoughts about the separation.

For me, self-doubt had given way to the simpler feeling of regret. The feeling didn't trouble me. There is nothing wrong with regret. It is a way of honoring what we once had. Life without regrets is superficial. My regret, I also felt, implied a measure of hope. It meant I still believed, in a way I couldn't have expected, in the possibility of marriage.

After I hung up the phone, I turned on the television. The Knicks were leading the Suns in the fourth quarter. It was an ordinary evening, but for some reason, as I settled down to watch the game that night, as the Knicks scored and I took a sip of Scotch, I experienced, despite the persistence of regret, a small but distinct, almost thrilling, stir of vindication. I knew that this was dangerous to say, even to myself—that it tempted fate—but for the moment all our lives seemed in order. We had done, not the right thing, perhaps, but the necessary thing.

POSTSCRIPT

Is Divorce Necessarily Bad for You?

Divorce is costly, even deadly, to adults and to their children, says DiIulio. Taylor's wife, Maureen Sherwood, seems to agree with DiIulio. In "An Emptiness I Didn't Know Existed," *Esquire* (May 1997), Sherwood states that even though she felt unloved, rejected, ignored, and frustrated much of the time, she regrets having asked Taylor to leave, and she asserts that one should hesitate before saying, "We have to separate."

Bill Galston of the Progressive Policy Institute recently summarized the social science literature and determined that divorce in and of itself has, in many ways, an independent negative effect on the well-being of minor children. In "Marriage Protection and Marriage Selection—Prospective Evidence for Reciprocal Effects of Marital Status and Health," *Social Science and Medicine* (July 1996), researchers Ingrid Waldron, Mary E. Hughes, and Tracy L. Brooks determine that the benefits of marriage on health are present to a great extent, but only for unemployed women. Differential lifestyles associated with being married may also play a role in the correlation between marriage and health. See, for example, "The Influence of Women on the Health Care Seeking Behavior of Men," *Journal of Family Practice* (November 1996) and "Work, Marriage, Lifestyle, and Changes in Men's Physical Health," *Journal of Behavioral Medicine* (April 1995).

Taylor notes that a complex avoidance system had evolved between his wife and himself, that they both lacked the will to improve the marriage, and, as a consequence, that they were left with the choice of ending it or enduring it. Taylor might agree that it is the quality of the marital interaction and not the role benefits of marriage that influence health and decision making regarding divorce. "Long-Term Marriage: Age, Gender, and Satisfaction," *Psychology and Aging* (June 1993) states that women in unsatisfying marriages have more mental and physical health problems than their husbands.

Some studies show no association between marriage and health, or they show negative associations. According to "Marital Status, Change in Marital Status, and Mortality in Middle-Aged British Men," *American Journal of Epidemiology* (October 1995), a nationally representative sample showed that, in general, divorced and separated men are not at increased risk of mortality in association with their marital status. "Work and Family Roles in Relation to Women's Well-Being: A Longitudinal Study," *British Journal of Social Psychology* (March 1995) suggests that family roles are unrelated to stress for women. However, marriage has been shown to be associated with weight gain for women. See "The Role of Change in Marital Status on Weight Change Over One Year," *Obesity Research* (July 1995).

ISSUE 12

Is Finding a Husband a Major Concern for African American Women?

YES: Debra Dickerson, from "She's Gotta Have It," *The New Republic* (May 6, 1996)

NO: Linda Blum and Theresa Deussen, from "Negotiating Independent Motherhood," *Gender and Society* (April 1996)

ISSUE SUMMARY

YES: Attorney Debra Dickerson maintains that she (and, presumably, other African American women like her) would like to marry but that the dearth of marriageable African American males is a crisis that she lives with daily.

NO: Linda Blum, an associate professor of sociology, and Theresa Deussen, a doctoral candidate in sociology, assert that African American women utilize community-based independence in order to resist assumptions based on a need for legal marriage. These women seek to carve out alternative relationships based on nonmarital relationships with male partners.

Currently in the United States about 43 percent of African American homes are headed by women, while numbers of marriageable African American men continue to decline. The U.S. Census Bureau reports a continued drop in the prevalence of African American husband-wife families and an associated drop in the percentage of resident children and marital births in these families. In 1960 the percentage of African American children living in husband-wife families in southern, nonmetropolitan areas was 66 percent. By 1990 it had dropped to 39 percent, indicating that changes in the structure of the African American family and concurrent increases in poverty have not been restricted to the urbanized North.

Forty-eight percent of all black women of marriageable age are either divorced or have never been married (compared with 31 percent of white women). Among African Americans aged 20–39, there are about 10 percent more women than men. An additional 10 percent of males are in prison, and another 10 percent are otherwise restricted by the legal system. Eighty percent of African American graduate students are women. For individuals between the ages of 25 and 55 there are 86.5 black men for every 100 black women. (In this same age group there are 100.5 white men for every 100 white women.) Other causes for this black male shortage include tragically high homicide rates (51.4 deaths per 100,000 black men), suicide rates

(9.9 deaths per 100,000 black men, compared with 2.0 per 100,000 for black women), and rates of death from disease and accidents.

In addition, black men are far more likely to marry nonblacks than are black women. According to the U.S. Census Bureau, the incidence of black-white married couples quadrupled between 1960 and 1990. However, writers have suggested that while black men often prefer fairer-skinned women, black women tend not to prefer fairer-skinned men. Also, African Americans are more in demand as husbands than as wives, some research suggests, partly because black men are seen as slightly more masculine than white men and black women are seen as slightly less feminine than white women. The media reinforces this image of black men through its stereotypes of African American males as rugged athletes. It has also been suggested that the American government promotes single motherhood for African American women by providing welfare aid and, along with it, a certain degree of economic freedom for these women. This governmental safety net may also aid men in rationalizing their refusal to marry.

Some writers claiming to represent African American females report that black women are resentful and bitter over the black male shortage and angry over the concept of interracial marriage. Such women presumably prefer the rewards of marriage over economic and social independence. Others suggest that African American women are not particularly interested in marriage *per se* and that their concerns are concentrated more in other areas.

In the following selections, Debra Dickerson expresses cynicism, hopeless-ness, and anger over the black male shortage and sees the dearth of black men as a crisis that she lives with daily. Linda Blum and Theresa Deussen assert that black women are more interested in increased autonomy than in any agenda that seeks to strengthen the African American family by reasserting the masculine family headship.

YES

Debra Dickerson

SHE'S GOTTA HAVE IT

The February 1996 issue of *Essence* features an adapted excerpt from Dr. Ronn Elmore's ... book, *How To Love a Black Man.* The cover presents four shirtless, simmering hunks promising all sorts of sweaty naughtiness with their x-ray eyes; a bonus two-page spread inside adds two more barely dressed, steroidal brothers. I ogled them appreciatively even as the nagging suspicion grew that I was about to be schooled, yet again, on how unsupportive and emasculating I am to the legion of together brothers eager to make me their queen. Sorta like the jiggling blonde in the car commercials who simultaneously excites and angers because you can afford neither her nor the vehicle.

The manipulative appeal of an article like the one in *Essence* is obvious enough, but the questions behind it still demand consideration. Does loving black men really require special training and, if so, why? How difficult is it to learn? Is it inherently difficult or difficult only because it requires abasing, or in some other way minimizing, ourselves?

Loving, healthily and reciprocally—isn't that really the only true difficulty, all other considerations mere distractions? The white Princeton graduate downsized from Wall Street may well consider himself just as victimized and punished for his race as the last-hired, first-fired inner-city brother booted out of the mailroom. He may be wrong, but trying to convince him of that will only make him pack his bags. All that really matters is that he's going to bring his wounded pride home with him for you to deal with. Mia and Woody, Lorena and John, Jim and Tammy Faye: all white, but it didn't make their relationships any easier, did it? Doesn't it all just come down to two clueless humans desperate to wrest something meaningful from the complicated tangle of their baggage?

Well, no. At least not according to the black section at book stores. The recent explosion in black-oriented self-help and relationship books—most of them aimed at women—is astounding. *How To Love a Black Man; How to Marry a Black Man; Black Pearls Book of Love: Romantic Meditations and Inspirations for African Americans; Girlfriend to Girlfriend: Everyday Wisdom and Affirmations from the Sister Circle; The Black Woman's Guide to Financial Independence; Success Runs in Our Race; In the Company of My Sisters: Black Women and Self-Esteem;*

In the Spirit: Lessons in Living; Black Sun Signs; Acts of Faith: Daily Meditations for People of Color; Getting Good Loving; and *The Best Kind of Loving.* "*Essence's* Best-Sellers," a monthly feature modeled on *The New York Times's* best-seller list, identifies many more. What exactly is going on between black men and black women? And whatever it is, is it really race-specific?

* * *

The short answer is yes and no. Susan Faludi, in *Backlash,* challenges the notion that it's women who crave marriage and provides some convincing data: 90 percent of the women surveyed in one recent study said they could be "happy and complete" without marriage; 90 percent of never-married women said "the reason they haven't [married] is that they haven't wanted to yet"; and nearly 60 percent of single women thought they were a lot happier than their married friends. As Faludi points out, "men far outnumber women in dating services, matchmaking clubs, and the personals columns" and, once they marry, seem to fare better in all sorts of areas, including mental health, than their single counterparts.

Trouble is, it's white people she's talking about. When somebody gave me Faludi's book for Christmas a few years ago, I stayed up until 6 a.m. devouring it. But even as I amen-ed every page, I knew it didn't include me. Any black woman, especially one with a college education, knows she will not be outnumbered by black men *anywhere* unless she does community service at the city jail. In the African American dating game, men occupy the driver's seat, and they bloody well know it. College-educated or college groundskeepers,

substance abusing or born again, living in his mama's basement or running his own company: a brother knows he's worth his weight in gold chains. While Faludi trashes the notion of a man shortage, she really only means a white man shortage. That's where black relationship books come in—they give substance, not to mention validation, to what a black woman's common sense has already told her.

* * *

In the best of the books I read, *Getting Good Loving: How Black Men and Women Can Make Love Work,* Audrey B. Chapman, a talk-show host and therapist, makes clear the chasm between black men and women. While the family has taken a beating across all racial and economic strata in America, blacks, as usual, got ebola while everyone else caught a cold. In 1970, 68 percent of black families were headed by couples; it's 44 percent today. The black divorce rate tripled from 100 per 1,000 married persons to 300 per 1,000; only 35 percent of adult black women are married now, compared to 70 percent in 1960. Jesse Jackson made it clear to the nation that there are more young black men in jail than in all our colleges combined. Quoting *Black Enterprise,* Chapman says that "for black males under the age of 25, marriage is virtually nonexistent." Twenty-three percent of single black men state an intention *never* to marry (compared to 13 percent of white men).

Hence, *How to Marry a Black Man* by *MRS.* de Jongh and *MRS.* Cato-Louis. Like most self-help books, this one posits individual solutions to what is essentially a social problem: in this case the shortage of marriageable black men. I need their book, the *MRS.*s scold affectionately, because "[a]nswer[ing] the soul-searching questions and do[ing] the meditations and the exercises [will] force [me] to face the only real obstacle between [me] and marriage: [me]!" They believe that I have probably already met my ideal black man. "It's just that deep down inside, you believe that you don't deserve him.[I do? why?] *We know you do!*" [They do? how?] They further inform me that it will take approximately two years to "transform from the single career partygirl diva [I] now [am] into the Mrs. [I am] destined to become." I haven't had a date in nearly three years; I haven't danced with another human present in two. My bare ring finger, I suspect, has more to do with my two-page résumé than anything else. A diva I ain't. And, anyway, since when do divas suffer from low self-esteem?

It's easy to poke fun at *How to Marry a Black Man*. Pocket-sized and repetitive, it purports to be a workbook—this, of course, because the blank spaces required for the fill-in answers are the main reason the book's length. "List a few things that you love about yourself." *That I refuse to answer questions like this.* "What is it about making decisions that causes you anxiety?" *Being really, really wrong.*

Still, for all its twaddle, *How to Marry a Black Man* impressed me. Not that it isn't replete with New Age silliness, Afrocentric babblings and pseudo-feminist apologia. But it's also dead-on in many of its observations and definitely useful for women who want to transcend their cynicism, hopelessness and anger (well-deserved though it is. Not that I'm bitter). What's wrong with wanting to marry? What's wrong with going about it with the same vigor and zip with which we attack our educations, careers and the Electric Slide? Nothing and nothing. (If they

could just stop referring to it as "getting him to marry you" like "getting him to give you a kidney"; there *is* something in it for him, after all.)

The secret of a book like this, though, is that the advice it dispenses has nothing to do with being black (even if the problem it addresses does). That's just niche marketing, like the "ladies" tool set, complete with bilious pink handles and frilly cozy-covers that so thoroughly pissed me off at Sears a few years ago. These books? Hammers with kente cloth handles.

Los Angeles psychotherapist Ronn Elmore, the author of *How To Love a Black Man*, offers insightful advice boiled down to snappy one-liners; reading the book feels like watching an infomercial, but for something useful. Obviously successful at his chosen line of work, Elmore offers a running patter that is far and away the most entertaining and easily digested of the lot. His word usage is pleasantly snappy, though not in the least "black" —he says "darndest" sans quotations marks, but "half-assed" is just that, self-consciously bracketed. In any event, the mostly sound advice in both books is easily applied across cultures.

* ˙ *

It is Chapman's book alone that sheds light on the problems specific to black men and women; thank God she doesn't embarrass herself scattering hip-hop terminology "willy-nilly." Hers was the only book I actually *read* for its own sake and intend to spend more time with. She made me check myself. She talks about the unrealistic expectations we saddle each other with because of the "Entitlement Syndrome" (which, no doubt, will be gleefully pounced upon by the right). Some blacks, she posits, expect their partners to make up for everything their parents and society couldn't or wouldn't give them and to which they feel entitled; these kinds of expectations can be, to say the least, rough on a relationship. Do others have the same problems? Yes, but they don't play themselves out in the same ways.

Being one of those East Coast elites that the dead-white-men-in-training at *National Review* so hypocritically dismiss, I am not embarrassed to say that I do not read self-help/relationship books, and I do not adhere to the idea that if it's black it must also be good. Can I now go so far as to admit that I was nonplused to find, in the black aisle at Crown Books, Ellison's *Invisible Man* next to Elmore's *How To Love a Black Man*? Baldwin's the *Fire Next Time* next to Boyd's *Girlfriend to Girlfriend*? What have they in common besides melanin and the alphabet?

My snobbery aside, these books reflect the prevailing angst of the critical mass of blacks who have struggled their way up the national food chain and into the middle class. *Girlfriend to Girlfriend* may not be great literature, but the dearth of black men *is* a crisis I live with daily. I would fear for my people and for my country if *Native Son* could still be written today.

NO

Linda Blum and Theresa Deussen

NEGOTIATING INDEPENDENT MOTHERHOOD

The authors examine the experiences and ideals of African American working-class mothers through 20 intensive interviews. They focus on the women's negotiations with racialized norms of motherhood, represented in the assumptions that legal marriage and an exclusively bonded dyadic relationship with one's children are requisite to good mothering. The authors find, as did earlier phenomenological studies, that the mothers draw from distinct ideals of community-based independence to resist each of these assumptions and carve out alternative scripts based on nonmarital relationships with male partners and shared care of children.

Fully 30 years after the Moynihan (1965) report pathologized the Black mother as "matriarch," policy analysts debate the same linkages among Black masculinity, men's unemployment, women's nonmarital childbearing, and poverty. Two lines of argument continue to predominate: the cultural argument, emphasizing that welfare dependency discourages marriage and stable employment (exemplified by Murray 1984 and now sweeping across the political spectrum), and the structural argument, emphasizing that the lack of stable employment for men discourages marriage (exemplified by Wilson 1987, 1994). Although the two sides clash bitterly, they share a common, if unacknowledged, gendered agenda. Both assume that strengthening the Black family requires the (re)assertion of masculine family headship.

When Black mothers are referred to in the public discourse, they are portrayed stereotypically—if not as the Moynihan matriarchs, then as weak and irresponsible teen mothers (e.g., DeParle 1994; Murray 1993). Such treatments obscure the structural causes of poverty and ignore women's interests. The work of Black feminist scholars who challenge such stereotypes and articulate autonomous interests (e.g., Collins 1990; Morton 1991) has transformed academic feminist discussion, but it is ignored in the public discussion. Earlier phenomenological studies that directly confronted the pathologized portrayals are also ignored (Dill 1980; Ladner 1972; Stack 1974). In this article, we return to the phenomenological tradition and place Black mothers' voices at the center of a look at motherhood and families.... We find, as did earlier phenomenological studies, that the mothers express a distinct ideal of community-based independence involving shared caregiving and nonmarital partnerships with men.

BACKGROUND

Powerful racist imagery of dependent teen mothers frames current welfare debates, reversing earlier stereotypes of "super-strong" Black matriarchs. Single parenthood, in fact, has risen among all U.S. racial-ethnic groups, yet 70 percent of nonmarital births are to women age 20 years or older and the rate of increase in teen births among African Americans has been flat since 1970. Significant racial differences, however, do fuel stereotyped portrayals: Births to single mothers now represent 22 percent of white births yet fully 66 percent of African American births (DeParle 1994). To debunk stereotypes, some scholars show how Aid to Families with Dependent Children (AFDC) has provided diminished rather than increased incentives for nonmarital childbearing (summarized in McLanahan 1994). Wilson (1987) takes a different tack, demonstrating that it is capitalism, particularly its deindustrializing phase, that threatens Black manhood. Multiracial feminists go even further, challenging the preoccupation with male family headship and the model of rationality that assumes women prefer the "rewards" of marriage over social and economic independence (e.g., Baca Zinn and Eitzen 1992)....

We organize the following discussion of African American mothers' norms of independent motherhood around two issues, starting with the attachment of normative motherhood to marriage and male family headship. We start with this because of its centrality in the public debate on the Black family and because, in our interviews, such assumptions of "marital rationality" so obscured women's experiences and understandings of their relationships with men. The second stems from the "epoxy glue" norm of exclusive motherhood; we examine the women's resistance to such norms and the alternative models drawn from shared child-rearing traditions....

TALKING ABOUT MARRIAGE AND MEN

... Of the 20 African American mothers we interviewed, 17 were unmarried, and their discussions evidenced the detachment of mothering from marriage so repudiated in the policy debates. Some of the mothers offered reasons for not marrying the fathers of their children, and at times such reasons did express the structural argument of Wilson. For example, Sharona had four children, and the father of the younger two wanted to marry her; she explained that it was difficult to refuse:

> It's hard to bring up the subject. "Well, I don't want to marry you because you don't have a job." You know, I kind of hint around what I'm trying to say to him. It makes him feel bad.... He wants to get married.

Sharona was unusual in her singular emphasis on (his) economic obstacles to marriage, with only 1 other woman telling a similar story. Sharona acknowledged, however, some conflicting feelings. Considering the length of the relationship and her partner's desire to marry, she concluded, "It's like a total war in my mind."

Other women we spoke with, by contrast, raised issues of independence, extended family, and public support, and they demonstrated much less interest in marriage.

In fact, in our interviews we found little direct or spontaneous interest in marriage even though only 5 of the 20 women were not involved in significant male-female relationships. The mothers, however, did emphasize the significance of fathers' continued relationships with children; only 4 of 23 living men who had fathered children with mothers in our group were truly "absent." When we asked questions about future hopes and goals, most spoke first of increased autonomy as working mothers and of wanting better jobs and public entitlements. None mentioned gaining a family wage through marriage to a "manly provider," even if (when prodded) they said they might want to get married. The African American mothers we spoke with claimed that they had been raised with expectations to achieve on their own, most repeatedly using the terms "independence" and "strength."

Jenny was 31 years old and the mother of three daughters. Although her parents had a traditional marriage, she had chosen not to marry or cohabit with the father of her children, her stable partner of 15 years. In her discussion of the future, Jenny included the upcoming completion of her associate's degree, transfer to a 4-year college, and plans for a job in the court system. She did not once mention marriage in connection with the future, although her partner was stably employed in construction. She expressed her ideal situation as follows: "I would like to be working and supporting my family and having a job that I truly loved, plus including my children in that, and they would be all happy and everything. That would be my fantasy."

Deb was similarly uninterested in legal marriage, although she and the father of her infant son had been together for six years: "Everybody keeps asking me when we're going to get married. No! ... I'm not thinking about it, and he's not either." Raised by a divorced working mother, Deb found in her a role model for independent motherhood: "You know, my son can have a nice life even if I'm with his father or without his father." She noted that dependence on a man was a potential liability if he were then to leave: "It's nice for him [the boy's father] to be working and helping out but ... I grew up under my mother's standards. She never depended on nobody, so I know I don't want to!"

One working mother, Kerry, stated this as a general rule: "Every woman needs her own money so she can take care of her kids." Elise, divorced from her first son's father and involved with her second son's father, exemplifies how these mothers looked to public entitlements to protect their autonomy. After five years of stable employment in a low-paying white-collar job, Elise quit and went on AFDC for six months in lieu of paid maternity leave; at the time of our interview, she had a new job lined up. When asked what would improve her situation, she mentioned neither marriage nor improved job options for her partner: "More help with day care because it's not affordable at all.... The government can kind of help you with ADC [Aid to Dependent Children] ... but if you're making six dollars, seven dollars, even eight dollars an hour, there is really no help in there!"

Nearly all the women we spoke with also emphasized desires for independence that went beyond the economic, speaking of "needing space" or even of "never letting a husband boss me around." One mother, Ramona, for example, corrected the interviewer's query about a time when she and her partner had lived together: "It was always my place." In our view, the women were not rejecting marriage per se. Many said that they liked the idea of getting married and finding life partners, if often placing this in the future. For example, Cynthia, a 29-year-old mother employed in food service, had stopped cohabiting with her partner after three years together. Since then, she felt that they got along better and enjoyed sharing care for their daughter. She mused that they might marry someday, with pleasurable thoughts of a church wedding.

Simply put, this group of mothers did not seem to feel an imperative to marry the men with whom they had children. The presumption that a "good mother" must be married was not evident.... Elise aptly expressed this, stating, "[My household] is a happy and healthy one," and Cynthia characterized herself, without contradiction, as a "homebody" who was "not ready for marriage." Kerry exemplified this positive, optional sense of marriage, after other priorities, when asked what would make her life better:

> If I went back to school and got a better paying job... I guess if I was to get married, to fall in love and marry somebody that I know would accept my kids, even though they weren't his, but would really love them and care about them.

Bernice simply laughed as she said, "I hope to be married one day, yeah, but I can't say I will be."

... Research is often conducted with a dichotomous model that recognizes only the presence or absence of marriage.

Our participants recounted many stories of extralegal relationships, and at times we fell into this presence/absence model with its tacit assumption of "marital rationality." Like those who problematize feminist methodology, we had trouble hearing across differences....

In retrospect, we can see that we were hindered by our lack of language for extralegal relationships as well as by our marriage "blinders." In one telling interview, at least eight different terms were used, creating gaps and misunderstandings between participant and interviewer. The interviewer supplied in turn "going out," "man you were sharing stuff with," "living with," and "roommate," whereas the participant, Ramona, countered with "talking with," "settle down with," "stayng with," and "friend." ...

The few married women in the study (three and one recent widow) supported the pattern of marriage as nonimperative, noneconomic, and distinct from motherhood; all claimed to have wed because they had found true partners. For all four, marriage had followed pregnancy; for three, it had followed birth. Joy's story is indicative. The mother of two, she worked full-time in a male-dominated blue-collar job, earning more money than her husband of 12 years. Sometimes, she said, he did feel threatened, although overall he was "pretty cool." Joy and her husband did not marry until their first child was 2 years old: "I've always been independent, and I just felt like that's part of everyone, to take their own independence.... And I didn't think that just because we had a child that we needed to get married."

Women's autonomy has long historical roots among African Americans, in part because mothers had a common experience of combining paid work and family. In the 20th century, public assistance programs made it (marginally) possible for white working-class mothers, especially widows, to remain out of the paid labor force, but "employable mother" and "suitable home" rules denied African American mothers this option and kept them in low-wage agricultural and domestic labor (Rose 1993). During the 1950s and 1960s, when the labor force participation of white mothers was still low, the employed mother had long been the norm for African American women. Perhaps, as Farley (1988) suggests, this legacy contributes to Black women's greater equality in marriage and reduced "need" to marry; nevertheless, much research has left an important question unasked: Do Black mothers want to be married? Listening to the women in this study suggests that the answer may often be negative and that economic considerations may not be at the heart of decisions (also see Amott 1993)....

In contrast to the public emphasis on men, manhood, and female dependency, these Black working-class mothers expressed ideals centered on autonomy and independence. This was not an isolated independence like the middle-class family and exclusively bonded mother-child dyad; rather, it was based on the kin networks and shared responsibility for children that earlier phenomenological research had emphasized. For these women, more isolated mothering would have been impractical, but it was also an undesirable ideal; they resisted assumptions that the deserving mother must be singularly and exclusively present. Their community-based independence, therefore, provides a better basis for policy design.

The women also resisted the assumption that legal marriage is required for good mothering, and they did not express strong desires to marry or rely on male breadwinners; yet, mothers valued long-term partnerships and the presence of fathers in their children's lives, and they framed marriage in pleasurable, if nonimperative, terms. Our trouble hearing such alternatives, based on economic and noeconomic independence from male family headship but no rejection of men, was very instructive. It reminded us that feminist qualitative methods are valuable for having subjects speak and for allowing participants to talk back to us, the researchers who frame and represent. This talking and talking back (and then trying again and correcting again) suggest a helpful model for speaking across differences among women in that it also evokes the great persistence required to challenge the current public debate about the deserving mother.

REFERENCES

Amott, Teresa. 1993. Caught in the crisis. New York: Monthly Review.

Baca Zinn, Maxine, and D. Stanley Eitzen. 1992. Diversity in families. New York: Harper & Row.

Collins, Patricia Hill. 1990. Black feminist thought. Cambridge, UK: Unwin Hyman.

DeParle, Jason. 1994. Scrap welfare? Surprisingly, the notion is now a cause. New York Times (22 April): A1.

Dill, Bonnie Thornton. 1979. The dialectics of Black womanhood. Signs: Journal of Women in Culture and Society 4: 543–55.

Farley, Reynolds. 1988. After the starting line: Blacks and women in an uphill race. Demography 25: 477–95.

Ladner, Joyce. 1972. Tomorrow's tomorrow: The Black woman. Garden City, NY: Doubleday.

McLanahan, Sara. 1994. The consequences of single motherhood. The American Prospect 18: 48–58.

Morton, Patricia. 1991. Disfigured images: The historical assault on Afro-American women. New York: Praeger.

Moynihan, Daniel Patrick. 1965. The Negro family: The case for national action. Washington, DC: U.S. Department of Labor. Office of the Policy Planning and Research.

Murray, Charles. 1984. Losing ground: American social policy, 1950–1980. New York: Basic Books.

———. 1993. The coming white underclass. Wall Street Journal (29 October): A12.

Rose, Nancy E. 1993. Gender, race, and the welfare state: Government work programs from the 1930s to the present. Feminist Studies 19: 319–42.

Stack, Carol B. 1974. All our kin: Strategies for survival in a Black community. New York: Harper & Row.

Wilson, William J: 1987: The truly disadvantaged: The inner city, the underclass, and public policy. Chicago: University of Chicago Press.

———. 1994. The new urban poverty and the problem of race. Michigan Quarterly Review 33: 247–73.

POSTSCRIPT

Is Finding a Husband a Major Concern for African American Women?

Blum and Deussen refer to "marital rationality," a concept that incorporates the attachment between "normative" motherhood and male family headship. People who are troubled by disproportionately lower numbers of marriageable African American males point to problems associated with single parenting and to problems exhibited by children who are raised in families without fathers. Do you think that these critics show a gender bias toward African American families by placing too much emphasis on a masculine family headship? Do some children show strengths in association with a predominantly female upbringing? Are concerns about what is best for the children paramount, or should the needs and desires of their mothers also carry some weight?

Economic independence reduces women's financial incentives to marry, to remain married, or to remarry, according to "Mate Availability and African American Family Structure in the U.S. Non-metropolitan South, 1960–1990," *Journal of Marriage and the Family* (February 1997). If financial incentives were completely removed, would African American women be motivated to marry at all? Some African American women express no interest in involving themselves in the kind of commitment required of close interpersonal relationships. For example, Judy Dothard Simmons, in "Mars Conjunct Neptune," in Marita Golden, ed., *Wild Women Don't Wear No Blues* (Anchor Books, 1994), says that she does not want a man for domestic and family life nor does she want to tie herself down with children. She believes that while the average, married, African American woman "works like a dog outside the home and in, in order to be a S.B.W. (Strong Black Woman)," she is, in fact, a "B.O.B. (Beast of Burden)." She believes that African American women have a tendency to "marry down" and asserts that, given only this choice, she would prefer to stay single.

In contrast, Bebe Moore Campbell, in "Black Men, White Women: A Sister Relinquishes Her Anger," also in *Wild Women Don't Wear No Blues*, suggests that most black women prefer a war zone to loneliness. She believes that white women succumb to highly sexualized images of the African American male as a phallic symbol and that black women "don't measure up to images of femininity that exclude them." Campbell also contends that black males think that white women are more willing to be subservient and that African American women make greater demands on men. Black women, she says, are perceived by black men as "too materialistic, too argumentative, too demanding, just too much." According to Steve Sailer, in "Is Love Colorblind?"

National Review (July 14, 1997), a startling number of black women are bitterly opposed to interracial marriage. The assertion that interracial marriage does not treat every sex and race fairly explains their concern, says Sailer. Furthermore, since 72 percent of black-white marriages consist of a black male and a white female, these marriages offer black men new opportunities while imposing competition on black women.

According to Audrey Edwards, in "Sleeping With the Enemy," in *Wild Women Don't Wear No Blues*, the African American male shortage has caused some women to make a conscious choice to look for a white mate. What strikes her, she says, is the extent to which white men are able to see the beauty and value of black women. Edwards says she enjoys being involved with white men because of what she sees as their power, their ability to move freely through life, and their sense of entitlement. She also points to differences in the ways that black and white men perceive their power, which helps to define the different natures of their relationships to women.

ISSUE 13

Do Family Courts Discriminate Against Fathers in Custody Hearings?

YES: Jeffrey M. Leving and Kenneth A. Dachman, from *Father's Rights* (Basic Books, 1997)

NO: Phyllis Chesler, from "Is Every Woman One Divorce Away from Financial Disaster?" *On the Issues* (Winter 1997)

ISSUE SUMMARY

YES: Attorney Jeffrey M. Leving and professor of psychology Kenneth A. Dachman argue that mothers are disproportionately more likely to benefit from judiciary protections in family courts than are fathers and that mothers are consistently and unfairly awarded custody of the children.

NO: Editor and author Phyllis Chesler asserts that most women do not win custody unfairly and that when fathers truly want custody, they are more likely to have the financial resources to help win the case.

Child custody decisions, which were regulated by common law in America well into the nineteenth century, were profoundly patriarchal. For example, when a child's parents were married, that child was the legal beneficiary of all aspects of entitlement, but a child who was fathered outside of wedlock had no legal claim on his or her biological father. Fathers had complete custodial authority over marital children, which was an extension of their authority over their wives, who were barred from engaging in legal transactions or owning property and could not legally deny their husbands sexual access. A father was also permitted by law to name a third party to be the guardian of his children upon his own death and could convey parental rights to a third party at any point in time, all without the consent of the mother.

Later in the nineteenth century legislatures began to replace common law with statutes that granted wives equal custodial rights over their children. By the early twentieth century mothers had become the preferred parent and were typically awarded custody when parents divorced. This was based upon the "tender years doctrine," a tenet of family law that required that young children (of tender years, typically under 7 or 10 years of age) be kept with their mothers. It was commonly believed that women were more "naturally suited" to parenthood.

In the early 1970s the tender years doctrine was repealed. The new custody law advocated decision making based upon the "best interests of the children." Individuals on both sides of the debate about which parent should be granted custody agree that the "best interest" standard is highly subjective. It is loosely defined in statutory law as "the needs and circumstances of the child including emotional ties, child preferences, stable environment, and proposed plans for care and upbringing." This doctrine is often criticized for privileging the apparent advocates of the children rather than determining the actual best interests of the children.

Those who believe that men are subject to discrimination in child custody hearings, often speaking as representatives of various fathers' rights groups, have proposed several versions of joint custody. They frequently define joint custody as that which allows both parents to have equal voices in child-rearing decisions. It need not involve joint living arrangements, and children may continue to live solely with their mothers under such an arrangement. These joint custody advocates believe that they have every right to be involved in decisions that impact their children's lives, an option that is not available if the mothers have full and exclusive custody. They assert that a faulty belief in the mother as the child's *real* parent and a bias inherent in the "antiquated tender years doctrine" still permeate the system.

Some who do not believe that courts discriminate against fathers assert that most of these men have no desire for custody of their children and that when they actually do want the children, they receive full custody 50 to 80 percent of the time. They believe that many men use the threat of a custody lawsuit as a bargaining chip in seeking a settlement when what they really want is power and control over the lives of their children (and indirectly over the children's mothers) with minimal personal financial liability.

In the following selections, Jeffrey M. Leving and Kenneth A. Dachman maintain that mothers are disproportionately likely to benefit from judiciary protections in family courts, are consistently and unfairly awarded custody of their children, and receive excessive child support settlements. Phyllis Chesler argues that most women do not win custody unfairly and that more often it is assigned to them whether they want it or not. Furthermore, she contends that most women do not have the economic resources to utilize the court system the way that most men do.

YES

Jeffrey M. Leving and
Kenneth A. Dachman

INEXCUSABLE BIAS, UNACCEPTABLE CONSEQUENCES

Not long ago, Rollo Norton, the president of a large insurance company, attended a "collaborative management" seminar on a secluded island near Vancouver. What Rollo learned (from inspirational speakers, slick videos, and team-building games in the woods) was that a corporate culture stressing teamwork and shared responsibility offered substantial benefits—happier customers, happier employees, and higher profits. Dictatorial leadership and crusty, inflexible policies, Rollo was told, bred stagnation and inefficiency in customer service, and created a surly, uncaring workforce.

Rollo returned to his office aglow with evangelical fervor. Believing in his heart and mind that collaborative management was indeed a wonderful thing, Rollo immediately launched an intensive campaign to transform his company's authoritarian "hit the mark or hit the street" style into an open, cooperative culture in which employees would be treated as valuable partners, not disposable-wage slaves.

Memos flew. Happy, hyperkinetic meetings that employees soon labeled "love-ins" were held in every department of the company. Workers felt the spirit. Hundreds of fine ideas poured forth from every level of the organization. Rollo beamed.

Six months later, the company commissioned a climate survey to measure the improvements that the new culture surely had wrought. Minutes after digesting the survey's results, Rollo called together his senior executives.

"Nothing has changed," Rollo said. "In fact, in our employees' opinion, we've gotten worse."

"I don't understand," said the vice president of human resources. "We've spent sixty thousand dollars explaining and promoting the new culture."

The puzzle was solved the next day, when the consultant who had conducted the climate survey came across this anonymous comment from someone in accounting:

"Our managers came to us with open arms and smiling faces. They promised us empowerment, involvement and respect, but nothing happens. They talk the talk, but they don't walk the walk."

It's important for a father who must rely on the family court system to protect and preserve his paternal rights to recognize and accept the central message of this modest parable:

Policies, rules, procedures, clear directives in black and white, are not easily converted to meaningful action.... Sadly, there's often a troublesome variance between a legislature's instructions (the talk) and a judiciary's actions (the walk).

Tony

Our first glimpse of a judge's possible baffling disregard for the basic tenets of family law comes through the eyes of Tony, a divorced father who lives in New Jersey. Here, in Tony's own words, is what happened to him and to his children. (Tony's story is adapted from *Fathers and Grandfathers Under Siege* by Sal Fariello and Jerome A. Wisselman.)

"My wife walked out on me and the kids. I had sole custody for six years. I raised those kids from diapers. My wife was a drunk, she slept around, she had a criminal record. She couldn't have cared less about the kids.

"Then one day she got religion. She joined some bogus church and started going to Alcoholics Anonymous meetings. After a couple of weeks, she decides she's saved, she's sober, she's a new woman. So she petitions the court for custody of the kids.

"When I show up to fight her petition, the judge comes after me. What's the matter with me, he wants to know. Why do I want to keep the kids from their mother?

"I can't believe I'm hearing this. Keep them from their mother? Where the hell has she been for six years? In a goddamn stupor, that's where. I'm surprised she remembers she has kids. I told the judge that maybe some visits would be okay if the ex proves she's really off the sauce, but custody? No way.

"The judge didn't like me suggesting what he might want to think about doing. He got real superior, and real nasty. He told me that deciding what was best for the kids was his call, not mine. In other words, he was in control, not me.

"So now I'm steamed. I ask him why the courts are all of a sudden so interested in my kids. I wanted to know where the court was when I was raising them. The courts gave me no money, no help, nothing.

"You don't know me or my kids, I told the judge. I'm their father, I said, I should have some say in what happens to them.

"Now the judge is pissed. He tells me I'm being selfish and that young children need their mother. Then he says I'm no prize as a father, anyway.

"I'm so mad now I can hardly see straight, but I manage to ask him what he's talking about. He says he's got a social worker's report that says I'm no more than 'adequate' as a parent. I admit I'm no father-of-the-year candidate, but I take care of my kids. They've got a house, food, clothes, toys, whatever. I make sure they do their schoolwork and stay out of trouble. I have to work a lot, but I'm with them as much as I can be.

"Near the end of the trial, when I realized that this judge was calling me a lousy father and when I saw he was about to turn the kids over to their mother, I went completely nuts. I called the judge an idiot.... He cited me for contempt and had the bailiff handcuff me.

"I spent the night in jail still fuming. About three A.M. I realized that no matter what I said or did, this asshole in his black robes would always have more of a right to decide how my kids would grow up than their own father."

* * *

Like many of his family court colleagues, Tony's judge actually believed that Tony's children "belonged" with their mother, that she was the children's "real parent." The tender years doctrine was banished from domestic relations law long ago, but, as I see it, the notion that a mother is a child's "real" parent remains alive and kicking in this judge's mind. Most states now have laws specifically excluding even the suggestion that a parent's gender will be given any weight in custody, support, or access decisions. It doesn't seem to matter. The pure, clear equity promised by family law statutes filters through a thick labyrinth of deep-seated and widely held prejudices before delivery of real-life "justice" occurs. Often enough to trigger valid outrage, certain family court decisions plainly indicate that the influences of outdated cultural stereotypes and social presumptions can overwhelm reasonable and gender-neutral application of the law —and, in some cases, defy simple common sense.

A number of studies have found that although fathers are generally granted statutory equality by domestic relations law, they do not always receive fair treatment from family courts. Legislative inquiries in several states throughout the 1990s overwhelmingly support the conclusion of the Colorado Supreme Court Task Force on Gender Bias. This task force examined hundreds of family court rulings and found "a clear preference for the mother." In fact, the study team wrote, a mother had to be "nearly dysfunctional" not to win custody of her children.

The foundation of the pro-female bias that permeates too many domestic relations courtrooms is part myth, part social history.

During the first one hundred or so years of American history, a father was, by law and in practice, both head of the family and his children's primary caregiver. Fathers were actively involved in every aspect of their children's growth, education, development, and well-being. Fathers taught life skills, both through formal instruction and by example. Fathers decided who their children would marry and managed their children's entry into the world outside the home. The United States was a patriarchy, and when divorce occurred, courts almost always awarded full custody of children to fathers.

Early in the nineteenth century, the Industrial Revolution forced a dramatic change in family structure and a radical shift in parental roles and responsibilities. The family home became the mother's domain, and child care became a mother's primary responsibility. Fathers spent much of their time (an average of more than fifty hours a week) working outside the home. By the end of the nineteenth century, society had imposed gender-based identities and expectations on both mothers and fathers, assigning to each parent qualities and capacities based on his or her day-to-day duties within the family unit. Parental roles and capabilities were considered to be mutually exclusive. Women were seen as "natural" caretakers of children, endowed with special nurturing skills— an array of inherent instincts and talents that men simply did not possess. The aggressive, competitive, and analytical elements of a man's "nature," on the other hand, equipped fathers to fulfill their destinies as breadwinners, financial managers, protectors, and disciplinarians.

As these social stereotypes took root and hardened, the notion that mothers were superior parents—biologically programmed to love, care for, and nurture children—became a widely held belief, then accepted fact, and, ultimately, a tenet of law. Custody statutes across the United States mandated strict adherence to the "tender years" doctrine, a family court rule requiring that when divorce occurred, mothers were always to be presumptively awarded custody of children "of tender years" (age five and under). The presumption leading to establishment of the tender years doctrine—that mothers were children's "real" parents —effectively widened the rule's scope to the point that, in divorces involving children of any age, mothers (unless proven clearly unfit) were routinely awarded custody. In 1938, in a decision explaining his belief that "no child should be deprived of that maternal influence," a Missouri judge wrote: "There is but a twilight zone between a mother's love and the atmosphere of heaven."

Decades passed without a serious challenge to the tender years doctrine. Then, in the early 1970s, a somewhat odd, certainly ironic, convergence of civil rights and gender-equity activism (which included efforts of the feminist movement) led to the rule's demise.

In a 1973 ruling typical of this era, a New York court noted: "Apart from the question of legality, the tender years presumption should be discarded because it is based on outdated social stereotypes rather than a rational and up to date consideration of the welfare of the children involved. The simple fact of being a mother does not, by itself, indicate a capacity or willingness to render a quality of care different than that which a father can provide."

Abolishment of the tender years doctrine forced revision of custody laws in most states. New family court rules required each parent to be given equal consideration in custody cases, and legislators installed "the best interests of the children" as the single most important aspect of custody decisions.

Unfortunately for divorcing fathers, all the noble judicial talk and all the "gender-neutral" custody statutes enacted by suddenly caring, suddenly sensitive legislatures have had almost no consistent impact on family court policies and practices throughout America.

The belief that women are blessed with a "maternal instinct" is still widely held and rarely questioned—despite the fact that no scientist has ever been able to confirm its existence. A century of reverence for the traditional roles and trappings of motherhood have become embedded in our culture, continuing to influence judges, lawyers, and the general public long after women's roles in the family, and in society, have changed dramatically.

A brief return to a time when the tender years doctrine governed custody decisions provides disturbing but useful insights into the size and strength of the maternal preference.

Remember, the tender years presumption—a concept formally incorporated into family law in 1839 *required* that custody of young children be presumptively awarded to their mothers. Only a mother, the law stated, was capable of providing the nurturance and love children needed. The doctrine, although purged from most states' custody laws in the 1970s, lives on in the minds of many family court judges. But courts today must disguise their preference for mothers; they can't blatantly ignore the law's demand for gender equity. Current decisions are careful to cite some element of the child's best interests when a mother wins custody.

When adherence to the tender years doctrine *was* legal, judges freely expressed their respect and admiration for motherhood. A Wisconsin court declared that "nothing can be an adequate substitute for mother love... a nurture that only a mother can give because in her alone is service expressed in terms of love." In Washington State, a family court judge found "mother love" to be a "dominant trait in even the weakest of women, surpassing the paternal affection for the common offspring." The same judge suggested: "A child needs a mother's care much more than a father's." In Iowa, motherhood was described as "God's own institution for the rearing and upbringing of the child." A North Dakota court decided that no judiciary should ever "rend the most sacred ties of nature which bind a mother to her children."

Since most states have outlawed gender bias in custody cases, eloquent essays on the celestial nature of motherhood no longer clutter family court transcripts. That doesn't mean, however, that pro-female bias has been eliminated.

A brief examination of the outcomes in several recent cases from all over the United States reveals how family courts manage to bend, stretch, and twist the law to defy fathers the equitable treatment they deserve. . . .

Alex and Nell

At the time of their divorce, custody of Alex and Nell's fifteen-year-old son, Jon, was awarded to Nell. A year later, Alex asked a Minnesota court to reverse that decision. The reason for this request, Alex's petition stated, was that Jon was "not adjusting well to living with his mother. He has become withdrawn and depressed, and has demonstrated impulsive behavior, angry outbursts and insensitivity. He has expressed a strong desire to live with his father and has indicated that he might run away from home if that request cannot be granted."

During the evidentiary hearing held in response to Alex's petition, a psychologist testified that Jon's emotional development did indeed appear to be in jeopardy. The expert also told the court that Jon believed Alex was a better parent for him than Nell. Alex, Jon said, was much more able to provide support, understanding, and pleasant family activities. The psychologist concluded by expressing the opinion that Jon's "best interests would be most effectively served by granting Alex primary physical custody of the child, with an award of liberal visitation rights to Nell." A court-appointed therapist agreed with this recommendation.

The court listened, nodded, and decided that Jon would remain with his mother. In explaining its decision, the court acknowledged that Jon's "present home environment" (with Nell) was "not as suitable as the proposed environment" (with Alex), and that Jon would probably benefit from a change in custody. But there would be no change, the court ruled, because although a potential danger to Jon's emotional health had been demonstrated, the risk shown wasn't severe enough to warrant taking Jon from his mother.

In other words, while Jon obviously would be better off living with his father, nobody had proved that life with Mom would kill Jon or drive him crazy.

Here again we see a family court judge possibly disregarding the law to honor a mother's request—and, in the process, rejecting the recommendations of two child-care professionals and ignoring the wishes of the child himself....

Mike and Lila

When the marriage of Mike and Lila ended, a Wyoming court granted Lila custody of the couple's three children. Within two years of their divorce, both Mike and Lila remarried.

Lila left the children with Mike for an extended visit one summer. Mike was to return the kids before school resumed in August. He didn't. Instead, Mike filed a petition to modify the original custody decree, asking the court to make him the children's custodial parent.

While Mike's petition was pending, the children were returned to Lila. She and the children moved to Colorado. Because Lila failed to appear at the custody hearing, a default judgment awarded custody of the children to Mike. Three years passed before Lila and the kids moved back to Wyoming. (By then Lila had divorced her second husband.) Lila asked the Wyoming courts to return custody of the children to her.

When the custody matter finally came to trial, Mike produced evidence that Nate, a man who had been living with Lila and the children, had pled guilty to sexually molesting Mike and Lila's eleven-year-old daughter. Testimony revealed that the abuse occurred over a nine-month period. The child asked a teacher for help, and it was this contact that led to Nate's arrest and incarceration for second-degree sexual assault.

In addition to citing the dangers posed to his children by Lila's choice of companions, Mike complained that Lila's "nomadic" lifestyle deprived the children of stability and security. He also offered proof that while in their mother's care, the children's school performance had deteriorated to the point where they were all held back a year.

Lila responded that she had been unaware of Nate's deviant behavior and that Mike had expressed no interest in the children's lives, contacting them only once during the three years she and the children lived in Colorado.

In announcing its decision, the court noted that, while Lila's association with Nate was "unfortunate and deplorable," there was "no excuse for Mike ignoring the children and leaving the mother alone to raise them." Ruling that Lila would be awarded custody of the children, the court said, "She gave birth to them. She was there for all those years alone. I can't forget that. No evidence has been shown that she isn't a good and loving mother."

What?

Remarkably, the state's supreme court affirmed the trial court's decision. A dissenting opinion, apparently unmoved by the apparent maternal bias of the majority, called the lower court's ruling "a clear and grave abuse of discretion." The award of custody to Lila was contrary to the "great weight of the evidence," the dissent declared. Lila had continued to see Nate *after* his sexual assault conviction, the dissent noted, and she had allowed her children (except for the daughter Nate had molested) to be alone with him. Lila's conduct and lifestyle were "clearly detrimental to the welfare and best interests of the children," the dissent noted, and the children should have been "the trial court's paramount concern."

* * *

The experiences of Tony, Alex, ... and Mike are unusual only because the pro-mother bias that these men encountered was so extreme. In most jurisdictions across the United States, a predisposition favoring mothers in custody issues exists quietly, an integral element of business as usual. Raw numbers demonstrate the depth and breadth of the judicial prejudice facing fathers expecting equal treatment from family courts: Mothers win 85 percent of all custody disputes.

A strong pro-female bias is also evident in the courts' allocation of support obligations. A noncustodial father is almost always ordered to pay child support; judges rarely ask a noncustodial mother to contribute to the economic support of her children. A recent week in domestic relations court offers examples of this distorted principle in action.

On Tuesday of this sample week, a family court judge ordered a father to pay his former spouse child support in the amount of $1,200 a month—about half the father's income. Three days later, in the same courtroom, the same judge ruled that a noncustodial mother was not required to pay child support, even though she owned and operated a successful business.

Another clear indicator of the over-powering influence of gender discrimination in family court policies can be seen by examining the system's enforcement practices. Courts typically deal swiftly and harshly with fathers who violate orders and decrees. In many jurisdictions, a father who returns his child two hours late after visitation will often have his visitation rights suspended or revoked. And, of course, most family court judges deal swiftly and harshly with fathers who fail to meet their child support obligations. Wage garnishment, seizure of assets, criminal prosecution, and jail time are freely and frequently employed to enforce support orders.

A mother needing help to collect child support can rely on an extensive enforcement structure built and operated at taxpayer expense. On the other side of the aisle, a father seeking a court's help in protecting or preserving his parental rights too often spends a lot of money and a lot of time securing the judicial equivalent of a smile and a shrug. ...

THE ULTIMATE OLD WIVES' TALE

The ingrained presumption that femininity and parental ability are "naturally" intertwined is a hardy, durable myth, apparently immune to the forces of science, social reality, political pressure, and public opinion.

Numerous studies of single-parent households have reached similar conclusions: There is no correlation between gender and child-rearing competence. While several differences in parenting styles were noted by researchers, both mothers and fathers were found to be equally capable as caregivers. (Parental competence, in all the studies cited, was measured through comprehensive evaluation of children's behavior, attitudes, school performance, and social skills.)

The results of these academic investigations are validated every day, in homes all over the country. Mothers and fathers are sharing child-care duties, often not because they want to but mainly because that's the way it has to be. That reality leads us to the aspect of the bias evident in many family courts that fathers, their attorneys, and social scientists find most unbelievable: Many judges continue to decide children's fates based on narrow, sexist stereotypes that no longer exist.

The fact is that the family roles assumed by both men and women have been changing for decades. Current Census Bureau statistics indicate that 68 percent of U.S. mothers with children under eighteen work outside the home. The "typical" postwar nuclear family is almost extinct. Ward and June Cleaver live on only in television reruns. Their pristine black-and-white family world has evolved into an unruly mélange of inventive family lifestyles.

June Cleaver's days were spent in an eternal marathon of housework, baking, and beauty shop visits. Today, women have made substantial advances in industry, government, the arts, and the professions. Inescapable economic forces, coupled with a wide range of personal fulfillment needs, have swept mothers out of the kitchen into the business world. While complete equality in the workplace has not been achieved, a woman's right to demand respect, status, and compensation based solely on job performance is no longer seriously questioned.

Ward Cleaver spent his days at the office, his evenings in the den. His parental duties consisted solely of delivering serious but amiable lectures nudging Wally and the Beaver back toward the straight and narrow. Men today routinely attend prenatal classes, assist in the births of their children, and take an active role in all facets of child rearing. Self-worth for men is no longer simply a function of success at work. Millions of fathers have discovered the joys and satisfactions of parenting. The following observation, from an essay on fatherhood by newspaper editor David Blasco, conveys an attitude now shared by countless fathers. Blasco,

several months after arranging his work schedule to be able to spend his days caring for his young children, wrote this:

"I am the breadwinner. It's an old pattern, perhaps one of the oldest on earth. My father would be familiar with it. But my father never had the chance to know what it was like to be with his child much of the day. I've been lucky. I've had all that time in the park."

Teacher and historian Michael Kort is another father who found time for both full-time parenting and a traditional career.

"I'd be the first to admit that raising children is not easy," Kort wrote. "It takes much of my time and most of my patience. But in return, aside from happiness, pride and love, my daughters have given me some simple pleasures... appreciating a butterfly, watching with fascination a perfectly ordinary bird in flight, playing Wiffle Ball, riding a bike, building a sand castle at the beach... They've given me, in short,... a remarkable gift which could have come from nowhere else, [a gift] worth far more than it cost."

An accurate distillation of the feelings many fathers experience as they shift focus from career to family was offered by David Riley, a lobbyist from Washington, D.C.

"I never knew how much you could get by giving," Riley wrote. "Jake [Riley's infant son] takes a lot of my time, but he gives back a dimension to my life that I cherish. And I've come to think that the world might be a very different place if its workaholics had more of this dimension in their lives."

In most homes today, mothers and fathers share child-care duties and the daily labors necessary to operate a family (cooking, cleaning, shopping, feeding and bathing the kids, helping with homework, and so forth). With both parents working in so many modern families, child rearing often involves day care, baby-sitters, or an infinite array of creative scheduling choices. Both mothers and fathers have become, in the words of one pediatric psychologist, "executive parents"—more parental care managers than direct caregivers. In other words, families today are a lot like small businesses, with dads, moms, relatives, and hired help doing whatever must be done, with little regard for titles or status.

Over the past thirty years, women have made remarkable progress in areas of society that had been dominated by men for centuries. The women's movement was responsible for much of this advancement, and it was feminists who first pointed out that traditional gender roles were oppressive and demeaning to both men and women. Interestingly, only half of feminism's message has made a meaningful impression on our collective consciousness. Women are now viewed as being capable of success in the workplace. Men, however, are not yet seen as being capable of providing competent, attentive child care—at least not in the eyes of many family court judges.

In a recent *USA Today* poll, 88 percent of the eleven thousand Americans surveyed believed that mothers and fathers should share equally in all child-rearing activities. Because local judiciaries usually are in tune with prevailing public opinion, many political experts find the invincibility of the maternal presumption in family law to be remarkable. As one veteran analyst commented, "Walking into some of these courtrooms is like traveling back in time."

Years of experience and research have convinced me that to understand the gender bias condoned by many family courts, we must recognize the interaction of all elements of the phenomenon. An inappropriate reverence for a long extinct ideal of motherhood is certainly one important piece of the puzzle. The belief that fathers can't handle the rigors of child care is another. The conviction that children need a father's money much more than the father himself also plays a part. The final key might be the perception—widely held within the judiciary and shared by many "civilians" —that fathers don't really want, or need, parental rights or responsibilities.

Society's lack of respect for fatherhood and the inaccurate assumption that fathers are not truly interested in parenting combine to perpetuate a comfortable rationalization, a judicial delusion that plays out something like this: Mothers and children need each other. Fathers and children don't, or at least not as much. Accept that dubious premise and gender bias, although illegal and unfair, doesn't seem all that harmful. It's not like real bigotry. There's no violence, no blatant oppression. No one is lynching anyone; no flaming crosses are showing up on fathers' lawns.

The insensitivity and inaccuracy of the notion that divorced or otherwise estranged fathers really don't want or need continuing involvement with their children immediately became clear to me within days after my decision to represent fathers in family court. A client I'll call Jim sat in my tiny office weeping uncontrollably. He had only one request: an hour or two with his six-year-old son. "His mother has my kid believing that his dad hates him," Jim said. "I need to tell him that's not true."

Since that day, I've become too familiar with the very real pain and overpowering sense of loss suffered by fathers excluded from their children's lives. All kinds of fathers from all walks of life find separation from their children to be a torturous, devastating experience. The father might be a glib advertising exec or a quiet factory foreman. The agony is the same.

"The silence I thought would be so welcome turned out to be the most oppressive experience of my life," an estranged father told author Howard Irving.

"When my boy was with me, I felt whole," said another divorced dad. "When he was gone, I felt empty. This is the writhing in the soul divorced men feel. When he goes back to his mom, a part of you dies. Something in your manhood suffers a profound assault that you're powerless against."

Divorced novelist C. W. Smith's reflections on the loss of his children are particularly relevant. Like many fathers pushed to the periphery of their children's lives, Smith didn't appreciate the inestimable value of what he had—until it was gone.

"I read the kids Curious George and Dr. Seuss books," Smith wrote. "Once, when a heavy snowfall closed the schools, we made an igloo in the yard.... Giving them a hug, or an off to school scuff on the head... making cheese toast, cheering while running behind my cycling novice son with one hand clutching the waistband of his jeans —these humble pleasures vanished the moment I decided to leave. To provide, to protect, and to guide... these had constituted the dogma of fathering I had learned as a son, and I didn't know that performing these ritual duties was such good spiritual nutrition."

The close involvement and deep affection for their children that so many modern fathers feel free to express has, of course, always existed, as has the realization that fatherhood is as precious to fathers as it is to children. More than two hundred years ago, Jean-Jacques Rousseau wrote that "paternal love" was the source of one of the "sweetest sentiments known to man." A century later, philosopher Lafcadio Hearn declared, "No man can possibly know what life means, what the world means, what anything means, until he has a child and loves it. And then the whole universe changes and nothing will ever again seem exactly as it seemed before."

I'm certain that most fathers know exactly the feelings that Rousseau and Hearn described. The belief that destruction of the father-child bond is a victimless crime is an utterly appalling, incredibly cruel fallacy.

NO

Phyllis Chesler

IS EVERY WOMAN ONE DIVORCE AWAY FROM FINANCIAL DISASTER?

She had a hard time getting up on those days when she had to appear in court on her petition for child support. She knew the court system rarely worked. Judges had staggering caseloads, archaic methods of case management, and limited power to wield against a male citizenry that neither feared nor respected the law. Fathers with money routinely hid their assets or paid a lawyer to appeal every order of child support. Appeals, trials, motions—these could go on for 5, 10, 15 years. A child could become a man, his mother a ghost, before her motion for half the summer camp tuition was ever heard.

Summer camp? Is that what her battle was about? Every day in America, she knew, electricity and heat are turned off, apartments padlocked, homes foreclosed on, and women and children fatally impoverished because women can't afford a lawyer/their lawyer is incompetent/their lawyer is incomparable, a jewel, but can't get a judge to make or enforce a decision. The truth: It's almost impossible to collect money from a father who doesn't have any, or who doesn't want to pay.

Nevertheless, she had decided to fight for her own—and her son's—economic rights, not on principle, but because they needed the money for her son's necessities. She hoped that, in her case, justice might prevail. Sometimes, it did.

Her mistake—her crime?—was not that she'd married the wrong man or had chosen to become a mother. In fact, her ex-husband had once been a very decent human being. Her crime was that, five years ago she became ill, could no longer work her usual four jobs, had cashed in her life insurance policy, borrowed heavily against her home, and now faced mounting medical bills with no savings to "run through." How could she save? For 14 years, she had been her son's sole support. She had paid for his food, clothing, shelter, education, entertainment, doctors, dentists, orthodontists, vacations, birthday parties, religious training, rites of passage, and for all the baby-sitters and live-in housekeepers without which she could not have worked or led her life.

* * *

I am that woman. My case is typical, almost humdrum. I have been in court for nearly four years now. I may very well still be there four years from now. And that's the good news. Most women can't economically afford to turn to the courts.

It's important that those of us who can fight for our economic rights do so. Women usually compare themselves, guiltily, to other women, not to men. Any woman (me too) can be easily shamed into settling for "less" and not complaining about it because other women have it "even worse." It is important that each woman compare herself with the men in the class above her, not just with the women in the class below her.

The class below middle class is abysmal. For years, below-poverty levels of welfare set the standard for what mothers—and the judges who sometimes decided their cases—viewed as what could be "worse." Now, "going under," i.e., going on welfare, has just been closed out as an unlimited option in America.

Let me be clear: Not all mothers are saints; many men are "good enough" fathers. Upon divorce, not all fathers desert their children. But many do. And although my case is hardly the neediest case of the week—chances are, I won't starve—what's at issue is my own and my son's right versus my ex-husband's right to remain in the middle class.

We all know at least one professional-class tale of outrage: the millionaire father who, without warning, closes out the brokerage accounts, turns off the electricity, sells the house, packs up all the furniture and disappears, leaving his stay-at-home wife and three young kids literally stranded in the snow—and who is never heard from again.

These days, my ex-husband, like so many, simply cannot conceive of having to sacrifice, even slightly, his own steadily escalating standard of spending in order to "do right" by his firstborn. Many otherwise perfectly nice men are like this. They tend to support a child as long as that child's mother is performing wifely services for them. Not otherwise. Men tend to sacrifice the children of their first wives when they remarry. Men are not legally prohibited from fathering more children simply because they do not—or cannot—support the children they already have.

And no, mothers do not "win" custody unfairly; more often, they are stuck with it, whether they want it or not. When fathers really do want custody, they tend to win it anywhere from 50 to 80 percent of the time. However, most fathers still do not want custody. Many use the threat of a custody battle as an economic bargaining chip.

* * *

My ex-husband tried that early on, then backed off—but since then, has never been forced to pay a dime. For years, I didn't press him. Then, when I became ill with chronic fatigue/immune-dysfunction syndrome in 1991, I had to. Since November of 1992, I have had a supremely skilled lawyer whom I can absolutely trust. We sued. On January 26, 1994, after 13 months, four motions, and four days in court, Brooklyn Family Court Judge Richard Spegele ruled that my ex did not have to pay any child support. The judge did not care that my ex was earning far more money than I or that I was living on disability. In his view, I was better off than most of the women whose cases he heard. He refused to believe that I couldn't support our son by myself, at some acceptable level of poverty. He was comparing me with the women in the class below me.

Wearily, we went to Manhattan Supreme Court. After only four months, Judge David Saxe ordered my ex to pay $250 a week in temporary child support, all the medical insurance, half the private school tuition, and all our son's unreimbursed health expenses. (Dear Judge: Thank you.) I am now owed approximately $30,000 in court-ordered temporary child support and $10,000 in legal fees for the period from June of 1995 to November of 1996. My lawyer hired detectives, obtained a court order to examine portions of my ex's financial records, served 150 restraining orders, and at least 50 income-execution orders. To date, I owe her more than $75,000 in fees and expenses. To date, she has been able to collect approximately $10,000 in child support, which my ex did not voluntarily turn over.

I can afford to keep fighting only because my lawyer took my case for no fee up front. (Susan Bender, counselor extraordinaire: Thank you.) Without such a resource, I, like most women, could not have gotten so far. Believe it or not, I am "winning" simply because I am able to keep fighting. Most mothers can't. While they and their lawyers wait for court dates, furniture is repossessed, electricity turned off—homes foreclosed.

My ex-husband, who in one recent year reported earning more than a quarter of a million dollars, refuses to pay court-ordered child support. He continues to refuse to turn over documents, appear for depositions, explain financial inconsistencies, or prove that, as he claims, he is unable to support our son. On February 22, 1996, 17 months after temporary child support was first ordered, Referee Frank Lewis recommended that the court find my ex in contempt of court. As of October 1996, 8 months later, I am still waiting for the judge of record to certify Referee Lewis's recommendation.

When you read this, my ex might well be on his way to jail. I would rather have had the money; I would have liked a "good enough" father too.

Then again, our son has turned out rather splendidly without one.

Lesson 1: My son's father is no one special, i.e., he has no special connections in the courts. Nevertheless, simply because he's a man, he has felt entitled and been allowed to get away without paying child support and without being an involved, responsible parent. He didn't always have a large income, but in recent years he has; my lawyer discovered that he had numerous bank and brokerage accounts, investments in the Cayman Islands, a recently purchased expensive home. He assumed monthly mortgage payments far in excess of his court-ordered child-support payments. Once Judge Saxe rendered his order, my ex quickly emptied his accounts. He claims that he is "broke" and "disabled" too.

Lesson 2: Even ill, I have more leverage, more resources, than most women in America. If this is what can happen to me, just think about the women with no or fewer resources. I want Every woman who gets no (or minimal and sporadic) child support to know that she's not alone; that even if she has done everything "right" (earns a "male" salary, chooses to be an unsalaried stay-at-home mother), she/we cannot easily, or even close to equally, hold our own against a man in court: that our achieved status and blameless records as "good enough" mothers are still not equivalent to having a penis.

* * *

I had married a "gentle" man. He attended natural childbirth classes, remained by my side when I was in labor, roomed in with me at the hospital. He was more expert than I at snappy diaper-changing, calmer in emergencies. I was nine years his senior and earned most of the money. Over the years, a number of newspapers had profiled us as a New Age/European kind of Older Woman, Younger Man couple.

Maybe I thought that my seniority, both economically and in terms of age, might balance out our gender differences. I was wrong.

After our son's birth, my husband refused to work or resume his studies, even part time. OK: Maybe he really did want to be a primary caregiver, right? Wrong. He conceived of his role as that of my overseer and "helper." Although I was breast-feeding, I had to return to work to support us. That meant traveling —and weaning too soon, against my will. I employed a live-in baby nurse and a housekeeper. My husband kept them company. OK: Maybe the man was suffering from postpartum depression; maybe he couldn't handle the bottom-line responsibility for such low-status "female" work. (I jest.) In 1978, everyone in our building and all the women in the park thought the man was a saint whenever he turned up during the day, alone, for an hour or two, with an infant, whom he fed, changed, and expertly calmed. Back then, few white middle-class men did this.

After a year, my husband started having affairs, openly, with girls literally half my age. OK: He was freaking out. I loved him, I'd wait until he came to his senses. Fat chance. My husband moved out. He began demanding money he knew I didn't have, perhaps for having married me or for having provided the sperm. When he demanded that his name be put on the deed of any house I might purchase in the future, I quickly moved for divorce.

He, in turn, moved for sole custody, alimony, child support, and all the marital assets on the basis that I was a totally unfit mother given my firebrand commitment to feminism. In his court papers, my husband also charged that I was an opium addict. An opium addict? No more ridiculous than his charge that I was a well-known lesbian man-hater. At the time, I was well-known for having remained hopelessly, even "rabidly," heterosexual. My husband then threatened to kidnap my son so that I'd never see him again. I believed him.

In fear, I settled with him privately. And then he tried to do me out of my half of that financial agreement. We ended up in court and in the newspapers too. Eventually, he walked away with $40,000, which bought him his chiropractic education. I persuaded the judge to set aside one seventh of my ex's financial settlement for our son, to be doled out at the rate of $500 a year for 12 years. I settled for vague but legally real language about his paying child support "in the future as best he can."

I know: I could have fought for stronger language but I was a busy woman. Like so many mothers, I did not want to further alienate the father my son didn't but might yet have if only I was demanded nothing. I tried to persuade my ex to live near us so that we could have joint custody. "I don't want to be your baby-sitter," said he.

My ex was soft-spoken, easy going. It was years before I understood that his abandonment of our son was a supremely violent act.

Over the years, my ex-husband saw our son whenever he wanted to, whenever it was convenient for him. He saw him every other weekend, overnight, for nearly three years. (See how good he was?) True, he'd pick him up two to four hours late, return him wearing dirty clothes and wet diapers, his undone laundry rolled up in a smelly snarl. Sometimes he'd return him hungry, or with a fever. I was shocked. Outraged. This was a father who knew the drill. Over the years, he did not feel obliged to meet with our son's teachers, attend school, sports, or music events, transport our son to Hebrew School or to doctors and dentists. He never once invited our son to join him for any national or religious holidays. No matter what I said, I could not get this man to take any bottom-line parenting responsibility.

However, after nine years, I was exhausted and desperate for a break. In the summer of 1987, I dropped our son off at his father's for an overnight and took a brief sabbatical. I called, said he had to keep our son for awhile, there was no alternative. This arrangement only lasted a few months, and was incredibly harried and labor-intensive. (Ex: "You have to be here to pick him for the weekend by 5 p.m. or I'll leave him on the street; you haven't given me enough money for his food; he needs a new pair of sneakers.") I missed my son more than I prized my time off from being overwhelmed by single-parenting responsibilities. Happily, I retrieved him.

At the time, I remember feeling grateful that my ex "let" me have him back.

I faithfully invited my ex and his girlfriend-of-the-moment to every one of our son's birthday parties. He often came late, and left early, but at least he came. I refused to risk even this little by turning to the courts.

When my ex opened a second office, remarried, and had a second child, even I had to realize that the man had moved on and was not taking our son along for the ride. Still, I figured: The man had to grow up someday, he's not all bad. In 1992, after years of begging, I'd finally persuaded him to start contributing half to our son's tuition at a private school. True: That left me also paying the other half and all the mounting costs of child support myself, but hey, I wanted a child, right?

Eventually, our son grew reluctant to visit his father overnight. He said that his dad went out to parties with his wife on the nights he was there, refused to spend time alone with him, give him a closet or a shelf of his own. Once a half-brother was born, my son was told he had to sleep on the couch and help the baby-sitters take care of his half-brother. Whenever my ex would slip his firstborn a five- or a ten-dollar bill, our son claimed that his father's wife would burst into tears, argue, retreat to her bedroom, or storm out of the apartment.

When I became ill, I asked my ex to allow our then-13-year-old son to stay with him for one summer month until I could figure out what was wrong with me. He said, "No, it wasn't convenient." The only thing left to fight for, both for myself and my son, was money. There was nothing left to lose.

I was wrong. In 1992, when I turned to the courts, my ex stopped seeing our son almost entirely. He made dates, then canceled them at the last minute; sometimes he simply stood him up. He saw our son for an hour or two at most and, according to our son, spent most of that time haranguing him about the child-support lawsuit.

Most women are facing far more hardship than I am. A violent father can do more to destroy a mother and child than economically impoverish them. He can also beat, rape, kidnap, brainwash, or kill them. Most mothers consider themselves lucky if all that happens is that they "go under" economically, learn to live on the edge for the rest of their lives.

However, economic crimes against mothers and children are deadly. Sooner or later, deprivation and constant worry about money kills. Lead on the wall, fatty junk foods, dangerous housing, no housing, living from hand to mouth, breaks the spirit and dulls the mind. Too much worry for too long, overwork, no paid work, the absence of hope, kills. Slow killing does not make the evening news: not dramatic enough, too ordinary, the plight of the poor is boring/their fault/not our problem. Impoverished American women and children are our "untouchables," our national shame.

My son—not our son—is 18 and a half now and has just begun college. What happened—and continues to happen to me as a mother—happens to most divorced women, whether they are feminists or not. Until now, I have kept silent. I hereby add my name to the long, exceedingly honorable roster of women who are bringing children up alone, under siege, in poverty far more bone-crushing than my own.

Most women are used to fighting for others, not for themselves. Me too. This, finally, is a fight for my own rights, for tangible, not symbolic justice.

POSTSCRIPT

Do Family Courts Discriminate Against Fathers in Custody Hearings?

Some of the most vocal groups in support of the ideas of Leving and Dachman are members of fathers' rights movements. In "Will Paternal Paranoia Triumph?" *On the Issues* (Winter 1997), Trish Wilson argues that these groups often use Internet sites to harass and demean women and that they are essentially composed of men who are angry over diminished power and control over their families. Accusations against these groups include that they attack single mothers, petition courts for sole paternal custody regardless of circumstances, argue for immediate reassignment of children to the father if the mother applies for welfare, and lobby for legislative reforms to empower themselves. Wilson asserts that they seek to discourage "all types of transfers of assets which encourage or support fatherlessness" and that they have a political agenda, which often is not connected with any desire to be with their children. Although fathers' rights groups argue that 75 percent of fathers are paying all or some child support in a timely fashion, Wilson says, a recent U.S. census has determined that 50 percent of women receive only partial payments or no payments and that payments are rarely made voluntarily. Despite these alleged illegalities and irresponsibilities, she notes that fathers' rights movements receive tax-free federal funding and dues.

Additional criticism is found in C. Bertola and J. Drakich, "The Fathers' Rights Movement," *Journal of Family Issues* (December 1993), in which contradictions between public and private rhetoric are examined. The authors assert that concepts such as coparenting and continuing parent-child relationships are embedded in such deeply held principles as "equality" and "rights," while, in truth, these terms may be employed to obscure the contradictory and statistically supported realities of divorce and shared custody. Other readings that question the integrity of fathers' rights groups include Martha Fineman, *The Illusion of Equality: The Rhetoric and Reality of Divorce Reform* (University of Chicago Press, 1991) and S. Boyd, "Investigating Gender Bias in Canadian Child Custody Law: Reflections on Questions and Method," in Joan Brockman and Dorothy E. Chunn, eds., *Investigating Gender Bias: Law, Courts, and the Legal Profession* (Thompson Educational Publishing, 1993).

What rights do biological, unwed fathers have to custody of their infant offspring? "Fathers' Rights and Mothers' Wrongs? Reflections on Unwed Fathers' Rights and Sex-Equality," *Hypatia* (Winter 1995) provides a complete review of five decisions of the U.S. Supreme Court that have been rendered over the past 20 years. After reviewing *Stanley v. Illinois, Quilloin v. Wolcott, Caban v. Mohammed, Lehr v. Robertson,* and *Michael H. v. Gerald D.,* the authors suggest that these cases established, at least in instances where a substantial relationship has been developed between child and unwed father, that the father's right to continue the relationship may be constitutionally protected. Some argue that a child's "best interest" test is a no-win situation for unwed fathers of infants because of long waiting lists of adoptive couples and because there is a bias in favor of rearing children in two-parent homes. Furthermore, the notion that a mother who decides to give up her child is indifferent to that child's fate distorts and denigrates her experience of pregnancy and the nature of her decision, say the authors. Katha Pollitt argues in support of unwed fathers paying child support in "Subject to Debate," *The Nation* (January 30, 1995), while David Blankenhorn takes the opposing view in "Pay, Papa, Pay," *National Review* (April 3, 1995).

Readings that unequivocally support the fathers' rights movement include "Fathers Have Rights Too," *Essence* (June 1995); "You've Come a Long Way, Daddy," *Policy Review* (July/August 1997); "The Fatherhood Movement," *The World and I* (June 1995); "They're Not All Deadbeat Dads," *The World and I* (April 1994); and "Fatherhood Aborted," *Christianity Today* (December 9, 1996), which addresses whether or not fathers should have a say in abortion decisions.

ISSUE 14

Do Lesbian Couples Naturally Adopt Separate Gender Roles?

YES: Joan Nestle, from *A Restricted Country* (Firebrand Books, 1987)

NO: Beverly Burch, from "Heterosexuality, Bisexuality, and Lesbianism: Rethinking Psychoanalytic Views of Women's Sexual Object Choice," *Psychoanalytic Review* (vol. 80, no. 1, 1993)

ISSUE SUMMARY

YES: Writer Joan Nestle maintains that the butch-femme experience is complex and authentic—a natural way of life for a majority of lesbian couples.

NO: Psychotherapist Beverly Burch argues that boundaries are fluid in typical lesbian relationships and that these relationships are not likely to function within the context of a butch-femme dichotomy, which allows lesbian couples to avoid any consistent dominance of one partner over the other.

Laypeople often assume that a lesbian is simply "a woman who has sexual desire for, or relations with, other women," but a more complete definition of lesbianism expands to emotional, social, and political dimensions. The butch-femme dichotomy in lesbianism describes traits of masculinity in one partner and traits of exaggerated femininity in the other. In 1928 well-known psychologist Havelock Ellis became one of the first to observe and reflect the prevailing view of the time. He reported that lesbian relationships embody a natural gender polarization.

During a period of sexual repression from the 1940s through the mid-1960s, the butch-femme identity became part of a social code, and lesbians often engaged in self-labeling as part of a cultural ritual. The prevailing wisdom of the time was that in any lesbian relationship, one partner must be the "man." It was commonly believed that if one explored the lives of a lesbian couple, one would find two latent or incompletely expressed heterosexuals. Butch-femme roles were therefore seen as essential components of lesbianism.

In the 1970s role-playing went underground, and the lesbian-feminist culture offered a new identity: that of the androgynous, politically aware, and politically correct lesbian who wanted egalitarian sexual relationships. Lesbians of this era generally did not wish to be seen as embodying twisted imitations of straight relationships. A trend began whereby lesbians began to dress and act alike and in which gender roles were dismissed as an unwelcome carryover from the 1950s. Then, in the 1980s and 1990s, butch-femme roles reemerged in the sexual arena, and they now seem to be even more intricately intertwined with lesbian sexuality than they were in the past.

Some of those opposed to lesbian expression in the form of butch-femme identities argue that butch and femme roles are nonegalitarian and lead to sadomasochistic sex that degrades women. Opponents define any sexuality based entirely on "self-other complementarity" as sadomasochistic sex. They claim that the intensely felt eroticism of dominance and submission, which are often associated with heightened arousal, tend to invoke notions of a patriarchal control of women's sexuality. Furthermore, the butch-femme dichotomy may also embody a power asymmetry that is problematic. Concerns have been expressed that the femme gets a bad deal because the butch calls all the shots.

On the other hand, advocates of sexual diversity argue that excessive concerns with politically correct behavior will lead to the death of sexual desire and, ultimately, to asexual relationships. Sex is not about equality, they say, but about tension, power, and dominance—about primitive instincts. Moreover, butch-femme roles are "adopted" to enliven sexual experience, and gender roles may be simply less extreme versions of sadomasochistic roles.

Other views suggest that the gendered sense of self is more fluid in the lesbian than in the heterosexual woman and that it shifts between various representations and expressions of masculine and feminine. Lesbians may not identify in any internally or consistent way as being butch or femme. On the other hand, many lesbians now strongly advocate for the butch-femme role dichotomy. They believe that butch-femme roles, by their very essence, are different from gender roles.

In the following selections, Joan Nestle indicates that she does not feel oppressed as a self-identified femme. She celebrates her role yet does not connect it with traditional notions of masculinity or femininity. Beverly Burch does not see a clear dichotomy in gender roles in lesbian relationships. She cites studies suggesting that the existence of stereotyped roles is rare and that lesbians often prefer relationships in which there is little or no role-playing; equality between partners is the norm.

YES

Joan Nestle

A RESTRICTED COUNTRY

For many years now, I have been trying to figure out how to explain the special nature of butch-femme relationships to Lesbian-feminists who consider butch-femme a reproduction of heterosexual models. My own roots lie deep in the earth of this Lesbian custom, and what follows is one Lesbian's understanding of her own experience.

In the late 1950s I walked the streets looking so butch that straight teenagers called me a bulldyke; however, when I went to the Sea Colony, a working-class Lesbian bar in Greenwich Village, looking for my friends and sometimes for a lover, I was a femme, a woman who loved and wanted to nurture the butch strength in other women. I am now forty years old (1981). Although I have been a Lesbian for over twenty years and I embrace feminism as a world view, I can spot a butch thirty feet away and still feel the thrill of her power. Contrary to belief, this power is not bought at the expense of the femme's identity. Butch-femme relationships, as I experienced them, were complex erotic statements, not phony heterosexual replicas. They were filled with a deeply Lesbian language of stance, dress, gesture, loving, courage, and autonomy. None of the butch women I was with, and this included a passing woman, ever presented themselves to me as men; they did announce themselves as tabooed women who were willing to identify their passion for other women by wearing clothes that symbolized the taking of responsibility. Part of this responsibility was sexual expertise. In the 1950s this courage to feel comfortable with arousing another woman became a political act.

Butch-femme was an erotic partnership serving both as a conspicuous flag of rebellion and as an intimate exploration of women's sexuality. It was not an accident that butch-femme couples suffered the most street abuse and provoked more assimilated or closeted Lesbians to plead with them not to be so obvious. An excerpt from a letter by Lorraine Hansberry, published in the Ladder[1] in 1957, shows the political implications of the butch-femme statement. The letter is a plea for discretion because, I believe, of the erotic clarity of the butch-femme visual image.

> Someday I expect the "discrete" lesbian will not turn her head on the streets at the sight of the "butch" strolling hand in hand with her friend in their trousers

and definitive haircuts. But for the moment it still disturbs. It creates an impossible area for discussion with one's most enlightened (to use a hopeful term) heterosexual friends.[2]

A critic of this essay has suggested that what was really the problem here was that "many other Lesbians at that time felt the adoption of culturally defined roles by the butch-femme was not a true picture of the majority of Lesbians. They found these socialized roles a limiting reality and therefore did not wish to have the butch-femme viewpoint applied or expressed as their own."[3]

My sense of the time says this was not the reason. The butch-femme couple embarrassed other Lesbians (and still does) because they made Lesbians culturally visible, a terrifying act for the 1950s. Hansberry's language—the words *discrete* and *definitive*—is the key, for it speaks of what some wanted to keep hidden: the clearly sexual implications of the two women together. The *Ladder* advocated a "mode of behavior and dress acceptable to society," and it was this policy Hansberry was praising. The desire for passing, combined with the radical work of survival that the *Ladder* was undertaking, was a paradox created by the America of the fifties. The writing in the *Ladder* was bringing to the surface years of pain, opening a door on an intensely private experience, giving a voice to an "obscene" population in a decade of McCarthy witch hunts. To survive meant to take a public stance of societal cleanliness. But in the pages of the journal itself, all dimensions of Lesbian life were explored including butch-femme relationships. The *Ladder* brought off a unique balancing act for the 1950s. It gave nourishment to a secret and subversive life while it flew the flag of assimilation.

However, it was not the rejection by our own that taught the most powerful lesson about sex, gender, and class that butch-femme represented, but the anger we provoked on the streets. Since at times femmes dressed similarly to their butch lovers, the aping of heterosexual roles was not always visually apparent, yet the sight of us was enraging. My understanding of why we angered straight spectators so is not that they saw us modeling ourselves after them, but just the opposite: we were a symbol of women's erotic autonomy, a sexual accomplishment that did not include them. The physical attacks were a direct attempt to break into this self-sufficient erotic partnership. The most frequently shouted taunt was, "Which one of you is the man?" This was not a reflection of our Lesbian experience as much as it was a testimony to the lack of erotic categories in straight culture. In the fifties, when we walked in the Village holding hands, we knew we were courting violence, but we also knew the political implications of how we were courting each other and chose not to sacrifice our need to their anger.[4]

The irony of social change has made a radical, sexual political statement of the 1950s appear today as a reactionary, nonfeminist experience. This is one reason I feel I must write about the old times—not to romanticize butch-femme relationships but to salvage a period of Lesbian culture that I know to be important, a time that has been too easily dismissed as the decade of self-hatred.

... [I]n Kansas at the National Women's Studies Association Conference, a slide show was presented to the Lesbian caucus in which a series of myths about

Lesbians was entertainingly debunked. The show was to be used in straight sex-education classrooms. One of the slides was a comic representation of the "myth" of butch-femme relationships with voiceover something like: "In the past, Lesbians copied heterosexual styles, calling themselves butch and femme, but they no longer do so." I waited until the end to make my statement, but I sat there feeling that we were so anxious to clean up our lives for heterosexual acceptance that we were ready to force our own people into a denial of some deep parts of their lives. I know what a butch or femme woman would feel seeing this slide show, and I realized that the price for social or superficial feminist acceptance was too high. If we deny the subject of butch-femme relationships, we deny the women who lived them, and still do.

Because of the complexity and authenticity of the butch-femme experience, I think we must take another look at the term *role-playing*, used primarily to summarize this way of loving. I do not think the term serves a purpose either as a label for or as a description of the experience. As a femme, I did what was natural for me, what I felt right. I did not learn a part; I perfected a way of loving. The artificial labels stood waiting for us as we discovered our sexualities.

We labeled ourselves as part of our cultural ritual, and the language reflected our time in history, but the words which seem so one-dimensional now stood for complex sexual and emotional exchanges. Women who were new to the life and entered bars have reported they were asked: "Well, what are you— butch or femme?" Many fled rather than answer the question. The real questions behind this discourse were, "Are you

sexual?" and "Are you safe?" When one moved beyond the opening gambits, a whole range of sexuality was possible. Butch and femme covered a wide variety of sexual responses. We joked about being a butchy femme or a femmy butch or feeling kiki (going both ways). We joked about a reversal of expectations: "Get a butch home and she turns over on her back." We had a code language for a courageous world for which many paid dearly. It is hard to re-create for the 1980s what Lesbian sexual play meant in the 1950s, but I think it is essential for Lesbian-feminists to understand, without shame, this part of their erotic heritage. I also think the erotic for us, as a colonized people, is part of our social struggle to survive and change the world.

A year ago some friends of mine were discussing their experiences in talking about butch-femme relationships to a women's studies class. Both had been gay since the 1950s and were active in the early gay liberation struggles. "I tried to explain the complex nature of butch sexuality, its balance of strength and delicacy," Madeline said. "The commitment to please each other was totally different from that in heterosexual relationships in which the woman existed to please the man."

As she spoke, I realized that not only was there the erotic statement made by the two women together, but there was and still is a butch sexuality and a femme sexuality, not a woman-acting-like-a-man or a woman-acting-like-a-woman sexuality, but a developed Lesbian-specific sexuality that has a historical setting and a cultural function. For instance, asa femme I enjoyed strong, fierce love-making; deep, strong givings and takings; erotic play challenges; calculated teasings that called forth the butch-femme encounter. But the essential pleasure was that we were two women, not masqueraders....

For me, the erotic essence of the butch-femme relationship was the external difference of women's textures and the bond of knowledgeable caring. I loved my lover for how she stood as well as for what she did. Dress was a part of it: the erotic signal of her hair at the nape of her neck, touching the shirt collar; how she held a cigarette; the symbolic pinky ring flashing as she waved her hand. I know this sounds superficial, but all these gestures were a style of self-presentation that made erotic competence a political statement in the 1950s. A deep partnership could be formed with as many shared tasks as there are now and with an encouragement of the style which made the woman I loved feel most comfortable. In bed, the erotic implications of the total relationship only became clearer. My hand and lips did what felt comfortable for me to do. I did not limit my sexual responses because I was a femme....

As a way of ignoring what butch-femme meant and means, feminism is often viewed as the validating starting point of healthy Lesbian culture. I believe, however, that many pre-Stonewall Lesbians were feminists, but the primary way this feminism—this autonomy of sexual and social identities—was expressed, was precisely in the form of sexual adventuring that now appears so oppressive. If butch-femme represented an erotically autonomous world, it also symbolized many other forms of independence. Most of the women I knew in the Sea Colony were working women who either had never married or who had left their husbands and were thus responsible for their own economic survival. Family connections had been severed, or the families were poorer than the women themselves. These were women who knew they were going to work for the rest of their Lesbian days to support themselves and the homes they chose to create. They were hairdressers, taxi drivers, telephone operators who were also butch-femme women. Their feminism was not an articulated theory; it was a lived set of options based on erotic choices.

We Lesbians from the fifties made a mistake in the early seventies: we allowed our lives to be trivialized and reinterpreted by feminists who did not share our culture. The slogan "Lesbianism is the practice and feminism is the theory" was a good rallying cry but it cheated our history. The early writings need to be reexamined to see why so many of us dedicated ourselves to understanding the homophobia of straight feminists rather than the life-realities of Lesbian women "who were not feminists" (an empty phrase which comes too easily to the lips). Why did we expect and need Lesbians of earlier generations and differing backgrounds to call their struggle by our name? I am afraid of the answer because I shared both worlds and know how respectable feminism made me feel, how less dirty, less ugly, less butch and femme. But the pain and anger at hearing so much of my past judged unacceptable have begun to surface. I believe that Lesbians are a people, that we live as all people do, affected by the economic and social forces of our times. As a people, we have struggled to preserve our people's ways, the culture of women loving women. In some sense, Lesbians have always opposed the patriarchy; in the past, perhaps most when we looked most like men....

Butch-femme women made Lesbians visible in a terrifyingly clear way in a historical period when there was no Movement protection for them. Their appearance spoke of erotic independence, and they often provoked rage and censure both from their own community and straight society. Now it is time to stop judging and begin asking questions, to begin listening. Listening not only to words which may be the wrong ones for the 1980s, but also gestures, sadnesses in the eyes, gleams of victories, movements of hands, stories told with self-dismissal yet stubbornness. There is a silence among us, the voices of the 1950s, and this silence will continue until some of us are ready to listen. If we do, we may begin to understand how our Lesbian people survived and created an erotic heritage.

NOTES

1. The *Ladder*, published from 1956 to 1972, was the most sustaining Lesbian cultural creation of this period. As a street femme living on the Lower East Side, I desperately searched newspaper stands and drugstore racks for this small slim journal with a Lesbian on its cover. A complete set is now available at the Lesbian Herstory Archives in New York.

2. The *Ladder*, No. 1, May 1957, p. 28.

3. Letter from Sandy DeSando, August 1980.

4. An article in *Journal of Homosexuality* (Summer 1980), "Sexual Preference or Personal Styles? Why Lesbians are Disliked" by Mary Reige Laner and Roy H. Laner, documented the anger and rejection of 511 straight college students toward Lesbians who were clearly defined as butch-femme. These results led the Laners to celebrate the withering away of butch-femme styles and to advocate androgyny as the safest road to heterosexual acceptance, a new plea for passing. This is the liberal voice turned conservative, the frightened voice that warns Blacks not to be too Black, Jews not to be too Jewish, and Lesbians not to be too Lesbian. Ironically, this advice can become the basis for a truly destructive kind of role-playing, a self-denial of natural style so the oppressor will not wake up to the different one in his or her midst.

NO

Beverly Burch

HETEROSEXUALITY, BISEXUALITY, AND LESBIANISM

GENDER IDENTITIES: TRANSITIONS AND AMBIGUITIES

There is in everyone some degree of identification with both parents, which allows the child to embody both genders within the self, what Joyce Mc-Dougall (1986) discusses as our psychic bisexuality, our wish to *be* as well as to possess the opposite-sex parent. Irene Fast (1990) suggests that before children undergo gender differentiation, maleness and femaleness are not experienced as mutually exclusive categories. As anatomical differences are observed and gender categories are differentiated, masculinity and feminity become opposites, not merely in anatomy but also in behaviors and personal characteristics associated with them. Assignment of gender brings a profound sense of limitation. This account again omits the crucial awareness that culture has already determined gender's meaning, and the child is acculturated by sorting out gender "appropriateness." We may ask why it is necessary that anatomical differences carry such psychological limitations.

In the endeavor to articulate a more adequate conception of gender identities in lesbian women, I draw upon both clinical experience and interviews with lesbians. The interviews, which addressed lesbian relationships (Burch 1992), afforded me an opportunity to explore that question of gender. Eight individual women and four couples, all between the ages of thirty six and fifty-two, were interviewed for approximately one to one and a half hours. The value of these informal interviews is purely descriptive. They are not necessarily representative of other lesbians, of course, but these women's self-reflective comments yield another account of how gender develops and is expressed. The interviews focused on conscious narratives of gender, but they allowed me to explore the subject more freely than in clinical work. Two specific questions related to gender: (a) "How do you experience your family ties and alignments—that is, in your family whom do you identify with or feel close to?" and (b) "How do you think about or identify with the terms *butch* and *femme*?"

From Beverly Burch, "Heterosexuality, Bisexuality, and Lesbianism: Rethinking Psychoanalytic Views of Women's Sexual Object Choice," *Psychoanalytic Review,* vol. 80, no. 1 (1993), pp. 82–99. Copyright © National Psychological Association for Psychoanalysis. Reprinted by permission. References omitted.

GENDER ROLES IN LESBIAN RELATIONSHIPS

In the terms of much of psychoanalytic and popular literature, there is the *butch*, the pseudomasculine lesbian who takes the part of the male lover in both behavior and dress, and the *femme*, who is not quite a true woman, being lesbian, but a caricature of femininity: helpless narcissistic, hysterical, maternal, or wifely. Through their mimicry of heterosexual love they may find some measure of satisfaction. The concepts of butch and femme linger, often a matter of parody or in-group humor that nevertheless carries real meaning.The fact that lesbians both deny these roles and continue to be interested in them led me to inquire about them in the interviews.

When I asked women whether they used or identified with these terms, all but one said no. However, many understood two levels of meaning here. The caricatured conception of butch and femme just described did not interest them, but the need for a way to express their different sense of gendered self— different from conventional feminine or masculine roles—did interest them. For example, several women used terms like *butchy femme* or *femmy butch* to describe themselves or their partner. One woman said, "I always felt more identified as femme, although I think I actually come off as more butch.... But in relationships I've always been more femme.... I like femmy butches, and I think I'm a butchy femme." These paradoxical terms do not simply mean "masculine woman"; they are efforts to articulate a complex gendered experience, which our language collapses into two, and only two, categories. Such terms also provide an internal continuity to the various identities that emerge in discrete experiences.

Lesbians cannot fail to be aware that in their choice of women as partners, and in the nontraditional life that accompanies this choice, they defy usual female roles. I think there is always some interplay between masculinity and femininity in lesbianism, not because lesbians are enacting gender roles in conventional ways but because these are the cultural givens. To understand the metapsychological significance of gender and roles in lesbian relationships we need to know the historical-cultural context. What may be meaningful for particular reasons in a particular historical period may be differently understood in later periods. As Katz pointed out, "All homosexuality is situational, influenced and given meaning and character by its location in time and social space" (Katz 1976:7). The same is true of heterosexuality, of course.

Several shifts in the meaning of lesbian gender roles in this century illustrate the necessity of this perspective. Lesbians struggled in the 1920s for public recognition of their relationships. The thinking about homosexuality at the time was determined largely by Havelock Ellis's work, which equated homosexuality with gender inversion. By cross-dressing, these women proclaimed in effect that their relationships were fully sexual ones, not the more acceptable, but asexual, Boston marriage (Newton 1984). They were concerned with establishing their relationships as sexual, not with challenging distortions of gender conceptions. Male homosexual identity was a fairly recent construct, less than a century old. As Elizabeth Wilson writes, "It is not surprising that lesbians, emerging at the same time with a conscious identity, had, during these years, accepted the sexologists' definition of their 'condition' as biologically determined and clinical, one to which masculinity was the key" (1984:215–216).

In the 1950s other concerns were influential. Philip Blumstein and Pepper Schwartz (1983) concluded that "homosexual couples went through the familial fifties along with the rest of the country ... when traditional assumptions about sex roles in marriage remained unchallenged ... many gay and lesbians couples fell into a pattern of role-playing" (1983:44). In other words they saw lesbians as attempting to normalize their relationships by conforming to the conventions of the time in their own way.

By the 1970s feminist and gay liberation movements were critiquing the distortions required by gender rules, arguing that women incorporate supposedly masculine attributes as women, not as men. Proclaiming a masculine identity became questionable; it suggested a devaluation of women. Wilson noted that "the role-playing falsity of gender was, according to this scenario, the mark of heterosexuality, while lesbianism by contrast became the arena for the flowering of real womanhood" (1984:216). Role-playing ceased to be a viable expression of lesbian identity and relationship.

The meaning of gender roles in lesbian relationships continues to evolve as feminist and lesbian movements change their focus. Some lesbians again consider role-playing of a very fluid kind intriguing and erotic. Wendy, a forty-two-year-old white woman raised in a middle-class southern family, was the only woman I interviewed who felt that her relationship incorporated a degree of role-playing. She also revealed a personal "history of identifications."

Over the years I've identified with the terms butch and femme in different ways. Initially it was kind of disgusting to me.... I remember reading about role-playing and thinking it was very heterosexual. I didn't understand it except that it was sort of archaic, that it was the way it had been, and it wasn't like that anymore.... After coming out and being a lesbian for a while, I took a neutral stance. One of my first girlfriends identified as butch. I had very short hair then and didn't wear makeup or jewelry. I couldn't think of myself as butch exactly, but [laughs] I didn't like the idea of femme, so it was hard to identify with either.... I remember when I started wearing make-up or earrings or whatever again. Maybe I put on some lipstick. Now I don't think about it much at all, but I think I would identify as a femme, whatever that means. Some women I've been with feel like they move back and forth, but they identify more as butch. You know [she laughs again], they pack the car and I pack the lunch.... I've been with my lover for five years now, and we play around with it. It's fun. We're not role-bound, but we have an acceptance of those ideas [butch and femme], that they're okay, and that they're okay as sexual roles.

Most of the women I talked to made some differentiations about gender between themselves and their partners. It seemed to me that here there was ample room for projection. Because the partners in a lesbian couple may themselves have different conceptions of what each represents in gendered expression, they may make use of it according to their own interests and desires. As some have argued, "In same-sex couples ... even small differences in the gender identities of the partners might lead them to play different gender roles" (Marecek, Finn, and Cardell 1982:48).

This possibility recalls Winnicott's (1971) concept of potential space, the psychological arena where partners can put their differences (real or imagined) to use. Potential space has been defined as the arena "where meaningful communication takes place.... the common ground in affectionate relationships" (Davis and Wallbridge 1981:63). Through psychic play with intimacy and identity, a new creation of self comes into being. As Winnicott wrote:

The interplay between originality and the acceptance of tradition as the basis for inventiveness seems to me to be just one more example, and a very exciting one, of the interplay between separateness and union.... The place where cultural experience is located is in the potential space between the individual and the environment (originally the object). (1971:99–100)

The exchanges that take place in this space provide a kind of complementarity founded on personal conceptions or even fantasies about gender rather than on actual gender-linked behavioral roles. Heterosexual couples may similarly exaggerate gender roles to enhance their sexuality. These interpretations suggest that role-playing is context specific, a form of social and psychological communication. So much constraint is placed upon human development by the demands of gender conformity that unexpressed dimensions of the personality seek new opportunities for appearance here. Again, as Winnicott said, "It is creative apperception more than anything else that makes the individual feel that life is worth living. Contrasted with this is a relationship to external reality which is one of compliance, the world and its details being recognized but only as something to be fitted in with or demanding adaptation" (1971:65).

In their relationships lesbians may draw upon fantasies about what the partner embodies. Complementarity around gender issues sometimes evolves in paradoxical ways. The relationship of Alix and Carol illustrates this point. Alix, forty-three, Jewish, from a working-class background, was married for many years before her involvement with forty-one-year-old Carol, who was raised in a white middle-class Protestant family in the Northeast. When married, Alix had disliked dressing and behaving in typically feminine ways, which she felt objectified her. Now, with a woman, she enjoyed dressing and acting in these same ways. She felt she would not be misunderstood or categorized. She projected onto her lover a familiarity with these things that in fact Carol did not corroborate. At the same time, Alix no longer worried about what she had always considered her more masculine qualities—aggressiveness and ambition—because she assumed they too would be appreciated. I interpret these changes as an expression of an increased sense of subjectivity: looking feminine became an expression of self as subject, with a more self-defined meaning, no longer the object of someone else's meaning. Freed from the confines of conventional gender roles within heterosexual culture, Alix found a personal meaning within her own conceptions of lesbian culture.

Carol shifted, also, toward some traditionally feminine signifiers or attributes: she began wearing more jewelry and she became more emotionally expressive. As she described it, she acquired a defensive sense of emotional invulnerability in her early years as a lesbian, a protective armor against a world that did not value her as she was. Her attachment to this more "masculine" attitude gave way to a greater desire to be expressive and responsive. To her this reflected a revaluing of what was feminine in herself. As Carol and Alix ascribed new meanings to their behavior, appearance, and feelings, various experiences of self opened up correspondingly, which each experienced as a redemption of her feminine self.

Another couple, Miriam, forty-two, and Ellen, thirty-nine, discussed how each had revised her own sense of herself and the other. Miriam was raised in a middle-class urban East Coast Jewish family and Ellen grew up in a white, upper-middle-class suburban California town. Among their many differences, they speculated about their differences in gender positioning. Ellen thought that she had been attracted to Miriam's apparent femininity because it gave her the idea that she would be in control. Instead Miriam turned out to be more often in control, sexually and otherwise. Ellen recognized a femininity in herself through this relationship that surprised her, and they both thought Miriam looked less feminine now. Miriam described a favorite fantasy in which she and Ellen, both in dresses, high heels, and pantyhose, go out to an expensive restaurant. She runs her hand up Ellen's thigh during dinner, realizing how female she is. Miriam says of this fantasy: "This is really lesbian. This is two women. I mean, silky pantyhose and everything. It's a real turn-on—being in a restaurant and sliding my hand under her skirt and over her leg."

RESHAPING GENDERS, TRANSCENDING GENDERS

Suzanne and Abby, both in their mid-thirties and also from very different Jewish and Protestant backgrounds, did not relate to the terms *butch* and *femme* at all. Regarding their appearance, one said: "We can both get very dressed up and be very feminine. We both started wearing makeup after we got together. We can both look like real jocks. We certainly don't use those categories in the way we relate, and we try not to use them sexually."

Wilson (1984) argued that feminism's antagonism to role-playing or lesbian expressions of gender differences denies the potential of homosexuality—its room for psychic play, its capacity for transformation and transcendence of gender. She suggested that "normalizing" lesbianism by denying its use of gender play may itself be homophobic and that feminism has erred in the direction of a new moralism about sexual behavior that emphasizes relationship over sexuality, woman-identification and bonding over eroticized Otherness. Paula spoke about the importance of this kind of psychic play in her life:

I love role stuff. This is one of the things I really love about being lesbian. I love switching roles.... There are days I like to look "butch"—wear a leather jacket, look tough. And there are days I like to wear makeup and "femme out." I like both parts of myself, and I have the most latitude to express them as a lesbian. That's true sexually as well.

Homosexuality moves beyond either an affirmation of gender differences or a denial of them. Instead, in Wilson's analysis, it destabilizes our gender conceptions by questioning the construction of gender. This is the threat of homosexuality: "For to insist on lesbianism as a challenge to stereotypes of gender is ultimately... political" (1984:224). It points toward an alternative to institutionalized relationships of domination. Some writers (cf. Dimen 1991; Goldner 1991; Harris 1991) have recognized the potential of conceptualizing gender as something other than a binary system. We can observe the presence of this unnamed multiplicity within our culture most visibly in homosexual communities....

The figure of the butch redefines the feminine. For lesbians it is appropriate to speak of differently developed versions of femininity rather than of masculinity versus femininity. Several women I interviewed broached this idea. Carol articulated it in terms of social power:

> It seems to me it's all layers. The more extremely feminine someone is, the more aggressive and power seeking she is, which brings her around to the other side. It just has to do with... how you want to convey your sense of power to the world. Either extreme, you're trying... to do that, so it evens out in the end.

Thinking of the feminine this way, as multifaceted experience, is how one comes to understand lesbianism as woman-to-woman love rather than as disguised heterosexual pursuit. The lover seeks the woman in her partner, but it may be a different woman than herself. She seeks the nurturing woman, she seeks the masterful woman, or some less clearly dichotomized femininity, in her lover, and she seeks to know it in herself, in her own grasp of what it is to be female. This is not necessarily the "phallic woman" of psychoanalytic theory, but the woman who does not require the phallus to be empowered, who is empowered by her enhanced experience of what is female.

For many lesbians the choice of another woman as a partner expresses a deep desire not to suffer the constrictions of femininity as mandated in heterosexuality. It is paradoxically a desire to seek within the self a fuller expression of being female or of femininity, if you will. The alternative woman, the woman who spans both ends of the gender continuum, is a woman who exists only in the absence of the male. Her lineage goes back to the mythical Greek women who disavow marriage and heterosexuality: Athena, Artemis, and Atalanta. Like them, like the "marriage resisters" in China, like women elsewhere who remain single even when the social cost is high, the lesbian seeks to bring herself into being in a way that seems to be possible in patriarchal cultures only when the male is absent (cf. Raymond 1986; Rich 1980).

The underlying theme that emerged from the interviews was that gender is a fluid experience, shifting over time and in the context of one's environment. Through the potential space of conscious and unconscious relatedness, a lesbian may use this fluidity to find a place for herself in the world, to create her own expression of self, and to have it recognized by others. Women draw upon this fluidity in ways that add interest, mystery, and sometimes tension to their intimacy. Their interrelatedness becomes a medium for adult developmental changes.

I am suggesting that everyone, but perhaps lesbians in particular, has a diversity of gender representations and identifications and that there is usually an unconscious, and sometimes a conscious, oscillation of gender dimensions in lesbian relationships. The gender play might be found along the lines of masculine-feminine complementarity, but it commonly seeks to explore a feminine-feminine connection. Not all couples participate in these interactions, and certainly couples who do so do it to different degrees. Though all couples can engage in this kind of exchange, perhaps homosexual couples have both a greater freedom and a greater desire to do so in what are sometimes fairly conscious ways.

Some psychoanalytic writers suggest the potential in heterosexuality for projected and introjected elements of masculinity and femininity between the man and woman (Bergmann 1980; Knight 1940; Murstein 1976). They understand them to strengthen the individual's conventional gender identity: "Feminine wishes in the man and masculine wishes in the woman are projected onto the part-

ner, enhancing one's own gender identity and therefore the boundaries of the self" (Bergmann 1980:74). This kind of exchange may be more important to heterosexual relationships, as these relationships confirm the individual's place within a social institution based upon entrenched gender differences. Between lesbians gender exchanges may expand the woman's sense of gender as well as confirm it. This alternative is also possible heterosexually, of course, but it may be more threatening there.

Perhaps lesbians are not escaping the constraints of femininity into masculinity, or even into androgyny, although that is how many would express it. Instead perhaps they strive to escape some of the limitations of gender categories altogether, into something more variable and fluid, a transcendence of gender rules. These different expressions of gender require us to rethink rigid notions of gender identities as fixed at an early age or as unitary and one-dimensional.

POSTSCRIPT

Do Lesbian Couples Naturally Adopt Separate Gender Roles?

Jane Cordova, in "Passing a Memoir," *Lesbian News* (October 1996), describes what it was like for her to try to pass as a femme or as an androgynous (neither male nor traditionally female) partner. She found it uncomfortable and gives the impression that the butch role, with which she feels comfortable, is not just about sexual interaction nor is it simply a role that she is playing. There are similarities between her story and that of Nestle. Another who writes from personal experience is Jeannine Delombard, in "Femmenism," in Rebecca Walker, ed., *To Be Real: Telling the Truth and Changing the Face of Feminism* (Anchor Books, 1995). She suggests that her identity as a femme was not something that she had constructed, nor was it something external.

Kristin G. Esterberg, in *Lesbian and Bisexual Identities: Constructing Communities, Constructing Selves* (Temple University Press, 1997), suggests that some lesbians take the process too seriously and play up a facade, or image. To her, the dichotomy is about role *playing*. The notion of play surrounds "butchness" and "femmeness," and these are important themes in lesbian history and culture. Butch-femme roles are appropriate, Esterberg says, if the women are not wholly serious about them. Some lesbians are not involved in playing or performing any of these identities, she notes. Pat Califia, in the chapter entitled "Genderbending: Playing With Roles and Reversals" of her book *Public Sex: The Culture of Radical Sex* (Cleis Press, 1994), agrees about the importance of not taking these roles too seriously. She believes that the roles should be changeable but asserts that there is "nothing oppressing about getting off on polarized roles during sex." However, Califia has been troubled by power differentials between butch and femme, finding that butches "have all the power, do most of the talking, take up more social space, and are more dominating (possessive)." She believes that roles should be identified as such and not as intrinsic to the woman. She states, "It wouldn't hurt to put a little more slack in the whole gender system." Do butch-femme relationships break the grip of patriarchal definitions of sexuality for women? Are butch-femme identities just another form of male-female norms that insinuate themselves into gender relationships by making heterosexuality a measure for any relationship?

According to Kath Weston, in *Render Me, Gender Me* (Columbia University Press, 1996), the belief that gay relationships mirror straight relationships is "the stuff of fantasy, fiction and stereotype." Lesbian relationships, she says, are about shared gender, not gender differences. Weston notes that lesbian "gendering" can be separated from heterosexual relationships and that *femme* need not be equivalent to femininity and *butch* need not be equivalent to masculinity. Studies that demonstrate how rarely stereotyped roles occur in lesbian relationships include M. S. Schneider, "The Relationships of Cohabiting Lesbian and Heterosexual Couples: A Comparison," *Psychology of Women Quarterly* (vol. 10, 1986); Philip Blumstein and Pepper Schwartz, *American Couples: Money, Work, Sex* (William Morrow, 1983); and Alan Bell and Martin Weinberg, *Homosexualities: A Study of Diversity Among Men and Women* (Simon & Schuster, 1978). Studies that show an absence of role-playing with a preference for equality between the partners include "The Balance of Power in Lesbian Relationships," *Sex Roles* (vol. 10, 1984); "Role Relationships: Lesbian Perspectives," *Journal of Homosexuality* (vol. 12, 1985); and "Gender Roles in the Relationships of Lesbians and Gay Men" and "Satisfaction in Lesbian Relationships," *Journal of Homosexuality* (vol. 8, 1982).

Are these writings on lesbian sexuality useful in establishing viable representations of female sexuality? Do they help lesbians develop a clearer sense of their own sexuality? Is it necessary for sex to determine whether or not two people are a couple?

On the Internet...

The Breast Implant Controversy: A Snapshot in Documents and Pointers

This 60-Minute Intellectual page provides information on silicone breast implants, a critique of implant manufacturers, and personal testimonies. It serves as a coalition of silicone survivors and provides public interest reporting and information on what others are saying about the controversy.
http://www.marmoset.com/60minute/Webnav/breast.html

A Status Report on Breast Implant Safety

This article contains information from the perspective of the Food and Drug Administration (FDA) on silicone breast implants, links to the FDA home page, and information on and links to status reports on implant safety, known and possible risks, manufacturers' studies, saline implants, surgical risks, and other concerns.
http://www.fda.gov//fdac/features//995_implants.html

Feminist.com

This site provides information and links in four areas: reproductive health, women and AIDS, women's health in general, and cancer and breast cancer. Links include the American Medical Women's Association, the Canadian Women's Health Network, the Feminist Women's Health Center, Internet resources for depression, and a women's health clinic.
http://www.feminist.com/health.htm

Handilinks™ to Women's Health

This Handilinks™ category provides a listing of links related to women's health, including magazines and journals, studies, listings of women's centers, an index of women's health issues, wellness programs, resource centers, consulting services, and university listings.
http://www.ahandyguide.com/cat1/w/w165.htm

The Female Genital Mutilation Research Homepage

This site reproduces and links to resources on female genital mutilation (FGM) as seen from religious, feminist, health, and human rights perspectives. It contains a networking page on which organizations engaged in FGM-related work can include information about their research, along with contact addresses.
http://www.hollyfeld.org/fgm

PART 4

Gender and Health

Men and women in the United States continue to face a variety of severe health problems. With traditional gender roles and values continually changing, some health issues have become politically popular as gender issues. Competing groups debate the importance of health research and health care allocations for one sex versus the other, and political controversy surrounds a variety of issues that disproportionally affect one or the other gender. The five debates in this section address the possible presence of a sex bias in medicine, premenstrual syndrome, post-abortion syndrome, the possible dangers of silicone breast implants, and whether or not ritual female genital surgery should be banned.

■ Is There a Male Sex Bias in Medicine?

■ Is Premenstrual Syndrome a Clear Medical Condition?

■ Do Women Suffer from Post-Abortion Syndrome?

■ Are Silicone Breast Implants Dangerous for Women?

■ Should Ritual Female Genital Surgery Be Regulated World-wide?

ISSUE 15

Is There a Male Sex Bias in Medicine?

YES: Gayle Feldman, from "Women *Are* Different," *Self* (July 1997)

NO: Andrew G. Kadar, from "The Sex-Bias Myth in Medicine," *The Atlantic Monthly* (August 1994)

ISSUE SUMMARY

YES: Health writer Gayle Feldman contends that heart disease—along with almost every other disease outside of the female reproductive system—was, until recently, studied almost exclusively in men, with the results extrapolated, undifferentiated, to women.

NO: Physician Andrew G. Kadar maintains that American health care delivery and research efforts actually benefit women at the expense of men, which explains women's longer average life expectancy.

According to women's rights advocates, most women are completely unaware of the fact that heart disease is the number-one killer of women, with symptoms and risk factors that show themselves differently in women than in men. According to these advocates, this lack of awareness is to be expected because heart disease, along with almost every other disease outside of the female reproductive system, has been studied almost exclusively in men until recently. Results of largely all-male research studies have been generalized to women, without attempts to account for possible differences in female anatomy and physiology.

Others have argued that claims of male-as-norm biases in medicine are not only wildly exaggerated but unfair. Some even suggest that the reverse is true, that women have received a disproportionate amount of medical funding, research, and attention while men have been neglected. For example, laparoscopic surgery and ultrasound are two advanced techniques that were first developed for use on women's bodies; the procedures were only later adapted for men. Women's diseases, such as breast cancer, have received research money that far exceeds the amount of money allocated for male diseases, such as prostate cancer. In proportion to the numbers of people who die from these cancers, some feel that women have received more than their fair share.

Studies show that women see their physicians more frequently, have more surgery, and are admitted to hospitals more often than men. In 1994 two out of three medical dollars were spent on women. A 1981 study conducted at the University of California at San Diego reviewed over 40,000 patient office visits and determined that the health care that men and women received was similar just over two-thirds of the time. When health care differed, it was the women who benefited.

Claims that health care and research in the United States benefit men at the expense of women are not taken lightly. A new medical frontier, gender-based medicine, is aggressively setting out to learn from the differences between the genders and to make up for years of perceived neglect. The Women's Health Initiative (WHI) has been funded as the largest-ever prevention study. It emphasizes variables and issues that are primarily female, including lifestyles and hormones and their effect upon disease development over time. Drug industry surveys now show that more products are being developed specifically for women, whereas in the past, women had been uniformly excluded from clinical drug trials, especially in the earlier phases.

Doctors grounded in gender-based medicine know that the symptoms and the courses of heart disease are often different for female sufferers. For example, smoking creates the likelihood that a man will get heart disease 7 years earlier than normal onset, while women who smoke develop heart disease an alarming 19 years earlier than normal onset. Furthermore, failure to use the best diagnostic tools for women may be one reason why many women, when diagnosed with heart disease, are far sicker than men are when they are diagnosed with heart disease. Critics assert that generalizing from male experience to human experience not only distorts what human experience is but also distorts what is specifically male, to say nothing of what is specifically female.

In the following selections, Gayle Feldman highlights details of research showing that men have been the primary beneficiaries of more than their fair share of medical research and funding. Andrew G. Kadar maintains that the widespread discrimination in medical research and practice has been against men, not women, and has resulted in a shortened life span for men.

YES   Gayle Feldman

WOMEN *ARE* DIFFERENT

Linda is 36 years old, on the go all day, and can hardly spare the time for her annual physical. She knows what the doctor will tell her: Lose weight, quit smoking, work out. Fat chance, given her schedule. In fact, she would like to put off the physical, but she's been feeling so tired and short of breath lately. On top of that, the past couple of weeks she's been sick to her stomach. She can't figure out why—she hasn't changed her diet or routine, and she's on the Pill, for goodness' sake, so she can't be pregnant. She'd better get the physical over with and find out what's going on.

What's going on, the doctor tells her, is that Linda has heart disease; in fact she's already had a mild heart attack. It's a complete shock. Like most women, Linda thinks heart disease is something that happens to men. Her image of a heart attack is a man clutching his chest or doubling over in life-stopping pain. The truth is, heart disease is the number-one killer of women, too; it kills more women than all cancers, AIDS, domestic violence and osteoporosis combined.

Most women are like Linda, not only completely unaware that heart disease could happen to them, but also that its symptoms and risk factors are often very different in women and in men. Their ignorance isn't surprising since heart disease—along with almost every other disease or condition outside the reproductive area—was until recently studied almost exclusively in men, and the results extrapolated, undifferentiated, to women.

But ignorance is not bliss; it's dangerous. Women are not simply pint-size men with different sexual plumbing. Now a new medical frontier is opening up, one that researchers are calling gender-based medicine. It is not only saying vive la différence but is aggressively setting out to learn from that difference and to make up for the years of neglect. It's looking at the biological specifics in areas that range from heart disease to pain management to how our bodies metabolize drugs.

Government and business are paying attention. Procter & Gamble is investing more than $2.5 million over the next few years to help establish the Partnership for Women's Health at Columbia University, located at Columbia–Presbyterian Medical Center in New York City, precisely to study gender-based medicine. Drug industry surveys show that more products are being developed specifically for women. And the Women's Health Initiative (WHI), the largest-ever prevention study funded by the U.S. government, is, among other things, researching how female hormones and lifestyles affect the development over time of heart disease, osteoporosis and other conditions in women.

Researchers know that women are far more prone to certain diseases or conditions than men. For example, we are:

- Twice as likely to suffer from major depression, anxiety disorders and phobias.
- Fifteen times more likely to have autoimmune or thyroid diseases.
- Three times more prone to rheumatoid arthritis and irritable bowel syndrome.
- Far more likely to suffer from migraine headaches.

The challenge that gender-based medicine has set for itself is to find out what causes the disproportion in women, and how treatment options might eventually be tailored more specifically—and more successfully—to help them.

Think about Linda's situation: A doctor grounded in gender-based medicine would recognize that her fatigue, shortness of breath and nausea were common heart disease symptoms in women. This doctor would know the best tests for coronary disease in women and would recognize that Linda is putting herself at risk for major heart problems by the very fact that she smokes while taking birth-control pills, which can cause the development of life-threatening blood clots. Smoking while on the Pill is something no woman over age 35 should ever do. A gender-based approach would rec-

ognize the heart benefits of hormone-replacement therapy after menopause for a woman like Linda.

Unfortunately, though, many primary-care physicians aren't yet looking at patients through a gender-specific lens. Astonishingly, a 1995 Gallup survey for the American Medical Women's Association (AMWA) found that one out of three of the 300 primary-care doctors surveyed didn't know that heart disease is the number-one cause of death in American women; two out of three didn't know risk factors for women are different; and nine out of 10 thought that male and female symptoms were the same. All the more reason for women to be educated participants in their own care.

One of the easiest ways to begin to appreciate what gender-based medicine is about is to look more closely into the female heart. Women's hearts are smaller, they weigh 50 to 100 grams less, and they beat more often and more quickly than men's. Our arteries also tend to be smaller, so it takes less fatty plaque to block them. When these arteries do become blocked and bypass operations, balloon angioplasty or other procedures are necessary to open or circumvent them, it can be trickier and riskier for heart surgeons to use on their female patients the standard instruments that have been designed to go into bigger male arteries. Sometimes they have to use surgical instruments that were designed for use on children; on other occasions, they just can't operate on certain arteries.

Statistically, our 36-year-old friend Linda was unlucky, since most premenopausal women are—to a large degree—protected against heart disease by their own estrogen. Once a woman enters menopause, heart problems can mushroom. One in nine women ages 45 to 64 has some cardiovascular disease, and the statistics skyrocket to one in three after age 65. Of course, until modern medical advancements like antibiotics extended women's life spans from an average of 48 years in 1900 to 79 years today, chronic illnesses such as heart disease, stroke and late-onset diabetes were hardly a problem at all: Women tended to die of infectious diseases or during childbirth; many never reached menopause. That is one of the reasons why the study of these diseases in women has lagged.

Although we know that estrogen protects the cardiovascular system, we still don't completely understand how. Traditionally, doctors thought that the hormone's beneficial effect was to help maintain a high level of high-density lipoproteins (HDLs, or "good cholesterol") and a low level of low-density lipoproteins (LDLs, or "bad cholesterol"). Now it has become clear that LDL levels are a better predictor of heart disease risk for men; HDL and triglyceride levels (triglycerides are another kind of fat, not found in cholesterol) are a better predictor for women, according to Debra R. Judelson, M.D., the Beverly Hills cardiologist who is the current president of AMWA. Linda's HDL level was found to be low and her triglyceride level was very high.

A unique benefit of estrogen that we do know is that it preserves the normal dilating response of blood vessels during stress. "You preserve the dilating response even in damaged blood vessels, an effect that is totally different between men and women," Dr. Judelson says.

Women often have very distinctive cardiovascular disease symptoms. According to Elizabeth Ross, M.D., author of *Healing the Female Heart*, the pain that a man with heart disease in danger of a heart attack feels tends to be severe and sudden. A woman may feel that, too, or, like Linda, may only feel nausea, pain in the arm or shoulder or jaw, extreme fatigue or shortness of breath. Or, she might only suffer from swelling in the ankles or lower legs.

Thanks to her estrogen, a woman tends to get heart disease, on average, 10 years later than a man, and yet she is twice as likely to die after a heart attack. How can that be? First, many women are so completely unaware of their risk that they don't realize their bodies are giving them warning signs. Second, many primary-care physicians are unaware of women's more subtle symptoms. Third, Dr. Ross emphasizes, the traditional gold-standard exercise stress test "is not as accurate in women as it is in men, because women's physiology of response to exercise may be different." Some doctors still don't realize that heart disease can be diagnosed more accurately in women by two other tests (a nuclear stress test or a stress echocardiogram). So by the time many women are diagnosed, they are far sicker than men.

Knowing already that heart disease was a factor in her life, Linda's physician wasn't surprised to find some evidence of mild diabetes when her blood test results cam back from the lab. Diabetes is a stronger cardiovascular risk factor in women than in men, and as our population ages, its prevalence is greatly increasing, even more so in the African American population. Obesity and a sedentary lifestyle are the two biggest predictors of diabetes risk. Ross reminds us that "one third of American women past the age of 30 are obese, and too many subscribe to the concept that dieting makes you healthy. But unless you also begin to exercise regularly, dieting will accomplish nothing useful in the long term."

Then, of course, there's smoking. Quite simply, it cancels out the beneficial effects of estrogen. According to Judelson, "smoking makes a man get a heart attack seven years earlier than usual, but a woman 19 years earlier than usual."

In fact, one of the major goals of gender-specific medicine is to determine how much lifestyle factors (regular exercise, eating a low-fat diet and not smoking, for example) can affect a woman's health. Researchers already know that how a woman treats her body when she's young affects what happens after menopause. Yet findings also show that too many young women are ignorant about that relationship or feel immune to it.

A 1993 survey by the Commonwealth Fund's Commission on Women's Health found that nearly one out of three women never exercised, and one out of four smoked. In addition, tobacco seems to slow lung function and growth in adolescent girls more than in boys. Since cigarette manufacturers recognized the profits to be made in targeting advertising to women decades ago, preventive medicine has a lot of catching up to do to tailor antismoking campaigns specifically to young girls.

And, of course, the whole debate over whether women should take hormone replacement therapy (HRT) after they have reached menopause is connected to their risk of cardiovascular disease. The higher their risk, the more they should consider HRT. Hormone replacement also looms large in any discussion of osteoporosis.

The next time you're in a crowd, notice all the senior citizens whose shoulders and backs are stooped and bent. Most of them are women, not men. That's because older women are the main victims of the disentegrating bone disease osteoporosis. In fact, two out of five women now alive will have had an osteoporosis-related fracture by the age of 70, according to Marianne J. Legato, M.D., the Columbia University professor who is directing the Partnership for Women's Health. The loss of estrogen after menopause is the most obvious factor in female osteoporosis, so why should younger women pay attention to a disease of middle and old age? Simple: because how we treat our bodies when we're young affects development of the disease after menopause. The osteoporosis that younger women should be concerned about is Type 1, which affects women six times more often than men and is associated with estrogen decline. (Type 2 affects women twice as often as men, but isn't really a factor until after age 70).

Osteoporosis is the loss of bone mass or density, which leads to fragility and unexpected fractures. Throughout our lives, our bones are constantly being rebuilt, with new bone matter replacing the bone mass we lose. But around age 30, bone loss begins very subtly to exceed bone formation in both men and women. Once a woman reaches menopause— and for eight to 10 years immediately afterward—the hormonal changes cause increased breakdown of bone. During that decade, as much as 5 percent of bone mass can be lost in a single year.

BUILDING BETTER BONES

So it's essential to build maximum bone mass when young and lead a lifestyle that will help maintain as much of it as possible later on. But women's bones are at a disadvantage from a very early age. Since most women have smaller frames and are less physically active as teenagers, they have less bone density than men do. If a teenager does not eat well or diets a lot, she will have a calcium deficiency and never build optimum mass. Similarly, if a woman is an exercise fanatic and begins to have irregular periods (or none at all), her body isn't producing enough estrogen. She'll pay the price later on.

Obviously, estrogen deficiency is not the only factor in the disease, since not every postmenopausal woman has osteoporosis. All women require a certain amount of calcium, but many don't get it through their diet. Although researchers agree that calcium supplements can be a beneficial preventive measure, according to the Commonwealth Fund survey, four out of five women ages 18 to 44 (and three out of five women 45 and older) do not take them.

Smoking, caffeine, too much alcohol and lack of weight-bearing physical exercise throughout adulthood make a woman susceptible to the disease. So too, does the abuse of thyroid medications, which some women misguidedly use to speed up their metabolisms to lose weight.

Thyroid disorders predispose women to osteoporosis, and they are much more a woman's problem than a man's. One in eight women develops some thyroid problem during her lifetime; one in 20 does so after having a baby. That's why during the past few years some doctors have started to advocate the TSH (thyroid stimulating hormone) test as part of a regular physical exam.

DRUGS FOR WOMEN ONLY?

The drugs men and women take may affect them differently solely because of gender, and the instructions that come with them may one day contain dosage variations for sex, weight, age and other factors. Freda Lewis-Hall, M. D., who heads the Lilly Center for Women's Health in Indianapolis, says that drug companies will have to address two major questions when developing new medications: first, whether there are differences in their effectiveness or in adverse side effects in men and women; and, second, whether the effectiveness of the medicine varies during a woman's menstrual cycle.

Think of the changes the menstrual cycle imposes on women's bodies; indeed, consider the multiplicity of hormonal changes throughout a woman's life and the effects they can have. Judelson describes a scenario that is all too familiar to every woman: "When I'm premenstrual, my GI tract slows down, my stomach takes forever to empty, and my belly bloats—doesn't that affect medication absorption?"

Remember, standard dosages of most medications until very recently were designed for and tested on men. According to a 1993 research report by the Food and Drug Administration's Working Group on Women in Clinical Trials, the popular painkillers acetaminophen, aspirin and lidocaine take longer to be eliminated from a woman's body. Does that mean women need different dosages or need to time them differently for optimum effect? We don't know. Seventy percent of psychotropic drugs are prescribed to women, yet basic studies of them were done primarily on male rats.

We have only limited knowledge about how oral contraceptives lessen some of the gender differential effects for drug metabolism and heighten others; we know even less about how HRT enters into the equation. The tranquilizer Valium, for example, takes longer to clear a woman's body than a man's, but only until menopause. What happens if a menopausal woman is on both Valium and HRT? As yet, nobody knows.

Then, too, consider not only the variations of the monthly cycle, but also the fact that women's circadian rhythms are different from men's. There may be certain times of day when a woman's body would do a quicker, better job of absorbing a drug and circulating it throughout her system, and it may be very different from the timing that works best in a man. We need to find out.

One thing we do know is that our higher body-fat content and lower body-water volume contribute to higher blood-alcohol concentrations. Women produce less of a liver enzyme—alcohol dehydrogenase—that breaks down alcohol. This is why a woman who drinks a smaller amount of an alcoholic beverage than does a man of the same size will nevertheless get more intoxicated.

Then there are drugs that have been tested and abandoned in men-only clinical trials, but if given a chance might work beautifully in women. Take, for example, the recent discovery by a team of researchers at the University of California San Francisco regarding a group of painkilling drugs called kappa-opioids. These drugs do not have the significant side effects of the more familiar mu-opioids—morphine, codeine, etc.—and had originally been developed as an alternative to them. In men-only tests, their effectiveness had been disappointing.

The team at San Francisco decided to try them out again, this time on a group of 48 young men and women who were having impacted wisdom teeth removed. The kappa-opioids worked very well for the women in the group—so well that the leader of this National Institutes of Health (NIH)–funded project, Jon D. Levine, M.D., Ph.D., recommended that their use for women with moderate to severe pain be reevaluated. Further, Dr. Levine stated, "our studies provide evidence that biologically, women and men do not obtain pain relief in the same way. It may be that the brain circuitry regulating pain relief differs between the sexes."

There's much to find out about gender differentiation in brain function. Some experts, like Dr. Legato, speculate that it may reveal the most fascinating gender specificity of all. Sex differences have already been recognized in cognition as well as in epilepsy, Alzheimer's disease and sleep disorders.

While research is crucial, it must be accompanied by new attitudes in the medical profession. AMWA believes doctors must fundamentally change the way they think about women. The organization has developed an education program for practicing physicians, the Advanced Curriculum in Women's Health, to help them do so. "Instead of grouping information by organ systems, it's much more suitable to look at life phases and consider how to prevent illness and maintain health in each phase," says Lila Wallis, M.D., clinical professor of medicine at Cornell University Medical College, head of the team that designed the course. The five life phases are adolescence (12 to 20 years old); young adulthood (from 20 to 45); perimenopause (45 to 60); postmenopausal, "mature" (60 to 85); and "advanced" (85-plus).

Changes also must be made in the way future doctors are trained. In 1994, doctors at Philadelphia's Allegheny University of the Health Sciences joined with AMWA to create *Women's Health in the Curriculum*, a resource guide for medical school professors and health care educators. But experts say that curriculum shifts will only occur if gender-specific questions become part of the licensing exams that every aspiring physician must take. Florence Haseltine, Ph.D., M.D., director of the Center for Population Research at the NIH, doesn't see "real changes happening for another 10 years."

The research establishment needs to rethink the way it conducts medical studies and reports results. Experts like Vivian W. Pinn, M.D., director of the Office of Research on Women's Health at the NIH, are concerned that medical journal articles don't routinely address gender differences in studies. Hormonal variations are not typically taken into account; rarely does a study report whether the subjects were pre- or postmenopausal, or taking HRT.

Dr. Haseltine believes medical students will be the agents of change, actively seeking out gender-specific information in their courses, as will the pharmaceutical industry, which sees the profit potential in new, differentiated products for the two sexes. In the end, gender-specific women's health also implies gender-specific men's health. Learning more about the special characteristics of women will inevitably produce corresponding action for men. That can only be good for both.

NO

Andrew G. Kadar

THE SEX-BIAS MYTH IN MEDICINE

"When it comes to health-care research and delivery, women can no longer be treated as second-class citizens." So said the President of the United States on October 18, 1993.

He and the First Lady had just hosted a reception for the National Breast Cancer Coalition, an advocacy group, after receiving a petition containing 2.6 million signatures which demanded increased funding for breast-cancer prevention and treatment. While the Clintons met with leaders of the group in the East Room of the White House, a thousand demonstrators rallied across the street in support. The President echoed their call, decrying the neglect of medical care for women.

Two years earlier Bernadine Healy, then the director of the National Institutes of Health [NIH], charged that "women have all too often been treated less than equally in... health care." More recently Representative Pat Schroeder, a co-chair of the Congressional Caucus for Women's Issues, sponsored legislation to "ensure that biomedical research does not once again overlook women and their health." Newspaper articles expressed similar sentiments.

The list of accusations is long and startling. Women's-health-care advocates indict "sex-biased" doctors for stereotyping women as hysterical hypochondriacs, for taking women's complaints less seriously than men's, and for giving them less thorough diagnostic workups. A study conducted at the University of California at San Diego in 1979 concluded that men's complaints of back pain, chest pain, dizziness, fatigue, and headache more often resulted in extensive workups than did similar complaints from women. Hard scientific evidence therefore seemed to confirm women's anecdotal reports.

Men more often than women undergo angiographies and coronary-artery-bypass-graft operations. Even though heart disease is the No. 1 killer of women as well as men, this sophisticated, state-of-the-art technology, critics contend, is selectively denied to women.

The problem is said to be repeated in medical research: women, critics argue, are routinely ignored in favor of men. When the NIH inventoried all

From Andrew G. Kadar, "The Sex-Bias Myth in Medicine," *The Atlantic Monthly* (August 1994). Copyright © 1994 by Andrew G. Kadar. Reprinted by permission.

the research it had funded in 1987, the money spent on studying diseases unique to women amounted to only 13.5 percent of the total research budget.

Perhaps the most emotionally charged disease for women is breast cancer. If a tumor devastated men on a similar scale, critics say, we would declare a state of national emergency and launch a no-cost-barred Apollo Project–style program to cure it. In the words of Matilda Cuomo, the wife of the governor of New York, "If we can send a woman to the moon, we can surely find a cure for breast cancer." The neglect of breast-cancer research, we have been told, is both sexist and a national disgrace.

Nearly all heart-disease research is said to be conducted on men, with the conclusions blindly generalized to women. In July of 1989 researchers from the Harvard Medical School reported the results of a five-year study on the effects of aspirin in preventing cardiovascular disease in 22,071 male physicians. Thousands of men were studied, but not one woman: women's health, critics charge, was obviously not considered important enough to explore similarly. Here, they say, we have definite, smoking-gun evidence of the neglect of women in medical research —only one example of a widespread, dangerous phenomenon.

Still another difference: pharmaceutical companies make a policy of giving new drugs to men first, while women wait to benefit from the advances. And even then the medicines are often inadequately tested on women.

To remedy all this neglect, we need to devote preferential attention and funds, in the words of the *Journal of the American Medical Women's Association*, to "the greatest resource this country will ever have, namely, the health of its women."

Discrimination on such a large scale cries out for restitution—if the charges are true.

In fact one sex does appear to be favored in the amount of attention devoted to its medical needs. In the United States it is estimated that one sex spends twice as much money on health care as the other does. The NIH also spends twice as much money on research into the diseases specific to one sex as it does on research into those specific to the other, and only one sex has a section of the NIH devoted entirely to the study of disease afflicting it. That sex is not men, however. It is women.

* * *

In the United States women seek out and consequently receive more medical care than men. This is true even if pregnancy-related care is excluded. Department of Health and Human Services surveys show that women visit doctors more often than men, are hospitalized more often, and undergo more operations. Women are more likely than men to visit a doctor for a general physical exam when they are feeling well, and complain of symptoms more often. Thus two out of every three health-care dollars are spent by women.

Quantity, of course, does not guarantee quality. Do women receive second-rate diagnostic workups?

The 1979 San Diego study, which concluded that men's complaints more often led to extensive workups than did women's, used the charts of 104 men and women (fifty-two married couples) as data. This small-scale regional survey prompted a more extensive national review of 46,868 office visits. The results, reported in 1981, were quite different from those of the San Diego study.

In this larger, more representative sample, the care received by men and women was similar about two thirds of the time. When the care was different, women overall received more diagnostic tests and treatment—more lab tests, blood-pressure checks, drug prescriptions, and return appointments.

Several other, small-scale studies have weighed in on both sides of this issue. The San Diego researchers looked at another 200 men and women in 1984, and this time found "no significant differences in the extent and content" of workups. Some women's-health-care advocates have chosen to ignore data from the second San Diego study and the national survey while touting the first study as evidence that doctors, to quote once again from the *Journal of the American Medical Women's Association,* do "not take complaints as seriously" when they come from women: "an example of a double standard influencing diagnostic workups."

When prescribing care for heart disease, doctors consider such factors as age, other medical problems, and the likelihood that the patient will benefit from testing and surgery. Coronary-artery disease afflicts men at a much younger age, killing them three times as often as women until age sixty-five. Younger patients have fewer additional medical problems that preclude aggressive, high-risk procedures. And smaller patients have smaller coronary arteries, which become obstructed more often after surgery. Whereas this is true for both sexes, obviously more women fit into the smaller-patient category. When these differences are factored in, sex divergence in cardiac care begins to fade away.

To the extent that divergence remains, women may be getting better treatment.

At least that was the conclusion of a University of North Carolina/Duke University study that looked at the records of 5,795 patients treated from 1969 to 1984. The most symptomatic and severely diseased men and women were equally likely to be referred for bypass surgery. Among the patients with less-severe disease—the ones to whom surgery offers little or no survival benefit over medical therapy—women were less likely to be scheduled for bypass surgery. This seems proper in light of the greater risk of surgical complications, owing to women's smaller coronary arteries. In fact, the researchers questioned the wisdom of surgery in the less symptomatic men and suggested that "the effect of gender on treatment selection may have led to more appropriate treatment of women."

As for sophisticated, pioneering technology selectively designed for the benefit of one sex, laparoscopic surgery was largely confined to gynecology for more than twenty years. Using viewing and manipulating instruments that can be inserted into the abdomen through keyhole-sized incisions, doctors are able to diagnose and repair, sparing the patient a larger incision and a longer, more painful recuperation. Laparoscopic tubal sterilization, first performed in 1936, became common practice in the late 1960s. Over time the development of more-versatile instruments and of fiber-optic video capability made possible the performance of more-complex operations. The laparoscopic removal of ectopic pregnancy was reported in 1973. Finally, in 1987, the same technology was applied in gallbladder surgery, and men began to enjoy its benefits too.

Years after ultrasound instruments were designed to look inside the uterus, the same technology was adapted to search for tumors in the prostate. Other pioneering developments conceived to improve the health care of women include mammography, bone-density testing for osteoporosis, surgery to alleviate bladder incontinence, hormone therapy to relieve the symptoms of menopause, and a host of procedures, including in vitro fertilization, developed to facilitate impregnation. Perhaps so many new developments occur in women's health care because one branch of medicine and a group of doctors, gynecologists, are explicitly concerned with the health of women. No corresponding group of doctors is dedicated to the care of men.

So women receive more care than men, sometimes receive better care than men, and benefit more than men do from some developing technologies. This hardly looks like proof that women's health is viewed as secondary in importance to men's health.

* * *

The 1987 NIH inventory did indeed find that only 13.5 percent of the NIH research budget was devoted to studying diseases unique to women. But 80 percent of the budget went into research for the benefit of both sexes, including basic research in fields such as genetics and immunology and also research into diseases such as lymphoma, arthritis, and sickle-cell anemia. Both men and women suffer from these ailments, and both sexes served as study subjects. The remaining 6.5 percent of NIH research funds were devoted to afflictions unique to men. Oddly, the women's 13.5 percent has been cited as evidence of neglect. The much smaller men's share of the budget is rarely mentioned in these references.

As for breast cancer, the second most lethal malignancy in females, investiga-tion in that field has long received more funding from the National Cancer Institute [NCI] than any other tumor research, though lung cancer heads the list of fatal tumors for both sexes. The second most lethal malignancy in males is also a sex-specific tumor: prostate cancer. Last year approximately 46,000 women succumbed to breast cancer and 35,000 men to prostate cancer; the NCI spent $213.7 million on breast-cancer research and $51.1 million on study of the prostate. Thus although about a third more women died of breast cancer than men of prostate cancer, breast-cancer research received more than four times the funding. More than three times as much money per fatality was spent on the women's disease. Breast cancer accounted for 8.8 percent of cancer fatalities in the United States and for 13 percent of the NCI research budget; the corresponding figures for prostate cancer were 6.7 percent of fatalities and three percent of the funding. The spending for breast-cancer research is projected to increase by 23 percent this year, to $262.9 million; prostate-research spending will increase by 7.6 percent, to $55 million.

The female cancers of the cervix and the uterus accounted for 10,100 deaths and $48.5 million in research last year, and ovarian cancer accounted for 13,300 deaths and $32.5 million in research. Thus the research funding for all female-specific cancers is substantially larger per fatality than the funding for prostate cancer.

Is this level of spending on women's health just a recent development, needed to make up for years of prior neglect? The NCI is divided into sections dealing with issues such as cancer biology and diagnosis, prevention and control, etiology, and treatment. Until funding allocations for sex-specific concerns became a political issue, in the mid-1980s, the NCI did not track organ-specific spending data. The earliest information now available was reconstructed retroactively to 1981. Nevertheless, these early data provide a window on spending patterns in the era before political pressure began to intensify for more research on women. Each year from 1981 to 1985 funding for breast-cancer research exceeded funding for prostate cancer by a ratio of roughly five to one. A rational, nonpolitical explanation for this is that breast cancer attacks a larger number of patients, at a younger age. In any event, the data failed to support claims that women were neglected in that era.

Again, most medical research is conducted on diseases that afflict both sexes. Women's-health advocates charge that we collect data from studies of men and then extrapolate to women. A look at the actual data reveals a different reality.

The best-known and most ambitious study of cardiovascular health over time began in the town of Framingham, Massachusetts, in 1948. Researchers started with 2,336 men and 2,873 women aged thirty to sixty-two, and have followed the survivors of this group with biennial physical exams and lab tests for more than forty-five years. In this and many other observational studies women have been well represented.

With respect to the aspirin study, the researchers at Harvard Medical School did not focus exclusively on men. Both sexes were studied nearly concurrently. The men's study was more rigorous, because it was placebo-controlled (that is, some subjects were randomly assigned to receive placebos instead of aspirin); the women's study was based on responses to questionnaires sent to nurses and a review of medical records. The women's study, however, followed nearly four times as many subjects as the men's study (87,678 versus 22,071), and it followed its subjects for a year longer (six versus five) than the men's study did. The results of the men's study were reported in the *New England Journal of Medicine* in July of 1989 and prompted charges of sexism in medical research. The women's-study results were printed in the *Journal of the American Medical Association* in July of 1991, and were generally ignored by the nonmedical press.

Most studies on the prevention of "premature" (occurring in people under age sixty-five) coronary-artery disease have, in fact, been conducted on men. Since middle-aged women have a much lower incidence of this illness than their male counterparts (they provide less than a third as many cases), documenting the preventive effect of a given treatment in these women is much more difficult. More experiments were conducted on men not because women were considered less important but because women suffer less from this disease. Older women do develop coronary disease (albeit at a lower rate than older men), but the experiments were not performed on older men either. At most the data suggest an emphasis on the prevention of disease in younger people.

Incidentally, all clinical breast-cancer research currently funded by the NCI is being conducted on women, even though 300 men a year die of this tumor. Do studies on the prevention of breast cancer with specifically exclude males signify a neglect of men's health? Or should a disease be studied in the group most at risk? Obviously, the coronary-disease research situation and the breast-cancer research situation are not equivalent, but together they do serve to illustrate a point: diseases are most often studied in the highest-risk group, regardless of sex.

What about all the new drug tests that exclude women? Don't they prove the pharmaceutical industry's insensitivity to and disregard for females?

The Food and Drug Administration [FDA] divides human testing of new medicines into three stages. Phase 1 studies are done on a small number of volunteers over a brief period of time, primarily to test safety. Phase 2 studies typically involve a few hundred patients and are designed to look more closely at safety and effectiveness. Phase 3 tests precede approval for commercial release and generally include several thousand patients.

In 1977 the FDA issued guidelines that specifically excluded women with "childbearing potential" from phase 1 and early phase 2 studies; they were to be included in late phase 2 and phase 3 trials in proportion to their expected use of the medication. FDA surveys conducted in 1983 and 1988 showed that the two sexes had been proportionally represented in clinical trials by the time drugs were approved for release.

The 1977 guidelines codified a policy already informally in effect since the thalidomide tragedy shocked the world in 1962. The births of armless or otherwise deformed babies in that era dramatically highlighted the special risks incurred when fertile women ingest drugs. So the policy of excluding such women from the early phases of drug testing arose out of concern, not out of disregard, for them. The policy was changed last year, as a consequence of political protest and recognition that early studies in both sexes might better direct testing.

* * *

Throughout human history from antiquity until the beginning of this century men, on the average, lived slightly longer than women. By 1920 women's life expectancy in the United States was one year greater than men's (54.6 years versus 53.6). After that the gap increased steadily, to 3.5 years in 1930, 4.4 years in 1940, 5.5 in 1950, 6.5 in 1960, and 7.7 in 1970. For the past quarter of a century the gap has remained relatively steady: around seven years. In 1990 the figure was seven years (78.8 versus 71.8).

Thus in the latter part of the twentieth century women live about 10 percent longer than men. A significant part of the reason for this is medical care.

In past centuries complications during childbirth were a major cause of traumatic death in women. Medical advances have dramatically eliminated most of this risk. Infections such as smallpox, cholera, and tuberculosis killed large numbers of men and women at similar ages. The elimination of infection as the dominant cause of death has boosted the prominence of diseases that selectively afflict men earlier in life.

Age-adjusted mortality rates for men are higher for all twelve leading causes of death, including heart disease, stroke, cancer, lung disease (emphysema and pneumonia), liver disease (cirrhosis), suicide, and homicide. We have come to accept women's longer life span as natural, the consequence of their greater biological fitness. Yet this greater fitness never manifested itself in all the millennia of human history that preceded the present era and its medical-care system—the same system that women's-health advocates accuse of neglecting the female sex.

To remedy the alleged neglect, an Office of Research on Women's Health was established by the NIH in 1990. In 1991 the NIH launched its largest epidemiological project ever, the Women's Health Initiative. Costing more than $600 million, this fifteen-year program will study the effects of estrogen therapy, diet, dietary supplements, and exercise on heart disease, breast cancer, colon cancer, osteoporosis, and other diseases in 160,000 postmenopausal women. The study is ambitious in scope and may well result in many advances in the care of older women.

What it will not do is close the "medical gender gap," the difference in the quality of care given the two sexes. The reason is that the gap does not favor men. As we have seen, women receive more medical care and benefit more from medical research. The net result is the most important gap of all: seven years, 10 percent of life.

POSTSCRIPT

Is There a Male Sex Bias in Medicine?

Why are certain medical problems such as clinical depression, autoimmune disease, thyroid disease, and irritable bowel syndrome so disproportionately represented in women? How can treatment options be tailored to offer more successful and specific help for these problems? Or should energy and resources instead be focused on some of the typically male diseases that have received so little funding and attention in the past? Who should decide, and how should they decide?

Ruth Conniff, in "Warning: Feminism Is Hazardous to Your Health," *The Progressive* (April 1997), maintains that libertarian feminist groups have conspired with the conservative right to make a mockery of legitimate health concerns of women. She describes a recent conference sponsored by the Independent Women's Forum (IWF) entitled "Women's Health, Law, and the Junking of Science." With the partial aim of distorting medical research, warns Conniff, such groups' motives appear to be based on their interest in maintaining free-market capitalism and consumer choice at any cost. The consensus of such groups is that women should be allowed to assume the risk in receiving procedures for which the long-term consequences are not known, as is the case with silicone breast implants.

Libertarian feminist groups, along with public-interest research organizations and trial lawyers, are criticizing the feminist concern for women's health as "encouraging paranoia and displaying excessive preoccupation with their own bodies." Psychiatrist David Murray, representing Statistical Assessment Service, a conservative group dedicated to improving media coverage of scientific and statistical information, has stated that "feminists have managed to convince the media they are suffering from strange diseases." Another psychiatrist has suggested that it is a bad idea to include women in clinical trials because this makes the trials cumbersome and more expensive.

Evelyn L. Barbee and Marilyn Little, in "Health, Social Class, and African American Women," in Stanlie M. James and Abena P. Busia, eds., *Theorizing Black Feminisms: The Visionary Pragmatism of Black Women* (Routledge, 1993), suggest that a litany of health problems plagues African American women at alarmingly high rates in the United States. Historically victimized in the health care arena, they say, African American women suffer excessively from cervical cancer, lupus, hypertension, diabetes, and maternal mortality. The authors accuse racist and sexist health policies of exacerbating these problems by allowing unequal access to resources in a hierarchically arranged social order. While African American women may be invisible in many spheres of life, their visibility vis-à-vis the medical establishment appears to be dependent upon drugs that need to be tested and procedures that need to be perfected. An ominous example is illustrated in Barbee and Little's article: In a Cook County hospital in Chicago in 1988, more than 200 pregnant African American women were given the drug Dilantin without their knowledge. Fortunately, to date, the drug, which is used only to treat epilepsy, has not caused observable damage to the resulting offspring or their mothers.

Readings that support the argument against past male favoritism or against future female favoritism (in an attempt to rectify alleged wrongs) include "Equality Law Could Backfire on Researchers," *New Scientist* (August 7, 1993); "Absence of Sex Bias in the Referral of Patients for Cardiac Catheterization," *The New England Journal of Medicine* (April 21, 1994); "Why Do Women Last Longer Than Men?" *New Scientist* (October 23, 1993); and "Survey Shows Women May Live Longer, but Not Healthier Than Men," *Nation's Health* (August 1993). The article "Group Therapy," *The New Republic* (April 5, 1993) suggests that it would not be beneficial to study men and women separately because in most cases the gender-related biological differences are not important enough to justify different approaches.

ISSUE 16

Is Premenstrual Syndrome a Clear Medical Condition?

YES: Sally K. Severino and Margaret L. Moline, from "Premenstrual Syndrome: Identification and Management," *Drugs* (vol. 49, no. 1, 1995)

NO: Maria Gurevich, from "Rethinking the Label: Who Benefits from the PMS Construct?" *Women and Health* (vol. 23, no. 2, 1995)

ISSUE SUMMARY

YES: Psychiatrist Sally K. Severino and physician Margaret L. Moline argue that premenstrual syndrome (PMS) is a legitimate illness consisting of cyclic recurrence of physical, mental, and behavioral symptoms in the late luteal cycle sufficient to require medical treatment.

NO: Psychology professor Maria Gurevich suggests that PMS is not simply a biomedical entity but instead a complex, ideologically and culturally constructed category that imposes a label that is socially and politically damaging to women.

Are women at the mercy of "raging hormones" prior to and during menstruation? In 1981 the *Journal of the Medical Association* described premenstrual syndrome (PMS) as "the newest women's health issue in the United States." Today it remains one of the most controversial. The debate ranges from questions of etiology, diagnosis, and definition to whether or not the syndrome actually exists. In Western countries many physicians now assume that there is a specific clinical condition called PMS that has emotional, somatic, and behavioral components. Advertisements for sanitary products, magazine articles, even comedic routines frequently focus on women's unpredictability and irrationality before menstruation, reinforcing popular images of PMS.

PMS has been defined as a characteristic clustering of symptoms in the premenstruum and the absence of these same symptoms in the postmenstruum. Timing of symptoms is more important than the type of symptoms reported, and critical to the diagnosis is the fact that the symptoms are cyclical. Symptoms usually include those belonging to the "PMS triad": irritability, lethargy, and depression. Other symptoms may include feeling out of control or worthless, experiencing a desire to escape, sporadic crying, uncontrollable rage, paranoia, sadness, anger, anxiety, phobias, and guilt. Some physicians maintain that dysphoric premenstrual syndromes are quite prevalent and that in some women they are severe enough to warrant medical treatment.

While vast numbers of Americans believe that PMS is a valid medical syndrome, some people warn that PMS is a political construct that is used to invalidate the anger and distress of women. The concern is that PMS may provide too easy an explanation for women who, when they are legitimately angry and discouraged about discrimination or oppression that confronts them, have recourse to a well-accepted physiological syndrome to account for their anxiety, depression, and "unfeminine" anger. Feminists have always recognized the importance of health and control of women's bodies, and some now see PMS as encouraging medical dependence and allowing oppressive individuals to reframe a woman's expressions of anger. Legitimate complaints may easily be derailed, for example, when a man asks, "Is it your time of the month?"

Some say research has not supported this view of dramatic and possibly violent shifts in mood and behavior prior to the menstrual cycle, nor has it documented hormonal fluctuations and treatment for the syndrome in any definitive way. Some say that a placebo effect has been shown to exist, suggesting that beliefs and expectations may influence symptoms of PMS. Moreover, women in some cultures do not report experiencing any of the so-called negative premenstrual symptoms. After heated arguments about the existence of PMS as a category in the American Psychiatric Association's *Diagnostic and Statistical Manual of Mental Disorders*, PMS was ultimately renamed "premenstrual dysphoric disorder" (PMDD) and included in an appendix to the fourth edition of the manual (*DSM-IV*). It is also listed as a "depressive disorder not otherwise specified" within the main text.

In the selections that follow, Sally K. Severino and Margaret L. Moline state that PMS is a real, identifiable medical condition for which a range of biologically based therapeutic interventions are recommended. Maria Gurevich argues against the utility of the PMS construct and against the persistence of PMS as a medical category. She believes that it is a "socially constructed disease" used to stigmatize and disempower women.

YES

Sally K. Severino and
Margaret L. Moline

PREMENSTRUAL SYNDROME: IDENTIFICATION AND MANAGEMENT

Both the identification of women with premenstrual syndrome (PMS) and the management of their symptoms challenges the acumen of many healthcare professionals. This is due, in part, to the nature of the syndrome, which encompasses symptoms that can be emotional and/or physical, last for days to weeks and can vary from month to month. Despite decades of research, neither the cause nor the most effective treatment have been resolved.[1] This article describes what is known about PMS, methods of identifying women with PMS and management recommendations.

DEFINITION

PMS is the name given to the cyclic covariance of several premenstrual symptoms that appear during the late luteal phase of the menstrual cycle and disappear during the full flow of menses, but which do not occur during the mid or late follicular phase.

Symptoms can begin any time after ovulation. Four temporal patterns have been described.[2] Premenstrual symptoms can begin at ovulation, with gradual worsening of symptoms during the luteal phase (pattern 1), or can begin during the second week of the luteal phase (pattern 2). In both patterns, symptoms remit within a few days after the onset of the next follicular phase (i.e. during menses). Some women experience a brief, time-limited episode of symptoms at ovulation, followed by symptom-free days and a recurrence of premenstrual symptoms late in the luteal phase (pattern 3). The most severely affected women have symptoms that begin at ovulation, worsen across the luteal phase and remit only after menses ceases (pattern 4). These women describe having only 1 week a month that is symptom-free. More research is required to determine whether these patterns represent distinct subtypes of PMS or correspond to other conditions.

In addition, these patterns must be differentiated from premenstrual magnification (PMM), a pattern that is also cyclical in that symptoms are present in

From Sally K. Severino and Margaret L. Moline, "Premenstrual Syndrome: Identification and Management," *Drugs*, vol. 49, no. 1 (1995). Copyright © 1995 by Adis International. Reprinted by permission.

the follicular and early luteal phases and increase in severity premenstrually.[3-5] A large percentage of these women self-identify with PMS. These women deserve careful evaluation to determine whether they have a premenstrual exacerbation of another disorder, such as depression, anxiety, eating disorders, substance abuse, headaches, allergies, asthma, seizures or herpes, or whether the symptoms appear *de novo* during the premenstrual phase.

More than 100 symptoms have been attributed to PMS. The most common complaints include emotional symptoms (depression, mood swings, anger, irritability and anxiety), physical symptoms (breast swelling and tenderness, abdominal bloating, headaches, muscle aches and pains and oedema) and others (decreased interest in usual activities, fatigue, difficulty concentrating, increased appetite and food cravings and hypersomnia or insomnia).

DESCRIPTION

The prevalence of PMS is unknown. Although a prospectively confirmed community-based epidemiological study has yet to be published, it is estimated that 20 to 40% of women experience some premenstrual symptoms and that 5% of women report some degree of significant impairment on their work or lifestyle.[6] These estimates are consistent with retrospective epidemiological survey data that report the prevalence of PMS to be 6.8%[7] and with 2 population-based studies that report the prevalence of PMS to be 4.6%[8] and 9.8%.[4]

Although the first occurrence of PMS can be any time after menarche, women usually seek treatment for their symptoms in their third or fourth decades.

Symptoms are believed to remit with menopause and with any other condition, such as pregnancy or amenorrhoeic lactation, that interrupts ovulatory cycles. Symptoms may occur in the absence of menstrual bleeding in which ovarian cyclicity exits[9] and may coexist with other conditions such as dysmenorrhoea. The course of PMS is unknown. Women generally report symptoms worsen with age until menopause, when PMS symptoms cease.

Premenstrual symptoms are thought to affect women equally regardless of socioeconomic status or culture, but particular symptoms may be identified more frequently in one culture than in another.[10-12] These beliefs, however, are based on retrospective surveys of premenstrual symptoms, not PMS. The incidence of PMS in different cultures is unknown.

The role of genetics in the development or severity of PMS is suggested by research, but it has not been demonstrated conclusively.[13-15] Some evidence from developmental studies shows that daughters of mothers with premenstrual tension are more likely to complain of the syndrome than daughters of mothers who are symptom-free.[16] These researchers studied the incidence of premenstrual symptoms in 5000 adolescent Finnish girls and their mothers. They reported a high familial incidence of premenstrual tension based on the observation that 70% of daughters whose mothers had nervous symptoms also had symptoms themselves, whereas only 37% of daughters of unaffected mothers experienced symptoms.

The concordance rate (if both twins have PMS) of PMS was found to be significantly higher in monozygous twins (93%) than in dizygous twins (44%) and in non-twin control women (31%).[17] Van den Akker and associates[18] obtained information by questionnaire from 462 female twin pairs who were either members of the Institute of Psychiatry Volunteer Twin Register or of the Birmingham Population Register. Their data, like that of Dalton and coworkers,[17] suggest that premenstrual symptoms are hereditary. These data need to be compared with the occurrence of PMS in the general population to determine whether this familial relation is significant.

The aetiology of PMS is unknown. Since 1931, many hypotheses have been proposed including abnormalities in hormonal secretory patterns (ovarian steroids, androgens, prolactin, mineralocorticoids, thyroid, insulin), neurotransmitter levels (biogenic amines, endogenous opioids), circadian rhythms, prostaglandins and vitamin B_6 levels, nutrition, allergic reactions, stress and psychological factors.[19] However, none of these has been definitely implicated. Likely candidates include alterations in neurotransmitter levels in women with predominant affective symptoms.

The difficulty discovering the aetiology led Severino[20] to hypothesise an integration model. In other words, women are born with a genetically designed brain and body system that can be influenced and changed by experience and learning. Our perspective differs depending on whether we are viewing a woman's biology, her developmental history and/or her contemporary circumstances. The last include both the woman's internally represented image of her world and the actual socioeconomic cultural conditions of her world. The aetiology of PMS, according to Severino's hypothesis, may reside in the dynamic interaction of all 3 perspectives.

IDENTIFICATION

PMS is a diagnosis of exclusion (table 1). Other physical and mental disorders must be ruled out before this diagnosis can be made. Thus, a careful physical and mental history must be obtained. It is also recommended that a physical examination, including a pelvic examination, and blood tests be performed to exclude such disorders as anaemia, diabetes mellitus, thyroid disease, endometriosis and fibrocystic breast disease, among others.[19] It is possible for a woman to have both a mental or physical disorder in addition to PMS as long as the premenstrual symptoms are distinct from the other disorder and occur in the luteal phase and remit in the follicular phase.

The use of retrospective histories of premenstrual symptoms alone has led to the overdiagnosis of PMS.[21,22] Therefore, prospective daily ratings of symptoms are required to substantiate the woman's history of premenstrual symptoms. The clinician may use the average of ratings for several days in the follicular phase of the menstrual cycle (days 5 to 10) compared with the average of symptom ratings in the late luteal phase (last 6 days of the menstrual cycle). However, several methods are routinely used in both clinical practice and research venues.[23]

A diagnosis of PMS is made when:

- no other disorder is present that can account for the woman's symptoms;
- prospective daily symptom ratings demonstrate a marked change in severity of 5 or more symptoms premenstrually for at least 2 menstrual cycles; and
- there is a symptom-free week (usual days 5 to 10) during the same menstrual cycles.

Table 1
Identification of Premenstrual Syndrome (PMS)

Careful history from the woman
Retrospective history of PMS
Review of physical symptoms
  gynaecological
  endocrinological
  allergic
  others
Review of mental symptoms

Medical and psychological examinations
Rule out anaemia, thyroid disease, etc.
Rule out psychiatric illness

Prospective daily ratings of symptoms
At least 2 menstrual cycles

The predominance of emotional symptoms that seriously interfere with life indicates premenstrual dysphoric disorder,[24] formerly known as late luteal phase dysphoric disorder.[25]

MANAGEMENT

Management of patients who may have PMS begins with a review of the results of the physical and psychological diagnostic work-up and daily symptom ratings (if they were indicated) with the patient. Treatment of a physical problem (e.g. hypothyroidism) may eliminate the premenstrual complaints and thus should be done before PMS is diagnosed. Having ruled out other medical illnesses, clinicians can then assign patients to one of 5 categories: (i) women with PMS; (ii) women with premenstrual dysphoric disorder (PMDD); (iii) women with both a psychiatric disorder and PMS (or PMDD); (iv) women with only a psychiatric disorder (not PMDD); and (v) women without either PMS or a psychiatric disorder.

Women With Premenstrual Syndrome (PMS) or Premenstrual Dysphoric Disorder (PMDD)

Recommendations for the management of women with PMS or PMDD follow similar guidelines. As stated above, women with PMDD are a subgroup of women with PMS who have primarily emotional symptoms and meet criteria for the diagnosis as it appears in DSM-IV.[24]

Completing the daily symptom ratings is fundamentally important. First, the ratings define the pattern of symptoms, thereby supporting or negating the retrospective history of PMS that prompted the initial evaluation. Secondly, they are a visual adjunct for clinicians to use so that women can see their symptom profile, especially in instances where the pattern is not consistent with the diagnosis of PMS. Thirdly, through the rating process, an important first step in management has been taken. As they chart their symptoms, many women gain a sense of control over their problems. Visualising the type, severity and timing of symptoms can make them seem more manageable. This sense of control may be enough to relieve distress in some women and make other interventions unnecessary.

If a patient requires additional symptom management, then clinicians can adopt 1 of 2 main approaches: modify the menstrual cycle or treat the specific symptom(s).

Initial Management: Dietary and Lifestyle Changes

If a woman requires additional symptom management, 4 initial management steps can be considered (table 2). Education of the woman that PMS is a legitimate

Table 2
Initial Management Steps for Premenstrual Syndrome

Education and support
Restrict caffeine consumption
Limit salt consumption
Exercise

concern and how she can plan ahead for its occurrence can be very helpful. This effort can be expanded to include her spouse and children so that her support system is strengthened. Some women profit from a PMS support group that is time-limited and led by a professional.[26,27]

The literature suggests that women who consume large amounts of caffeine or its equivalent (theophylline and theobromine, or methylxanthines) in coffee, tea or colas report more severe premenstrual symptoms.[28] Because of this association of caffeine consumption with increased prevalence and more severe symptoms, it makes sense to recommend that women decrease caffeine consumption premenstrually to minimise its potential contribution to irritability and insomnia.

Decreasing salt intake is almost always recommended as a way to minimise premenstrual bloating. However, this has yet to be confirmed by research. Many people tend to consume more salt than necessary, and it seems reasonable to recommend limiting salt intake on the chance that temporary bodyweight gain could be avoided.[29]

Some research suggests that exercise can minimise some premenstrual symptoms related to fluid retention.[30] Exercise also may increase self-esteem. Thus, women should be encouraged to participate all month in some kind of regular physical exercise. It is the regularity, i.e. the frequency, rather than the intensity of exercise that seems to make a difference.[26,31]

Pyridoxine (vitamin B_6), while frequently mentioned as a treatment option in the lay press, has fallen from favour as a treatment for PMS. The rationale for its use was based on 5 hypotheses[19] including the knowledge that vitamin B_6 is a cofactor for enzymes involved in the synthesis of neurotransmitters that are thought to be associated with PMS. The literature regarding the efficacy is contradictory and there is concern about the neurotoxicity of pyridoxine. The most recent review of its efficacy[32] lends weak support to its use. If it is used, the dosage should be low (50 mg/day). This dose has been shown to be effective for symptoms of depression, irritability and tiredness.[33] While using pyridoxine, women should be monitored closely for muscle weakness, numbness, clumsiness, and paraesthesia.

Medication is appropriate if symptoms persist after these measures have been tried. Because the cause of PMS is not yet known, treatment is aimed either at control of the menstrual cycle or at specific symptom management.

Control of the Menstrual Cycle
If the menstrual cycle is to be manipulated, then clinicians can consider 4 alternatives (table 3).

Oral Contraceptives
Both retrospective[34,35] and prospective treatment studies[36,37] report that oral contraceptives may minimise symptoms of PMS. However, oral contraceptives have also been shown to be no more effective than placebo[38] and to worsen premenstrual symptoms in some women.[39] As

with all therapeutic interventions, benefit of treatment must be weighed against possible adverse effects. Particular attention should be given to cardiovascular risks. Migraine headaches may be precipitated. In addition, oral contraceptives may increase plasma triglyceride levels.

GnRH Analogues

Analogues of gonadotrophin-releasing hormone (GnRH) [luteinising hormone-releasing hormone (LHRH)] have been used to treat PMS symptoms.[40-44] Depending on the dose, menstrual cycles can be eliminated completely or ovulation only can be prevented. In women whose cycles were blocked by injection of a GnRH analogue,[43] premenstrual symptoms were not present. When the nasal preparation was used, the results were mixed.[40,41] A third method of administering GnRH analogues has been reported for PMS treatment—subcutaneous implantation.[45] Both physical and psychological symptoms of PMS improved significantly with treatment.

The main disadvantage of this technique is that estrogen levels are usually markedly reduced, with the accompanying risk of osteoporosis and other unpleasant symptoms of hypoestrogenaemia. However, the combined use of a GnRH analogue and estrogen with or without progesterone has been found to be successful.[46]

Ovariectomy

Following the same rationale as the use of chemical ovariectomies, surgical bilateral ovariectomies have been performed to treat PMS.[47,48] Although surgery eliminates symptoms, it is associated with the unwanted effects of low estrogen production, including decreased

Table 3

Control of the Menstrual Cycle

Oral contraceptives
GnRH analogues and ovariectomy
Danazol
Estradiol implants and patches

Abbreviation:
GnRH = gonadotrophin-releasing hormone [luteinising hormone-releasing hormone (LHRH)].

libido. Surgical menopause may also cause even greater bone loss than that which occurs after natural menopause.[49] In older women who are nearing natural menopause, oophorectomy may be less questionable.[50] However, no long term outcomes of bilateral oophorectomy have been published. Surgery is a last resort that should be reserved for women with incapacitating symptoms and who are over 40 years old in whom all other less invasive methods have failed.

Danazol

Menstrual cycles can be eliminated reversibly by the use of danazol. In a double-blind study, Watts and colleagues[51] showed that danazol was superior to placebo when given daily. However, many women withdrew from the study because of adverse effects of treatment. In a second double-blind test, danazol administration was begun at the onset of symptoms.[52] In this well designed study, overall symptom scores decreased significantly more in the active treatment months than in the placebo control cycles. Intermittent therapy was not associated with adverse effects. Subsequent studies have also shown the efficacy of danazol.[53-55]

Estradiol Implants

Estradiol implants have been used successfully by Magos and colleagues[56] to treat PMS. In their study, the addition of a monthly regimen of synthetic progestin (to promote endometrial shedding) was associated with the return of premenstrual-like symptoms, but these were significantly milder intensity than pretreatment. Transdermal estrogen with cyclic oral progesterone produced similar results.[57]

Progesterone, whether natural or synthetic, oral or suppository, is also a treatment option. However, the rationale for its use, i.e. that women with PMS are deficient in the hormone in the late luteal phase, has not been proven. Furthermore, studies of women receiving estrogen replacement who were given progesterone reported the symptoms appeared at the time of progesterone administration. Double-blind studies of progesterone have not demonstrated its superiority to placebo.[58]

Specific Symptom Management

Women With Predominantly Emotional Symptoms

Drugs used in the management of emotional symptoms are summarised in table 4. In general, short term use of a benzodiazepine, such as alprazolam, for the treatment of premenstrual depression (with or without anxiety) may be tried.[59-61] A problem with this class of drugs is that dependence and tolerance develop quickly. Thus, before a benzodiazepine is prescribed, the clinician should be familiar enough with the patient to know whether she manifests any sign of an addictive personality. In addition, the drug must be tapered gradually during menses to avoid withdrawal symptoms such as exacerbation of anxiety, shakiness, palpitations, tremor and seizures.[62] In addition to the problem of addiction potential, alprazolam is not a uniformally effective treatment.[63]

If alprazolam is the drug of choice for a particular woman, however, the following schedule may be used. Treatment may begin in the luteal phase at the onset of premenstrual symptoms with 0.25 mg at bedtime. This may be increased in increments of 0.125 mg 3 times daily, until either a satisfactory effect is obtained or adverse effects preclude further dosage increases. Smith and colleagues [64] do not exceed 0.25 mg 3 times daily. Tapering the dose by no more than 25% daily to avoid withdrawal symptoms should begin on day 2 of menses. If the initial intermittent use (i.e. during the premenstruum only) of a benzodiazepine is successful, the patient should be monitored regularly to determine whether continued use remains effective and to prevent addiction to the medication.

Buspirone has been reported to be effective in treating women with severe premenstrual anxiety[65] and with PMS.[66] This drug can be prescribed after ovulation until menses; the recommended dosage is 5 to 10mg 3 times daily. Further research is required to validate whether this drug is a useful therapeutic option.

Nortriptyline, a tricyclic antidepressant drug, has been shown to be effective in an open trial of women with severe premenstrual depression.[67] Nortriptyline (50 to 175mg at bedtime) must be administered on a daily basis, therefore the severity of symptoms must be weighed against the possible adverse effects of long term administration.

Five drugs with serotonergic activity have been reported to have efficacy in the treatment of premenstrual

Table 4
Management of Emotional Symptoms

Alprazolam
Buspirone
Nortriptyline
Clomipramine
Fluoxetine

emotional symptoms: buspirone, fluoxetine, *d*-fenfluramine, clomipramine and fluvoxamine. These have been carefully reviewed.[68] At this time, fluoxetine, a selective serotonin (5-hydroxytryptamine; 5-HT) reuptake inhibitor, is the selection of first choice on the basis of the research literature.[69] The recommended dosage is 20 mg/day administered in the morning. In women who are concerned about taking medication all month long when they are symptomatic only a few days, there is 1 case report in the literature that describes the successful use of fluoxetine during the symptomatic phase only.[70]

There is no specific treatment for irritability. In fact, there have been comments that irritability has not been given enough attention in treatment studies.

Women With Predominantly Physical Symptoms

The management of physical symptoms is summarised in table 5. If one of the following symptoms is the major complaint of the patient, a treatment trial with the suggested medication is in order.

Fluid retention Diuretics have been shown to be useful in treating women with symptoms of bloating and bodyweight gain. Bodyweight gain seems to be required for a diuretic to help symptoms of fluid retention.[71] Not all women who complain of bloating actually gain bodyweight.[72] When choosing a diuretic, practitioners must be careful to avoid hypokalaemia and adlosteronism.

Mastodynia Women with symptoms of breast swelling or pain could first try one of the nonprescription remedies that have shown some efficacy in treating these problems. There is some data to support the efficacy of tocopherol (vitamin E) [400 units/day] and evening primrose oil (1 capsule of 500mg daily up to a maximum of 2 capsules 3 times daily).[73]

For serious cases of mastodynia, bromocriptine has been shown to be successful. Use of this drug should not be routine, however, because several unpleasant adverse effects occur frequently with the dosages that are usually prescribed to control the symptoms.[74-78] Another option may be tamoxifen,[79] an oral nonsteroidal antiestrogen, in dosages of 10 mg/day from day 5 to day 24. Animal studies, however, raise concern about the carcinogenic effects of tamoxifen.[80]

Fatigue or insomnia Women whose primary complaints include fatigue or insomnia should be instructed about sleep hygiene. Recommendations made by the Sleep Wake Disorders Center of the Westchester Division, New York Hospital[19] are summarised in table 6.

Prescribing a sedative hypnotic for premenstrual insomnia is not recommended, because tolerance and dependence may occur, and residual daytime sedation usually ensues. Tryptophan, which had been recommended until several years ago for its sedative properties, has been withdrawn from the nonprescription market because of concerns about eosinophilia and blood dyscrasia. Alternatively, women may try foods rich in tryptophan such as milk at bedtime.

Table 5
Management of Physical Symptoms

Symptom	Treatment
Fluid retention	Spironolactone
Mastodynia	Tocopherol (vitamin E), bromocriptine
Fatigue and/or insomnia	Sleep hygiene (see table 6)
Headaches	Aspirin (acetylsalicylic acid), paracetamol (acetaminophen), ibuprofen
Food cravings	Behaviour modification, fenfluramine

Headaches and menstrual migraine Because migraine headaches can be an adverse effect of oral contraceptive use, oral contraceptives should be discontinued or avoided in patients who have histories of migraines. Women who are not taking oral contraceptives who experience premenstrual headaches should try 1 of the common nonprescription analgesics [aspirin (acetylsalicylic acid), paracetamol (acetaminophen), ibuprofen] as soon as possible after the start of the headache. Treatment for menstrual migraine is the same as treatment for migraine at any other time of the month.

Several combinations of drugs are available for treating migraine: (i) 'Cafergot', a combination of ergotamine tartrate and caffeine; (ii) 'Fiorinal', a combination of butalbital, aspirin and caffeine; and (iii) 'Midrin', a combination of isometheptene mucate, dichloralphenazone and paracetamol. Each of these drugs can cause adverse effects, including nausea. In addition, the number of days for which 'Cafergot' can be prescribed is limited. If migraine headaches occur more frequently than once a week, prophylactic treatment should be considered. A variety of drugs are available for this purpose, including propranolol and 'Bellergal' (a combination of ergotamine, belladona alkaloids and phenobarbital), which have been the subject of some research in treating PMS.[81,82]

Food craving The craving for food is probably best treated with behaviour modification techniques addressing eating habits and diet. Based on research findings suggesting that carbohydrate intake increases premenstrually in some women and may influence mood,[83,84] women with this symptom may be encouraged to plan diets that incorporate frequent small meals and adequate nutrition, with an emphasis on complex carbohydrates and the elimination of caffeine, alcohol (ethanol) and salt.[26]

Fenfluramine, an anorectic drug, has been proposed as a treatment for seasonal affective disorder, a syndrome that shares the symptoms of carbohydrate craving with PMS.[85] Results of a small trial suggested that this drug may be effective for PMS.[86]

Other symptoms A brief mention is needed regarding calcium supplements. These have been shown to be effective in treating symptoms of PMS.[87,88] However, a calcium deficiency should be treated before a diagnosis of PMS is made, just as anaemia or hypothyroidism would be treated first. Thus, it may be worthwhile to ensure that a patient has an adequate daily consumption of calcium (1 g/day for women aged 25 through to menopause) either before or while she is rating her symptoms so that additional treatment can be avoided if possible.

Table 6
Sleep Hygiene

Sleep on a regular schedule, including weekends
Do not spend too much time in bed. 30 min more than an individual's average amount
   of sleep per 24h is sufficient
Avoid caffeinated beverages after noontime, and if this does not help, avoid them altogether
Avoid alcohol within 4h of bedtime, if not altogether
Exercise, but do so in the morning or afternoon, not within 3 or 4h before bedtime
Do something relaxing in the hour or so before getting into bed–avoid arguments,
   excitement, and bill paying during this time
A light bedtime snack is permissible, but avoid eating a full meal just before bedtime
An occasional sleeping pill is permissible but should be reserved for special
   circumstances. More than 1 a week is too many
Stop trying to make sleep happen. Let it happen

Constipation and haemorrhoids related to the late luteal phase of the menstrual cycle should be treated the way constipation and haemorrhoids are treated at any other time of the month. A diet high in fibre and fluids together with sufficient exercise are a good focus. Fruits, especially prunes, are effective. Laxatives should be a last resort. Hemorrhoids often become less problematic when constipation is no longer a problem. In more acute situations, over-the-counter preparations are effective.

Women With a Psychiatric Diagnosis and PMS

Women with a psychiatric diagnosis and PMS may have premenstrual exacerbations of their current psychiatric illness as well as the new symptoms related to PMS. It is important to treat the underlying psychiatric disorder first before tackling the premenstrual symptoms. Doses of psychotropic medication may need to be increased premenstrually to control symptoms.[89]

Women With Only a Psychiatric Diagnosis (Not PMDD)

These women should be shown how their pattern of symptom ratings differs from those of women with PMS, i.e. that their symptoms are not limited to the premenstrual phase of the menstrual cycle, but occur at any time during the month. These women should be referred to an appropriate mental health professional.

Women Without PMS

As with the patients in the previous group, women without PMS should be shown: (i) that their daily symptom ratings do not meet the criteria for PMS; (ii) that their physical examination and tests do not suggest another medical illness; and (iii) that their psychological evaluation has ruled out a mental disorder.

They should be reassured, however, that this does not mean that their symptoms are not real. Indeed, their symptoms are real. However, the meaning of their symptoms is unclear. Perhaps they are in the incipient phases of developing PMS where their symptomatology is inconsistent or of a low level of severity such that they do not qualify for the diagnosis of PMS. These women could be encouraged to continue charting their symptoms or return in 6 months for reevaluation. Alternatively, other sources of symptoms could be explored such as stressful life situations.

CONCLUSION

The aetiology of PMS is unknown. Providers of women's healthcare must listen carefully to what women say about their symptoms and be guided by the fact that each woman is an entire, biopsychosocial, unique human being, a person who seeks help, rather than a diagnostic category. Identification of women with PMS is based on thorough medical evaluations, both physical and mental, together with prospective daily symptom ratings.

Management of symptoms should begin with education and support. Specific symptom management can begin by: regulating food intake to ensure adequate nutrition and avoid symptom engendering items such as caffeinated beverages; regulating exercise, relaxation and sleep; and learning techniques for stress and conflict management. For women whose symptoms persist, pharmacotherapy must be chosen carefully, weighing the severity of impairment against short term and possible long term adverse effects of treatment.

REFERENCES

1. Gold JH, Severino SK, editors. Premenstrual dysphorias: myths and realities. Washington, DC: American Psychiatric Press, Inc., 1994.
2. Reid, RL, Yen SSC. The premenstrual syndrome. Clin Obstet Gynecol 1983; 26: 710–8.
3. Harrison M. Self-help for premenstrual syndrome. New York: Random House, 1982.
4. Mitchell ES, Woods NF, Lentz MJ. Recognizing PMS when you see it: criteria for PMS sample selection. In: Taylor DL. Woods NF, editors. Menstruation, health and illness. Washington DC: Hemisphere, 1991: 89–102.
5. Mitchell, ES, Woods NF, Lentz MJ. Differentiation of women with three premenstrual symptoms patterns. Nurs Res 1994 Jan-Feb; 43 (1): 25–30.
6. Committee Statement 66 of the American College of Obstetricians and Gynecologists. American College of Obstetricians and Gynecologists. Washington, DC, January 1987.
7. Stout AL, Steege JF. Psychological assessment of women seeking treatment of premenstrual assessment. J. Psychosom Res 1985; 29: 621–9.
8. Rivera-Tovar AD, Frank E. Late luteal phase dysphoric disorder in young women. Am J Psychiatry 1990; 147: 1634–36.
9. Backstrom T, Boyle H, Baird DT. Persistence of symptoms of premenstrual tension in hysterectomized women. Br J Obstet Gynasecol 1981; 88: 530–6.
10. Adenaike OC, Abidoye RO. A study of the incidence of the premenstrual syndrome in a group of Nigerian women. Public Health 1987; 101: 49–58.
11. Hasin M, Dennerstein L, Gotts G. Menstrual cycle related complaints: cross-cultural study. J. Psychosom Obstet Gynecol 1988; 9: 35–42.
12. Janinger O, Riffenburgh R, Karsh R. Cross cultural study of premenstrual symptoms. Psychosomatics 1972; 13: 226–35.
13. Wilson CA, Turner CW, Keye WR. Firstborn adolescent daughters and mothers with and without premenstrual syndrome: a comparison. J. Adolesc Health 1991; 12: 130–7.
14. Kendler KS, Silberg JL, Neale MC, et al. Genetic and environmental factors in the aetiology of menstrual, premenstrual and neurotic symptoms: a population-based twin study. Psychol Med 1992; 22: 85–100.
15. Condon JT. The premenstrual syndrome: a twin study. Br J Psychiatry 1993; 162: 418–6.
16. Kantero RL, Widholm O. A statistical analysis of the menstrual patterns of 8,000 Finnish girls and their mothers: IV. Correlations of menstrual traits between adolescent girls and their mothers. Acta Obstet Gynecol Scand 1971; 14 Suppl.: 30–6.
17. Dalton K, Dalton M, Guthrie K. Incidence of the premenstrual syndrome in twins. BMJ 1987; 295: 1027–8.
18. Van den Akker OB, Steen GS, Neale MC, et al. Genetic and environmental variation in menstrual cycle; histories of two British twin samples. Acta Genet Med Gemellol 1987; 36: 541–8.
19. Severino SK, Moline ML. Premenstrual syndrome: a clinician's guide. New York: Guilford Press, 1989.

20. Severino SK. Late luteal phase dysphoric disorder: a scientific puzzle. Med Hypotheses 1993; 41 (3): 229–34.

21. Morse CA, Dennerstein L, Varnavides K, et al. Menstrual cycle symptoms: comparison of a non-clinical sample with a patient group. J Affect Disord 1988; 14: 41–50.

22. Rapkin AJ, Chang LC, Reading AE. Comparison of retrospective and prospective assessment of premenstrual symptoms. Psychol Rep 1988; 62: 55–60.

23. Schnurr PP, Hurt SW, Stout AL. Consequences of methodological decisions in the diagnosis of late luteal phase dysphoric disorder. In: Gold JH, Severino SK, editors. Premenstrual dysphorias: myths and realities. Washington, DC; American Psychiatric Press, Inc., 1994: 19–46.

24. American Psychiatric Association. Diagnostic and statistical manual of mental disorders. 4th ed. Washington, DC: American Psychiatric Press, Inc., 1994: 715–18.

25. American Psychiatric Association. Diagnostic and statistical manual of mental disorders. 3rd rev. ed. Washington, DC; American Psychiatric Press, Inc., 1987: 367–9.

26. Pearlstein T, Rivera-Tovar A, Frank E, et al. Nonmedical management of late luteal phase dysphoric disorder: a preliminary report. J. Psychother Pract Res 1992; 1: 49–55.

27. Reid RL, Maddocks SE. A positive approach to PMS. Contemp Obstet Gynecol 1987 April; 41–54.

28. Rossignol AM, Zhang JY, Chen YZ, et al. Tea and premenstrual syndrome in the People's Republic of China. Am J Public Health 1989; 79: 67–9.

29. MacGregor GA, Markandu ND. Roulston JE, et al. is 'idiopathic' oedema idiopathic? Lancet 1979; 1: 397–400.

30. Prior JC, Vigna Y. Conditioning exercise and premenstrual symptoms. J Reprod Med 1987; 32: 423–8.

31. Steege JF, Blumenthal JA. The effects of aerobic exercise on premenstrual symptoms in middle-aged women: a preliminary study. J Psychosom Res 1993; 37: 127–33.

32. Kleijnen J, Riet GT, Knipschild P. Vitamin B6 in the treatment of the premenstrual syndrome—a review. Br J Obstet Gynaecol 1990; 97: 847–52.

33. Doll H, Brown S, Thurston A, Vessey M. Pyridoxine (vitamin B6) and the premenstrual syndrome: a randomized crossover trial. J Royal Coll Gen Pract 1989; 9: 364–8.

34. Andersch B, Hahn L. Premenstrual complaints: II. Influence of oral contraceptives. Acta Obstet Gynecol Scand 1981; 60: 579–83.

35. Kutner SJ, Brown WL. Types of oral contraceptives, depression and premenstrual symptoms. J Nerv Ment Dis 1972; 155: 153–62.

36. Herzberg B, Coppen A. Changes in psychological symptoms in women taking oral contraceptives. Br J Psychiatry 1970; 116: 161–4.

37. Graham CA, Sherwin BB. A prospective treatment study of premenstrual symptoms using a triphasic oral contraceptive. J Psychosom Res. 1992; 36: 257–66.

38. Backstrom T, Hansson-Malmstrom Y, Lindhe BA, et al. Oral contraceptives in premenstrual syndrome: a randomized comparison of tripha-sic and monophasic preparations. Contraception 1992; 46: 253–68.

39. Bancroft J, Rennie D. The impact of oral contraceptives on the experience of perimenstrual mood clumsiness, food craving and other symptoms. J. Psychosom Res 1993; 37: 195–202.

40. Bancroft J, Boyle H, Warner P, et al. The use of an LHRH agonist, buserelin, in the long-term management of premenstrual syndromes. Clin Endocrinol 1987; 27: 171–82.

41. Hammarback S, Backstrom T. Induced anovulation as treatment of premenstrual tension syndrome. Acta Obstet Gynecol Scand 1988; 67: 159–66.

42. Muse KN. Clinical experience with the use of GnRH agonists in the treatment of premenstrual syndrome. Obstet Gynecol Survey 1989; 44: 317–8.

43. Muse KN, Cetel NS, Futterman LA, et al. The premenstrual syndrome: effects of medical ovariectomy. N Engl J Med 1984; 311: 1345–9.

44. Reid RL, Yen SSC. LHRH agonists and antagonists: therapeutic possibilities for premenstrual syndrome. In: Vickery BH, Nestor JJ, Hafez ESE, editors. LHRH and its analogs. Lancaster, England: MTP Press, 1987: 279–93.

45. West CP, Lumsden MA, Baird DT. Modification of symptoms of the premenstrual syndrome during ovarian suppression with goserelin (Zoladex) depot: potential for research and clinical investigation. J Psychosom Obstet Gynaecol 1989; 10: 79–88.

46. Mortola JF, Girton L, Fischer U. Successful treatment of severe premenstrual syndrome by combined use of gonadotropin-releasing hormone agonist and estrogen/progestin. J Clin Endocrinol Metab 1991; 72: 252A–F.

47. Casper RF, Hearn MT. The effect of hysterectomy and bilateral oophorectomy in women with severe premenstrual syndrome. Am J Obstet Gynecol 1990; 162: 105–9.

48. Casson P, Hahn PM, Van Vugt DA, et al. Lasting response to ovariectomy in severe intractable premenstrual syndrome. Am J Obstet Gynecol 1990; 162: 99–105.

49. Riggs L, Melton LJ. Involutional osteoporosis. N Engl J Med 1986; 314: 1676–86.

50. Studd J. Prophylactic oophorectomy. Br J Obstet Gynaecol 1989; 96: 506–8.

51. Watts JF, Butt WR, Edwards RL. A clinical trial using danazol for the treatment of premenstrual tension. Br J Obstet Gynaecol 1987; 94: 30–4.

52. Sarno Jr AP, Miller Jr EJ, Lundblad EG. Premenstrual syndrome: beneficial effects of periodic, low-dose danazol. Obstet Gynecol 1987; 70: 30–6.

53. Derzko CM. Role of danazol in relieving the premenstrual syndrome. J Reprod Med 1990; 35 Suppl.: 99–102.

54. Deeny M, Hawthorne R, Hart DM. Low dose danazol in the treatment of the premenstrual syndrome. Postgrad Med J 1991; 67: 450–4.

55. Halbreich U, Rojansky N, Palter S. Elimination of ovulation and menstrual cyclicity (with danazol) improves dysphoric premenstrual syndromes. Fertil Steril 1991; 56: 1066–9.

56. Magos AL, Brincat M, Studd JWW. Treatment of the premenstrual syndrome by subcutaneous oestradiol implants and cyclical oral norethisterone; placebo-controlled study. BMJ 1986; 292: 1629–33.

57. Watson NR, Studd JWW, Savvas M, et al. Treatment of severe premenstrual syndrome with oestradiol patches and cyclical oral norethisterone. Lancet 1989; 2: 730–2.

58. Moline ML. Pharmacologic strategies for managing premenstrual syndrome. Clin Pharm 1993; 12: 181–96.

59. Smith S, Rinehart JS, Ruddock VE et al. Treatment of premenstrual syndrome with alprazolam: results of a double-blind, placebo-controlled randomized crossover clinical trial. Obstet Gynecol 1987; 70: 37–42.

60. Harrison WM, Endicott J, Nee J. Treatment of premenstrual dysphoria with alprazolam: a controlled study. Arch Gen Psychiatry 1990; 47: 270–5.

61. Schmidt PF, Grover GN, Rubinow DR. Alprazolam in the treatment of premenstrual syndrome. Arch Gen Psychiatry 1993; 50: 467–73.

62. Ayd Jr FJ. Benzodiazepine seizures: an update. Int Drug Ther News 1989; 24: 5–7.

63. Schmidt PJ, Grover GN, Rubinow DR. Alprazolam in the treatment of premenstrual syndrome: a double-blind, placebo-controlled trial. Arch Gen Psychiatry 1993; 50: 467–73.

64. Smith S, Rinehart JS, Ruddock VE et al. Treatment of premenstrual syndrome with alprazolam: results of a double-blind, placebo-controlled randomized crossover clinical trial. Obstet Gynecol 1987; 70: 37–42.

65. David D, Freeman A, Harrington, TM, et al. Buspirone for anxious women in a primary care environment; a multicenter open evaluation. Adv Ther 1987; 4: 251–64.

66. Rickels K, Freeman E, Sondheimer S. Buspirone in treatment of premenstrual syndrome [letter]. Lancet 1989; 1: 777.

67. Harrison WM, Endicott J, Nee J. Treatment of premenstrual depression with nortriptyline: a pilot study. J Clin Psychiatry 1989; 50: 136–9.

68. Severino SK. A focus on 5-hydroxytryptamine (serotonin) and psychopathology. In: Gold JH, Severino SK, editors. Premenstrual dysphorias: myths and realities. Washington, DC; American Psychiatric Press, Inc., 1994: 67–98.

69. Pearlstein TB, Stone AB. Long-term fluoxetine treatment of late luteal phase dysphoric disorder. J Clin Psychiatry 1994; 55(8): 332–5.

70. Daamen MJ, Brown WA. Single-dose fluoxetine in management of premenstrual syndrome. J Clin Psychiatry 1992; 53: 210–1.

71. Werch R, Kane R. Treatment of premenstrual tension with metolazone: a double-blind evaluation of a new diuretic. Curr Ther Res 1976; 19: 565–72.

72. Andersch B, Hahn L, Andersson M, et al. Body water and weight in patients with premenstrual tension. Br J Obstet Gynaecol 1978; 85: 546–50.

73. Rivera-Tovar A, Rhodes R, Pearlstein TB, et al. Treatment efficacy. In: Gold JH, Severino SK, editors. Premenstrual dysphorias: myths and realities. Washington DC: American Psychiatric Press, Inc., 1994: 99–148.

74. Andersen AN, Larsen JF, Steenstrup OR, et al. Effect of bromocriptine on the premenstrual syndrome: a double-blind clinical trial. Br J Obstet Gynaecol 1977; 84: 370–4.

75. Graham JJ, Harding PE, Wise PH, et al. Prolactin suppression in the treatment of premenstrual syndrome. Med J Aust 1978; 2: 18–20.

76. Kullander S, Svanberg L. Bromocriptine treatment of the premenstrual syndrome. Acta Obstet Gynecol Scand 1979; 58: 375–8.

77. Elsner CW, Buster JE, Schindler RA, et al. Bromocriptine in the treatment of premenstrual tension syndrome. Obstet Gynecol 1980; 56: 723–6.

78. Ylostalo P. Cyclical or continuous treatment of the premenstrual syndrome (PMS) with bromocriptine. Euro J Obstet Gynecol Reprod Biol 1984; 17: 337–43.

79. Messinis IE, Lolis D. Treatment of premenstrual mastalgia with tamoxifen. Acta Obstet Gynecol Scand 1988; 67: 307–9.

80. Seachrist L. Animal tests take back seat to clinical data. Science 1994; 264: 1525.

81. Robinson K, Huntington KM, Wallace MG. Treatment of premenstrual syndrome. Br J Obstet Gynecol 1977; 84: 784–8.

82. Barwin BN. The management of premenstrual tension syndrome. Fertil Steril 1980; 34: 187–8.

83. Wurtman J, Brzezinski A, Wurtman RJ et al. Effect of nutrient intake on premenstrual depression. Am J Obstet Gynecol 1989; 161: 1228–34.

84. Rossignol AM, Bonnlander H. Prevalence and severity of the premenstrual syndrome: effects

of foods and beverages that are sweet or high in sugar content. J Reprod Med 1991; 36: 131–6.

85. O'Rourke D, Wurtman JJ, Wurtman RJ, et al. Treatment of seasonal depression with d-fenfluramine. J Clin Psychiatry 1989; 50: 343–7.

86. Brzezinski AA, Wurtman JJ, Wurtman RJ, et al. d-Fenfluramine suppresses the increased calorie and carbohydrate intakes and improves the mood of woman with premenstrual depression. Obstet Gynecol 1990; 76: 296–301.

87. Thys-Jacobs S, Ceccarelli S, Bierman A et al. Calcium supplementation in premenstrual syndrome: a randomized crossover trial. J Gen Intern Med 1989; 4: 183–9.

88. Alvir JMJ, Thys-Jacobs S. Premenstrual and menstrual symptom clusters and response to calcium treatment. Psychopharm Bull 1991; 27: 145–8.

89. Severino SK, Yonkers K. A review of psychotic symptoms associated with the premenstruum. Psychosomatics 1993; 34: 299–306.

NO

Maria Gurevich

RETHINKING THE LABEL: WHO BENEFITS FROM THE PMS CONSTRUCT?

INTRODUCTION

Many important areas of women's health are under-researched and under-funded, and women are strikingly absent from numerous clinical trials and research protocols, even when the health issues and treatment interventions under investigation affect both women and men (Rodin & Ickovics, 1990). A notable exception is the great popularity of the premenstrual syndrome (PMS) as a focus of scientific inquiry. Since Frank first described premenstrual tension (PMT) in 1931, this diagnostic category has generated over 60 years of research. Despite such efforts, work in this area continues to be characterized by a pervasive lack of consensus about the definition, aetiology, and treatment, nor is there agreement regarding the utility of this construct.

Much of both the biological and psychological theorizing about PMS is predicated on the assumption that PMS is a *real* identifiable, biological 'disease'. The message conveyed is sometimes ambiguous, notably when some authors acknowledge the importance of social and cultural influences on women's premenstrual experiences, but continue to give preeminence to biological forces and biologically-based therapeutic interventions (Laws, 1983). Feminist researchers are also frequently thwarted by "their *own* tacit acceptance of the biomedical world view" (Koeske, 1985, p. 2). In this way, although newer definitions and explanatory devices are invoked, the basic construct remains intact.

As Sophie Laws (1983) contends, "to enter a debate about causes would be to accept the ground on which that debate is based, the belief that a treatable medical condition called PMT exists" (p. 29). Similarly, a debate about definition and treatment is founded on the belief in the existence of this "illness."

The present paper is *not* intended to examine the prevailing theories of PMS and the limitations of current research methodologies. Numerous authors have provided very cogent and comprehensive discussions of the limitations of PMS theorizing and research (e.g., Koeske, 1973; McFarlane & Williams,

1990; McFarlane, Martin, & Williams, 1988; Parlee, 1973; 1974; Ruble & Brooks-Gunn, 1979) and the reader is referred to these works for a closer examination of these issues. Rather, this paper provides a review of the feminist theoretical literature on PMS.

Based on this perspective, the aim of this paper is threefold:

1. To point, only briefly, to some of the most problematic aspects of the biomedical research in this area to illustrate that the PMS construct has, at best, limited diagnostic, therapeutic or epistemological utility;

2. To examine the historical, social, political, and economic forces that have led to the development and maintenance of this construct; and finally,

3. To argue that retaining the PMS label is not only likely to be damaging to women medically, socially and politically, but that it may also preclude potentially fruitful scientific inquiry into the normal cyclical fluctuations associated with menstruation.

LIMITATIONS OF PMS RESEARCH

Over 150 symptoms of PMS have been identified (e.g., Moos, 1969; Rubinow & Roy-Byrne, 1984). They vary greatly from study to study, from one woman to another, and even within the same woman, from one cycle to another (Golub, 1988). Typically women experience a combination of symptoms, which are broadly characterized as being either (a) psychological and/or behavioural or (b) somatic (Abplanalp, 1985; O'Brien, 1987). The most frequently cited symptoms, all of which may range from minor bouts to profound incidents, appear in Table 1.

In the absence of reliable diagnostic criteria, a comprehensive universally-agreed-upon definition of PMS cannot and has not been formulated. The definitions of PMS range from very broad and imprecise to overly pedantic (O'Brien, 1987). The more problematic aspects include: frequent failure to consider severity; lack of complete agreement about the precise timing of the symptoms; and failure to specify which symptoms or how many symptoms are needed to be diagnostic.

A prototypical definition was presented in 1983 by the Premenstrual Syndrome Workshop at the Royal College of Obstetricians and Gynaecologists for use in both clinical treatment and for scientific research. To be classified as PMS symptoms, the menstrual changes must be "regularly recurring psychological or somatic symptoms, or both, which occur specifically during the luteal phase of the cycle. The symptoms must be relieved by the onset of, or during, menstruation; there must be a symptom-free week following menstruation" (cited in O'Brien, 1987, p. 6). The symptom-free week is the key feature of this definition, which is intended to distinguish PMS from other gynecological or psychological complaints. Severity of symptoms are not considered within this definition, and all symptoms are given equal weight, irrespective of their origin.

Given the abundance of symptoms and the variability among definitions, it is not surprising that the prevalence rates reflect this lack of consensus and, therefore, vary from 5% to 97% (e.g., Coppen & Kessel, 1963; Moos, 1968; Sutherland & Stewart, 1965; Woods, Most, & Dery, 1982).

Attempts to identify the aetiology of PMS have been equally unsatisfactory;

Table 1

Common PMS Symptoms[*]

Psychological

mood swings
irritability
depression
hostility
anxiety

Behavioural

Increased tendency to engage in conflicts
crying spells
changes in motor coordination
changes in concentration levels
sleep disturbance
alterations in libido
increase/decrease in hunger and thirst

Somatic

abdominal bloating
abdominal cramps
weight gain
water retention
breast tenderness
fatigue
skin changes
headaches
backaches

[*]See the review by Abplanalp (1985) and O'Brien (1987).

"it would appear that no hormone or chemical has escaped implication in the aetiology of PMS" (O'Brien, 1987, p. vii).... The data do not provide consistent support for a single unifying aetiological theory (Golub, 1992).

Treatments proffered for this presumed disease are in excess of 327 (Hamilton, Parry, Alagna, Blumenthal, & Herz, 1984).... Methodoligically sound, double-blind, controlled studies have not demonstrated that such treatments are more beneficial than placebos (Golub, 1992). Exercise is the only technique that has been empirically demonstrated to be effective in alleviating the negative premenstrual symptoms (McFarlane & Williams, 1990).

A significant portion of this conflicting research on PMS has been used by the American Psychiatric Association to support the inclusion of Premenstrual Dysphoric Disorder (PMDD) in the DSM-IV, the most recent edition of the Diagnostic and Statistical Manual of Mental Disorders (Caplan, McCurdy-Myers, & Gans, 1992). PMDD, which was first introduced into the DSM-III-R in 1987 as Late Luteal Phase Dysphoric Disorder, is a psychiatric diagnostic category which essentially refers to a very severe form of PMS. Although PMDD is more stringently defined than PMS, this new diagnostic category is based largely on the PMS research literature. This literature has been extensively criticized by numerous researchers (e.g., Parlee, 1973; Fausto-Sterling, 1985), and many of these criticisms can be leveled against the research on PMDD (Caplan et al., 1992).

EPISTEMOLOGICAL UNDERPINNINGS

PMS does not meet the usual criteria for a disease as the aggregate of specific symptoms and signs, nor is there empirical support for the accumulated list of treatments. The unwavering insistence upon retaining PMS as a disease category in the face of such obvious "methodological chaos" suggests that "shared cultural knowledge," rather than objective facts dictate the scientific inquiry about PMS (M. Rodin, 1992, p. 52). These accumulated cultural beliefs, as they pertain to the conduct of science in particular, include a number of unstated and long-entrenched biases, such as: the presumption that scientific facts and methodologies are objective and value-free; the reliance upon reductionistic and decontextualized investigative approaches; the dominance of and preference for "expert" medical knowledge; and the acceptance of a biologically deterministic and essentialist view of human behaviour (Koeske, 1985).

An analysis of the influence that underlie the popularization and medicalization of the PMS construct (which may eventuate in a shift to alternative ways of conceptualizing the premenstruum) requires a recognition, an explicit articulation and a reevaluation of "the basic assumptions of the biomedical world view" (Koeske, 1985, p. 2). Randi Koeske (1985) provides an excellent critique of these normative foundations of the scientific perspective, which contain "the accumulated common experience of membership in Western culture and modern medicine" (p. 4).

According to Koeske (1985), the preponderance of menstrual cycle research is guided by two types of "taken-for-granted" assumptions—conceptual and methodological—all of which are used in the service of establishing a causal "link between the menstrual cycle... and behavior" (Koeske, 1985, p. 3)....

HISTORICAL AND CULTURAL TRENDS

The development and reification of a 'disease entity' called *the premenstrual syndrome* has elevated the traditional "raging hormones" conceptualization of women to a legitimate scientific status (Ussher, 1989).

Medical Analogues

Several authors have pointed out the striking similarity between the nineteenth-century concept of hysteria and this century's PMS construct (e.g., Lander, 1988; M. Rodin, 1992; Ussher, 1989). The general consensus among physicians at this time was that the uterus was the root of this and all other nervous disorders that were peculiar to women (Ussher, 1989). The preeminence of the womb, the widely-accepted notion that the brain and the reproductive organs were directly linked (Showalter, 1987), and a cultural norm that prescribed motherhood, passivity, and subservience as the only acceptable and natural functions of women, all conveniently supported the diagnosis that hysteria was the inevitable result of women defying their 'natural destiny' (Ussher, 1989). Among the numerous symptoms that typified this 'illness', "sobbing, ... general unhappiness, nervousness, or discontent" (cited in Ussher, 1989, p. 4) were common. Several authors have argued that having a 'hysterical fit' was the only vehicle available to women to express their anger, opposition to and rejection of the socially-prescribed role (Smith-Rosenberg, 1972; Ehrenreich & English, 1979). Thus, hysteria can be seen as a metaphor for women's disavowal of the traditional feminine prototype.

A similar analysis can be applied to the twentieth-century female 'malady'— PMS. Like hysteria, PMS has arisen out of and is maintained by a cultural ideology that dictates that a woman's most natural functions lie in the realm of childbearing and caretaking. Therefore, when women transgress by stepping out of or, worse yet, by completely abandoning their 'natural' sphere of domesticity, they are inevitably subject to psychological disturbances, such as PMS (M. Rodin, 1992).

Despite the obvious similarities between hysteria and PMS—the association between women's reproductive systems and their mental and physical health—there are some differences between the two illness categories. First, as Erin Hewitt (personal communication, August, 1993) has pointed out, hysteria was viewed as being much more incapacitating than PMS is considered to be. Nor was it cyclical in nature—the disease state persisted until an appropriate 'cure' could be found. It is also arguable that the diagnosis of hysteria was more evidently applied as punishment for women's disavowal of their limited role. PMS is not so clearly a punishment for rejecting the traditional feminine role. Rather, the label provides women with a legitimate vehicle for the expression of feelings and behaviours that are not consistent with the accepted 'normal' feminine script. That is, certain aspects of a woman's personality are only deemed acceptable if their manifestation is relegated solely to the premenstrual phase. Nineteenth-century treatments for hysteria, which included clitoridectomies, ovariectomies, seclusion, and immobility (Ussher, 1989), were undoubtedly more extreme and invasive than those offered for PMS. Yet, many of the currently used treatments for PMS, such as lithium, progesterone, and estrogen (Abplanalp, 1985) are also quite invasive and potentially detrimental to women's health.

Neurasthenia, a disease characterized by generalized "nervous exhaustion" of uncertain origins is another nineteenth-century illness that bears close resemblance to today's premenstrual syndrome (King, 1989; Snow & Johnson, 1978). King (1989) has outlined the parallels between neurasthenia and PMS which led both to be classified as medical disorders. These include:

1. A misunderstanding of and misguided cultural beliefs about the normal aspects of menstruation;
2. An absence of known, identifiable causes of the presumed 'disease';
3. An overabundance of symptoms that could easily be indicative of other diseases;
4. No valid and reliable diagnostic criteria;
5. An absence of scientifically substantiated and effective therapeutic techniques;
6. And finally, a diagnosis of neurasthenia or PMS led (and leads) to women's behaviour being "confined by the personal, professional and societal expectation of the diagnosis" (King, 1989, p. 2).

The historical evidence surrounding hysteria and neurasthenia clearly illustrate that the conceptualization (and construction) of disease is powerfully influenced by personal, professional and cultural norms and expectations.

Employment Patterns

Martin (1987) has identified some very revealing historical trends in the menstrual cycle research that coincided with women's participation in the work force. Researchers during the early 1930s (e.g., Billings, 1933; Brush, 1938; McCance, Luff, & Widdowson, 1937; Seward, 1934) who were concerned about premenstrual women's ostensibly diminished abilities as employees were working during the Depression, following World War I, when women were being forced to give up their jobs to men. Martin (1987) has observed that Frank's introduction of the term "Premenstrual Tension" in 1931, was the result of his particular interest in the possible detrimental effects of PMS (then called PMT) on women's capacity to be effective workers. Accordingly, he advised employers about the kinds of provisions and sick leaves they would need to allow for women at these times.

At the start of Word War II, studies documenting *no* deleterious effects of the menstrual cycle on women's work performance were being published (e.g., Altmann, Knowles, & Bull, 1941; Anderson, 1941; Brinton, 1943; Novak, 1941; Percival, 1943); coincidentally, women were also once again required in the work force during this period. An obvious instance of a change in the research agenda was displayed by one researcher (Seward, 1934) who had considered menstruation to be problematic in 1934, but had altered her opinion about the matter completely after World War II had begun. In 1944 she wrote: "Any activity that may be performed with impunity at other times, may be performed with equal impunity during menstruation" (Seward, 1944, p. 95). She contradicted her earlier findings further still by claiming that if women fail to turn up for work due to menstrual difficulties, they are wallowing in "a bit of socially acceptable malingering by taking advantage of the *popular stereotype* of menstrual incapacitation" (Seward, 1944, p. 95) [my emphasis].

The most damning evidence about the disabling influences of PMS emerged following World War II, when men needed the jobs previously held by women. Katharina Dalton was the biggest promoter of the dangers of menstruation (e.g., Dalton & Greene, 1953; this research was begun in the 1940s). She wrote numerous articles throughout the 1950s

which conveyed this message clearly: "The Effect of Menstruation on Schoolgirls' Weekly Work," "Menstruation and Crime," "Menstruation and Accidents," "Menstruation and Acute Psychiatric Illness," "The Influence of Mother's Menstruation on Her Child" (quoted in Tavris, 1992, p. 140).

The mid to late 1970s witnessed the most fervent interest in PMS research. This coincided with the second wave of the feminist movement and the reentry of women into the paid labour force in growing numbers (e.g., Laws, 1985; Lander, 1988) "for the first time without the aid of a major war" (Martin, 1987, p. 120). Martin views this trend in recent history as being indicative of a familiar pattern: "when women's participation in the labor force [is viewed] as a threat," rather than a necessity "menstruation [becomes] a liability" (Martin, 1987, p. 121).

Cultural Specificity

A discussion of the historical parallels surrounding PMS would be incomplete without reference to the culture-specific nature of this phenomenon. T. Johnson (1987) has observed that while premenstrually-specific experiences have been described since the time of Aristotle, the reification of the premenstrual syndrome as a 'disease' can best be understood in the current historical context of Western society. The notion that PMS is a culture-bound phenomenon is supported by evidence that PMS is not a universally embraced concept. One study of tribal societies reported that women in some cultures do not experience any negative menstrual symptoms (Paige & Paige, 1981). A World Health Organization survey of 500 women from ten different countries around the world, found that although women universally report similar physical symptoms associated with menstruation (e.g., cramps, breast tenderness), PMS and its attendant mood fluctuations is a singularly Western phenomenon (Ericksen, 1987). The available statistics also suggest that the incidence of PMS is much higher in the U.S. than in other places (Ramey, 1982). Taken together, these studies point to the importance of culture in the framing of women's premenstrual experiences.

THE POPULARIZATION OF PMS

Louise Lander (1988) has remarked that PMS achieved its greatest prominence in the U.S. in the early eighties, when it became "both a media and a medical marketing event" (p. 90). In 1981, PMS was described as "the newest women's health issue in the United States" by the *Journal of the American Medical Association* (Gonzalez, 1981, p. 1393). American PMS clinics began to dispense progesterone as a treatment, PMS support groups flourished, and newspapers, popular books and pamphlets, women's magazines and television talk shows brought PMS to the public's attention (Lander, 1988; Martin, 1987; see also Chrisler & Levy, 1990; Pugliesi, 1992; & Rittenhouse, 1991, for more extensive discussions of the role of the media in the popularization of PMS).

PMS and the Press

Both the scientific and popular press have played a significant role in widely disseminating information about PMS. A computer search conducted by Carol Tavris (1992) on PMS-related articles in medical and psychological journals revealed that in 1964, only one article on PMS appeared in medical journals and not one in the psychological journals.

In 1974–75, 114 articles were found in medical journals, while the psychological journals contained only 16. By 1984–85, 218 PMS papers were included in medical journals and there were 77 in their psychological counterparts.

An examination of popular women's magazines in the U.S. from 1980 to 1987, relying on the Readers' Guide to Popular Literature and other online data bases, yielded 89 articles which referred extensively to PMS (Pugliesi, 1992). A content analysis of these articles revealed that not only were the symptoms of PMS quite numerous (as many as 67 in some cases), but the focus was predominantly on the more negative and debilitating ones.

Chrisler and Levy (1990) found 81 articles on PMS during the period of 1980–1987 in their search of the Reader's Guide to Periodical Literature. The prevailing tone of these articles was overwhelmingly negative. The titles of these articles reflect an emphasis on the more incapacitating (particularly with respect to emotional states) aspects of the premenstruum: "Premenstrual Frenzy," "Dr. Jekyll and Ms. Hyde," "Once a Month, I'm a Woman Possessed," "How to Beat the Pre-period Uglies," "The Taming of the Shrew Inside You" (Chrisler & Levy, 1990, p. 97). Approximately 20% of the (131 different) symptoms described in these articles have not appeared in the scientific literature on PMS. Although there was disagreement about prevalence rates, just as in the scientific literature, some writers claimed that "most women experience PMS, although they may not know it!" (Chrisler & Levy, 1990, p. 97).

Such compelling journalistic testimonies can be very effective in persuading women that they are afflicted with this latest female malady; particularly, in light of the fact that the majority of the population rely extensively on the media for most of their information about health and illness, thereby making the media a powerful regulator of attitudes and beliefs about these issues (Parlee, 1987; Weston & Ruggiero, 1985). It is also the more unusual stories that are generally reported by the media. Accounts of PMS, similar to all other issues, are documented based on their newsworthiness, which explains the focus on the more negative aspects of the premenstrual phase (Parlee, 1987). The fact that most women function very well while premenstrual is not notable, but "it is news when a woman cannot restrain her violent urges or becomes too depressed to go to work" (Chrisler & Levy, 1990, p. 91).

PMS as a Legal Defense

PMS also gained considerable attention from the general public in 1980 during two much-publicized murder trials in England (Walsh, 1987). The murder charges in both women's cases were reduced to manslaughter "by reason of diminished responsibility due to PMS" (Zita, 1989, p. 188). This event marked the acceptance of the premenstrual syndrome as "a disease of mind" in England's law courts (see Brahams, 1981; Luckhaus, 1985). Shortly thereafter, an American attorney attempted to set a precedent of using PMS as a defense in the case of a 25-year-old mother of six, charged with assault (beating her four-year-old daughter) (Lander, 1988). But the defendant's own words precluded the success of the PMS plea: "My nerves are not that bad that I am just going to beat up on my kid because my period comes down" (quoted in Lander, 1988, p. 95).

THE APPEAL OF PMS FOR WOMEN

There has been some suggesting that the admission of PMS into the medical sphere was largely due to the pressure exerted by women (T. Johnson, 1987). Regardless of the veracity of this speculation, PMS is not merely an externally imposed label —it is also a useful survival device for women.

PMS as an Emotional Valve

Women may (and frequently do) embrace the term PMS because such a framework appears to provide a vehicle for articulating the psychological distress in women's lives (Lander, 1988; Laws, 1985; 1990; Parlee, 1989), albeit in a very circumscribed way. This feature of the PMS lexicon can be advantageous because they render "experiences that were previously ignored, trivialized, or misunderstood" medically and socially real (Tavris, 1992, p. 143). In this way, PMS appears to "offer a way of getting one's troubles listened to; it enables a medical solution to be found which avoids us being labeled as neurotic or inadequate" (Laws, 1985, p. 58). Unfortunately, PMS is also frequently used to dismiss women's legitimate concerns. The underlying message is: " 'Yes, let's talk about how your menstrual cycle affects you, but it'll be your fault if it only turns out to discredit you further' " (Laws, 1990, p. 205, 206). In this way, women's attempts to describe their lives in their own words are thwarted by culturally-imposed beliefs.

PMS as Role Renegotiation

T. Johnson (1987) argues that PMS represents "a 'negotiated reality' between women and society" (McFarlane & Williams, 1990, p. 103) in response to the role strain women experience, created by "conflicting societal expectations that women be both productive and reproductive" (T. Johnson, 1987, quoted in M. Rodin, 1992, p. 55). PMS is a vehicle by which "Western culture translates the ambiguous and conflicted status of woman into a standardized cultural idiom which makes her position 'meaningful' " (T. Johnson, 1987, quoted in M. Rodin, 1992, p. 55). In this way, the PMS concept can be adopted by women "strategically" as "a means of renegotiating roles," specifically household divisions of labor (Pugliesi, 1992, p. 144). Although role negotiation clearly has political overtones, "PMS effectively depoliticizes discourse surrounding issues of roles and obligations" (Pugliesi, 1992, p. 145). This can be beneficial in achieving short-term goals for the individual woman, but contributes little to redressing larger social inequities. T. Johnson (1987) predicts that the incidence of PMS will decrease once the multiplicity of women's roles is adequately resolved.

PMS as Preservation of the Feminine Script

Of the vast array of symptoms that are said to characterize PMS, feelings of *anger, irritability* and a sense of being *out-of-control* appear to be the most frequent and the most problematic for the women themselves (Golub, 1992). This faulty 'emotion management' (Pugliesi, 1993) is highly undesirable because it disrupts the accepted gender-role script (Martin, 1988). Because the overt expression of anger is incompatible with the accepted norm of a 'healthy' feminine personality, PMS has become an acceptable mode of expressing women's distress (Martin, 1988; Laws, 1983; 1990). Similarly, the feeling of losing control can be viewed as "a metaphor for women's common

position of not being in control of their life situation" (Lander, 1988, p. 97), and its explicit manifestation premenstrually serves as a convenient superficial outlet.

By containing her anger, dissatisfaction, and feelings of impotence throughout the month, and deferring their expression to one particular time of the month, women can give voice to their legitimate discontent without disturbing the acceptable image of the "Good Woman" (M. Rodin, 1992), without losing their "feminine allure" (Gottleib, 1988). In fact, women frequently refer to their premenstrual selves as being "possessed" (Martin, 1988), thereby denying the unfavourable parts of themselves. In this way, the artificial dichotomy between the 'Bad Woman' and the 'Good Woman' is retained, and little or no change need be affected to remove the sources of women's distress or to reconceptualize our notions of femaleness.

BENEFICIARIES OF THE PMS MOVEMENT

Economic Considerations

"PMS cures are a thriving business" (Tavris, 1992, p. 137). And the greatest beneficiaries of the PMS movement have been the medical and research establishments, and the pharmaceutical industry. The medical profession has acquired a substantial and compliant patient population. PMS clinics, books, tapes, and seminars are being advocated by all sectors of the medical profession—from nutritionists to nurses, from psychologists to physicians (Lander, 1988; Tavris, 1992). Some PMS Medical Groups are being funded by drug companies, and many pharmaceutical products as well as natural remedies are being promoted, albeit in the absence of sufficient evidence of their efficacy (Tavris, 1992). For instance, Midol, a popular treatment for physical menstrual discomforts, has now developed Midol PMS for premenstrual afflictions. Another product called "premsyn PMS" is comprised of "premenstrual syndrome caplets" which "the sufferer is to 'take at the first signs of PMS.' These products consist of acetaminophen (an aspirin substitute used in Tylenol), pamabrom (a diuretic), and pyrilamine maleate (a common ingredient in all pain relievers)" (Tavris, 1992, p. 137).

Parlee (1987, 1989) has observed that the focus of earlier psychological research on menstruation was on normal menstrual cycles. But increasingly "the big money, the big grants" were awarded to the biomedical researchers, "on the assumption that PMS was a disease or a physiological abnormality that was best studied by radioimmunoassays of gonadal hormones and by other new weapons in the medical arsenal" (Tavris, 1992, p. 141). Drug companies have and continue to actively endorse(d) the trend toward the medicalization of PMS (Parlee, 1989). There is a clear financial benefit to be obtained if menstruating women can be convinced to consume medication every month. Parlee goes on to say that if the small minority of women with premenstrual difficulties are inadvertently lumped together with the majority of women who experience their menstrual cycles as normal and uneventful, this can only be economically advantageous for the drug companies.

The Classification Imperative
The *sine qua non* of medicine is classification and diagnosis. They have succeeded in dividing up various aspects of the menstrual cycle into "discrete sections of varying lengths—before, during and after, and so on, flying in the face of all the evidence to create tidy categories out of what is essentially an untidy process" (Laws, 1983, p. 21). The menstrual cycle, and in particular the premenstrual phase, thus contained and classified becomes more manageable and numerous treatment options can now be advanced.

An obvious instance of this classification imperative is the inclusion of PMDD (Premenstrual Dysphoric Disorder) in the DSM-IV. Part of the controversy surrounding this label is centered around the sex-specific nature of this diagnostic category. Men also experience fluctuations in gonadal hormone levels which affect their psychological and behavioural functioning (Ramey, 1982; Caplan et al., 1992). Yet the APA has developed a psychiatric category for women, while no DSM equivalent exists for men (Caplan et al, 1992). Although cyclicity is neither a disease nor a uniquely female phenomenon, fluctuations in mood and behaviour are treated as abberations to be medically managed when they occur in women, while similar changes in men are not publicly and medically scrutinized (Taylor, 1988; Laws, Hey, & Eagen, 1985). One might wonder: "if LLPDD [now PMDD] is a medical condition, why is a psychiatric diagnosis necessary? Thyroid abnormalities cause mood and behavior changes, but we don't consider these physiologically based changes a psychiatric disorder" (Tavris, 1992, p. 142). Despite the inconclusiveness of the research on PMDD, "nevertheless, there it sits, a convenient label for physicians and psychiatrists to use in diagnosing patients and in turn receiving insurance compensation" (Tavris, 1992, p. 142). The medical community is, thus, well served financially and professionally, albeit possibly to the detriment of women.

REFERENCES

Abplanalp, J. M. (1985). Premenstrual syndrome: A selective review. In S. Golub (Ed.), *Lifting the curse of menstruation; A feminist appraisal of the influence of menstruation on women's lives* (pp. 107–123). New York: Harrington Park Press, Inc.

Altmann, M., Knowles, E., & Bull, H. D. (1941). A psychosomatic study of the sex cycle in women. *Psychosomatic Medicine, 3,* 199–225.

Anderson, M. (1941). Some health aspects of putting women to work in war industries. *Industrial Hygiene Foundation 7th Annual Meeting,* 165–169.

Billings, E. G. (1933). The occurrence of cyclic variations in motor activity in relation to the menstrual cycle in the human female. *Bulletin of Johns Hopkins Hospital, 54,* 440–454.

Brahams, D. (1981). Premenstrual syndrome: A disease of mind. *The Lancet, 2,* 1238–1240.

Brinton, H. P. (1943). Women in industry. In the *National Institutes of Health, Division of Industrial Hygiene, Manual of Industrial Hygiene and Medical Service in War Industries* (pp. 395–419). Philadelphia: W. B. Saunders.

Brush, A. L. (1938). Attitudes, emotional and physical symptoms commonly associated with menstruation in 100 women. *American Journal of Orthopsychiatry, 8,* 286–301.

Caplan, P. J., McCurdy-Myers, J., & Gans, M. (1992). Should 'premenstrual syndrome' be called a psychiatric abnormality? *Feminism and Psychology, 2,* 27–44.

Chrisler, J. C. & Levy, K. B. (1990). The media construct a menstrual monster: A content analysis of PMS articles in the popular press. *Women & Health, 16,* 89–104.

Coppen, A. & Kessel, N. (1963). Menstruation and personality. *British Journal of Psychiatry, 109,* 711–721.

Dalton, K. & Green, R. (1953). The premenstrual syndrome. *British Medical Journal, 1,* 1016–1017.

Ehrenreich, B. & English, D. (1979). *For her own good: 150 years of experts' advice to women.* London: Pluto Press.

Ericksen, K. P. (1987). Menstrual symptoms and menstrual beliefs: National and cross-national patterns. in B. E. Ginsburg & B. F. Carter (Eds.), *Premenstrual syndrome.* New York: Plenum.

Fausto-Sterling, A. (1985). Hormonal hurricanes, menstruation, menopause, and female behavior. In *Myths of Gender: Biological Theories about Women and Men.* New York: Basic Books.

Golub, S. (1988). A developmental perspective. In L. Hartley Gise, N. G. Kase & R. L. Berkowitz (Eds). (1988). *The Premenstrual Syndromes: Contemporary Issues in Obstetrics and Gynecology, Vol. 2* (pp. 7–19). New York: Churchill Livingstone, Inc.

Golub, S. (1992). *Periods: From menarche to menopause.* Newbury Park, CA: Sage Publications, Inc.

Gonzalez, E. (1981, April 10). Premenstrual syndrome: An ancient woe deserving of modern scrutiny. *Journal of the American Medical Association, 245,* 1393–1396.

Gottleib, A. (1988). American premenstrual syndrome: a mute voice. *Anthropology Today, 4,* 10–13.

Hamilton, J. A., Parry, B. L., Alagna, S., Blumenthal, S., & Herz, E. (1984). Premenstrual mood changes: A guide to evaluation and treatment. *Psychiatric Annals, 14,* 426–435.

Johnson, S. R. (1987). The epidemiology and social impact of premenstrual symptoms. *Clinical Obstetrics and Gynecology, 30,* 367–376.

Johnson, T. M. (1987). Premenstrual syndrome as a western culture-specific disorder. *Culture, Medicine and Psychiatry, 11,* 337–356.

King, C. R. (1989). Parallels between neurasthenia and premenstrual syndrome. *Women & Health, 15,* 1–23.

Koeske, R. D. (1973). Physiological, social, and situational factors in the premenstrual syndrome. Unpublished MS.

Koeske, R. D. (1985). Lifting the curse of menstruation: Toward a feminist perspective on the menstrual cycle. In S. Golub (Ed.), *Lifting the curse of menstruation: A feminist appraisal of the influence of menstruation on women's lives* (pp. 1–16). New York: Harrington Park Press, Inc.

Lander, L. (1988). *Images of bleeding: Menstruation as ideology.* New York: Orlando Press.

Laws, S. (1983). The sexual politics of pre-menstrual tension. *Women's Studies International Forum, 6,* 19–31.

Laws, S. (1985). Who needs PMT?: A feminist approach to the politics of premenstrual tension. In S. Laws, V. Hey, & A. Eagen (Eds), *Seeing red: The politics of premenstrual tension.* London: Hutchinson & Co.

Laws, S. (1990). *Issues of blood: The politics of menstruation.* London; Macmillan Press, Ltd.

Laws, S., Hey, V., & Eagen, A. (Eds.). (1985). *Seeing red: The politics of premenstrual tension.* London: Hutchinson & Co.

Luckhaus, L. (1985). A plea for PMT in the criminal law. In S. Edwards (Ed.), *Gender, sex, and the law.* Great Britain: Croom Helm Ltd.

Martin, E. (1987). *The woman in the body: A cultural analysis of reproduction.* Boston: Beacon Press.

Martin, E. (1988). Premenstrual syndrome: Discipline, work, and anger in late industrial societies. In T. Buckley & A. Gottlieb (Eds.), *Blood magic: The anthropology of menstruation* (pp. 161–181). Berkeley and Los Angeles, CA: University of California Press.

McCance, R. A., Luff, M. C., & Widdowson, E. E. (1937). Physical and emotional periodicity in women. *Journal of Hygiene, 37,* 571–605.

McFarlane, J., Martin, C. L., & Williams, T. M. (1988). Mood fluctuations: Women versus men and the menstrual versus other cycles. *Psychology of Women Quarterly, 12,* 201–223.

McFarlane, J. & Williams. T. M. (1990). The enigma of the premenstrual syndrome. *Canadian Psychology, 31,* 95–108.

Moos, R. H. (1968). The development of a menstruation distress questionnaire. *Psychosomatic Medicine, 30,* 853–867.

Moos, R. H. (1969). A typology of menstrual cycle symptoms. *American Journal of Obstetrics and Gynecology, 103,* 390–402.

Novak, E. (1941). Gynecologic problems of adolescence. *Journal of the American Medical Association, 117,* 1950–1953.

O'Brien, P. M. S. (1987). *Premenstrual syndrome.* Oxford: Blackwell Scientific Publications.

Paige, K. & Paige, J. (1981). *Politics and reproduction rituals.* Berkeley; University of California Press.

Parlee, M. B. (1973). The premenstrual syndrome. *Psychological Bulletin, 80,* 454–465.

Parlee, M. B. (1974). Stereotypic beliefs about menstruation: A methodological note on the MDQ and some new data. *Psychosomatic Medicine, 36,* 229–240.

Parlee, M. B. (1987). Media treatment of premenstrual syndrome. In B. E. Ginsburg & B. F. Carter (Eds), *Premenstrual Syndrome: Ethical and Legal Implications in a Biomedical Perspective* (pp. 189–205). New York: Plenum.

Parlee, M. B. (1989). The science and politics of PMS research. Invite address presented at the annual meeting of the Association for Women in Psychology. Newport, RI.

Percival, E. (1943). Menstrual disturbances as they may affect women in industry. *The Canadian Nurse, 39,* 335–337.

Pugliesi, K. (1992). Premenstrual syndrome: The medicalization of emotion related to conflict and chronic role strain. *Humboldt Journal of Social Relations, 18,* 131–165.

Pugliesi, K. (1993). Premenstrual syndrome: A sociological perspective. Paper presented at the Society for Menstrual Cycle Research conference, Boston, MA.

Ramey, E. (1982). The endocrinologist's approach. In C. Debrovner (Ed.), *Premenstrual tension—A multidisciplinary approach* (pp. 33–45). New York: Human Sciences Press.

Rittenhouse, C. A. (1991). The emergence of premenstrual syndrome as a social problem. *Social Problems, 38,* 412–425.

Rodin, J. & Ickovics, J. R. (1990). Women's health: Review and research agenda as we approach the twenty-first century. *American Psychologist, 45,* 1018–1034.

Rodin, M. (1992). The social construction of premenstrual syndrome. *Social Science and Medicine, 35,* 49–56.

Rubinow, D. R. & Roy-Byrne, P. (1984). Premenstrual syndromes: Overview from a methodological perspective. *American Journal of Psychiatry, 141,* 163–172.

Ruble, D. N. & Brooks-Gunn, J. (1979). Menstrual symptoms: A social cognition analysis. *Journal of Behavioral Medicine, 2,* 171–193.

Seward, G. H. (1934). The female sex rhythm. *Psychological Bulletin, 31,* 153–192.

Showalter, E. (1987). *The female malady: Women, madness, and English culture, 1830–1980.* London: Virago.

Smith-Rosenberg, C. (1972). The hysterical woman: Sex roles in nineteenth-century America. *Social Research, 39,* 652–678.

Snow, L. F. & Johnson, S. M. (1978). Myths about menstruation: Victims of our own folklore. *International Journal of Women's Studies, 1,* 63–72.

Sutherland, H. & Stewart, I. (1965). A critical analysis of the premenstrual syndrome. *Lancet, 1,* 1180–1183.

Tavris, C. (1992). *The Mismeasure of Woman.* New York: Simon & Schuster.

Taylor, D. (1988). *Red flower: Rethinking menstruation.* Freedom, CA: The Crossing Press.

Ussher, J. (1989). *The psychology of the female body.* London: Routledge.

Walsh, M. R. (Ed.) (1987). *The psychology of women: Ongoing debates.* New Haven, CT: Yale University Press.

Weston, L. C. & Ruggiero, J. A. (1985). The popular approach to women's health issues: A content analysis of women's magazines in the 1970's. *Women & Health, 10,* 47–74.

Woods, N. F., Most, A., & Dery, G. K. (1982). Prevalence of perimenstrual symptoms. *American Journal of Public Health, 72,* 1257–1264.

Zita, J. N. (1989). The premenstrual syndrome: "Diseasing" the female cycle. In N. Tuana (Ed.), *Feminism and science* (pp. 188–210). Bloomington: Indiana University Press.

POSTSCRIPT

Is Premenstrual Syndrome a Clear Medical Condition?

In 1863 Dr. Isaac Ray made the following statement: "With women it is but a step from extreme nervous susceptibility to downright hysteria, and from that to overt insanity. In the sexual evolution, in pregnancy, in the parturient, extraordinary feeling, criminal impulses, may haunt a mind at other times pure and innocent." See *Mental Hygiene* (Hafner Publishing, 1968). A paper by R. T. Frank, "The Hormonal Causes of Premenstrual Tension," *Archives of Neurology and Psychiatry* (1931), is usually credited with being the first modern account of PMS.

Those who argue that PMS exists believe that as many as 40–60 percent of women suffer from the symptoms. Five to 10 percent of women find symptoms incapacitating and see a need for them to be treated medically. Mangos et al., in "Effects of Subcutaneous Implants on Ovarian Activity," *British Journal of Obstetrics and Gynecology* (1987), found that estradiol (estrogen) implants were a most effective treatment for PMS, with patients showing significant improvements compared to those administered a placebo. Smith and Studd, in the chapter entitled "Estrogens and Depression in Women" from *Treatment of Postmenopausal Women* (Raven Press, 1994), claim that none of the published double-blind, placebo-controlled studies have shown progesterone to outperform a placebo, and they contend that "the continuing widespread use of progesterone for treatment of PMS is a therapeutic aberration which is hard to understand. It is the 20th century equivalent of bleeding for anemia." Also see "Premenstrual Syndrome: A Disease of Mind," *The Lancet* (vol. 2, 1981); "Hormones and Depression: What Are the Facts About Premenstrual Syndrome, Menopause, and Hormone Replacement Therapy?" *American Journal of Obstetrics and Gynecology* (August 1995); and "Altered Serotonergic Activity in Women With Dysphoric Premenstrual Syndromes," *International Journal of Psychiatry in Medicine* (vol. 23, no. 1, 1993).

Sophie Laws, in the chapter entitled "Who Needs PMT?" from *Seeing Red: The Politics of Premenstrual Tension* (Hutchinson, 1985), agrees with Gurevich about the political dangers of understanding cyclical changes in women's bodies in terms of an illness. As a dramatic example, she points to cases where marital counseling was postponed until the woman had moved out of the premenstrual phase so that she could be taken seriously. Throughout history, according to Laws, women's thoughts and feelings have been reduced to "something wrong with their reproductive organs." Changes constitute part of a woman's being; they are not signs of sickness. A woman's life should not be characterized as phases of normality interrupted by times of illness, asserts Laws.

Critics of the PMS construct suggest that claims to knowledge about women's psychology/biology are structured according to the power and interest of the dominant social grouping—exclusionist men whose goal is to protect their privileged status. When scientific findings are broadcast, individuals can become so familiar with them that when these individuals are studied, they can do nothing but reflect the earlier findings, which they have incorporated as true. Critics say that contemporary versions of psychiatry suggest women are vulnerable, illogical, and intellectually impaired prior to menstruation but that this is not supported in the research. See also "The Selling of Premenstrual Syndrome: Who Benefits from Making PMS 'The Disease of the 80's'?" *Ms.* (October 1983); "The Media Constructed a Menstrual Monster: A Content Analysis of PMS Articles in the Popular Press," *Women and Health* (vol. 16, 1990); A. Fausto-Sterling, *Myths of Gender: Biological Theories About Women and Men* (Basic Books, 1985); and R. D. Koeske, "Premenstrual Emotionality: Is Biology Destiny?" in Mary Roth Walsh, ed., *The Psychology of Women: Ongoing Debates* (Yale University Press, 1987).

ISSUE 17

Do Women Suffer from Post-Abortion Syndrome?

YES: Celeste McGovern, from "Hag-Ridden by Post-Abortion Guilt," *Alberta Report/Western Report* (October 4, 1993)

NO: Joyce Arthur, from "Psychological Aftereffects of Abortion: The Rest of the Story," *The Humanist* (March/April 1997)

ISSUE SUMMARY

YES: Freelance reporter Celeste McGovern states that induced abortion is often psychologically harmful and that post-abortion symptoms include feelings of guilt, regret, and remorse, and suicidal thoughts.

NO: Technical writer Joyce Arthur asserts that there is a consensus in the medical and scientific communities that most women who elect to have an abortion experience little or no psychological harm.

The concept of "post-abortion syndrome" has become a controversial issue between the pro-choice left and the pro-life, or antiabortion, right. If the antiabortion groups could prove that a damaging syndrome affects a majority of women who have undergone elective abortion, they might gain some ground in their political efforts to overturn *Roe v. Wade* (1973), the Supreme Court case that made abortion safe and legal in the United States. Pro-choice groups, in contrast, can further their cause by uncovering facts that signify the absence of any type of severe and pervasive post-abortion syndrome. For purposes of this debate, we will be dealing only with elective abortion (and ignoring the emotional consequences of spontaneous abortion).

To be diagnosed with post-abortion syndrome a woman must have two positive indications. The first is that she has undergone an elective abortion that she later perceives to have been a "traumatic event." The second is the presence of a cluster of symptoms that reflect those typically seen in individuals diagnosed with post-traumatic stress disorder (PTSD). Symptoms of PTSD include emotional numbing, dissociative defenses, flashbacks, denial, fantasy, nightmares, intrusive thoughts, substance abuse, oversleeping, fear of punishment, and self-destructive acts, including promiscuity (among others).

With regard to the subsequent perception of abortion as a traumatic event, it is helpful to delineate criteria used by the *Diagnostic and Statistical Manual of Mental Disorders* (*DSM-IV*) for definition. To be considered as having experienced a traumatic life event, a person must exhibit one or both of the following in relation to that event. First, the person must have experienced, witnessed, or have been confronted with an event or events that involved actual or threatened death or serious injury, or a threat to the physical integrity of self or others. Second, the person's response must have involved fear, helplessness, or horror. If a woman meets one or both of these criteria in connection with her attitude toward her abortion and suffers from a range of the symptoms of PTSD, she may be experiencing a form of post-abortion syndrome.

Currently, there are no national data sets that provide information on incidence and prevalence of post-abortion syndrome. Absence of conclusive information exacerbates the controversy. There are, however, a variety of academic studies on the topic, studies with widely disparate levels of methodological rigor. General findings suggest that about 20 percent of women suffer some type of post-abortion emotional discomfort, but the intensity, nature, and pervasiveness of the problems appear to be at the heart of the controversy. There are, of course, a variety of confounding variables that might influence the mental status of the post-abortive woman, including length of pregnancy, feelings of coercion, the state of emotional and mental development of the female, and perceived external stressors. Obviously, how well a woman recovers after an abortion is related to her overall understanding of the experience.

Many experts believe that the medical and scientific communities have come to a consensus within the last decade and that most women who have an abortion experience little or no psychological harm. Still, the woman's ability to cope continues to be a subject of heated debate, and pro-life advocates continue to argue for the presence of post-abortion syndrome as a common phenomenon. In the following selections, Celeste McGovern contends that there is a prevalence of post-abortion syndrome, while Joyce Arthur argues that most women come through the experience unscathed.

YES

Celeste McGovern

HAG-RIDDEN BY POST-ABORTION GUILT

Pro-life activists have been making steady gains in the abortion debate by pointing to the widespread phenomenon of post-abortion guilt, a guilt so severe that it has been known to drive women insane. Now the pro-choice side is fighting back. [In September 1993], the *Globe* and *Mail* ran a front-page story headlined "Guilt over abortion is rare." It was based on personal interviews by Paul Sachdev, a militant pro-choice professor of social work at Memorial University in St. John's Newfoundland. However, a close look at the research Prof. Sachdev published in his new book *Sex, Abortion and Unmarried Women* might lead less partisan readers to a very different conclusion.

Dedicated by Prof. Sachdev to the pioneers of abortion on demand, "so that every child is a wanted child," the book recounts, in fragments, the experiences of 70 Ontario women.

"I am extremely depressed and emotionally upset," one young woman told Prof. Sachdev. "I am sad and on the verge of tears right now because of having the abortion. I don't feel unhappy for ending a life. I don't condemn myself. I know I can start another life if I want to; I can go sleep with my boyfriend right now and get pregnant again. I'm sad that the whole thing had to have happened and that George had to go through with this. I still feel depressed and cry a lot, not for having an abortion, but for having to have one..." Prof. Sachdev's diagnosis: "Her depression was not related to the act that she had her pregnancy terminated." Turning to his table entitled "Degree of Guilt or Depressive Reactions as Reported by Seventy Women," Prof. Sachdev marked the young woman under the subtitle "None."

Prof. Sachdev insists his sample was "randomly selected," but his book suggests otherwise. "A list containing the names of 114 women who met the study criteria was drawn up from the records of three hospitals and one [abortion] referral and counselling agency." Fourteen of those women were personally introduced to the professor by a social worker, head nurse or abortionist. The women on the list were all between ages 18 and 25, white, unmarried, pregnant for the first time when they aborted, and had first-trimester D&E (suction) abortions in a hospital between six months and one year earlier. This allowed for a homogenous sample, explains Prof. Sachdev,

From Celeste McGovern, "Hag-Ridden by Post-Abortion Guilt," *Alberta Report/Western Report*, vol. 20 (October 4, 1993). Copyright © 1993 by United Western Communications Ltd. Reprinted by permission of *Alberta Report/Western Report*.

although he concedes that adolescents were excluded from the study because "as a group, compared to adult women, [they] are more likely to have psychological distress," as are women having repeat abortions or later abortions.

Of the 114 women, 24 could not be traced. Eleven refused to participate because "they feared the interview would stir up painful memories." Two women had recently married and "their husbands would not let them discuss their past." Three lived too far away.

Contacted by telephone, the 70 women who agreed to meet Prof. Sachdev were asked to check off symptoms on cue cards describing their guilt or depression.

How many women in the sample reported they felt depressed or guilty? "I don't know," replies Dr. Sachdev. "I can't remember. That was not the purpose of my study," he explains. "I was only looking for how many seemed depressed or guilty from the abortion experience." Raw data was not published in the book.

Based on their remarks, Dr. Sachdev says he decided if they were suffering severe, moderate, mild or no reaction from the abortion. Thirty percent, like the woman on the verge of tears, he concluded, had no reaction to the abortion. One half felt "mild" reactions, 10% experienced "moderate" guilt and depression and the final 10% were categorized as "severe" reactors.

The following testimony from a 24-year-old, was given to describe a typical "mild" abortion reaction: "I felt a bit guilty for about two months for doing this to something living, but I don't feel anymore. I have dreamt a few times after the abortion. I saw that I have a child with me and was just playing with it and then the child just disappeared. Then something would happen to me.

Somebody was always trying to kill me. I had this dream quite often."

A 23-year-old teacher, classified as having a "moderate" guilt reaction had this to say to the professor: "I still regret the fact that I had to do this sort of thing. The thought of abortion, I think, will always bother me. Before I felt these feelings more often than I do now. I'm trying to forget about it, but it's still there.

"[Four days after the abortion] I went to the washroom and there was a fetus, and I thoroughly examined it. I held it on a piece of Kleenex. I kept saying to myself, 'Don't do that, you are hurting it,' even though it was dead already [R's voice choked]. I started thinking that it could have been a person; it could have possibly been loved by somebody else who could have taken care of it. I thought as if it was almost still alive. That really shocked me.

"For about a week I had it wrapped up in that Kleenex and in the cabinet underneath the sink. I couldn't bring myself to throw it in the garbage or do anything like that. And then every time I came into the washroom I knew it would be in there and I wouldn't dare open the door of the cabinet.

"After about a week I worked up enough nerve to take another look at it. But by this time it was all sticking to the Kleenex and I just didn't want to start tearing it apart. So I ended up putting it in the garbage. It sounds so horrible saying it that way. It really affected me."

The young woman was not actually seeing a fetus, insists Prof. Sachdev, but only thought she was. What she saw was endometrial tissue, he presumes. Hallucinations of this sort, he adds hastily, do not suggest mental instability; they are rather "typical conditioned responses of women who have seen pictures of unborn fetuses."

"Any woman who has seen that film by Bernard Nathanson [*The Silent Scream*, an ultrasound depiction of the actual killing of a fetus] will be severely traumatized," says Prof. Sachdev. Women who have seen pictures of fetuses in biology textbooks or pro-life literature, or ultrasound photos of developing babies are also at "serious risk" of psychological reaction, he adds. Why? "It looks like a baby to them. Maybe it's sucking its thumb or something. These women can't tell the difference."

Prof. Sachdev emphatically objects to women being given any information about prenatal development before abortions. "I know some people argue that a woman should make a decision based on everything available, that she should make an informed choice," he ruminates. "But scientists have been given these pictures and they can't decide where life begins. The Supreme Court of Canada cannot even decide unanimously based on these pictures. Why show them to women when it will just upset them?"

"It is an extremely patronizing point of view he's taking," scoffs June Scandiffio, president of Toronto Right To Life. She thinks Prof. Sachdev is trivializing the intense guilt and depression that many women experience after abortion. "Any woman who does feel guilty is being made to think she's aberrant."

"There's no room at the psychological inn for these people," agrees Vincent Rue, psychologist at Portsmouth, New Hampshire's Institute for Pregnancy Loss. Dr. Rue has worked in concert with Vancouver psychiatrist Philip Ney, an international expert in the now medically recognized Post Abortion Syndrome field. He has written that induced abortion is more often psychologically harmful than helpful to women.

Similarly, a 1987 study of 262 post-abortion women by David Reardon found 61% had flashbacks of their abortion, 33% imagined suicide, and 49% had since started using or increased using drugs. A 1993 Akron Pregnancy Service study of 344 post-abortive women found 66% felt guilty, 22% had nightmares, 38% had lowered self-esteem, 46% were unable to forgive themselves, 27% felt despair, 54% experienced regret and remorse and 16% had suicidal impulses. Curiously, although Prof. Sachdev claims to have based his research on "every North American post-abortion study," these researchers' names weren't listed in his bibliography.

Dr. Sachdev says: "To anyone who suggests that I am injecting my own bias into this study I tell you that when I began it [in 1990] I was leaning to the pro-life point of view." (As it happens, however, he did write a pro-choice *International Handbook On Abortion* in 1988.)

Prof. Sachdev's study states that 81.5% of the women sampled "had completely or considerably adjusted six months to one year following the abortion." But he also states that more than half (55%) of the women were suppressing memories (keeping themselves excessively busy and forcing themselves never to think about it). A further 20.4% of the women were rationalizing their abortions ("thinking that it was 'for the sake of the child or the parents or the career or preserving the partnership with the male.'") Another 24.5% "intellectualized" the abortion impact, reports Prof. Sachdev. That is, "they could only talk about it in analytical terms and would not associate any feelings with it." A full

100% were using these "defense coping mechanisms" with varying success.

Pro-choice psychiatrist Keith Pearce, former chairman of the Calgary Foothills Hospital Abortion Committee, disagrees. "Those three defense mechanisms are what are known as primitive defense mechanisms," he says. "They're the sort of thing we use if we're told we have cancer and we're going to die. They're good protection in the short term, but not in the long term."

"You have to let feelings surface to cope with them," says Beverly Daw. Much energy is consumed in deliberately not thinking about something. She had an abortion when she was 16. "I went for years, not knowing why I was depressed, why I was suicidal," she explains. "I went to a psychiatrist who told me it had nothing to do with my abortion." It took her 11 years to realize that "the underlying root of the problem was that I killed my baby." After spending six years counselling "hundreds" of women who called or visited her Ottawa hotline for women in post-abortion distress, Mrs. Daw retired to raise her two children. "Aborted women desperately need inner healing," she says. "As long as we're not allowed to recognize the source of our grief, and to grieve, we won't get it."

NO

Joyce Arthur

PSYCHOLOGICAL AFTEREFFECTS OF ABORTION: THE REST OF THE STORY

Over the last decade, a consensus has been reached in the medical and scientific communities that most women who have an abortion experience little or no psychological harm. Yet, a woman's ability to cope psychologically after an abortion continues to be the subject of heated debates. Vocal anti-abortion advocates claim that most women who have abortions will suffer to some degree from a variant of post-traumatic-stress disorder called *post-abortion syndrome*, characterized by severe and long-lasting guilt, depression, rage, and social and sexual dysfunction. Why is there such a major discrepancy between the scientific consensus and anti-abortion beliefs?

Conflicting studies done over the last thirty years have contributed to this atmosphere of confusion and misinformation. A 1989 review article that evaluated the methodology of seventy-six studies on the psychological aftereffects of abortion noted that both opponents and advocates of abortion could easily prove their case by picking and choosing from a wide range of contradictory evidence. For example, many studies—especially those done between 1950 and 1975—purport to have found significant negative psychological responses to abortion. Such studies, though, often suffer from serious methodological flaws. Some were done when abortion was still illegal or highly restricted, thereby biasing the conclusions in favor of considerable (and understandable) psychological distress. In some cases, research was based on women who were forced to prove a psychiatric disorder in order to obtain the abortion. Further, a large number of studies, both early and recent, consist simply of anecdotal reports of a few women who sought psychiatric help after their abortion. In short, many studies which favor anti-abortion beliefs are flawed because of very small samples, unrepresentative samples, poor data analysis, lack of control groups, and unreliable or invalid research questions.

Researcher bias on the part of scientists and physicians has also been a serious problem. In earlier times, society's views on how women "should" feel after an abortion were heavily skewed toward the traditional model of women as nurturing mothers. In one study done in 1973, postdoctoral psychology students taking psychoanalytic training predicted psychological effects far more

From Joyce Arthur, "Psychological Aftereffects of Abortion: The Rest of the Story," *The Humanist* (March/April 1997). Copyright © 1997 by Joyce Arthur. Reprinted by permission.

severe than those predicted by women themselves before undergoing an abortion. This might be because traditional Freudian theory teaches that a desire to avoid childbearing represents a woman's denial of her basic feminine nature.

Some psychiatric studies, along with much of today's anti-abortion literature, tend to cast women who have abortions into one of two roles: victim or deviant (although these terms are not necessarily used). Victims are coerced into abortion by others around them, in spite of their confusion and ambivalence, and against their basic maternal instincts. Deviants have little difficulty with the abortion decision, which is made casually for convenience sake. Such women have no maternal instinct and are often characterized in a derogatory or pitying fashion as selfish, callous, unfeminine, emotionally stunted, and neurotic.

Books written by anti-abortion advocates that deal with post-abortion effects are, by and large, heavily infected with bias. Not only is contrary evidence unrefuted, it is rarely even mentioned. Incorrect and out-of-date "facts" abound. The authors' pop psychology often seems to be based on little more than their own wishful projections about the nature of women and how they should feel. Here are two typical examples from essays in the anti-abortion book The *Psychological Aspects of Abortion* (1977):

> It is interesting that women who need self-punishment do not abort themselves more often.... Abortion is done "to" the woman, with her as only a passive participant. This is further indication of masochism.

—(Howard W. Fisher, "Abortion: Pain or Pleasure")

... sooner or later [after the abortion], the truth will make itself known and felt, and the bitter realization that she was not even unselfish enough to share her life with another human being will take its toll. If she had ever entertained a doubt as to whether her parents and others really considered her unlovable and worthless, she will now be certain that she was indeed never any good in their eyes or her own. A deep depression will be inevitable and her preoccupation with thoughts of suicide that much greater.

—(Conrad W. Baars, "Psychic Causes and Consequences of the Abortion Mentality")

With the advent of safe, legal, routinely performed abortions, a wealth of good evidence has come to light that is quite contrary to common anti-abortion assertions. The typical abortion patient is a normal, mentally stable woman who makes a strongly resolved decision for abortion within a few days after discovery of the pregnancy and comes through the procedure virtually unscathed. Several scientific review articles—published from 1990 to 1992 in highly respected journals such as *Science* and *American Journal of Psychiatry*—support this conclusion. The reviews evaluated hundreds of studies done over the last thirty years, noting the unusually high number of seriously flawed studies and pointing out common methodological problems. Based upon the more reliable studies, all the reviews concluded that, although psychological disturbances do occur after abortion, they are uncommon and generally mild and short-lived. In many cases, these disturbances are simply a continuation of negative feelings caused by the pregnancy itself. Serious or persistant problems are rare and are frequently related to the circumstances surrounding the abortion rather than the abortion itself.

Further, many women who were denied an abortion showed ongoing, long-term resentment, and their resulting children were more likely to have increased emotional, psychological, and social problems in comparison with control groups of wanted children. These differences between children widened throughout adolescence and early adulthood. Finally, many studies show that giving birth is much more likely than abortion to be associated with severe emotional aftereffects, such as postpartum depression.

The review articles largely concluded that the most frequently reported emotions felt by women immediately following an abortion (experienced by about 75 percent of women) are relief or happiness. Feelings of regret, anxiety, guilt, depression, and other negative emotions are reported by about 5 percent to 30 percent of women. These feelings are usually mild and fade rapidly, within a few weeks. Months or years after an abortion, the majority of women do not regret their decision. In fact, for many women, abortion appears to improve their self-esteem, provide inner strength, and motivate them to refocus their lives in a meaningful way.

Studies on abortion are done primarily through self-report measures, however, and it is possible that some women may be reluctant to admit negative feelings after their abortion. To help quantify this, consider these figures: every year since 1977, 1.3 million to 1.6 million abortions are performed in the United States; about 21 percent of all American women between the ages of fifteen and forty-four have had an abortion.

These are very large numbers indeed. The American Psychological Association has pointed out that, even if only 10 percent of the millions of women who have had abortions experienced problems, there would be a significant mental health epidemic, clearly evident by large numbers of dysfunctional women requesting help. There is no evidence of any such epidemic, thereby supporting the general reliability of self-report measures.

Some women who are disturbed or unhappy with their abortion decision belong to support groups like Women Exploited by Abortion and Victims of Choice. Several anti-abortion studies and books purporting to demonstrate the overall harmfulness of abortion limit their samples to the membership of such groups. Not only does this introduce an immediate and fatal flaw to their argument, it shows deliberate obfuscation on the part of the authors. This does not mean, however, that post-abortion support groups are valueless to women. The very existence of such groups points to the strong need for health professionals to identify and provide extra help to women who are most at risk for developing psychological problems related to abortion. Many studies have shown that women at greater risk tend to include:

- emotionally immature teenagers
- women with previous psychiatric problems
- women aborting a wanted pregnancy for medical or genetic reasons
- women who encounter opposition from their partner or parents for their abortion decision
- women who have strong philosophical or religious objection to abortion

- women who are highly ambivalent or confused about their abortion decision and had great difficulty making it

- women who are coerced by others into having an abortion

- women undergoing second-trimester abortions

In spite of psychological problems suffered by a few women after abortion, the existence of post-abortion syndrome is doubted by most experts. There is little need to posit a unique disorder in this case, since abortion is not significantly different from any other stressful life experience that might cause trauma in certain people. Former Surgeon General C. Everett Koop, himself anti-abortion, noted this in 1988. Unfortunately, facts, evidence, and common sense rarely get in the way of anti-abortion advocates who are determined to prove that women suffer terribly from post-abortion syndrome. Certainly, if this syndrome were real it would be a lethal weapon in the fight to reverse *Roe* v. *Wade.* This was, in fact, the motivation behind a 1989 surgeon general's report on the health effects of abortion on women, which was called for by former President Ronald Reagan on behalf of anti-abortion leaders. Although the report was duly prepared, the surgeon general chose not to release it, apparently because it did not support the anti-abortion position. Meanwhile, anti-abortion literature continues to churn out the myth that women are severely harmed by abortion.

Because abortion is such a volatile issue, it is probably unrealistic to expect this aspect of the controversy to die down soon, if at all. However, by recognizing that a small subset of women may require increased counseling and support during their abortion decision and afterward, the women's community and health professionals can do much to minimize the damage wrought by the anti-abortion movement's dangerous and irresponsible campaign of misinformation.

POSTSCRIPT

Do Women Suffer from Post-Abortion Syndrome?

It is interesting to note that the author of each selection believes that research findings that do not support her view are methodologically flawed. For example, Arthur notes that studies conducted between 1950 and 1975—studies that are most likely to confirm the presence of post-abortion syndrome in larger numbers of women—coincide with a time when elective abortion was illegal in the United States. Naturally, the added challenges of defying the system in order to obtain an illegal abortion and the feelings brought about by such circumstances may confound research findings. Why would obtaining an illegal abortion be more traumatic than obtaining a legal one? McGovern faults studies for failing to compare post-abortion women with women who carried unwanted pregnancies to term. Why would she view this as problematic?

Candice DePuy and Dana Dovitch believe that post-abortion syndrome is enough of a problem that they have written a book to assist women in coming to terms with it. See *The Healing Choice: Your Guide to Emotional Recovery After Abortion* (Simon & Schuster, 1997). For a personal account of the negative emotional aftereffects of abortion experienced by a Catholic woman, see "Giving Up the Gift: One Woman's Post Abortion Decision," *Commonweal* (February 25, 1994). Yvette R. Harris writes about adolescent abortion in "Adolescent Abortion," *Society* (July/August 1997) and asserts that this group is uniquely vulnerable to post-abortion syndrome. In "Late Psychological Sequelae of Abortion," *Journal of Family Practice* (October 1996), cases are presented of two women who had negative effects at 5 and 19 years after their abortions.

Many recent quantitative articles support Arthur's viewpoint. For example, a Danish study of late-term abortion found that of 15 women, none expressed regret after the fact. See "Induced Abortion After the Twelfth Week of Pregnancy in the County of Ahrus, 1993–1994," *Ugeskrift for Laeger* (July 1996). A British study compared women who aborted with women who went to term voluntarily and with women who were denied abortion. It found that rates of psychiatric disorder were no higher after termination of pregnancy than after childbirth. See "Termination of Pregnancy and Psychiatric Morbidity," *British Journal of Psychiatry* (vol. 167, no. 2, 1995). A Scandinavian study found that both medical and vacuum aspiration abortion were psychologically safe and that abortion was associated with a high incidence of psychological benefit. See "Psychological Responses Following Medical Abortion," *Acta Obstretricia et Gynecologica Scandinavica* (vol. 73, no. 10, 1994). It has been reported that women who are currently affiliated with conservative churches, who had lower degrees of reported social support, and/or had lower confidence in their abortion decision were more likely to experience negative post-abortion symptoms than were those who had made firm decisions, are not associated with conservative churches, and/or who had higher perceived levels of social support. See "Post-Abortion Perceptions: A Comparison of Self-Identified Distressed and Non-Distressed Populations," *International Journal of Social Psychiatry* (vol. 39, no. 4, 1993). In Israel, evaluations of women both pre- and post-abortion showed that stress levels were lower after the abortion, although stress levels prior to abortion were higher than those experienced by a comparable population of women on the verge of delivery. See "Emotional Distress in a Group of Israeli Women Before and After Abortion," *American Journal of Orthopsychiatry* (vol. 63, no. 2, 1993).

ISSUE 18

Are Silicone Breast Implants Dangerous for Women?

YES: Lynette J. Dumble, from "Dismissing the Evidence: The Medical Response to Women With Silicone Implant–Related Disorders," *Health Care for Women International* (1996)

NO: Michael Fumento, from "A Confederacy of Boobs," *Reason* (October 1995)

ISSUE SUMMARY

YES: Lynette J. Dumble, a research fellow in the Department of Surgery at the University of Melbourne, asserts that a combination of medical politics and flawed research has unfairly weakened the cases of silicone breast implant recipients who claim that the implants have caused them to become ill.

NO: Author Michael Fumento states that solid research has proven that silicone breast implants are not dangerous. He believes that an anti-implant campaign has led medical public policy to be driven by anecdotal rather than epidemiological evidence.

Silicone breast implants used for cosmetic purposes in otherwise healthy women were taken off the market in 1992 by the U.S. Food and Drug Administration (FDA). Led by FDA commissioner David Kessler, the organization expressed concern about a possible connection between silicone leakages and a variety of disturbing medical conditions. Kessler claimed that a lack of adequate information on the lifespan of these implants was the reason for the moratorium. Prior to May 1995, when Dow Corning, a leading manufacturer of silicone breast implants, declared bankruptcy and placed itself beyond the reach of the trial courts, lawsuits were filed and large sums of money were awarded to women who claimed that implants had caused them to be seriously ill. The declaration of bankruptcy for Dow Corning came only days after the collapse of the Breast Implant Global Settlement, in which implant manufacturers had agreed to compensate hundreds of thousands of women who claimed to have developed, or who feared that they would develop, illnesses associated with the implants.

Some critics of this moratorium believe that breast implants symbolize the power of the FDA and the breakdown of the tort system. Many claim that there was never any credible evidence linking implants to disease, and they question why juries gave multimillion-dollar awards to women who asserted that implants had made them sick. It is their opinion that the government sees the cosmetic industry as promoting unnecessary and artificial procedures that could harm the consumer. According to these commentators, beauty is not a value recognized by the FDA, and a paternalistic American government is using this situation to further its position that alteration of genetic destiny is unwarranted without compelling health reasons.

In contrast, radical feminists and others see the availability of implants that have not undergone adequate testing as a "patriarchal plot" or, at the very least, as more evidence of a lingering medical negligence toward women. They are troubled to see women having their bodies altered and appalled at women's willingness to risk illness, even death, in order to meet beauty standards prescribed and enforced by males. It has been said that if women have been so brainwashed as to think that they must improve their appearance at any risk, then it definitely *is* the responsibility of the government to ensure that the cosmetic industry takes precautions to keep dangerous products off the market and out of women's bodies. From another view, many libertarian feminists are offended whenever women's options are reduced. They reason that women have a right to make informed choices about issues that concern their physical appearance. If a product has not been proven to be unsafe, women should have every right to use it. After all, current research in the social sciences has demonstrated that individuals deemed more attractive—male or female—consistently secure the best jobs and command the highest incomes. Why shouldn't women be able to choose to have larger breasts if this would make them feel more attractive and confident and bestow upon them a competitive advantage in the workplace?

The heart of the debate is about the appropriateness of, motive for, and ramifications of removing silicone implants from the market. A critical locus of the argument on both sides of the issue involves medical evidence. Have the implants in fact caused illnesses? In the following selections, Lynette J. Dumble asserts that a combination of medical politics and flawed research has unfairly served to weaken the case of implant recipients against the silicone industry's manufacturers and plastic surgeons. Michael Fumento maintains that medical evidence conclusively proves that implants have no potential to harm women in any serious way.

YES

Lynette J. Dumble

DISMISSING THE EVIDENCE

Financial and professional ambition have figured prominently in the medical dismissal of claims from implant recipients—the overwhelming majority of whom are women who have undergone breast augmentation—that silicone was the cause of their atypical autoimmune diseases. After examining the dubious history of silicone and the events that led the Food and Drug Administration to place a moratorium on its use in reconstructive surgery in 1994, discussion centers on the combination of medical politics and flawed research that has served to weaken the case of implant recipients against the silicone industry's manufacturers and plastic surgeons. Women's experiences from the silicone implant affair are compared with their experience from the human pituitary hormone affair, which in general failed to inform them that their gonadotrophin treatment had left them at risk of an invariably fatal neurological disorder known as Creutzfeldt-Jakob disease. The parallels between silicone implant and human pituitary hormone iatrogenic illness emphasize the urgent need to restructure medical understanding of what constitutes genuine informed choice and consent for health consumers.

Based on proclamations of silicone innocence, ruling medical opinion continues to dismiss claims from implant recipients, the overwhelming majority of whom are women, that their serious illnesses are connected to their reconstructive surgery. A number of landmark settlements—a US$4.2 billion award against the implant manufacturing companies of Dow Corning, Bristol-Myers Squibb, and Baxter International in the United States in 1994 (Brahams, 1994), followed in 1995 by another of US$6 million to an Alabama woman who developed potentially cancerous lumps and suffered immune damage when silicone spread throughout her body from rupturing breast implants (Associated Press, 1995), and Bristol-Myers Squibb's out-of-court $28 million (Canadian) reserve for Ontario and Quebec women suffering *any implant-attributed* disease as a result of implants supplied by its subsidiary Medical Engineering Incorporated (Kondro, 1995)—have uncovered the scandal of dismissing the link between illness and implant surgery. Added to accruing medical evidence of silicone toxicity (Campbell & Brautbar, 1995; Vojdani et al., 1995), the information revealed during the course of the legal proceedings suggests that the medical dismissal is part of a larger conspiracy to avoid responsibility for yet another chapter of medical misogyny (Dumble, 1995a).

SILICONE HISTORY

Despite the fact that silicone has been used in the breast reconstructive surgery of an estimated 3 million women worldwide since 1962, the substance has a long and dubious past that goes back to its use as an insecticide in the 1950s. A decade later, when the window of opportunity for artificial breasts emerged, scheduled silicone toxicology was pushed aside as the manufacturers and surgeons focused their attention on a mega-million dollar market (Dumble, 1995b). It is less than naive to assume that the silicone hazards were closely kept secrets known only to chemical companies with questionable ethics. Evidence debunking the myth that silicone was inert has been around in medical literature for more than 30 years. Countless articles within specialist journals of plastic and reconstructive surgery warned that silicone implants underwent detrimental changes after contact with body tissues and often leaked or bled silicone into surrounding tissues (Pearl et al., 1978). Animal studies demonstrated that silicone promoted inflammatory and fibrous tissue reactions (Ferriera et al., 1975) and that large amounts of escaping silicone migrated throughout the entire body. Imprudently, the animal studies were never extended to establish the long-term consequences of silicone migration following an implant leakage or rupture, nor was there any research in appropriate animal species to figure out the relationship between silicone and autoimmune disease.

Clinical results indicated that a silicone bleed or leak from an implant provoked an even more severe and extensive inflammatory response (Baker et al., 1978) and was probably the physiological equivalent of a silicone injection. Although the license to inject liquid silicone was withdrawn by the U.S. Food and Drug Administration (FDA) in 1976, the message of the annulment was either too subtle for manufacturers and surgeons to grasp, or the financial incentive, together with a surgeon's perspective that implant surgery was the solution to women's demeaned-body image, overshadowed the welfare of a vulnerable group of health consumers.

FDA REASSESSMENT OF SILICONE SAFETY

The first of the consumer organizations, the U.S.-based National Women's Health Network (NWHN), commenced to question silicone-breast implant safety before the FDA in 1983. One year after urging the FDA to require proof of silicone safety from manufacturers in 1988, NWHN used its newsletter to alert women to the dangers of implants in the absence of long-term safety data (Zones, 1989) and became a member of the Breast Implant Task Force established by the FDA Office of Consumer Affairs for the specific purpose of providing printed information for consumers. Since 1991, silicone's reputation has taken a downward turn; a new FDA commissioner, determined to amend the languishing issues of the 1980s, together with a rising incidence of autoimmune/connective tissue disease among women with breast implants, and a small number of men with penile and testicular implants, and the scrutiny of a congressional oversight committee, prompted the FDA to give breast implant manufacturers 90 days in which to submit pre-market approval applications (reviewed by Pearson, 1995). It soon surfaced that manufacturers held no evidence of breast implant safety and effectiveness. More shamefully, and to the contrary, testing over the prior two or more decades had already alerted the implant industry of immune dysfunction from silicone implants, and although this data was internally distributed within the manufacturer's environment from memoranda bearing an instruction to "disregard after reading" the information was concealed from authorities until the FDA renewed its consultations in the 1990s. At this same point in time, the plastic surgeons entered the fray, casting their reputations down the same shameful spiral as the manufacturers, with a US$4 million campaign designed to convince Congress, the FDA, and the public that women had the "right to choose" breast implants. NWHN countered that "The right to choose is meaningless without the right to know" and its media and congressional campaigns (Zones, 1991), together with these startling revelations and events, played a leading role in the FDA's 1994 moratorium on the use of silicone in reconstructive surgery.

MEDICAL POLITICS AND SILICONE IMPLANT-RELATED ILLNESS

An editorial in the *New England Journal of Medicine* instantly argued that the FDA had been "paternalistic and unnecessarily alarmist" in banning silicone implants (Angell, 1994). Across the Atlantic, an editorial in the *Lancet* (Bridges, 1994) took an opposite stance, pointing out that the dismissive viewpoint of the *New England Journal* was largely based on a study from the Mayo Clinic (Gabriel et al., 1994), which, despite the stature of the institution, was "insufficiently powerful" to detect an increased incidence of connective tissue disease. Put more bluntly, this implied that the Mayo Clinic study was impotent to answer whether silicone caused illness; as equally, it was virtually irrelevant to women with breast implants because it placed no emphasis on the atypical disorders on which they base their complaints (Solomon, 1994). Furthermore, the researcher interviewed only asymptomatic implant recipients, which, to paraphrase Andrew Campbell (Campbell & Brautbar, 1995), director of the Center for Immune, Environmental, and Toxic Disorders at the University of Texas Health Sciences in Houston, is as lame as asking a group who are constipated "What causes diarrhea?"!

Evidence demonstrating the unique physiological changes in silicone implant recipients strengthens the case that silicone-related illness in itself is more likely to be unique, or more specifically, atypical or different from other known illnesses. Equally, the fact that an illness is atypical in no way diminishes the distress to the individual who has the fate to develop symptoms outside the norm. Yet, despite the fact that the silicone affair is a global issue impacting on at least 3 million health consumers, articles supporting the claims of implant recipients are more likely to be found on the lower profile pages of major medical journals, such as the *Lancet* and *New England Journal of Medicine*, that are reserved for letters to the editor. In contrast, the editors of the same journals consistently publish denials of the link between silicone implants and a variety of serious disorders, including rheumatological and neurologic illnesses, as feature articles. In a recent example, the report (Wall et al., 1995) of the abnormal lipid profile (chylomicroanaemia) in 40% of women with silicone and saline breast implants, but in only 15% of matched controls, appeared in the Letters section of the *Lancet*. Almost certainly, had this novel lipid change occurred in tobacco users, vasectomized men, or women who refused to be good girls and take their menopausal hormone replacement therapy, the news would have been transmitted around the world by the print and electronic media following its publication on the pages reserved for breakthrough medical research.

Experts predict that 20% of women with silicone breast implants will develop mild, moderate, or severe symptoms of toxicity, and more than 4,000 women in Australia alone have registered their silicone-related illnesses with consumer organizations. A 1993 medical review of the history, complications, and safety of silicone breast implants noted that, given the large number of women with silicone implants and rheumatic disease, especially scleroderma, epidemiological studies were warranted. Yet, epidemiology, which frequently amounts to decades of follow-up years in sizeable populations, is neither appropriate nor essential to establish that silicone is the culprit. As Brautbar and Campbell (1995a) pointed out, epidemiology can be useful in risk assessment, but three decades of silicone implant case reports and population studies have already fulfilled the Bradford Hill (1965) benchmark[1] logic and criteria of disease causation; first, from the consistent association, or link, between a range of atypical, chiefly immunological, disorders in silicone implant recipients around the world for the past three decades (Myoshe et al., 1964;

Van Nunen et al., 1982; Vojdani et al., 1992); second, from the specific common factor, silicone, to implantees developing atypical health disorders, and by the emergence of silicone-specific antibody in more than half of both symptomatic and asymptomatic implantees (Bridges et al., 1993); third, from the temporal and dose relationship between ill health in silicone recipients, which is further proven by the frequent reversibility of disease symptoms on removal of the implants (Kaiser et al., 1990); and lastly, by the biological plausibility and coherence of the silicone blame whereby similar illnesses have been reproduced in experimental animals exposed to silicone (Ben-Hur et al., 1967).

SILICONE TOXICITY IN TERMS OF WOMEN'S LIVES

Largely due to the medical smokescreen, the devastating effects of silicone-related diseases not only on women's lives, and also on those who share their lives, has failed to prompt the outrage and sympathy warranted (Dumble, 1994b). Their situation, more often than not, adversely affects their personal relationships, and many (barely aged 50), unable to physically or psychologically tend for themselves, are permanently nursed in homes for the aged or the mentally ill. Some are confined to life in a wheelchair. Many require around-the-clock supervision to prevent self-injury because they have been robbed of their manual dexterity. Many endure constant pain, due in part to their silicone-related illness, but frequently worsened by botched attempts to surgically correct technical problems with their implants. The women's personal efforts to overcome low self-esteem are thwarted, not only by mirror images of their scarred and mutilated breasts, but also by the medical dismissal that their atypical illness has anything to do with their implant, or, more patronizingly, is merely a figment of their imagination.

Drawn-out legal battles and research by a handful of rheumatologists and immunologists both promise cold comfort for the large number of women who endure serious illness after implant surgery. The frequency and severity of implant-related illness is set to be grossly underestimated as cases inevitably escape the networks of an alert handful, while Dow Corning has already filed for Chapter 11 bankruptcy protection in response to the volume of private claims made after the product liability settlement awarded against the company in the United States (Kondro, 1995). More crucially, based on "severely flawed" studies from prestigious institutions such as Harvard (Brautbar & Campbell, 1995a) and the Mayo Clinic (Gabriel et al., 1994), the conspiracy to dismiss implant-related illness entices more and more women, and some men, to flirt with death for the perceived benefits of implant cosmetics. At the same time, other vital issues, such as whether breastfeeding mothers with implants transmit silicone and its toxic effects onto their children, have been largely ignored. Similarly, although the possibility of silicone-induced breast cancer is denied by some studies (Bryant & Brasher, 1995), there is clear clinical and experimental evidence (Brautbar & Campbell, 1995b; Potter et al., 1994) that silicone has the capacity to act as a carcinogen, thereby raising the question of whether an increase in the overall cancer rate may result from the implants. Important, too—given that the early diagnosis of recurrent malignancy is critical to the survival of women who have previously undergone surgery for a primary breast cancer—the mere fact that silicone implants conceal the mammography detection of recurrent tumors in 40% of women (Silverstein et al., 1991) gives an insight into the motives and preferences of certain medical prescribers when it comes to the welfare of health consumers who also happen to be women.

MEDICINE AGAIN PLACING WOMEN IN JEOPARDY

This is not the first time that health consumers, the majority of whom were women, have been placed in jeopardy by a medically prescribed program. Past experiences indicate that women have good reason to both shout foul and protest that their safety ran a poor second to the ambition and/or financial incentives of medical prospectors (Dumble, 1995b; Rowland, 1992). In 1994, an independent inquiry returned a damning indictment of the medical profession's role in the Human Pituitary Hormone Program (Cooke, 1994) that has left at least 2,300 infertile and short-statured Australians at risk of a cruel and invariably fatal brain illness known as CJD, or Creutzfeldt-Jakob disease (Cooke & Armstrong, 1992; Dumble & Klean, 1992). To this day, U.S. women treated with hormones manufactured from human cadaver pituitary glands in an identical infertility program remain unaware that their lives are in similar jeopardy, despite the enormity of an NIH-sponsored program that supplied human pituitary gonadotrophin to more than 250 infertility experts (U.S. National Pituitary Agency, 1980) more than two decades before it all came to a halt in 1985 with the emergence of the first cases of CJD in growth hormone-treated children.

Eminent surgical identities have anchored the silicone disaster in much the same manner as distinguished obstetricians, gynecologists, pediatricians, and endocrinologists from the most prestigious western universities and teaching hospitals underpinned the CJD affair. Australian health minister, Dr. Carmen Lawrence, in her criticism and promised overhaul of prevailing medical ethics (Cooke, 1994), both on announcing the verdict of the independent inquiry and when introducing a national CJD Trust Fund, should have sent shock waves through certain medical quarters, not the least of all in the space occupied by plastic surgeons. Gauged by the deafening silence, the Health Minister's message seems to have dumbfounded the usually outspoken presidents of the Australian Medical Association, and the respective Colleges of Surgeons, Physicians, and Obstetricians and Gynecologists. Alternatively, the silence may be a sign that those within the medical profession with unquestionable ethics actually welcome government intervention to straighten out the ethics of their ruthless minority.

Silicone implant recipients are due the same acknowledgment, support and compensation paid to victims of any iatrogenic disaster. At present, their plight is ignored or dismissed in much the same manner that medical decisions were initially made to leave infertile women treated with human pituitary gonadotrophin uninformed of the hormone's fatal CJD legacy. Self-funded consumer groups representing implant victims operate with precious little outside financial assistance to meet the spiraling demands. Legally, Judge Poyner's justice in the United States (Brahams, 1994) has virtually destroyed any hopes foreign claimants, like those from Australia,

may have held for a worthwhile settlement from the silicone industry. But the worst and most disempowering rebuff for implantees comes from the medical profession itself; in particular, from plastic surgeons who neglected to investigate whether the tools of their trade were as prudent as they led their patients to believe, and who now dismiss the women's problems as unrelated to implant reconstruction.

FUTURE DIRECTIONS FOR MEDICAL ETHICS AND DAMAGE CONTROL

A *handful* of concerned specialists is a disgraceful response to the medical *dismissal* that masks the silicone scandal. Women with silicone implants are owed immediate action; in the first place, a medical admission that the debilitating illnesses prevalent among implant recipients are the direct result of reconstructive surgery that was incorrectly and deceitfully sold to them as a safe procedure. Equally, or perhaps of greater importance, studies are warranted to (a) establish whether existing implants should be removed, replaced, or left undisturbed; (b) develop sensitive clinical and laboratory methods that detect silicone toxicity in its earliest stages; and (c) investigate the advantages and disadvantages of detoxification procedures that could prevent terminal illness as a result of silicone toxicity. While many within the medical profession are busily dismissing or dodging their responsibilities to silicone recipients, and manufacturers such as Dow Corning are fudging bankruptcy declarations, women, and perhaps some men, are dying marginalized and uncompensated. Others are placed in further jeopardy because appropriate management, including silicone detoxification, is not forthcoming, and additional health consumers are placed at similar risk because they too will dice with implant surgery for as long as the myth of silicone innocence survives.

Neither silence nor denial, nor low-priority pages within major medical journals (Dumble & Klean, 1992) permanently withheld the truth about the human pituitary hormone saga in Australia (Cooke & Armstrong, 1992) and the United Kingdom (Pallot, 1993) from the public sector. A second case of pituitary growth hormone-related CJD in New Zealand has recently shaken that country's wall of medical silence (Slinger, 1995a, 1995b), and the inevitable CJD epidemic in the United States is anticipated to bring its medical profession and institutions a due share of the disrepute for failing to inform human pituitary gonadotrophin recipients of the treatment's CJD legacy. There are some remarkable parallels between the silicone and pituitary hormone affairs, and based on the indications that the lessons from the CJD affair have gone unlearned, there is an urgency to reiterate that risks and benefits are about the welfare of health consumers rather than protecting the profits and reputations of groups with vested interests. Just as endocrinologists, pediatricians, and infertility specialists held sway over knowledge that warned of iatrogenic consequences from human pituitary hormones, so too implant manufacturers and plastic surgeons have restricted independent assessment of silicone safety, which, to paraphrase Melbourne barrister Jocelynne Scutt (1992), deprived each group of chiefly women health consumers of their entitlement to both genuine choice and truly informed consent. But, like pituitary hormone recipients before them,

implant recipients may have a lengthy wait for their already overdue apology for the prevailing medical morality that has dismissed their deadly inheritance.

NOTES

1. Medical epidemiology, since 1965, engages the Bradford Hill Criteria (1. Strength of Association, 2. Consistency, 3. Specificity, 4. Relationship of Time, 5. Dose Response, 6. Biological Plausibility, and 7. Coherence of the Evidence) to differentiate between scientific data and speculation in order to trace the cause(s) of health disorders.

REFERENCES

Angell, M. (1994). Do breast implants cause systemic disease? Science in the courtroom. *New England Journal of Medicine, 330,* 1748–1749.

Associated Press. (1995, February 5). Woman gets $6m for implant leak. *The Canberra Times,* p. 6.

Baker, D. E., Reisky, M. I., & Schultz, S. (1978). "Bleeding" of silicone from bag-gel breast implants, and its clinical relation to fibrous capsule reaction. *Plastic and Reconstructive Surgery, 61,* 836–841.

Ben-Hur, N., Ballantyne, D. L., Rees, T. D., & Seidman, I. (1967). Local and systemic effects of dimethylpolysiloaxane in fluid in mice. *Plastic and Reconstructive Surgery, 29,* 423–425.

Brahams, D. (1994). Breast implant compensation. *The Lancet, 344,* 1499.

Brautbar, N., & Campbell, A. (1995a). Silicone implants and immune dysfunction: Scientific evidence for causation. *International Journal of Occupational Medicine and Toxicology, 4,* 3–13.

Brautbar, N., & Campbell, A. (1995b). Silicone is a potential carcinogen. *International Journal of Occupational Medicine and Toxicology, 4,* 71–74.

Bridges, A. J. (1994). Silicone implant controversy continues. *The Lancet, 344,* 1451–1452.

Bridges, A. J., Conley, C., Wang, G., Burns, D. E., & Vasey, F. B. (1993). A clinical and immunological evaluation of women with silicone breast implants and immunological-mediated disease. *Annals of Internal Medicine, 234,* 929–936.

Bryant, H., & Brasher, P. (1995). Breast implants and breast cancer—reanalysis of a linkage study. *New England Journal of Medicine, 332,* 1535–1539.

Campbell, A. W., & Brautbar, N. (1995). Silicone breast implant recipients and autoimmune endocrinopathy. *International Journal of Occupational Medicine and Toxicology, 4,* 75–78.

Cooke, J. (1994, July 2). The shocking truth behind Australia's human hormone program. Medical Minefield. *Sydney Morning Herald*, p. 26.

Cooke, J., & Armstrong, D. (1992, November 28). The experiment that killed. *Sydney Morning Herald*, p. 1.

Dumble, L. J. (1994a). The dissection of women from conception to menopause: An urgent issue for bioethics in the 1990s. In *Bioethics 1971–2001*. Australian Bioethics Association, University of Adelaide, pp. 80–86.

Dumble, L. J. (1994b, December 12). Silence falls on silicone victims. *The Canberra Times*, p. 11.

Dumble, L. J. (1995a). Population control's medical paradigm: Regulation of fertility or disruption of lives? *Women's Global Network for Reproductive Rights Newsletter, 50*, ii–iv.

Dumble, L. J. (1995b, December 6). The scandal of silicone implants. *Green Left*, pp. 3–4.

Dumble, L. J., & Klean, R. D. (1992). Creutzfeldt-Jakob legacy for Australian women treated with human pituitary gland hormone for infertility [Letter to the editor]. *The Lancet*, 847–848.

Ferriera, M. C., Spina, V., & Iriya, K. (1975). Changes in the lung following injections of silicone gel. *British Journal of Plastic Surgery, 28*, 173–176.

Gabriel, S. E., O'Fallon, W. M., Kurland, L. T., Beard, C. M., Woods, J. E., and Melton, L. J., III. (1994). Risks of connective tissue diseases and other disorders after breast implantation. *New England Journal of Medicine, 330*, 1697–1702.

Hill, A. B. (1965). The environment and disease: Association or causation? [President's address]. *Proceedings of the Royal Society of Medicine, 9*, 295–300.

Kaiser, W., Biesenbach, G., Stubby, U., Graffinger, P., & Zazgornik, J. (1990). Human adjuvant disease: Remission of silicone-induced disease after explanation of breast augmentation. *European Journal of Surgery and Oncology, 16*, 468–469.

Kondro, W. (1995). First non-US breast-implant settlement. *The Lancet, 346*, 46.

Myoshe, K., Miyamura, T., & Kobayashi, Y. (1964). Hypergammaglobulinemia by prolonged adjuvanticity in men. Disorders developed after augmentation mammoplasty. *Japanese Journal of Medicine, 2122*, 9–14.

Pallot, P. (1993, September 4). Fertility treatment "killed my mother." *The Daily Telegraph [London]*, p. 3.

Pearl, R. M., Laub, D. R., & Kaplan, E. N. (1978). Complications following silicone injections for augmentation of the contours of the face. *Plastic and Reconstructive Surgery, 144*, 888–891.

Pearson, C. A. (1995). National Women's Health Network and the US FDA: Two decades of activism. *Reproductive Health Matters, 6* (Nov.), 132–141.

Potter, M., Morrison, S., Wiener, F., Zhang, X. K., & Miller, F. W. (1994). Induction of plasmacytomas with silicone gel in genetically susceptible strains of mice. *Journal of the National Cancer Institute, 86*, 1058–1065.

Rowland, R. (1992). *Living laboratories. Women and the new reproductive technologies.* Sydney: Macmillan.

Scutt, J. A. (1992). At issue. The right to say yes: The ethics of consent to medical treatment. *Issues in Reproductive and Genetic Engineering, 5*, 183–194.

Silverstein, M. J., Handel, N., & Gamagami, P. (1991). The effect of silicone-gel-filled implants on mammography. *Cancer, 68*, 1159–1163.

Slinger, S. (1995a, August 12). Killer disease in blood banks. *The Daily News [New Zealand]*, p. 1.

Slinger, S. (1995b, August 12). Hormone therapy leaves a deadly legacy. *The Daily News [New Zealand]*, p. 10.

Solomon, G. A. (1994). Clinical and laboratory profile of symptomatic women with silicone breast implants. *Seminars in Arthritis and Rheumatology, 24*, 29–37.

U.S. National Pituitary Agency. (1980). Report to National Institute of Arthritis, Metabolism and Digestive Disorders [NIAMDD], Bureau of Drugs, Food and Drug Administration. Progress report re human growth hormone IND 1163. July 1, 1979 to June 30, 1980, pp. 1–34. Submitted 19 August 1980.

Van Nunen, S. A., Gateby, P. A., & Basten, A. (1982). Post mammoplasty connective tissue disease. *Arthritis and Rheumatology, 25*, 694–697.

Vojdani, A., Campbell, A., & Brautbar, N. (1992). Immune functional impairment in patients with clinical abnormalities and silicone breast implants. *Toxicology and Industrial Health, 8*, 415–429.

Vojdani, A., Campbell, A. W., Karjoo, R., & Brautbar, N. (1995). Neuroimmunological evaluation of patients with silicone implants. *International Journal of Occupational Medicine and Toxicology, 4*, 25–62.

Wall, W., Martin, L., Frittzler, M. J., & Edworthy, S. (1995). Non-fasting chylomicroanaemia in breast implant recipients [Letter to the editor]. *The Lancet, 345*, 1380.

Zones, J. S. (1989). The dangers of breast augmentation. *Network News*, (July/Aug), 1–8.

Zones, J. S. (1991). New developments in silicone breast implant regulation. *Network News*, (June/Aug), 1–4.

NO

Michael Fumento

A CONFEDERACY OF BOOBS

"Not only are they abusing the judicial system, but they are emotionally abusing the women." That's what one silicone breast implant recipient told the *Boston Herald* following the decision of Dow Corning to file for bankruptcy. Dow Corning had contributed about half of a $4.2 billion settlement—the biggest ever—for women claiming to suffer various illnesses from their implants.

[In 1995], however, it became clear that there were far more women trying to get a piece of the pie than there were slices. Plaintiffs' attorneys were saying that $74 billion might be needed to satisfy just the first set of claims against the companies. Rather than close its doors forever, Dow Corning chose to try to limit its losses.

Financially, it's unclear where the bankruptcy leaves implant claimants. But what has become more and more certain since the settlement was reached back in 1993 is that while both the judicial system and silicone implant recipients have been terribly abused, the villain isn't Dow Corning or any other implant maker.

Indeed, women with breast implants have been nothing more than pawns in a bizarre game involving lawyers, feminists, headline hounds, and super-inflated bureaucratic egos. The stakes, however, go beyond the physical and mental health of women with implants to include the future health of millions of Americans who will need insertable medical devices. Indeed, the multimillion-dollar awards against silicone implant manufacturers have already triggered a wave of suits against medical implants made of solid silicone and even some containing no silicone at all.

"We have great concerns that any medical device with silicone in it will not survive," says Elizabeth Connell, a professor of gynecology and obstetrics at Emory University and head of two Food and Drug Administration [FDA] silicone breast implant panels that unsuccessfully recommended leaving the devices on the market. Since June 1992, most uses of silicone breast implants have been banned by the FDA. Annually, some 1.5 million patients receive silicone eye lenses; another 670,000 get artificial silicone joints. All told, about 7.5 million medical devices are implanted in Americans each year. Many of these devices—such as pacemakers, heart valves, and shunts which draw fluid off the brain—are life savers.

Hence, the misinformed campaign against silicone breast implants raises issues that go far beyond the not insignificant question of whether women should be able to change their appearance as they see fit. A strange alliance of diverse interests, including FDA bureaucrats interested in broadening their powers, feminists who equate boob jobs with mutilation, and reporters more interested in good copy than relevant medical research, worked together to take implants off the market. The anti-implant campaign is nothing less than a case study in how medical public policy is often driven by anecdotal rather than epidemiological evidence, formulated by ideologues who have little regard for what individuals might value, and discussed in a consistently one-sided manner.

The use of silicone implants to enlarge the size of the breast dates back to 1963. Somewhere around one million American women have received them. Implants may be used either for "augmentation"— making a healthy breast or pair of breasts larger—or to replace a breast removed during mastectomy. It appears that about 60 percent of breast implants have been used for augmentation.

While there has been mention of possible disease caused by implants as far back as 1978, the kick-off point of the scare that ultimately prompted the FDA to ban silicone implants may have been the airing of an implant feature on CBS's *Face to Face with Connie Chung* in 1990. Chung's graphic imagery—she called silicone gel "an ooze of slimy gelatin that could be poisoning" women —spurred one stampede of women to have their implants removed and another to file suits against implant makers.

As Chung herself later put it, the show "unleashed a torrent of protests and investigations around the country." Soon, women were bombarded with such stories as "Toxic Breasts," "The Hazards of Silicone," and "Time Bombs in the Breasts." The height of hysteria may have been reached when, after the FDA moratorium, two women removed their own implants with razor blades. They said they had no success in getting doctors to remove them.

A new front opened up in December 1991, when a California jury awarded a Marin County woman, Mariann Hopkins, $7.3 million from Dow Corning. She alleged aches, pains, and fatigue caused by her implants without citing any illness more specific than autoimmune disease, a catchall phrase for a variety of connective-tissue diseases such as rheumatoid arthritis, scleroderma, lupus, Sjogren's Syndrome, fibromyalgia, and Raynaud's Disease.

In January 1992, the FDA declared a voluntary (but strongly recommended) moratorium on the sale and use of silicone breast implants pending review of additional information, saying, "physicians should cease using them and manufacturers should stop shipping them." Four months later, the FDA essentially converted this to a ban, although the agency did allow continued use of the implants for women who had suffered mastectomies and permitted a small number of women who wanted implants for cosmetic purposes to enroll in long-term studies.

* * *

Like many health scares, the one over silicone implants is primarily American.

Only a few countries besides the United States forbid the devices within their borders. One is Canada, even though the Canadian Independent Advisory Committee review showed no causal link between silicone breast implants and serious illness. While most countries haven't even seriously considered removing silicone implants from use, some, such as the United Kingdom, have reviewed the evidence and affirmatively stated that implants should remain available. In June 1994, the 20-member European Committee on Quality Assurance and Medical Devices in Plastic Surgery declared it "does not support any restriction on the use of silicone-gel filled implants."

Because of the ban in the United States, American women have gone to other countries, including the United Kingdom, Mexico, France, and Germany, to get implants. One popular package mixing implantation in an English hospital with a trip to Shakespeare's birthplace is called "Boobs n' Bard." Having to go abroad for implants, of course, prices some women out of the market. Women who do travel for implants face different problems: If something goes wrong with the surgery, the doctor is thousands of miles away. And malpractice suits are difficult to pursue in much of the world and virtually impossible in South and Central America.

The FDA seriously considered pulling saline-filled implants off the market as well. But in late 1994, it decided to allow their continued use pending approval applications due in 1998. Silicone is generally preferred to saline because it gives the breast a more natural feel. To keep saline-filled breasts from swishing like a waterbed, it is necessary to pack them tight with the solution. In breasts that are quite small to begin with,

wrinkles or ripples in the implant surface are more easily visible through the skin and the breast may not move or hang as naturally as it would with silicone implants.

Whatever goes into the implant of the future, the silicone implants of today are in the bodies of a million or more women who need to know what risk, if any, these devices pose.

There are two ways that women can be exposed to silicone from an implant. One is when microscopic droplets of silicone fluid "bleed" through the envelope of a gel-filled implant. "Low-bleed" implants have been available since the early 1980s and have reduced the amount of silicone that escapes from the implant. In any event, because scar tissue quickly forms around the implant, the gel usually goes no further than one or two millimeters beyond the implant wall.

The other way women can be exposed is through rupture. According to the FDA, about 4 percent to 6 percent of silicone implants have ruptured, though studies in progress indicate this figure is probably too low.

Nonetheless, again the scar "capsule" that invariably grows around the implant tends to hold any silicone even if it breaks, which explains why so many ruptures are outwardly undetectable. While the gel has gone beyond the pouch, it still usually remains in place, although it has been found in the lymphatic system of some women.

That implants can cause physical problems is beyond doubt. It has long been known, for instance, that the scar capsule can harden and constrict, sometimes painfully so. This hardening can make necessary follow-up treatment to remove the scar tissue. Makers of later model implants claim to have reduced this problem, but it's too early to say what success they may have had.

But when critics warn of the dangers of silicone implants, this usually minor problem is seldom what they're talking about. According to Jack Fisher, a San Diego plastic surgeon and outspoken defender of implants, more than 50 symptoms are alleged to be caused by implants, including memory loss, dry mouth, cancer, bladder problems, difficulty swallowing, joint pain, decreased sex drive, and a host of autoimmune diseases. Some have referred to this broad constellation of symptoms as "silicone-gel syndrome." But if it is a syndrome it appears the proper definition would have to be any illness that any woman with implants ever contracts.

To sympathetic observers, such a wide array of symptoms must seem alarming. But a general rule of epidemiology is that the more diverse the symptoms allegedly related to a single cause are, the less likely it is that the suspected cause is real. This basic precept is, in a sense, the mirror image of snake-oil cures that promise to remedy all sorts of unrelated symptoms. Many of the most commonly cited symptoms of silicone exposure—such as fatigue, headaches, and difficulty swallowing—can be brought on by suggestion. As a result, people who hear that implants may cause certain problems may then develop them. These are the same "side effects" described by participants in drug studies who are actually receiving placebos.

And, in fact, most of the evidence against implants is anecdotal: It is based on reports from women who are sick and have implants and claim the two conditions are related. Thus, if a woman with implants ever develops symptoms that doctors can't readily explain, everyone simply assumes that silicone is the cause. Sometimes this sort of reasoning is expressed in the very titles (of the implant scare articles. Consider the headline for the *San Francisco Chronicle's* article about Mariann Hopkins: "After Breast Implant, Horror Began."

While such a loose correlation may be appealing to people looking for quick and easy answers, it is essentially the same logical fallacy that blames black cats for inexplicable illness. Yet, in some cases, the silicone-gel symptoms actually predate the implants. Indeed, such a curious time frame appears to have been the case even in the first big implant settlement.

One of Mariann Hopkins's treating physicians testified that, although her diagnosis of mixed connective-tissue disease did not come until after the implants were put in, she had already displayed symptoms of connective-tissue disease as early as two years before receiving implants. The doctor even testified that another physician was so concerned that he subjected her to a battery of tests for one type of connective-tissue illness called systemic rheumatic disease. Those came back negative, but they were not tests specifically for mixed connective-tissue disease. Had they been and had they come back positive, it's unlikely Hopkins would have ever received the $7.3 million award.

But then again, the jury did not seem overly influenced by those most knowledgeable of Hopkins's medical history. At the time of trial, Hopkins was basically free of symptoms, thanks to a low dose of medicine. And none of Hopkins's treating physicians testified at the trial that they believed her illness to be related to the implants.

Instead, the jury made its finding on the basis of outside testimony that implants could cause such disease, testimony from professional anti-implant witnesses such as Tampa, Florida, physician Frank Vasey, who makes his living by treating women he says are sick from their implants.

Perhaps the most serious charge against silicone implants is also the weakest—that they may cause breast cancer. Although such influential groups as Sidney Wolfe's Public Citizen (founded by Ralph Nader) have made the claim, repeated studies have shown no such link. The only cancers ever plausibly attributed to silicone—in a study released over 40 years ago—were connective-tissue sarcomas that appeared in strains of rodents especially susceptible to cancer.

* * *

The simple truth is that no epidemiological studies have linked cancer in people to implants. The largest study is also the most recent: After looking at a group of almost 11,000 women from the Alberta, Canada, area, the Alberta Cancer Board concluded, "The incidence of breast cancer among the women who had breast augmentation could not be said to be either significantly higher or lower than that among the general population.

Polyurethane implants, which make up about 10 percent of implants currently in use, are a special case. Manufactured by Surgitek Inc., a subsidiary (of Bristol-Myers Squibb Co., these implants featured a gel-filled pouch with a layer of polyurethane foam coating the silicone envelope. The implants were a special target of Connie Chung's *Face to Face* report. Under such heat, Surgitek felt it had no choice but to remove them from the market in 1991. (Nevertheless, a *USA To-day* illustration in May 1995 accompanying an anti-implant editorial depicted a polyurethane-coated implant.)

The purpose of the foam was to reduce the chance of scar tissue contracting around the implant. But when the foam breaks down chemically, it produces a substance called 2-toluene diamine (TDA) that is considered a probable animal carcinogen and a possible human one. Although that would seem to be an obvious source of trouble, it turns out that, like all the other serious accusations against breast implants, the charges against polyurethane implants don't hold up under epidemiological scrutiny. The only difference is that in this case the FDA has admitted it.

In late June, Bristol-Myers Squibb concluded an FDA-solicited study to determine how much TDA really ended up in the system of women with polyurethane implants. The amount (when any was found at all) was so small that even assuming it is a *definite* human carcinogen—using the FDA's own rating system—the risk of cancer was one in a million. Since only about 110,000 women have had such implants, the FDA stated in a position paper, "FDA estimates it is unlikely that exposure to TDA will cause cancer in even one of the women with these implants." The agency added, "The health risk connected with surgical removal of the implants is far greater than the risk of developing cancer."

There's another, deeper irony in the whole polyurethane controversy, one the FDA obviously couldn't state: that a product designed to alleviate the only absolutely certain health problem clearly linked to implants was forced off the market because of worries over other unproven health effects.

Since silicone gel from implants is most commonly accused of causing autoimmune disease, or connective-tissue disease, it isn't surprising that a large number of studies on both animals and humans have looked for a link between silicone exposure and autoimmune/connective-tissue disease. When the British Department of Health undertook a review of these studies earlier this year, it found approximately 270 papers published after 1971 alone.

The animal studies, the department concluded, "provide no immunological reason for concern over the use of silicone gels in implants." The report went even further, however: "None of these studies demonstrated that the coexistence of connective-tissue disease with silicone breast implants is any more prevalent than would be expected by chance."

The largest study of connective-tissue disease to date appeared in the *New England Journal of Medicine* [in] June [1995]. Conducted by the Harvard School of Public Health and the Brigham and Women's Hospital in Boston, the study looked for evidence of 41 types of connective-tissue disease among 87,501 nurses, of whom 1,183 had implants.

* * *

The results were unambiguous. The researchers found no "association between silicone breast implants and connective-tissue diseases, defined according to a variety of standardized criteria." Already anticipating the charge that they knew would be forthcoming from plaintiffs' lawyers—that silicone implants cause a special kind of autoimmune disease that doesn't show up with standardized criteria—the authors added, "or signs or symptoms of these diseases." In fact, they reported that women with silicone implants were significantly less likely to relate symptoms of these diseases or to complain of symptoms or signs of illness resembling connective-tissue disease.

For many health professionals, the *NEJM* study, added on top of all the others, was the final piece of proof needed. "I think we have enough data to end the moratorium," George E. Erlich, a Philadelphia rheumatologist and head of the FDA arthritis advisory committee, told *The New York Times*. Erlich emphasized he was speaking for himself and not the FDA committee, but he added that the International League of the Associations of Rheumatology also agreed unanimously there was no evidence linking implants to connective-tissue disease. And long before that, the American College of Rheumatology had already issued its own statement, saying, "There is no convincing evidence that these implants cause any generalized disease."

If the evidence against silicone implants is so weak—and has always been so—why have they inspired such commotion and fear? The chief reason has to do with the federal bureaucrat whose various power-grabbing machinations would embarrass a villain from Central Casting: David Kessler, commissioner of the FDA.

In December 1991, Kessler called together a panel of physicians, self-styled consumer representatives, and the like to evaluate the evidence of potential harm caused by implants. The verdict of the panel, though by no means unanimous, was that the devices should remain on the market pending collection of further data from studies already underway.

That, however, did not please Kessler, who ordered FDA staffers to solicit case histories from doctors of implant recipients who later claimed to have suffered ills as a possible result. Since lawyers had already begun soliciting women with complaints and sending them on to specially chosen doctors, finding such case histories was probably not difficult. In any event, case histories reveal little because they don't allow for comparison groups. That's what the epidemiological studies were, but Kessler couldn't wait for them.

In January 1992, Kessler implemented the moratorium, citing the case studies as the reason (and glossing over the fact that he himself solicited them). The next month, he reconvened the panel to ply them with his new "evidence." The panel didn't budge and Kessler once again ignored its advice.

"We still saw no clear evidence of danger, though there were a number of unanswered questions," says Emory's Connell, who served as the chair of both panels. "We felt breast implants should stay available to women who, with informed consent, wanted to use them." Three and a half years after the first panel voted to recommend keeping the implants available, Connell says she would clearly do so again. "I think the difference is we could say it this time with a great deal more assurance."

"A whole new literature has been developed since that time," she explains. "We were operating on anecdotal evidence and case history. Now the evidence has been gathered by good people in well-designed studies so it's an entirely different situation."

So why did the FDA ban silicone implants despite the lack of evidence that they are harmful? Pressure came from repeated anecdotal reports in both print and television media. The moratorium that became a ban occurred after more than a year of intense media pressure, including Connie Chung's inflammatory show, which was repeated a year later.

Congressional pressure, in the form of the late Rep. Ted Weiss (D-N.Y.), also came down on the FDA. Weiss, who chaired the House committee with jurisdiction over the FDA, accused Dow Corning of possible misconduct in its effort to document the safety of silicone implants and called for both the Justice Department and the FDA to investigate the company. ([In] May [1995], the Justice Department dropped the investigation for lack of evidence.) He also accused the FDA of dragging its feet over the polyurethane-implant issue.

To be sure, there was pressure to keep implants available, too. It came from the American Medical Association, implant makers, plastic surgeons, and breast-cancer groups. But this was not the sort of public pressure that can embarrass an agency, and the breast cancer groups' objections were dealt with by allowing continued use of silicone implants for breast reconstruction following mastectomy.

The decision to ban implants was just the sort of thing one would expect from a regulatory body that puts so much emphasis on safety that it can't take anything else into account. *New England Journal of Medicine* Editor Marcia Angell has said that the FDA probably acted the way it did because implants are cosmetic and are therefore of only subjective worth. Such worth, says Angell, can't be plugged into Kessler's cost-benefit analysis.

In an *NEJM* editorial, Angell noted that nobody questions allowing the use of automobiles, even though they kill over 40,000 Americans a year, because we all have a common understanding of the worth of cars. "In the case of breast implants" though, wrote Angell, "the benefit has to do with the personal judgments about the quality of life, which are subjective and unique to each woman." But given "the difficulty of assessing the benefits, the FDA has acted as though there were none—at least when implants are used for augmentation." The result, said Angell, "is that [FDA Commissioner Kessler] may be holding breast implants to an impossibly high standard: Since there are no benefits, there should be no risks."

* * *

The FDA's pseudo-scientific approach lends support to the more obviously ideological attack on breast implants from feminists. To many of the most vocal and influential feminists, a preference for big breasts represents female oppression. Susan K. Brownmiller, in her landmark 1984 book *Femininity*, opined that "[e]nlarging one's breasts to suit male fantasies" represents the exploitation of women. "Big breasts are one of many factors that have slowed women down in the competitive race of life," she said. "Symbolically, in the conservative Fifties, when American women were encouraged to stay at home, the heavily inflated bosom was celebrated and fetishized as the feminine ideal. In decades of spirited feminist activity such as the Twenties and the present when women advance into untraditional jobs, small, streamlined breasts are glorified in fashion."

If large breasts signal oppression, say these feminists, then the implants used to enlarge one's breasts are tools of oppression. Scarsdale psychologist Rita Freedman, writing in *Beauty Bound*, claims, "Having been taught that feminine beauty means having full, softly rounded breasts, women judge them-

selves against this standard. Missing the mark, they put on padded bras or suffer silicone implants." Naomi Wolf, in her 1991 bestseller *The Beauty Myth* , states, "Breast surgery, in its mangling of erotic feeling, is a form of sexual mutilation."

Having gone this far with imagery, it's s small step to start blaming implants for physical ills. This is precisely what happened after anecdotes began to appear linking implants to disease. Susan Faludi, in her popular book *Backlash: The War Against Women*, wrote matter-of-factly that leaking implants "could cause toxicity, lupus, rheumatoid arthritis, and autoimmune diseases such as scleroderma."

To such polemicists, it doesn't matter that the evidence for negative effects was weak. It was just too fitting that something in their minds so harmful to women as a class should be harmful to them as individuals.

Two women on the FDA panel translated such thoughts into direct action. Vivian Snyder, the panel's "consumer representative," told Kessler in a letter that "[t]he federal government now has the power to deliver a profoundly important message to the American public involving basic values, concepts of beauty and health," adding, "it would really be wonderful if the FDA could address such attitude-impacting mental health issues as what is really healthy and normal and maybe even beautiful...."

The other panelist was *Beauty Bound* author Rita Freedman. She sent a letter to Kessler decrying that implants "perpetuate the myth of Barbie Doll's Body" and asked whether breast augmentation will become, "like rhinoplasty [nose surgery], a rite of passage for affluent teens."

Such feminist participation in the anti-implant crusade has proven ironic, since the FDA's virtual ban has denied what feminists have always proclaimed as their goal—a woman's right to choose for herself. Faludi herself acknowledges that at one time the leading feminist journal, *Ms.*, "deemed plastic surgery a way of 'reinventing yourself—a strategy for women who dare to take control of their lives.' "

Writing in *NEJM*, Angell says, "It is possible to deplore the pressures that women feel to conform to a stereotyped standard of beauty, while at the same time defending their right to make their own decisions." If anything, says Angell, the act of withdrawing implants could be viewed as sexist because "people are regularly permitted to take risks that are probably much greater than the likely risk from breast implants," citing cigarette smoking and excess alcohol consumption.

* * *

When the FDA slapped the moratorium on implants, the impact went far beyond prohibiting a single surgical technique. "The widespread fear—and the multimillion-dollar lawsuits—have dated largely from the FDA's removal of breast implants from the market," says Angell.

One study comparing the attitudes of women with implants before and after the FDA moratorium found that after the moratorium the level of satisfaction dropped markedly, from 98 percent satisfied to 71–79 percent satisfied. The study authors said their findings were similar to those of the American Society for Plastic and Reconstructive Surgery in another poll.

As for prompting the "multimillion-dollar lawsuits," one need look no further for evidence than so many of the attorney advertisements soliciting silicone implant recipients. "THE FDA WARNS THAT SILICONE GEL-FILLED BREAST IMPLANTS PRESENT HEALTH RISKS" blared a typical ad of this sort in the Newark, New Jersey, *Star-Ledger*. Implant critics often cite money as the only concern of Dow Corning and other manufacturers. But few notice that the group which stands to gain the most from liability cases—trial lawyers—has a love of filthy lucre. In a single case involving three women complaining of implant-related illness, a jury in 1994 awarded $33.5 million, although the judgment was later reversed by an appeals court and then settled. Thirty-three percent of a multi million-dollar award—lawyers typically take a third off the top—can be a powerful incentive for a law firm.

It's hardly surprising, then, that the American Trial Lawyers Association conducts regular seminars for implant plaintiffs' attorneys. It does so using selected data provided by Sidney Wolfe of Public Citizen, the group most identified with criticism of implants. For $750, Public Citizen will also provide trial lawyers a list of medical experts and consultants, FDA reviews and FDA panel testimony, and a variety of other litigation documents. It will also refer clients to those lawyers.

Suing implant manufacturers has become a boom industry in the United States, with lawyers out to convince women that even though they may feel just fine they are really sick and must be properly compensated. With so much money to spread around, it also isn't difficult to get doctors to find patients.

"I get calls from women who say, 'I have implants. Where do I pick up the money?' " says Sandy Finestone of the Women's Implant Information Center in Irvine, California. The center disseminates information on implant safety. "You dangle $4 billion in front of them and it certainly gets their attention." Finestone has two polyurethane-coated implants that she makes clear will not be the subject of litigation.

Indeed, attorneys have not only ignored scientists, they've attacked them. After Mayo Clinic rheumatologist Sherine E. Gabriel published a study in *NEJM* in June 1994, a lawyer claiming to represent 2,000–3,000 implant recipients began filing legal demands against her. "The magnitude of the demands is staggering; the burden is staggering," she told *The New York Times*. "They want over 800 transcripts from researchers that were here, they want hundreds of data bases, dozens of file cabinets and the entire medical records of all Olmsted County [Michigan] women, whether or lot they were in the study."

Not surprisingly, Gabriel says the demands have "severely compromised" her ability to do research and made colleagues of hers back off from doing their own implant research, for fear their findings would also infuriate plaintiffs' lawyers. "Some," she says. "determined that the price in terms of their own research careers is too high to pay."

The widespread association of silicone implants with various illnesses is largely the result of unsophisticated reporting on the topic. "The media may be portraying a closer link between implants and autoimmune disease that is actually merited because younger women tend to he more prone to autoimmune disease than other groups," explains David Leffell, associate professor of dermatology at the Yale School of Medicine. But the real question, says Leffell, is whether women with silicone implants are getting these diseases at levels higher than expected. All signs point to no.

With silicone implants, the media have managed to make news as much as report it. Clearly, they have had a significant impact on public perceptions, which then fueled both litigation and contributed to the FDA moratorium. This in turn fueled more litigation.

Whatever role sheer confusion—and ignorance of scientific data and principles —played on the part of the media, it is disturbing to realize that opportunities to present the other side were often ignored. In 1991, for instance, CBS reran the Connie Chung show that did so much to kick off the implant scare. But at the last minute, the network yanked a Dow Corning rebuttal to the program's charges. CBS didn't explain its decision. Apparently it felt its viewers would not benefit from an airing of both sides of the issue.

Unfortunately, the anti–silicone implant crusade has given women something very tangible to fear. Because of the negative publicity, as early as 1991 insurance companies were already denying or restricting medical coverage to women with implants. Now, because some doctors and lawyers have tied various illnesses to implants, women with implants who do eventually get any of those illnesses may find themselves without medical coverage. The founder of the Washington, D.C., chapter of the Y-ME National Breast Cancer Organization told a congressional panel, "In some instances, it is easier for a cancer patient to obtain insurance than one who has implants."

* * *

In early June, even before the *NEJM* connective-tissue disease study, Y-ME Executive Director Sharon Green wrote to Kessler asking him to "make a public statement regarding the most recent epidemiological studies... to stop the current frenzy." The only statement he issued that month was a response to the *NEJM* study saying yet more evidence was needed.

Emory's Connell says the FDA's actions and the legal profession's high-tech ambulance chasing are "costing us not only what we [already] have but the chance for new and better products in the future. I think we're in a worse mess in American medicine than we've ever been in. Instead of leading the world, we're now a third-rate country in terms of our ability to develop new drugs and devices."

Indeed, J. Donald Hill, chairman of cardiovascular surgery at California Pacific Medical Center, worries that the anti-implant crusade will broaden into an at-tack against a wide variety of medical aids already on the market. The first device to go down the tubes may be the Nor-plant contraceptive, which after implan-tation into the arm releases a tiny amount of silicone into the system. While no suits have yet been filed, lawyers are encour-aging women with the devices who have any sort of illness to contact them. Trial lawyer seminars are already being held, using some of the same instructors and same self-styled medical experts who tor-pedoed breast implants.

In a country so heavily dependent on science to improve the quality of our lives, to defend our shores, to feed our growing population, to prevent and cure illness, the resoundingly anti-scientific and successful crusade against silicone implants portends problems that right now cannot even be guessed.

POSTSCRIPT

Are Silicone Breast Implants Dangerous for Women?

Defense attorneys often speak of "assuming the risk" when they are representing an organization against a consumer who was aware of the questionable safety of a product or service. When it comes to silicone breast implants, what constitutes an acceptable medical risk? Who should make this decision? Should women and those who love them trust the government to take appropriate precautions before sanctioning medical options, especially when these options are merely cosmetically desirable instead of medically necessary? Why have silicone implants been left on the market for breast cancer patients, a group of individuals whose immune systems are already compromised? Should silicone implants be categorized as a "treatment" for them? If the government regards implants as posing no health threat to its recipients, why are implants only appropriate for those who have previously endured mastectomy? If we believe that the threats of silicone implants are sufficient to warrant policing the lives of healthy women, why should we allow the lives of recovering cancer patients to be further endangered?

Jennifer Washburn, in "Reality Check: Can 400,000 Women Be Wrong?" *Ms.* (March/April 1996), accuses silicone manufacturing companies of having in their possession internal documents that address the dangers of liquid silicone inside the body, yet they insist that the autoimmune diseases thousands of women claim to suffer from (and have been diagnosed with) do not exist. She reveals that the two studies cited most commonly on behalf of implant manufacturers—studies conducted by researchers at Harvard and the Mayo Clinic, which were published in the June 22, 1995, issue of the *New England Journal of Medicine*—were methodologically flawed. Furthermore, she points out that Dow Corning did not fully disclose the results of their own silicone testing. For more from this perspective, see the special report "Beauty and the Breast," *Ms.* (March/April 1996).

In February 1997 the Independent Women's Forum (IWF) sponsored a conference titled "Women's Health, Law, and the Junking of Science." Claims were made at the conference that the silicone implant moratorium was based on "junk science." Their views were recently supported by federal judge Robert E. Jones in Portland, Oregon. Judge Jones found that the evidence for a connection between implants and illness was not confirmed after he appointed four independent experts to examine the situation. This ruling may have substantial legal fallout across America. See "Ruling Out 'Junk Science,'" *Time* (December 30, 1996/January 6, 1997).

ISSUE 19

Should Ritual Female Genital Surgery Be Regulated Worldwide?

YES: Efua Dorkenoo, from "Combating Female Genital Mutilation: An Agenda for the Next Decade," *World Health Statistics Quarterly* (vol. 49, no. 2, 1996)

NO: Eric Winkel, from "A Muslim Perspective on Female Circumcision," *Women and Health* (vol. 23, no. 1, 1995)

ISSUE SUMMARY

YES: Efua Dorkenoo, a World Health Organization (WHO) consultant on women's health, argues for worldwide regulation of ritual female genital surgery (RFGS) based on human rights standards, including the right to health.

NO: Scholar Eric Winkel suggests that Islamic legal discourse be utilized as a forum for resolving issues associated with RFGS. He believes that change should not be imposed by Westerners but should instead be brought about via existing channels and traditional formats.

Ritual female genital surgery (RFGS), also known as female genital mutilation (FGM), is a widespread practice in Africa and in the Middle East. Muslims in many countries practice RFGS, although the custom is not based on the Koran (Muslim law based on Allah's teachings) nor is it part of Islamic ritual. On March 29, 1997, a new law banning the practice of female circumcision went into effect in the United States, making it illegal for women under 18 years old to be subjected to the practice. Offenders will be sentenced with up to five years in prison The law, which gained congressional approval in 1996, was authored by former congresswoman Pat Schroeder (D-Colorado) and cosponsored by Barbara-Rose Collins (D-Michigan). The Centers for Disease Control (CDC) estimate that some 150,000 girls and women of African descent in the United States either risk undergoing or have already undergone the procedure.

RFGS entails the removal of part or all of the external female genitalia and/or injury to the female genital organs for cultural or other nontherapeutic reasons. The WHO Technical Working Group developed the following definitions: Type I, when the prepuce (clitoral hood) is removed, sometimes with part or all of the clitoris; Type II, when both the prepuce and some or all of the clitoris are removed, along with part or all of the labia minora (inner vaginal lips); and Type III (known as infibulation), when the clitoris and labia minora are completely removed together with the inner surfaces of the labia majora. The raw edges of the labia majora are then stitched together with thorns or silk or catgut sutures so that when the skin of the remaining labia majora heals, a bridge of scar tissue forms over the vagina. A small opening is preserved by the insertion of a foreign body to allow the passage of urine and menstrual blood. The most common procedure is Type II, constituting up to 80 percent of all female genital mutilation practiced. Another 15 percent or so involves the most extreme form, infibulation. RFGS takes place at any age, but most experts agree that the age is falling for females undergoing these procedures. It is not known when or where this tradition originated. Reasons cited for maintaining it are aesthetic, psychosexual, hygienic, sociocultural, and religious. There is no comprehensive global survey of the prevalence of RFGS, although fragmented data puts the prevalence at 5–98 percent in African countries.

Those who object to RFGS are fighting to have it banned in all areas of the world in the name of human rights. There is widespread belief that the procedure has nothing to do with race or religion but, instead, is a patriarchal procedure related to slavery and designed to maintain polygamy for men and monogamy for women. In short, critics see the procedure as a vestige of unbridled domination designed to elaborate an ideal of masculinity, which requires a brutal exercise of power and which feeds on the weakness and vulnerability of women.

Many of the representatives from cultures that practice FGM are offended by the regulatory efforts of countries like the United States. In fact, parents can now be barred from leaving the United States if it is determined that they are taking their daughters back to their home country to have the surgical procedure conducted. The fact that Western observers cannot understand why women would want to practice clitoridectomy is not relevant, according to representatives of involved countries. They believe that it is not appropriate for another country to try to understand their cultural practices and rituals, let alone to tell them what to do.

In the selections that follow, Efua Dorkenoo argues for the regulation of female genital mutilation based upon human rights standards, including the right to health. Eric Winkel asserts that it is the business of the Muslims to handle their own internal situations and that if anything should be done, it should be initiated from within, through well-established Islamic legal discourse.

YES

Efua Dorkenoo

COMBATING FEMALE GENITAL MUTILATION: AN AGENDA FOR THE NEXT DECADE

Hosken *(1)* and Toubia *(2)* estimate that there are at present over 120 million girls and women who have undergone some form of female genital mutilation [FGM]—sometimes referred to as "female circumcision"—and that 2 million girls per year are at risk of mutilation. Most of the girls and women who have undergone mutilation are reported to live in 28 African countries where it is practised by many ethnic groups, in northern, eastern and western Africa. Some female genital mutilation is practised in the southern parts of the Arabian peninsula and along the Persian Gulf and increasingly, among some immigrant populations in Europe, Australia, Canada and the United States of America. It has also been reported to be practised by a minority ethno-religious group—the Daudi Bohra Muslims, who live in India—and among Muslim populations in Malaysia and Indonesia *(3)*.

The arguments against this traditional practice are based upon recognized human rights standards including the right to health. It is known that the physical and psychological effects of the practice are very extensive and irreversible, affecting the health of girls and women, in particular sexual, reproductive and mental health and well-being. Furthermore, female genital mutilation reinforces the inequities suffered by women in the communities where it is practised, and must be addressed if the health, social and economic development needs of women are to be met.

Despite recognition of the importance of this sensitive issue, there are still major gaps in knowledge about the extent and nature of the problem and the kinds of interventions that can be successful in eliminating it. To begin the process of developing a sound technical basis for policy and action, WHO [World Health Organization] convened a Technical Working Group Meeting on Female Genital Mutilation in July 1995 *(4)*. The recommendations which emanated from this meeting have drawn international attention to female genital mutilation and its health consequences and have contributed to setting the agenda for the next decade for accelerating the elimination of this practice.

DEFINITION

Female genital mutilation entails the removal of part or all of the external female genitalia and/or injury to the female genital organs for cultural or other non-therapeutic reasons. This definition, adopted by the WHO Technical Working Group Meeting on Female Genital Mutilation, encompasses the physical, psychological and human rights aspects of the practice.

CLASSIFICATION OF THE TYPES OF FEMALE GENITAL MUTILATION

In order to strengthen policy formulation including legislation and to clear the path for research and training, the WHO Technical Working Group recommended for adoption the following classification for the different types of female genital mutilation. In Type I, the prepuce (clitoral hood) is removed, sometimes along with part or all of the clitoris. In Type II, both the prepuce and the clitoris and part or all of the labia minora (inner vaginal lips) are removed. Type III (known as infibulation) involves the complete removal of the clitoris and labia minora, together with the inner surface of the labia majora. The raw edges of the labia majora are then stitched together with thorns or silk or catgut sutures, so that when the skin of the remaining labia majora heals, a bridge of scar tissue forms over the vagina. A small opening is preserved, by the insertion of a foreign body, to allow the passage of urine and menstrual blood. Since a physical barrier has been created for sexual intercourse, the infibulated woman has to undergo gradual dilatation by her husband over a period of days, weeks or months to allow for penetrative intercourse. This painful process does not always result in successful vaginal penetration and the opening may have to be re-cut.

Type IV is a new category that encompasses other surgical procedures including manipulation of the genitalia. These include pricking, piercing or incision of the clitoris and/or labia, stretching of the clitoris and/or labia, cauterization by burning of the clitoris and surrounding tissue, introcision, scraping of the vaginal orifice, cuts into the vagina and introduction of substances into the vagina with the aim of tightening or narrowing the vagina.

The commonest type of female genital mutilation is Type II. This constitutes up to 80% of all female genital mutilation practised. The most extreme form is infibulation. This is thought to constitute 15% of FGM and is widespread in Somalia, northern Sudan and Djibouti. It has been reported in parts of Ethiopia, Eritrea, and northern Kenya and small parts of Mali and northern Nigeria.

PRACTITIONERS

Female genital mutilation is usually performed by a traditional practitioner with crude instruments and without anaesthetics. Although WHO has consistently issued statements opposing medicalization of any form of female genital mutilation, among the more affluent and in urban centres, female genital mutilation is increasingly being performed in health care facilities by qualified medical personnel.

AGE

The age at which female genital mutilation is practised varies from area to area. It is performed at a few days old (for example among the nomads of Sudan), at about 7 years old (as in Egypt and in countries in eastern Africa and the horn of Africa) or in adolescence. In Nigeria, for instance, FGM takes place shortly before marriage among the Ibo, but only before the first child among the Aboh in the midwest (5). Most experts agree, however, that the age of which FGM takes place is falling.

REASONS

It is not known when or where the tradition of female genital mutilation originated and a variety of reasons (sociocultural, religious, psychosexual, hygienic, and aesthetic) are given for maintaining it. Female genital mutilation is practised by followers of a number of different religions including Muslims, Christians (Catholics, Protestants and Copts) and animists, and also by non-believers in the countries concerned. Although female genital mutilation is not mentioned in the Koran, it is frequently carried out in some Muslim communities in the genuine belief that it forms part of Islamic tradition.

THE HEALTH COMPLICATIONS OF FEMALE GENITAL MUTILATION

The health effects of FGM depend on the extent of cutting, the skill of the operator, the cleanliness of the tools and the environment, and the physical and psychological state of the girl or woman concerned.

Immediate Complications
Immediate physical complications include haemorrhage and severe pain which can lead to shock and in some cases death. Acute urinary retention and in-

fections are common. Injury to adjacent tissue of the urethra, vagina, perineum and rectum can result from the use of crude instruments. Fractures of the clavicle, femur or humerus or dislocation of the hip joint can occur if heavy pressure is applied to the struggling girl during the operation, as often occurs when several adults hold down the girl during the procedure. Group mutilations, in which the same unclean cutting instruments are used on each girl may give rise to a risk of transmission of HIV and hepatitis B but this has not been confirmed. Medium-term problems include delayed healing and the formation of abscesses due to primary infections resulting from faulty healing.

Long-Term Complications
The long-term complications include keloid scar formation, the formation of dermoid cysts and clitoral neuroma, dyspareunia (painful intercourse), chronic pelvic infections and difficulties in menstruation as a result of partial or total occlusion of the vaginal opening. Problems in pregnancy and childbirth are common, particularly following type III mutilation, because the tough scar tissue that forms causes partial or total occlusion of the vaginal opening and prevents dilatation of the birth canal. Prolonged and obstructed labour can lead to tearing of the perineum, haemorrhage, fistula formation and uterine inertia, rupture or prolapse. These complications can lead to neonatal harm (including stillbirth) and even maternal death.

Psychosexual and Psychological Health
Almost all the types of female genital mutilation involve the removal of or damage to part or the whole of the clitoris, which is the main female sexual organ,

equivalent in its anatomy and physiology to the male organ, the penis. Infibulation removes larger parts of the genitals, and closes off the vagina, leaving areas of tough scar tissue in place of the sensitive genitals, thus creating permanent damage and dysfunction. Sexual dysfunction in both partners may be the result of painful intercourse and reduced sensitivity following clitoridectomy and narrowing of the vaginal wall.

FGM may leave a lasting mark on the life and mind of the woman who has undergone it. The psychological complications may be submerged deeply in the child's subconscious mind, and may trigger the onset of behavioural disturbances. The possible loss of trust and confidence in care-givers has been reported as another serious effect of female genital mutilation. In the longer term, women may suffer anxiety, depression, chronic irritability, frigidity and marital conflicts. Many girls and women, traumatized by their experience of FGM, may have no acceptable means of expressing their fears, and suffer in silence.

HUMAN RIGHTS AGREEMENTS TO GUIDE ACTION

There are various international agreements in place that are legally binding on the parties (states) and which prohibit the practice of female genital mutilation. The *United Nations Convention on the Elimination of All Forms of Discrimination Against Women* promotes the rights of women and specifically addresses discriminatory traditional practices (6). The *Convention on the Rights of the Child* protects the right to gender equality, and Article 24.3 of the Convention explicitly requires States to take all effective and appropriate measures to abolish traditional practices prej-

udicial to the health of children (7). Similarly, there are regional human rights agreements such as the *African Charter on Human and Peoples' Rights* and the *African Charter on the Rights and Welfare of the Child* which protect women and children against harmful traditional practices (8, 9). Article 18 of the African Charter on Human and Peoples' Rights specifically requests states to "ensure the elimination of every discrimination against women and also ensure the protection of the rights of women and the child as stipulated in international declarations and conventions."

Article XXI of the African Charter on the Rights and Welfare of the Child obliges state parties to eliminate harmful social and cultural practices affecting the welfare, dignity, normal growth and development of the child.

The *Programme of Action of the International Conference on Population and Development (ICPD)* held in Cairo in 1994 also included recommendations in regard to female genital mutilation, which commit governments and communities to "urgently take steps to stop the practice of female genital mutilation and to protect women and girls from all such similar unnecessary and dangerous practices." (10)

The *Platform for Action of the World Conference on Women*, also included a special section on the girl child and urged governments, international organizations and nongovernmental groups to develop policies and programmes to eliminate all forms of discrimination against the girl child including female genital mutilation (11).

GAPS IN KNOWLEDGE

There have been no comprehensive global surveys of the prevalence of female genital mutilation. Current information on types of mutilation and their prevalence is derived from inadequate, fragmentary data. On the basis of government reports, anecdotal evidence and limited surveys with samples that are not always representative, the prevalence of female genital mutilation is estimated to range from 5% to 98% in African countries (1, 2). Sudan is the only country to have carried out nationwide surveys (12-14). They were based on a national sample which excluded the three southern provinces, where the practice is unknown (except by adoption through marriage to the dominant northern ethnic groups practising FGM), and indicated an initial prevalence of 89% which subsequently declined by 8%. A study by the Nigerian Association of Nurses and Nurse-Midwives (15) conducted in Nigeria in 1985–1986, using a sample of 400 women and men in each state, showed that 13 out of the 21 states had populations practising some form of female genital mutilation, with prevalence ranging from 35% to 90%. However, the data could not be extrapolated to give a national picture. Similar limited surveys exist for Chad, Ethiopia, Gambia, Ghana and Kenya.

Reliable and accurate data on the prevalence, incidence and recurrence rates of the different forms of female genital mutilation or its health consequences will provide baseline information for subsequent evaluations and to inform policy makers and national decision-making processes. At the local level, a rapid-intervention survey may be the most appropriate step. At the national level, more detailed incidence and prevalence rates can be obtained by incorporating modules on female genital mutilation into existing surveys. Existing government surveys (for example, national Demographic and Health Surveys (DHS), household income and expenditure surveys, and fertility surveys) can, with the addition of some extra questions, be used to provide data on female genital mutilation at a fraction of the cost of a specific survey. As has been noted, questions on female genital mutilation were incorporated in the 1989–90 Demographic and Health Survey (DHSI) in the Sudan. The Central African Republic and Côte d'Ivoire have also incorporated a few questions on FGM into their national Demographic and Health Surveys (1994 and 1994–95). Egypt integrated 34 questions on female genital mutilation into its national Demographic and Health Survey in 1995. A full module on female genital mutilation with 20 questions (DHS III) was field-tested in Mali and Eritrea in 1995. These efforts will help to generate reliable incidence and prevalence data for countries in future years.

Where studies of FGM are to be conducted, the magnitude of the practice should be reported for different socio-demographic groups and for each type of genital mutilation. The magnitude of the problem should be expressed in terms of prevalence, incidence and recurrence rates. Repeat surveys of prevalence, incidence and recurrence rates over time will help to establish trends of genital mutilation in a given community or nation.

Further descriptive research providing quantitative and qualitative information is needed to characterize the different forms of genital mutilation and the socio-demographic characteristics of those who practise FGM versus those who do not. Other sociological variables such as the age of the girl, the location, and the persons involved in performing or assisting in the practice are essential information for planning target interventions and health education programmes aimed at certain locations (for example, schools or homes) or populations (for example, nurses, midwives, doctors and traditional birth attendants) that could help eliminate the practice at the source.

Investigations are also needed to gain a better understanding of the sociocultural factors that influence female genital mutilation, including beliefs, class differences, power structures within society, the social/festive character that has built up around mutilation rituals and the links with marriageability. Some beliefs recur in a number of population groups, but there are notable differences and some themes are exclusive to certain areas. Efforts are needed to analyse these factors within countries so that information and communication materials can be adapted to take account of local conditions. Similarly, an accurate analysis of the existing economic incentives that promote the continuation of the practice will suggest measures to counteract them and indicate appropriate areas for intervention.

With regard to the health complications, the physical complications are well known. What is unclear, however, is the actual prevalence of complications and their long term sequelae in relation to gynaecological and obstetric morbidity and their impact on maternal and childhood mortality. The nature and the degree of psychological and sexual damage in different groups are still largely unexplored. Given the scale of the practice of female genital mutilation in many communities, this information is most important for developing clinical support for girls and women who are suffering from the health complications of female genital mutilation.

LESSONS LEARNED

In the last decade, a wide range of organizations and individuals have attempted community-based activities to eliminate FGM. Women's organizations from communities where the practice persists have been leading the campaign for the last decade. With very little resources, they embarked on awareness-raising campaigns and have managed to break the taboo surrounding FGM in their communities. They have also brought the problem to the attention of political, religious and community leaders. Some governments have made statements condemning female genital mutilation; a few have adopted a policy or passed laws banning the practice; but often they have taken little action on the issue. FGM is an issue that cuts across both health and human rights and a major lesson learned from past community actions is that efforts to stop the practice need to go beyond the medical model of disease eradication. A multidisciplinary approach must be developed.

An Agenda for Action

To achieve real change at the grassroots will require more planning, and more sustained commitment from governments and international agencies to the elimination of FGM. The gaps in knowledge that need to be addressed have been outlined. While voluntary organizations can play a pivotal role in the elimination of FGM, it is important that governments act to initiate, support and coordinate actions against this practice. The broad actions to be taken at the national level, include the need to:

- adopt a clear national policy for the abolition of FGM. This should focus on prevention and rehabilitation. It should also incorporate clear goals, targets and objectives, and schedules for their attainment. Legislation is important, but legislation alone is insufficient. It should be accompanied by appropriate community-based action. Laws and professional codes of ethics should prohibit the medicalization of all the different forms of FGM;

- establish inter-agency coalitions with members from relevant government ministries, nongovernmental organizations and professionals to follow up action on FGM;
- promote research on FGM, including the incidence, prevalence, and health consequences, particularly the impact of FGM on mental and sexual health as well as on the sociocultural determinants of FGM, in order to develop more effective approaches to its elimination;
- organize strong community outreach and family life education programmes for all sectors of the public including village and religious leaders, men and young people; and
- organize training for health workers—physicians, nurses, midwives and also traditional birth attendants and healers —to enable them to work for the abolition of female genital mutilation and to provide clinical and psychological care and support for girls and women who have undergone FGM.

In order to sustain action for the elimination of FGM, activities on FGM must be integrated into existing health education programmes, reproductive health services and population and development strategies at national, regional and at community level.

Given the United Nations commitment to human rights, with emphasis on ad-

vancing and protecting the health and the lives of women and children, including their mental and sexual health, it is the duty of WHO, UNICEF, UNFPA and other UN agencies, as well as bilateral, multilateral and international development agencies, to support policies and programmes that bring an end to this damaging practice in all its forms. Various approaches will need to be developed such as promotion, providing technical support, and mobilizing resources, so that national and local groups can initiate community-based activities aimed at eliminating all harmful practices that affect the health of women and children, especially FGM. WHO, in particular, has a special responsibility to increase knowledge of FGM and promote technically sound policies and approaches for the elimination of FGM, including developing training guidelines to equip health care workers with the appropriate knowledge, skills and attitudes for preventing and eliminating FGM, providing clinical management of the health complications, and ensuring that FGM is incorporated into broader concerns of women's health, reproductive health and human rights.

CONCLUSIONS

Harmful practices such as female genital mutilation persist today in many communities for a variety of reasons. However, the roots of the practice lie in the patriarchal family and in society at large. Although women who are the victims of FGM are the gatekeepers of the practice in their communities, this should be understood within the context of their general powerlessness in male-dominated societies. Promoting gender equity and women's empowerment will invariably lead to a decrease in the incidence and prevalence of FGM within communities and to its total elimination. It has taken some time for women's and children's rights to be accepted as human rights. It is vital that efforts now be made to give the human rights declarations and conventions on women's and children's rights meaning at the national and local levels. A significant shift in societal attitudes towards women and girls is called for. Young people are the adults of tomorrow. Early introduction of gender-sensitive education in schools will help to foster respect for girls' and women's human rights. Finally, as increased education of women appears to be a major factor in decreasing the practice of FGM, efforts to promote female education would have to be central to the long-term strategy for the elimination of this harmful traditional practice.

SUMMARY

Female genital mutilation (FGM)—sometimes locally referred to as "female circumcision"—is a deeply rooted traditional practice that adversely affects the health of girls and women. At present it is estimated that over 120 million girls and women have undergone some form of genital mutilation and that 2 million girls per year are at risk. Most of the girls and women affected live in 28 African countries where the prevalence of female genital mutilation is estimated to range from 5% to 98%. The elimination of female genital mutilation will not only improve women's and children's health; it will also promote gender equity and women's empowerment in the communities where the practice persists. To achieve change will require more planning, and more sustained programmes for its elimination. The political will of governments is essential in order to eliminate this harmful traditional practice and concerted efforts from all concerned are required.

REFERENCES

1. Hosken, F. P. Female genital mutilation, estimate: total number of girls and women mutilated in Africa, Lexington, Women's International Network News, 1995.
2. Toubia, N. Female genital mutilation, a call for global action, second edition, New York, RAINBO, 1995, 24–25.
3. Hosken, F. P. The Hosken report, genital and sexual mutilation of females, fourth revised edition, Women's International Network News, 1993.
4. Report of a WHO Technical Working Group Meeting on Female Genital Mutilation, 17–19 July, 1995. Geneva, WHO (forthcoming).
5. Dorkenoo, E. Cutting the rose: female genital mutilation, the practice and its prevention, London, Minority Rights Group, 1994.
6. Convention on the elimination of all forms of discrimination against women, in: Brownlie, I. (ed) Basic documents on human rights, 3rd edition, Oxford, Oxford University Press, 1992 (pp. 169–181).
7. Convention on the rights of the child, in: Brownlie, I. (ed) Basic documents on human rights, 3rd edition, Oxford, Oxford University Press, 1992 (pp. 182–202).
8. African charter on human and peoples' rights, in: Brownlie, I. (ed) Basic documents on human rights, 3rd edition, Oxford, Oxford University Press, 1992 (pp. 555–566).
9. African charter on the rights and welfare of the child. Organization of African Unity, Doc. CAB/LEG/153/Rev. 2 (1960).
10. International Conference on Population and Development (ICPD), Report of the International Conference on Population and Development, UN Doc. A/CONF. 171.13 (1994).
11. Platform for Action of the World Conference on Women, in Report of the Fourth World Conference on Women, UN Doc. A/CONF. 177/20.
12. El Dareer, A. Woman, why do you weep? London, Zed Books, 1982.
13. The Sudan fertility survey, Department of Statistics, Ministry of Economic and National Planning, Khartoum, Sudan, 1979.
14. Sudan demographic and health survey. Department of Statistics. Ministry of Economic and National Planning, Khartoum, Sudan, 1989/1990.
15. Adebajo, C. O. Female circumcision and other dangerous practices to women's health. In: Kisekka, M. N. Women's health issues in Nigeria, Zaria, Tamaza Publishing Company, 1992, 1–11.

NO

Eric Winkel

A MUSLIM PERSPECTIVE ON FEMALE CIRCUMCISION

ABSTRACT. Western observers are unable to understand why women would want to practice clitoridectomy, just as they are perplexed at the vocal, if mostly inarticulate, rejection by many Muslims of the Cairo conference. The battle lines which get drawn have on one side public health professionals, development organizations, and feminists and on the other side conservative and "fundamentalist" Muslims who, if they are heard at all, sound impossibly antediluvian. Many Muslims, including myself, are uncomfortable with both sides. What is needed is an alternative to this polarization. The alternative I propose is the Islamic legal discourse, which might best be described as the discursive arena in which issues of societal importance get worked out.

That positive change can come about from within—using the Islamic discourse—is possible because Islamic discursive systems are broad and nuanced enough to accommodate a wide variety of medical and public health endeavors. Meaningful social change and improved public health could come about by stimulating and recovering the many Islamic sunnah (exemplary) practices which are so conducive to physical and material well-being. By dealing change through existing, and proven, traditional formats, Muslims would be able to effect valuable and meaningful change in their communities. Muslim communities should not become dependent on and indentured to Western agencies and their own nation-states to solve the problems they face, including the tragic consequences of widely practiced infibulation and clitoridectomy; instead we need to apply our own traditional practices and to support an indigenous Islamic legal discourse.

The practice of clitoridectomy has become for western observers a shibboleth which does not admit the possibility of complexity. It is taken as a sure sign of peculiarly backward behavior, an issue "we" all can get behind. It is

From Eric Winkel, "A Muslim Perspective on Female Circumcision," *Women and Health*, vol. 23, no. 1 (1995), pp. 1–7. Copyright © 1995 by Haworth Press, Inc., Binghamton, NY. Reprinted by permission.

such that one would be hard pressed to find a debater to argue "for" female circumcision, at least in English. But western observers are often surprised to find that "in fact, most of the women, regardless of age, social status, or ethnic extraction, favored the continuation of this way of life."[1] Similarly, western observers were perplexed at the vocal, if mostly inarticulate, rejection by many Muslims of the Cairo conference. The fact is that the practice of clitorectomy is often linked to Islam, even though those who so link it often admit that it is not found in the Qur'an. Those who link clitorectomy to Islam, then, imply that *Islam* is something which stands in the way of progress, along with related superstitions. Exemplifying this attitude are statements like this: "The convictions" of some observers "are so strong that until significant educational inroads are made... and superstitions give way to scientific reasoning and objective rationalization," this backward practice will continue.[2]

Female circumcision and other issues arising from the Cairo conference seem to bring out a stark polarization. On the one side are public health professionals, development organizations, and feminists. On the other side are conservative and "fundamentalist" Muslims who, if they are heard at all, sound impossibly antediluvian. The two sides seem to be characterized by observers variously as good and bad, pro-woman and anti-woman, or forward and backward. Perhaps it is more accurate to say that female circumcision and issues of the Cairo conference divide people into two groups, those who believe that the western model of development is universal and universally beneficial and those who do not.

Many Muslims, myself included, are in an awkward position when the battle lines get drawn. We agree with the points of the first side without accepting their agenda; and we agree with the agenda of the second side without accepting their points. For example, the agenda of international and national campaigns to eradicate female circumcision is widely perceived by Muslims as racist and ethnocentric. The entire thrust of "development," after all, includes paternalistic and racist notions of who stands in need of education and development, and why. So whether international or national, a campaign to eradicate female circumcision will carry with it a largely hidden agenda to change people's lives according to a particularly western model of development. One observer writes that "the government in Somalia launched a campaign with the help of the Women's Democratic Organization with Edna Ismail (a Christian by name) as one of the local leaders."[3] In such a situation, Muslims will quickly suspect that "female circumcision" is not what is really at stake: what is at stake is Islam itself, the presence of a Christian as a campaign leader suggesting yet another missionary assault on Islam. The code word "Democratic" might also suggest to Muslims, who are so widely portrayed as terrorists, or at least undemocratic, that they and Islam are under attack.

What is needed is an alternative to the polarization presented above. The alternative I propose is the Islamic legal discourse, which might best be described as the discursive arena in which issues of societal importance get worked out. The legal discourse of Islam may be conceived of as a more or less flexible superstructure erected over the shari'ah, which in turn may be defined as the set of injunctions emanating from the Qur'an and sunnah (exemplary prophetic practice). Those who deal with this superstructure, and help it flex and bend to meet new circumstances, may be loosely defined as the 'ulama', those who have knowledge. This amorphous group of people, women and men, are recognized in their communities by their knowledge. There is no institution or bar which certifies them, and their independence is so vital to their cause that they continually warn themselves against "going to kings." Needless to say, the "official 'ulama" usually do not meet either criterion.

The alternative I propose, the Islamic legal discourse, serves three purposes in this paper. First, it clarifies the issue of female circumcision. Second, it demonstrates, to many people for the first time, that Muslims can have articulate and authentically Islamic responses to issues of concern. Finally, this legal discourse is an important way for Muslim communities to deal with new situations in authentic ways.

Without becoming a nominalist, one may appreciate deeply the clarity that the legal discourse of Islam gives issues through its basis in *names*. The first thing the practitioner of the Islamic legal discourse does is to get the names straight. Let us do that now. We have something called male circumcision where the foreskin covering the head of the penis is trimmed back. The legal position is that Muslim males should be circumcised, although some classical scholars produce evidence which suggests that male converts to Islam need not get circumcised if they are fearful of the procedure. Cutting the actual penis is in the same category as amputation of foot or ear or other bodily part, and there is a complex legal discussion about penalties for inten-

tional and unintentional amputation. Female circumcision is classified as sunnah, which in this context means optional. There is no harm in not doing it, and there is some reward in doing it. But removal of the clitoris, clitorectomy, is in the same category as cutting the actual penis. Clitoridectomy is legally parallel to castration, and that is forbidden as an "alteration of Allah's creation." The phrase in the Qur'an is "Let there be no alteration in Allah's creation" [30:30] and has traditionally been used to explain the unlawfulness of tattoos, disfiguration, and castration. It may be explicitly applied to infibulation.

Infibulation is not unique to Muslim societies; nor do the majority of Muslim communities have this practice. Because it is a harm to women—in Islamic terms —and because it is an "alteration of Allah's creation," Muslims should work to eradicate the practice. The following are ways in which Muslims can articulately frame an approach.

Ibn Qudamah [620 A.H./1223 C.E.] is a major commentator to the work of Ahmad ibn Hanbal, who is himself one of the four sunni imams to whom schools of legal discourse trace their origins. The Hanbalis (followers of Ahmad ibn Hanbal) are generally considered the most "strict." Ibn Qudamah writes that "As for circumcision, it is obligatory on men and admirable [*makrumah*] for women, but it is not obligatory on them. This is the position of the majority of people of knowledge. Ahmad [ibn Hanbal] said ... the women's circumcision is much less [than the man's]." He cites then as evidence for the lightness of the female circumcision a hadith where the prophet, Allah bless and give him peace, says to the "khafidah" (the word means "one who trims back"), "Do not overdo it, because it [the clitoris] is a good fortune for the spouse and a delight to her."[4] Let us look at this hadith in detail.

In the collection of hadith of Abu Dawud [275/888], we have the following, where *haddathana* means "We were told in the form of a hadith".[5]

haddathana Sulayman ibn 'Abd al-Rahman [of Damascus] and 'Abd al-Wahhab ibn 'Abd al-Rahim al-Ashja'i who both said *haddathana* Marwan *haddathana* Muhammad ibn Hasan that 'Abd al-Wahhab (of Kufah) said, from 'Abd al-Malik ibn 'Amir, from Umm 'Atiyah the Ansar, that a women was circumcising in Madinah and the prophet, Allah bless him and give him peace, said to her, "Do not overdo it, because that [clitoris] is lucky for the woman and dear to the husband." [I,] Abu Dawud, am mentioning that the narration from 'Abid-Allah ibn 'Amr from 'Abd al-Malik is narrated according to its meaning [i.e., not narrated literally; we see above that Ibn Qudamah has a slightly different version]. This hadith is not strong. It is *mursal*.[6] Muhammad ibn Hasan is unknown [to the hadith biographers], so this hadith is *da'if* [weak].[7]

The hadith is not considered revelational proof because the chain is not completely secure in its all links from the prophet, Allah bless and give him peace, to the hadith scholars, and because, according to the vast majority of scholars, a hadith, to be part of the sunnah, must be correctly transmitted word for word. But what is interesting is that despite its weak nature, the hadith is transmitted and becomes part of the Islamic legal discourse. It means that the scholars find it important, even though it does not have the exalted status of a verse from the Qur'an or a strong hadith.

What we have here (and this is supported in many other places as well) is that the traditional scholars have posited that their understanding of Islam (that is, their fiqh) is that female circumcision is not required, and if performed, it should be slight, and that the clitoris contributes to the woman's sexual enjoyment, and that that is an enjoyment which is both hers and her husband's.

I have heard that one reason clitorectomy is performed is to make sex unpleasant as a way of maintaining control over unmarried girls' sexuality. Such reasoning clearly goes against the hadith cited above, because there the woman's sexual pleasure is desired by both the woman and the man; as "sex" and "marriage contract" are synonymous in the legal discourse (the word is *nikah*), sexuality is "controlled" by marrying early and often (for example, a divorced woman should be able to find another husband easily). I have heard other reasons proffered as well. The legal discourse insists that every reason must be put to the test of authenticity, which means in this case that clitorectomy to control sexuality or eliminate female sexual pleasure will be found to be illegitimate. And as with the awkwardly drawn battle lines mentioned above, the entire issue of "control" and "autonomy" needs to be reexamined from an authentic discursive perspective.

It is true that sexuality is controlled internally by individuals themselves (men and women) and by a superstructure which carefully maps relationships of daughters, wives, mothers, sons, husbands, and fathers, but this control gets distorted by a male discourse which seeks to apply violent punishments to "dangerous" women to restore an imagined past. The west struggled for three centuries to dismantle a system of gender control—we have or had "good girls" who got married and "bad girls" who had sex—and yet, for many different reasons, women are still not safe, popular music extols humiliating women, and women are special targets of commodification. Muslims need to find a healthy and authentic alternative to both systems.

In the one system, for example, governments have thinly veiled motives for eliminating female circumcision. One researcher writes that "many African countries, including Somalia, took a hard look at the liabilities female circumcision holds for national development."[8] But the interest of "national development" takes no account of the aspirations, traditions, and beliefs of individuals and communities. The motives for eliminating female circumcision are as important as the motives for practicing female circumcision. They equally must be put to the test of Islamic authenticity, and clearly "national development" is a reason not found in the Islamic legal discourse.

That positive change can come about from within is possible because Islamic discursive systems are broad and nuanced enough to accommodate a wide variety of medical and public health endeavors. Valuable social change comes from within. Some Muslim feminists, for example, have found that their voice is most effective when articulated within an Islamic discourse,[9] noting that "feminism" has historically been tainted with colonialism.[10] And Sachiko Murata explains that "the rigidity 'patriarchal' stress of some contemporary Muslims is to be softened," but "Muslims will be able to do this as Muslims—not as imitation Westerners—only if they look once again

at the spiritual and intellectual dimensions of their own tradition."[11]

Meaningful social change and improved health could come about first by stimulating and recovering the many Islamic sunnah practices which are so conducive to physical and material well-being. By dealing with change through existing, and proven, traditional formats, Muslims would be able to effect valuable and meaningful change in their communities. Muslim communities should not become dependent on and indentured to western agencies and their own nation-states to solve the problems they face, including the tragic consequences of widely practiced infibulation and clitoridectomy; we need to apply our own traditional practices and to support an indigenous Islamic legal discourse.

NOTES

1. Daphne Williams Ntiri [1993] 219.

2. Ntiri [1993] 225.

3. Ntiri [1993] 224.

4. Found in Ibn Qudamah's *al-Mughni Sunan al-Fitrah* pp. 70–71.

5. The practice of merely citing a hadith without citing the complete chain of transmission, or at least its ranking by classical scholarship, contributes to the particularly modern problem of "fundamentalism," which seems to enjoy statements like "Islam says" and "Islam is," based on evidence which is often highly discounted in or quite differently applied by classical sources.

6. *Mursal* means the hadith has a missing link in its transmission.

7. Abu Dawud in *Sunan Abu Dawud Kitab al-Adab*, hadith 5271.

8. Ntiri [1993] 224.

9. One group in Malaysia, called Sisters in Islam, assisted by Dr. Amina Wadud, then a colleague of mine in the International Islamic University, in Kuala Lumpur, formulated their projects for social change related to women's issues in distinctly Islamic modes.

10. Leila Ahmed remarks that "colonialism's use of feminism to promote the culture of the colonizers and undermine native culture has ever since imparted to feminism in non-Western societies the taint of having served as an instrument of colonial domination, rendering it suspect in Arab eyes.... That taint has undoubtedly hindered the feminist struggle within Muslim societies" in Leila Ahmed [1992] *Women and Gender in Islam* (New Haven: Yale University Press) 167.

11. Sachiko Murata [1992] *The Tao of Islam: A Sourcebook on Gender Relationships in Islamic Thought.* Albany: State University of New York Press. p. 323.

POSTSCRIPT

Should Ritual Female Genital Surgery Be Regulated Worldwide?

Winkel's view that the rest of the world should tend to their own affairs when it comes to the regulation of RFGS is reinforced in a 1993 article in the *American Journal of Obstetrics and Gynecology*. In the article—written as a guide for delivering a child vaginally from an infibulated woman—the author asserts, "The issue of whether the woman will want her own infant daughter circumcised also needs to be discussed so that she can make an individual, culturally appropriate and educated choice." In "Can the Government Legislate Female Circumcision?" *Afro-America* (March 17, 1997), Seble Dawit, who was born in Africa and underwent the procedure herself, says that culture cannot be legislated and that jailing participants in a 5,000-year-old practice would be counterproductive.

After CNN broadcast footage of a 13-year-old girl undergoing the procedure in Cairo, Egypt, and after the government promised to take action in 1994, Fad Haq Ali Gad Haq, then Egypt's senior religious figure and the sheik of Cairo's Al Azhar University, warned that "girls who are not circumcised when young have a sharp temperament and bad habits." Speaking out in support of the continued practice of female circumcision in his country, an Islamic cleric who sued to overturn the ban on performing the operation in Egypt was elated when the ban was overturned in June 1997. He stated, "I feel joyful. The judge returned to Islam, and he recognized that [the sayings of the Prophet Muhammad] ordered Muslims to do this operation.... A woman can enjoy her sexual feeling with her husband, but if we cut off this piece, she will be able to control herself." Both quotes are from the *Washington Post* (June 25, 1997). According to *U.S. News and World Report* (July 7, 1997), another plaintiff in the successfully overturned ruling stated, "Unless a woman's genitals are surgically reduced, wearing tight clothes will make her want any man, any boy, for sex."

However, even in the Muslim countries, not everyone supports this continued procedure. The sheik of Cairo's Al-Azhar Mosque has declared it un-Islamic, and most recently, Health Minister Ismail Awadallah Salaam filed an appeal with Egypt's Supreme Administrative Court challenging the recent decision to lift the ban. The ban will remain in place for now, according to the *Washington Post* (July 12, 1997). There is no shortage of writings that suggest that FGM should be abolished worldwide. Prior to the formal U.S. legislation that effectively outlawed the procedure, Barbara Reynolds stated, "It has nothing to do with race or religion, it is patriarchal, and is related to slavery. It is designed to maintain polygamy for men, and monogamy for women." See

"The Move to Outlaw Female Genital Mutilation," *Ms.* (July/August 1994). The Royal College of Nursing published an excellent pamphlet in 1994 outlining the practice of FGM and suggesting that nurses, midwives, and health visitors should assume an advocacy role and report cases to managers, the family's general practitioner, and the social service department. An article that recommends strategies for informing, educating, and supporting men and women to decrease the numbers of female circumcisions globally is "Female Genital Mutilation: An Overview," *Journal of Advanced Nursing* (vol. 24, 1996).

Other writings that focus on the dangers of FGM and/or recommend that the practice be abolished or controlled include Hanny Lightfoot-Klein, *Prisoners of Ritual: An Odyssey into Female Genital Circumcision in Africa* (Haworth Press, 1989); Olayinka Koso-Thomas, *The Circumcision of Women: A Strategy for Eradication* (Zed Books, 1987); "Female Circumcision Comes to America," *The Atlantic Monthly* (October 1995); and K. Tomaésevski, *Women and Human Rights* (Zed Books, 1993).

CONTRIBUTORS
TO THIS VOLUME

EDITOR

ALISON D. SPALDING received her B.A. in psychology in 1978 and her M.A. in social work in 1980 from Florida State University, and she earned her Ph.D. in social policy and social work from Virginia Commonwealth University in 1991. She served as a clinical social worker and mental health officer in the United States Air Force from 1982 to 1986. She currently teaches in the Department of Health Sciences at SUNY Brockport. She teaches and publishes in the areas of alcoholism, HIV/AIDS, and counseling, and her articles have appeared in *Alcoholism Treatment Quarterly* and *Social Work and Health Care*. She maintains a private counseling practice in Rochester, New York.

STAFF

David Dean   List Manager

David Brackley   Developmental Editor

Ava Suntoke   Developmental Editor

Tammy Ward   Administrative Assistant

Brenda S. Filley   Production Manager

Juliana Arbo   Typesetting Supervisor

Diane Barker   Proofreader

Lara Johnson   Graphics

Richard Tietjen   Publishing Systems Manager

AUTHORS

ROBERT L. ALLEN is senior editor of the *Black Scholar* and a former president of the Oakland Men's Project.

DONNA ALVERMANN is a research professor of reading education at the University of Georgia and codirector of the National Reading Research Center. Her work has been published in *Reading Research Quarterly, Journal of Reading Behavior, Journal of Educational Psychology,* and the *Journal of Adolescent and Adult Literacy.*

JOYCE ARTHUR is a freelance and technical writer from Vancouver, British Columbia, Canada. An activist in the abortion rights movement, she is the editor of the Canadian newsletter *Pro-Choice Press.*

LINDA BLUM teaches sociology and women's studies at the University of New Hampshire. She is the author of *Between Feminism and Labor: The Significance of the Comparable Worth Movement* (University of California Press, 1991) and of the forthcoming *At the Breast: Ideologies of Breastfeeding and Motherhood in the Late-Twentieth-Century United States.*

BEVERLY BURCH is the author of *Other Women: Psychoanalytic Views of Women* (Columbia University Press, 1997).

PHYLLIS CHESLER is the author of eight books, including *Women and Madness* (Harcourt Brace Jovanovich, 1989) and *Mothers on Trial: The Battle for Children and Custody* (Harcourt Brace Jovanovich, 1991).

JOAN C. CHRISLER teaches psychology at Connecticut College. She is best known for her research and writing on women's health issues. She is coeditor of a number of books, including *Lectures on the Psychology of Women* (McGraw-Hill, 1996), with Carla Golden and Patricia D. Rozee, and *Variations on a Theme: Diversity and the Psychology of Women* (State University of New York Press, 1995), with Alyce Huston Hemstreet. She is currently writing an undergraduate textbook on women's health.

MICHELLE COMMEYRAS is an associate professor of reading education at the University of Georgia in Athens, Georgia.

KENNETH A. DACHMAN is a doctor of psychology and an award-winning professor with numerous books to his credit.

RENE DENFELD is the author of *The New Victorians: A Young Woman's Challenge to the Old Feminist Order* (Warner Books, 1995).

THERESA DEUSSEN teaches sociology at Pacific Lutheran University in Tacoma, Washington, and writes on service workers' strategies to combine low-wage work with family responsibilities.

DEBRA DICKERSON is a lawyer in Washington, D.C.

JOHN J. DiIULIO, JR., is an associate professor of politics and public affairs at Princeton University in Princeton, New Jersey. His publications include *No Escape: The Future of American Corrections* (Basic Books, 1991).

EFUA DORKENOO is a consultant in women, health and development in the World Health Organization's Division of Family Planning and Reproductive Health in Geneva, Switzerland.

LYNETTE J. DUMBLE is a research fellow in the Department of Surgery at the University of Melbourne in Parkville, Victoria, Australia.

GAYLE FELDMAN is a writer living in New York City. She is the author of *You Don't Have to Be Your Mother* (W. W. Norton, 1994).

ELIZABETH FOX-GENOVESE is a professor of southern history and literature at Emory University in Atlanta, Georgia. Her publications include *Feminism Without Illusions: A Critique of Individualism* (University of North Carolina Press, 1991).

MICHAEL FUMENTO, a former AIDS analyst and attorney for the U.S. Commission on Civil Rights, is currently a fellow with Consumer Alert in Washington, D.C. The author of numerous articles on AIDS for publications worldwide, he has written two books, *The Myth of Heterosexual AIDS* (New Republic Books, 1990) and *Science Under Siege: Balancing Technology and the Environment* (William Morrow, 1993). He received the American Council on Science and Health's Distinguished Science Journalist of 1993 Award for *Science Under Siege*.

DAVID GELERNTER is a professor of computer science at Yale University in New Haven, Connecticut. He is the author of *1939, The Lost World of the Fair* (Free Press, 1995) and a contributing editor of the *City Journal* and *National Review*.

EDWARD GILBREATH is the associate editor of *New Man* magazine.

STEVEN GOLDBERG is an associate professor in and acting chair of the Department of Sociology at City College of the City University of New York, where he has been teaching since 1970. He is a contributor to the magazines *Psychiatry,*

Ethics, Yale Review, and *Saturday Review,* and he is the author of *The Inevitability of Patriarchy* (William Morrow, 1973).

MARIA GUREVICH is affiliated with the Graduate Programme in Psychology at York University, North York, Ontario, Canada.

STEPHANIE GUTMANN is a writer living in New York.

SHARON HAYS is an assistant professor of sociology and women's studies at the University of Virginia in Charlottesville, Virginia.

WILLIAM A. HENRY III was a Pulitzer Prize–winning culture critic at *Time* magazine.

SHEILA JEFFREYS teaches in the Department of History and Politics at the University of Melbourne in Australia. She is the author of *Anticlimax* (New York University Press, 1991) and *The Lesbian Heresy* (Spinifex, 1993).

ANDREW G. KADAR is an attending physician at Cedars-Sinai Medical Center in Los Angeles, California, and a clinical instructor in the School of Medicine at the University of California, Los Angeles.

LINDA ACHEY KIDWELL is an assistant professor of accounting at Niagara University in Niagara, New York.

ROLAND E. KIDWELL, JR., is an assistant professor of management at Niagara University in Niagara, New York.

ROBERT LERNER is cofounder of Lerner and Nagai Quantitative Consulting with Althea Nagai.

JEFFREY M. LEVING is a pioneer of fathers' rights. A sought-after speaker, he is a legislative analyst on laws that impact men and their children. He is coauthor of the Illinois Joint Custody Law and founder of the National Institute for Fathers and Families.

CELESTE McGOVERN is a freelance writer and a frequent contributor to the *Canadian Western Report*.

MARGARET L. MOLINE is director of the Manhattan Branch of the Sleep-Wake Disorders Center in New York.

ALTHEA NAGAI is cofounder of Lerner and Nagai Quantitative Counsulting with Robert Lerner.

JOAN NESTLE is the author of *A Restricted Country* (Firebrand Books, 1987).

CAMILLE PAGLIA is a professor of humanities at the University of the Arts in Philadelphia, Pennsylvania. She is the author of the best-selling *Sexual Personae* (Yale University Press, 1990).

JONATHAN RAUCH is a writer for the *Economist* in London and the author of *Kindly Inquisitors: The New Attacks on Free Thought* (University of Chicago Press, 1993).

DEBORAH L. RHODE is a professor of law at Stanford University in Stanford, California. She is a former director of Stanford's Institute for Research on Women and Gender and the author of *Justice and Gender: Sex Discrimination and the Law* (Harvard University Press, 1989).

STANLEY ROTHMAN is Mary H. Gamble Professor of Government Emeritus at Smith College in Northampton, Massachusetts, and director of the Center for the Study of Social and Political Change.

ELAYNE A. SALTZBERG is the author of *Exercise Participation and Its Correlates to Body Awareness and Self-Esteem*.

SALLY K. SEVERINO is a psychiatrist and an associate professor at Cornell University in New York City.

M. T. STEPANIANTS is head of the Oriental Philosophies Division, Institute of Philosophy at the USSR Academy of Sciences in Moscow.

JOHN SWOMLEY is a professor emeritus at the St. Paul School of Theology in Kansas City, Missouri. He serves on the national board of the American Civil Liberties Union, chairing its church-state committee.

JOHN TAYLOR is a senior writer for *Esquire* magazine.

ERIC WINKEL is a Fulbright Scholar in the Center for Area Studies at Quaid-i-Azam University in Islamabad, Pakistan.

KENNETH L. WOODWARD is a senior writer and longtime religion reporter for *Newsweek*. He is the author of *Making Saints: How the Catholic Church Determines Who Becomes a Saint, Who Doesn't, and Why* (Simon & Schuster, 1990).

AMY OAKES WREN is an assistant professor of business law at Louisiana State University at Shreveport.

INDEX